D1741498

Palgrave Studies in Cultural Heritage and Conflict

Series Editors
Ihab Saloul
University of Amsterdam
Amsterdam, Noord-Holland, The Netherlands

Rob van der Laarse
University of Amsterdam
Amsterdam, The Netherlands

Britt Baillie
Wits City Institute
University of the Witwatersrand
Johannesburg, South Africa

This book series explores the relationship between cultural heritage and conflict. The key themes of the series are the heritage and memory of war and conflict, contested heritage, and competing memories. The series editors seek books that analyze the dynamics of the past from the perspective of tangible and intangible remnants, spaces, and traces as well as heritage appropriations and restitutions, significations, musealizations, and mediatizations in the present. Books in the series should address topics such as the politics of heritage and conflict, identity and trauma, mourning and reconciliation, nationalism and ethnicity, diaspora and intergenerational memories, painful heritage and terrorscapes, as well as the mediated reenactments of conflicted pasts.

Professor Ihab Saloul is founder and research co-director of the Amsterdam School for Heritage, Memory and Material Culture (AHM) at University of Amsterdam and Professor of Memory Studies and Narrative at the Umberto Eco Centre at Bologna University. Saloul's interests include cultural memory and identity politics, narrative theory and visual analysis, conflict and trauma, Diaspora and migration as well as contemporary cultural thought in the Middle East.

Professor Rob van der Laarse is professor of Conflict and War Heritage, at the University of Amsterdam and VU University Amsterdam, and he was the founding director of the Amsterdam School of Heritage, Memory and Material Culture. Van der Laarse's research focuses on (early) modern European elite and intellectual cultures, cultural landscape, heritage and identity politics, and the cultural roots and postwar memory of the Holocaust and other forms of mass violence.

Dr. Britt Baillie is an Honorary Research Fellow at the Wits City Institute, University of the Witwatersrand and a founding member of the Centre for Urban Conflict Studies at the University of Cambridge. Baillie's interests include the politics of cultural heritage, urban heritage, religious heritage, living heritage, heritage as commons, and contested heritage.

More information about this series at
http://www.palgrave.com/gp/series/14638

Anna-Marie de Beer

Sharing the Burden of Stories from the Tutsi Genocide

Rwanda: écrire par devoir de mémoire

Anna-Marie de Beer
University of Pretoria
Pretoria, South Africa

Palgrave Studies in Cultural Heritage and Conflict
ISBN 978-3-030-42095-6   ISBN 978-3-030-42093-2   (eBook)
https://doi.org/10.1007/978-3-030-42093-2

This Palgrave Macmillan imprint is published by the registered company Springer Nature Switzerland AG.
The registered company address is: Gewerbestrasse 11, 6330 Cham, Switzerland

FOREWORD

The genocide against the Tutsi in Rwanda, like the Jewish Holocaust before it, has attracted a rich body of scholarship that is almost unprecedented on the African continent. Anna-Marie de Beer's new book is part of this incredible scholarly gaze that continues to be directed at this despicable act of human cruelty that engulfed this small nation in Africa as the world watched in silence. Perhaps this explains, at least in part, why the genocide has compelled so much intellectual attention—a shared guilt from those who remained silent in the face of tyranny. The intellectual and scholarly output referred to here has been largely sociological in approach, often seeking to offer some explanatory authority on how Rwanda arrived at this ghastly human tragedy—its underlying causes—and, indeed, its implications for social cohesion and national unity, now and in the future. Anna-Marie de Beer's book, while signaling the desire to grasp all these, is very different. By choosing to focus for the large part on literary creations, testimonies, and stories about the genocide, it is decidedly about the voyage into our human subjectivities in order to surface those insights that only narrative can offer. It is about how literature opens a window through which trauma, associated with genocide such as this one, can be seen and reduced to its essence. The fundamental question that this book seeks to ask is how fiction offers a discursive space for listening and witnessing trauma, especially mass trauma that invites a multiplicity of voices to take part in the dialogue. The most critical point that the book makes is that fiction opens up many paths for re-historicizing trauma as a way of working through it by, for example, establishing shared memories and re-examining shared histories, generating contestation, and creating a plurality of voices and perspectives. Without distancing herself from her work, de Beer draws attention to how art and the intellectual interlocutor offer precisely this possibility of plural and mediated perspective. In this sense, the writer/intellectual creates the space for speaking with and to others as opposed to speaking for others, and as a result avoiding the risk of committing what Gayatri Spivak equates with epistemic violence against the voiceless. The act of writing and the implied act of reading and listening is part of that process of working out the historical trauma. And yet the ultimate value of this book is how de Beer draws our attention to how the texts, by drawing on local cultural resources or indigenous resource base, forge a novelistic discourse of restoration, of healing, and working through trauma. The book lingers on the primacy of communal ethos, framed here through the use of Ubuntu and a form of Afropolitanism which valorizes oral testimonies, local healing modes, the presence of the invisible—the living dead—and mourning traditions, all of which aid and facilitate the sharing of the burden of trauma. Indeed the sharp intersection between life stories, history, and literature that the book surfaces can only point to its multifocal approach, and the act of writing, of translating experience into words, which enables the process of mourning and posits literary texts as vehicles for symbolic reparation, restitution, and restoration. What de Beer's book allows us to do is to grasp art's ability to re-symbolize trauma in order to work through it and in the process offer paths of healing, way beyond the reinstatement of trauma and its ramifications that a range of sociological scholarship on the Rwandan genocide has tended to do. Because narrative through its tropes of journey, travel, and listening aid the amplification of voices, it is also transformative. Again, because narratives studied here avoid the installation of monuments and instead point to traces of traumatic memories, the book is able to use this to complicate our reading of post-genocide realities as complex and layered, as defying monolithic narrative and closure, and therefore sees healing as a multidimensional process that requires constant renewal. The book invites us to be witnesses and to keep alive the difficult history of the genocide against the Tutsi, eked deeply in public memory, and to share the immense burden of pain that the narratives studied here open up. Finally, the text is written in an easy style, both accessible and reader-friendly, and strikingly free of the usual academic jargons that tend to bedevil similar studies. It is a book for all of us that are interested in the human subjectivities that accompany mass trauma, while equally relevant for undergraduates, graduates, and senior faculty alike.

Centre for the Advancement of Scholarship   James Ogude
University of Pretoria, Pretoria, South Africa

Professor and Director, Centre for the Advancement of Scholarship, University of Pretoria, and author of *Ngugi's Novels and African History*, and editor of *Ubuntu and the Reconstitution of Community*, among others.

ACKNOWLEDGMENTS

The work presented in this book would not have been possible without the contributions of numerous people and institutions over the years. I herewith acknowledge in particular the generous financial and institutional support of the African Humanities Program of the American Council of Learned Societies, the University of Pretoria, and the National Research Foundation of South Africa. For their feedback on my writing, I would like to thank Elisabeth Snyman, James Ogude, Pamela Nichols, and Simone Chiara van der Merwe. I am equally indebted to my two fellow travelers: Omar Ndizeye and Stephanie Wolfe. Finally, my sincere gratitude goes to those who encouraged me when I became weary: my parents, family and friends, and those who believed in me, Ingrid and Mariaan.

Small sections of this book first appeared in other sources and have been adapted, integrated, and developed here with the kind permission of the following publishers and journals: *French Studies in Southern Africa, Indiana University Press, Présence Africaine, Tydskrif vir Letterkunde,* and *Verbum et Ecclesia.*

CONTENTS

CHAPTER 1

Introduction: Leaning on the Shoulder of Another

I grew up in Rhodesia, during the Bush War. My father's cousin and his wife were among the first ambush victims. At the time I was seven. I did not understand about colonialism, liberation wars, or the people's *Chimurenga*,[1] neither the first one nor the second. I only saw the grief on my father's face when he told me of the death of his beloved cousin.

I would eventually come to see that history and war are more complex than I had thought. In the end, it was literature that helped open my eyes. This has become increasingly important to me: how and what can literature teach us about different people's perspectives, experiences, and pain? How did reading books such as Tsitsi Dangarembga's *Nervous Conditions* and NoViolet Bulawayo's *We Need New Names* make me revise what I thought of a period, a people, and a place?

Years later, when I was already living in South Africa, a colleague pushed a slim volume into my hands and wistfully remarked how lucky I was to be able to read French. She had done me an enormous favor; it was Véronique Tadjo's account of the genocide against the Tutsi in Rwanda and it started me off on a journey that I am still on. That journey has led to this book, in which I am reflecting, not about literature and the Zimbabwean Liberation War, but about literature and the genocide in Rwanda.

I subsequently discovered that Tadjo's book was one of several texts by authors, from across the continent, who had set off on their particular journeys to Rwanda, bravely attempting to see in their own ways what literature could do in the face of the collective and unimaginable trauma

© The Author(s) 2020
A.-M. de Beer, *Sharing the Burden of Stories from the Tutsi Genocide*, Palgrave Studies in Cultural Heritage and Conflict, https://doi.org/10.1007/978-3-030-42093-2_1

that we call genocide. Genocide is about dehumanization. Literature can be about rehumanization.

At a conference in 2014, I had the privilege of meeting Berthe Kayitesi.[2] She evoked the delicate relationship between survivors and those who listen to their stories, foregrounding the value of 'learning *with* survivors' as opposed to 'learning *from* them'. She spoke of the 'reconstruction' of a survivor, made possible by 'the presence of the other who is not a survivor', another who has what she qualified as a 'safe mind'.[3] Similarly, in his testimony Révérien Rurangwa doubts whether it would ever be possible to pick oneself up again without accepting the outstretched hand of a friend and leaning on the shoulder of another (2006: 95).[4] This focus on mutual responsibility is reminiscent of a comment made by Nocky Djedanoum on sharing the burden of mourning: '[P]erhaps it comes to us naturally, this modesty that requires of us to lean on the shoulder of another, one who reaches out a hand and wipes away our tears to ease our pain?' (2000: 11; my translation).[5] The crucial presence of another who listens appropriately to trauma has been widely debated and theorized[6] and the comments made by Kayitesi, Rurangwa, and Djedanoum indeed echo the assertion that the activity of witnessing necessitates 'the intimate and total presence of an other—in the position of one who hears' (Felman and Laub 1992: 70–1).

Genocide is not only a form of extreme trauma that requires of us to listen to and narrate its stories; it is also mass trauma and the sheer scale of it demands a shared effort of representation. It asks that we invite as many voices as possible to participate in the dialogue, including those of the people who experienced it (victim, perpetrator, and bystander) and those of the people who listen to and read these stories.

Many researchers[7] emphasize the importance of creating multivocal stories in order to narrate collective trauma affecting whole communities. They accentuate the importance of establishing a shared memory and re-examining and reinterpreting our histories together. Such a negotiation may provide us with ways to create space for the 'contesting representations cobbled together from the often fragmented and clashing memories of survivors, perpetrators, witnesses and bystanders' (Hinton and O'Neill 2009: 1). It could lead to a less 'monolithic' and more 'complex and differentiated' view of the society as well as a 'plurality' of perspectives on the origins and consequences of the genocide (Staub 2006: 877). This daunting process can hardly be envisaged without the mediating role of both art and the 'intellectual witness' (Hartman 1998: 37–40).[8]

At times, traumatized communities are not yet ready to tell their own stories, and others step up to help shoulder this heavy burden. The practice of speaking for another undoubtedly poses its own set of potential dilemmas including the danger of appropriating another's story (James Dawes 2009: 396). When speaking on behalf of another, an inclusive approach where everyone's account within the community is taken into account is essential because 'no embodied speaker can produce more than a partial account' (Alcoff 1991: 20). Such shared encounters may provide ways of complicating existing dominant and univocal narratives, allowing communities to problematize categorizations and harmful collective associations.

Reflecting on the value of engaging in a participatory mode in dealing with trauma that affects whole communities leads me to the notion of '*récit dialogué*',[9] a term which refers to the creation of a shared narrative which is in fact woven together from parts of different individual stories (Gallimore 2009: 15–22). In this book, I set out to explore ways in which narratives of genocide perform such a *récit dialogué*, thus transforming the undertaking into a collective effort. I consider the written memory of this event and its heritage by accentuating the plurality of narrative voices and modes of storytelling that have emerged, informed by the premise that trauma on such a large scale requires not only multivocal representation but also multiple forms of listening. Such an approach seems to be necessary for restoration in a context where extensive trauma has taken place.

When I first became interested in reading genocide accounts, I assumed that it would be essential to place the texts in well-defined categories—testimonies versus fictional texts, secondary witness versus eyewitness accounts, and direct victims versus 'absent'[10] or 'intellectual' witnesses—forgetting, however, that it was just such categorization, binaries, and absolutes that had been so detrimental in the history of the Rwandan people. Certainly, in the aftermath of genocide, many of these boundaries are blurred and it seems to be more meaningful to situate these texts on a fluid continuum (Kerstens 2006). Berthe Kayitesi had already taught me, in her soft-spoken manner, that when dealing with genocide stories, one should never hierarchize people's suffering, but rather provide a space to listen to them all.[11] The question I discovered was not so much who has the right to tell the story, although this is an interesting question, but how it can be told so that it invites dialogue, creates a multivoiced narrative, allows us to listen to the trauma of genocide, and involves the reader.[12]

Such a mode of joint, inclusive narrative becomes particularly interesting when explored through the lens of the African philosophical system of *ubuntu*; this is therefore a pivotal pillar of my reading of the genocide stories dealt with in this book. In my discussion of these texts, I place strong emphasis on the Afropolitan cultural frame in which they were conceived and written. Instead of using European tropes, the focus is on an African conflict written about by writers from African origin, enabling a more situated study in which it becomes possible to draw out the ideas of *ubuntu*, oral testimonies, local healing, the presence of the invisible, and mourning traditions. However, although I refer to realities, culture, real places, and people, this book lays no claim to being an anthropological study.[13] Instead, it is about discovering how literature opens our eyes and minds to what is not at first obvious, material and visible. I look at how literature, as presented through an Afropolitan frame, contributes to a deeper understanding of the Rwandan genocide and its aftermath. Throughout, my interest remains in the role of literature and its ability to help share in the burden of testimony. Literature can urge us to move beyond the parochial in order to situate the experience of genocide within the universal.

One of the fundamental moments in the ongoing process of representing the genocide was the landmark literary project '*Rwanda: écrire par devoir de mémoire*' (generally translated as 'Rwanda: Writing by Duty of Memory'), which included Véronique Tadjo's book that had so moved me. Initiated in 1998 by a group of largely outsider, intellectual, or absent witnesses, the project undertook to write the stories[14] of and about those who had experienced the trauma first-hand. This book focuses on this project and, although each contribution articulates it in a unique way, the project explores how writing, which is also a metaphor for traveling, may lead to different ways of listening and involving the reader. I read about the genocide of the Tutsi in these written narratives before ever setting foot in the country. And yet, years later, they would shape the way in which I listened to testimonies and the questions I asked myself about the country. Now that I have listened to many other stories, they have in turn started to shape the way I read these literary configurations. It is this constant interaction between life stories, history, and literature that I find so inspiring.

This book endeavors to accentuate the contribution of this literary initiative to the existing body of literature by focusing, firstly, on its polyphonic, dialogical nature and, secondly, on the African cultural perspective that it provides.[15] It looks at each of the nine texts that are commonly viewed as part of the project.[16] One of the challenges of analyzing a project such as this one in its entirety is indeed the diversity of genres and forms that it offers: from highly poetic and imaginative works of fiction to others that more closely resemble argumentative essays or eyewitness testimonies. These different genres have their own internal structures and logic, making it difficult to know which criteria to apply when evaluating or appreciating the texts produced for the project. One way of doing so could be to consider the collective objectives associated with the project, such as creating public awareness, or attempting to 'resurrect' the victims in imaginative and respectful ways, or else, sharing the pain and the process of mourning, exorcising the horror of genocide through writing, contributing to the preservation of communal memory, and so forth.

Of course, it remains a delicate exercise comparing the literary, and at times fictionalized, representations of experienced and renowned writers such as Véronique Tadjo and Boubacar Boris Diop, who had not personally experienced the genocide, to the work of a genocide survivor such as Kayimahe, who was not a writer by profession and had not published much before engaging in the project. However, my point in including all the works produced for the project in this comparative analysis is not to measure their worth or impact in the literary world, but rather to remain true to the principle that representing genocide should be a multivocal, multilayered enterprise and to acknowledge that works such as these contribute immensely to the heterogeneous nature of the project.

In Chap. 2, I set the scene for the ways in which I read the nine texts. Here, I reflect on the interrelated notions of community trauma, listening and intellectual witnessing, and how the project is situated in terms of these concepts. As many of these tenets are framed within Western definitions of trauma esthetics, I move on to speak to the African frameworks and lenses that constitute a strong presence in the project, and which I believe have been underemphasized thus far in studies on the project.

Chapters 3, 4, 5, and 6 analyze each of the texts from the perspectives outlined in Chap. 2. In Chap. 3, through my reading of Koulsy Lamko and Véronique Tadjo's texts, I dwell on the Afropolitan frame in which the writers (wittingly, unwittingly, or perhaps instinctively) clothed their stories, and I introduce the trope of transformative travel. Chapter 4 explores the literary representation of some of the societal conditions which led to the genocide: fear of the Other, dehumanization, propaganda, and the culture of submission to authority, as depicted in Abdourahman Waberi's and Boubacar Boris Diop's texts. In Chap. 5, I look at the consequences and aftermath of genocide, through the portrayal, proposed by Monique Ilboudo and Tierno Monénembo, of the worlds of those living dead who inhabit post-genocide Rwanda. Chapter 6 is a reflection on the heterogeneous subject and authorial positions, as well as on the ubiquitous traces of exile and diasporic living which plague the African continent, as embodied in the work of Nocky Djedanoum, Vénuste Kayimahe, and Jean-Marie Vianney Rurangwa.

Although I have chosen, in each chapter, a specific overarching frame to discuss the texts, these frames are often present in other texts from the project. Therefore, where relevant or useful, I do include selected examples from other texts. In my conclusion, I narrow my focus to a number of themes that surface strongly throughout the project; here I no longer work with isolated texts, but read the project as a whole.

I situate my approach to this project within the broader framework of attempts to decolonize trauma theory and hope that it demonstrates what Irene Visser calls an 'openness to non-Western belief systems and their rituals and ceremonies in the engagement with trauma' and an engagement with 'culturally specific spiritual and religious perspectives' (2015: 250, 259). Informed by Jeffrey C. Alexander's approach to collective trauma, Visser notes that literature plays an important role in the process of verbalizing and giving 'narrative shape and meaning' to the harmful consequences of colonialism which have impacted negatively on the collective identity of certain societies (ibid.: 258).

In that sense, my reading of the project engages with the increasing academic interest in the troubling relationship between Euro-American conceptualized trauma theory and literature on violence in postcolonial contexts. The origins of the mass trauma which is the subject of this project are indeed 'historical and political', making it a useful example to explore the concerns and aims of the current drive to decolonize trauma theory (ibid.: 251). As Visser points out (drawing from Michael Rothberg's work), the Western model with its focus on single traumatic events that are already in the past does not 'account for the sustained and long processes of the trauma of colonialism' which is often collective rather than individual and chronic rather than of a passing nature (ibid.: 252). This is why this approach has effectively been 'discarded' in terms of current postcolonial scholarship, which favors a focus on historical, societal, and 'cultural specificity' and engages with 'concrete' historical facts (ibid.: 253–4). It would be meaningful then to see how the project deals creatively with issues of collective trauma, ongoing trauma, cultural forms of mourning, the 'complexity of the entanglement of complicity, agency and guilt' (ibid.: 258) in the colonial process, as well as the aftermath of trauma; do they envisage possibilities of healing, 'renewed social inclusion', 'social activism, recuperation and psychic resilience' in their texts, or does the focus remain on the 'crippling' effects of trauma such as victimization, inaction, and weakness? (ibid.: 254, 263).

This project has been analyzed by various critics, to whom I refer throughout. They have, for the most part, dedicated their comments to a smaller selection of writers from the project. Few have discussed the project in its entirety or focused on what the project offers when read as a multivocal project, written within an Afropolitan frame. This entry point is, I believe, the crux of my contribution to the existing debate.

NOTES

1. A Shona word which refers to the armed uprising against the colonialists in Zimbabwe.
2. Dr. Kayitesi was a survivor of the genocide in Rwanda, where, at the age of 16, she lost both her parents. In 2009, she published her testimony, *Demain ma vie—enfants chefs de famille dans le Rwanda d'après*. She died of a brain hemorrhage at age 37 on 23 June 2015.
3. From a conference paper read by Berthe Kayitesi, entitled 'Testimonies, Trauma and Resilience: Learning and Coping with Survivors from the Genocide against the Tutsi of Rwanda', at the conference Rwanda 20 Years After: Memory, Justice and Recovery in the Shadow of Genocide, held 28–30 March 2014, at Weber State University, Utah.
4. « Peut-on se relever seul, sans saisir la main tendue, s'appuyer sur une épaule amie ? Je ne le crois pas » (Rurangwa 2006: 95).
5. « Peut-être que c'est dans le naturel de l'homme, cette pudeur qui veut que l'on s'appuie sur les épaules de l'autre, que l'autre nous donne la main et nous essuie les larmes pour nous soulager de notre blessure ? » (Djedanoum 2000: 11).
6. Consult, for example, Bal et al. (1999: 10), Dauge-Roth (2009: 168), Felman and Laub (1992: 71), LaCapra (2001: 98), Laub (1995: 73), and Semprun (1996: 26).
7. Consult, for example, Alcoff (1991: 20), Dauge-Roth (2010: 172), Gallimore (2009: 15–22), Hinton and O'Neill (2009: 1), and Staub (2006: 880–7).
8. Geoffrey Hartman uses the term 'intellectual witness' to refer to those who did not experience an event (such as the Shoah) first-hand, but who feel compelled to bear witness to it. The function of the intellectual is, then, to provide a 'witness for the witness', to 'actively receive words that reflect the

darkness of the event' (Hartman 1998: 37, 41). According to Hartman, this notion includes both witnesses who have contact with eyewitnesses, or what he calls the 'first generation', and those who see the Shoah not as merely a past event but as a 'contemporary issue requiring an intensity of representation close to eyewitness report'(1998: 38).

9. A type of narrative or account which is created through dialogue and sharing.
10. I borrow this term from Catherine Coquio, quoted in Viviane Azarian (2011).
11. Refer to notes 2 and 3.
12. For more on the reader's involvement, consult Kenneth Harrow (2005: 40).
13. In a collaborative project on the meaning of genocide memorials, which led us as a research team to visit all the districts and listen to testimonies, I found that many of the cultural and historical elements of Rwanda and the genocide that I had encountered by reading literary texts were confirmed by the stories we heard. These realities therefore do inform my analysis of the texts, but my focus is on how stories are told rather than on the social and historical content of the stories.
14. I use the term 'story' in a very broad sense, referring mostly to the act of narrating an event, in the sense ascribed to it by Paul Ricœur (1983: 116) in his discussion of 'mise en intrigue' through the process of mimesis I (prefiguration), mimesis II (configuration), and mimesis III (refiguration). I intend no connotation regarding the truthfulness or fictional value of the accounts in question to be derived from the term 'story'.
15. Small sections of this book were originally published in other sources—see De Beer (2015, 2016a, b, 2019) and De Beer and Snyman (2015)—and have been edited and reworked here within the framework of this text with the kind consent of the relevant journals/publishers.
16. The following texts were published as part of this endeavor:
    Murambi: le livre des ossements (2000) by Boubacar Boris Diop from Senegal;
    L'aîné des orphelins (2000) by the Guinean writer Tierno Monénembo;
    Murekatete (2000) by Monique Ilboudo from Burkina Faso;
    La phalène des collines (2002) by Koulsy Lamko from Chad;
    L'ombre d'Imana: voyages jusqu'au bout du Rwanda (2000) by Véronique Tadjo from Côte d'Ivoire;
    Moisson de crânes: textes pour le Rwanda (2000) by Abdourahman A. Waberi from Djibouti;
    Nyamirambo! (2000), a poetry anthology by Nocky Djedanoum from Chad;
    Le génocide des Tutsi expliqué à un étranger (2000), an essay by exiled Rwandan Jean-Marie Vianney Rurangwa; and
    France-Rwanda: Les coulisses du génocide, témoignage d'un rescapé (2001), a testimony by genocide survivor Vénuste Kayimahe.

REFERENCES

Alcoff, Linda. 1991. The Problem of Speaking for Others. *Cultural Critique* 20: 5–32.

Azarian, Viviane. 2011. Scholastique Mukasonga: le « témoignage de l'absent ». *Revue de Littérature Comparée* 4: 423–433.

Bal, Mieke, Jonathan V. Crewe, and Leo Spitzer. 1999. *Acts of Memory: Cultural Recall in the Present*. Hanover: Dartmouth College.

Dauge-Roth, Alexandre. 2009. Testimonial Encounter. *French Cultural Studies* 20 (2): 165–180. https://doi.org/10.1177/0957155809102632.

———. 2010. *Writing and Filming the Genocide of the Tutsis in Rwanda: Dismembering and Remembering Traumatic History*, After the Empire: The Francophone World and Postcolonial France. Lanham, MD: Lexington Books.

Dawes, James. 2009. Human Rights in Literary Studies. *Human Rights Quarterly* 31 (2): 394–409. https://doi.org/10.1353/hrq.0.0071.

De Beer, Anna-Marie. 2015. Ubuntu and the Journey of Listening to the Rwandan Genocide Story: Original Research. *Verbum et Ecclesia* 36 (2): 1–9.

———. 2016a. « La saison des pertes » dans *L'aîné des orphelins* de Tierno Monénembo. *French Studies in Southern Africa* 46: 30–45.

———. 2016b. Véronique Tadjo and the Masks and Shadows of Rwanda. In *Écrire, traduire, peindre—Véronique Tadjo—Writing, Translating, Painting*, Les cahiers, ed. Sarah Davies Cordova and Désiré Wa Kabwe-Segatti, 43–63. Paris: Présence africaine.

———. 2019. Ubuntu, Reconciliation in Rwanda and Returning to Personhood through Collective Narrative. In *Ubuntu: The Reconstitution of Community*, ed. James Ogude. Bloomington: Indiana University Press.

De Beer, Anna-Marie, and Elisabeth Snyman. 2015. Shadows of Life, Death and Survival in the Aftermath of the Rwandan Genocide. *Tydskrif vir letterkunde* 52 (1): 113–130. https://doi.org/10.4314/tvl.v52i1.8.

Djedanoum, Nocky. 2000. *Nyamirambo!: recueil de poésies*. Bamako, Lille: Le Figuier, Fest'Africa.

Felman, Shoshana, and Dori Laub. 1992. *Testimony: Crises of Witnessing in Literature, Psychoanalysis, and History*. New York: Routledge.

Gallimore, Rangira Béatrice. 2009. Souffrances individuelles et voix collectives: la stratégie orale des témoignages des femmes au Rwanda. *Cultures Sud: L'engagement au féminin*, March 5.

Harrow, Kenneth W. 2005. "Ancient tribal warfare": Foundational Fantasies of Ethnicity and History. *Research in African Literatures* 36 (2): 34–45. https://doi.org/10.2979/RAL.2005.36.2.34.

Hartman, Geoffrey. 1998. Shoah and Intellectual Witness. *Partisan Review—New York* 65 (1): 37–48.

Hinton, Alexander Laban, and Kevin Lewis O'Neill. 2009. *Genocide: Truth, Memory, and Representation*. Durham: Duke University Press.

Kerstens, Paul. 2006. "Voice and give voice": Dialectics between Fiction and History in Narratives on the Rwandan Genocide. *International Journal of Francophone Studies* 9 (1): 93–110. https://doi.org/10.1386/ijfs.9.1.93/1.

LaCapra, Dominick. 2001. *Writing History, Writing Trauma.* Baltimore: Johns Hopkins University Press.

Laub, Dori. 1995. Truth and Testimony: The Process and the Struggle. In *Trauma: Explorations in Memory,* ed. Cathy Caruth, 61–75. Baltimore: Johns Hopkins University Press.

Ricœur, Paul. 1983. *Temps et récit,* L'Ordre philosophique. Paris: Seuil.

Rurangwa, Révérien. 2006. *Génocidé: récit.* Paris: Presses de la Renaissance.

Semprun, Jorge. 1996. *L'écriture ou la vie.* Collection Folio; 2870. Paris: Gallimard.

Staub, Ervin. 2006. Reconciliation after Genocide, Mass Killing, or Intractable Conflict: Understanding the Roots of Violence, Psychological Recovery, and Steps Toward a General Theory. *Political Psychology* 27 (6): 867–894. https://doi.org/10.1111/j.1467-9221.2006.00541.x.

Visser, Irene. 2015. Decolonizing Trauma Theory: Retrospect and Prospects. *Humanities* 4 (2): 250–265. https://doi.org/10.3390/h4020250.

CHAPTER 2

Trauma and Storytelling in Africa

A LISTENING-WRITING PROJECT

The origin of the project entitled '*Rwanda: écrire par devoir de mémoire*' (hereafter referred to as 'the project') can be traced back to a writer's residency initiated in 1996 during Fest'Africa[1] by the Chadian author Nocky Djedanoum and Maïmouna Coulibaly from Côte d'Ivoire, both from journalistic backgrounds. Djedanoum explains that after an initial shocked reaction to the images of genocide that confronted him on the television screen, he felt compelled to do something concrete (in Mongo-Mboussa 2000).[2]

Djedanoum expressed surprise that the Westerners who came to write about the genocide seemed to have no need to ask permission from the Rwandan authorities, whereas he, an African writer, was initially treated with distrust (ibid.).[3] It was only in July 1998 that Djedanoum's group, consisting of African writers, film makers, and a sculptor,[4] left for Kigali. They spent several months in Rwanda, visiting genocide sites, prisons, and orphanages and meeting survivors, perpetrators, returnees from exile, foreigners, and other inhabitants of post-genocide Rwanda. Not all of the writers involved in the project were able to participate in the first journey and several returned later for further visits. The project extended over the following two years and resulted in, among other things, the publication of the texts that are analyzed in this book.

© The Author(s) 2020

A.-M. de Beer, *Sharing the Burden of Stories from the Tutsi Genocide*, Palgrave Studies in Cultural Heritage and Conflict, https://doi.org/10.1007/978-3-030-42093-2_2

A closer look at this commemorative initiative reveals that the majority of the participants were not genocide survivors or eyewitnesses. Seven of the texts were published by non-Rwandan authors and were based on the stories of survivors or adaptations thereof. These include four novels, two travel accounts, and a poetry anthology by authors from African countries as diverse as Djibouti, Chad, Senegal, Côte d'Ivoire, Guinea, and Burkina Faso.

These writers saw themselves as precursors of those who would one day find their own voices to narrate the genocide. The Senegalese writer Boubacar Boris Diop remarked that those who had seen their own mothers raped and their loved ones killed would eventually tell the story in depth, but that this would take time, if not generations, because novels are crafted with old memories, rather than with the 'immediate, raw reality' (Diop 2006).[5]

Certainly, at the time the project was initiated, few Rwandans appeared to have obtained the necessary distance from the genocide in order to be able to write literary or even testimonial texts about it (Kopf 2012: 67). Only a handful of personal testimonies, not to mention fictional representations, of the genocide had been published and what had been written mostly came from outside the continent. This situation has since changed, but at the end of the 1990s, the authors participating in the project were writing into a 'void' of representations of the genocide (ibid.). Indeed, only two of the project participants were Rwandan: one of them was a survivor who published a testimony and the other a Tutsi who lived in exile from a very early age and who wrote an essay undertaking to 'explain' the genocide to a stranger.

Fest'Africa established an office in Kigali, which continued the activities initiated by this group of intellectuals (Djedanoum, in Achariant 2002: 4). The endeavor eventually comprised various stages, and efforts were made to bring the texts and testimonies back to the people of Rwanda. In 2000, in an attempt to include Rwandans who could not read the texts, some of them were adapted for the theater and staged with the participation of actors and students from the University of Butare.[6] This event attracted the interest of other authors, artists, and researchers, both from the continent and elsewhere, and Djedanoum considered it to be the crowning moment of the project (ibid.). Although other texts, authors, and artists became associated with the project at different stages, my analysis is limited to the nine texts published initially.[7]

The project is exceptional in a number of ways, not only because of its interactive, collaborative nature, but also due to the coming together of a group of transnational African authors[8] to write on an event that took place on African soil, providing us with a seminal example of what Stef Craps would call the trauma esthetics that is relevant to a 'minority' trauma (2014: 46). Diop noted that, in contrast to their European and American counterparts, African intellectuals had initially reacted mostly with awkward silences or indifference (2005: 83).[9] This project surely added texture and nuances to the representation of the genocide, which had, until then, been largely dominated by Western and Eurocentric perspectives.

The period of the genocide in Rwanda and its aftermath were eventful times for the continent and its democracies in terms of Human Rights; some uplifting, other depressing. South Africa was joyfully celebrating its first democratic election (27 April 1994) and the end of the apartheid regime. In 1996, South Africa launched its Human Rights Commission. In Nigeria, however, the prominent activist and author Ken Saro-Wiwa was sentenced to death together with eight others, and executed by hanging in 1995, despite international protestation against the politically motivated trials. Much has been written about how the international community failed Rwanda and chose to focus on the events unfolding in South Africa at the time.

One of the challenges faced by the group of writers was keeping a suitable intellectual distance while at the same time providing appropriate listening: 'For the testimonial process to take place, there needs to be a bonding, the intimate and total presence of an *other*—in the position of one who hears. Testimonies are not monologues; they cannot take place in solitude' (Felman and Laub 1992: 70–1). This role required of them to 'actively receive' the words of those who did experience the genocide (Hartman 1998: 48): 'We had to learn to listen to irreparably broken human beings recounting our own novels to us before we could write down even the first word' (Diop 2003: 122). Their aim was to 'ponder, listen, observe, try to understand and reflect together' and hope that the Rwandans themselves would, in time, be able to take on the arduous task of narrating the genocide (Djedanoum 1999; my translation).[10]

The authors seemed acutely aware of the interactive, dialogical nature of witnessing. Abdourahman Waberi writes about searching for a form of poetry to express the pain in such a way that it could somehow be not universal, but at least 'shared' and 'shareable' (in Brezault 2000).[11] One can never truly share the experiences of others, nor speak of their pain; one can only listen to them silently and with modest humility: 'listen to them at length, brush against them lightly, caress them with awkward words and silences' (Waberi 2004: 15; my translation).[12]

Koulsy Lamko likens his role as a writer to that of a ferryman moving between two shores, a medium through whom words can pass and who hopes to transform his own life as well as that of others (in Kalisa 2005: 263).[13] The authors' intent was clearly not to silence or usurp the voice of the other, but rather to create spaces for encounters and plurality as well as open the way for Rwandans to start telling their own stories. The intention was *not* to provide a conclusive text on the genocide, but to be a type of humble listener and, at best, a precursor or interim measure until the Rwandans themselves could write their stories; this is to my mind precisely what defines the historic and literary value of the project.

An 'African Response'

This section deals with the African roots of the project participants. I also consider the communitarian notion of *ubuntu*,[14] with its focus on solidarity, as well as the capacity of the oral tradition to build bridges and share stories.

I have chosen this paradigm for various reasons. Firstly, the participants of the project all hail from the African continent and were therefore in a position to narrate the genocide in ways which take into account the cultural values of the continent they were writing about. Secondly, if the writers truly wanted to act as appropriate listeners[15] and display a sense of solidarity, it would make sense to write texts that engaged with the cultural and traditional framework of the witnesses they were listening to and whose stories they were telling.

Such a reading seems to cohere with the spirit of the project as it was originally conceived; it is commonly accepted that this joint effort by a transnational group of African authors was 'an unprecedented phenomenon' in African literature and that the 'old idea of Pan-Africanism, of an overarching African identity' was an important motivation for the participating writers (Cazenave and Célérier 2011: 84, 86). Furthermore, this project has been read from a variety of points of view; my intention is to add a fresh perspective by looking at their contribution to the existing body of knowledge on the genocide through this particular lens.

Never before in history had a group of African writers gathered, in the face of traumatic events which had taken place in an African country, to produce literary works which would be at the same time 'individual' *and* 'collective' (Djedanoum 1999).[16] It would seem that the collaborative nature of the project, in spite of the restrictions it may have introduced, offered a potentially more effective platform to respond to the duty of memory and reflected the communal scale of the trauma.[17] Through such an endeavor, it became possible to express not only a personal response to the genocide but also a polyphonic and mutual one; the writers were able to respond both as individuals and as a voice from the African continent.

Thus was conceived an attempt to redress the imbalance between the large-scale reporting by Western media and the near-silence and seeming indifference on the part of African intellectuals, by adding an 'African response' to the genocide (Small 2007: 85). This silence could easily (and erroneously) be interpreted as consensus with the Afro-pessimistic version of events offered by Western media, colored by a somber image of the 'dark' continent, associated with 'interethnic hatred' and 'savagery' (Small 2005: 122–3; my translation). The project was also an attempt to resist this prevailing sense of despair directed at the African continent (ibid.: 123–5).

One can ask whose memory is being represented here and, if it is a collective memory, whether we are dealing with Rwandan or African or even world memory (Kopf 2012: 67, 68). In this regard, the participants faced a dilemma: were they to write as individuals or as 'African citizens' (Hitchcott 2009: 153)? This is possibly why Nicki Hitchcott describes them as 'global African citizens', thus underlining the inherent tensions of such a collective identity—being at the same time African and world citizens (ibid.: 152–3).

Furthermore, the composition of the group was unusual: the authors hailed from various geographical locations but still had the 'colonial experience' in common (ibid.). Hitchcott has suggested that this composition is a reflection of the '*identité africaine*' in its diversity and plurality, while at the same time bringing together writers who had much in common (ibid.). Abdourahman Waberi claims that their initiative offered a way of 'inscribing' an African tragedy 'into the field of reflection and literature written by Africans themselves' (in Hirchi 2006: 601; my translation).[18] Their unique mandate, then, was to write the stories of their own continent in their capacity as African individuals against a backdrop of certain shared historical experiences.

Not only can such literature be rehumanizing, as I suggest in my introduction; it seems that it can also be a pre-emptive force which sensitizes us to conditions in our society that potentially lead to genocide (Montesano 2015: 88). Patrice Nganang (2007) argues that, after the genocide, literary testimony in Africa, which was traditionally written within a tradition of victimhood, should be replaced by a new type of writing: one which would prevent future tragedies on the continent.[19]

Afropolitan Authors

A quick glance at the body of authors that constituted the project reveals that it would be a misconception to classify them exclusively as 'African' writers. They have all lived and worked outside the continent and their approaches to writing have naturally been influenced not only by the cultures and paradigms of their countries of birth, but also by those of the other countries and continents they have inhabited. Indeed, Waberi would argue that it is this 'interstitial space' that they occupy that enriches their creative responses to a task such as writing about the genocide, in a way that takes into account the Rwandan context and paradigm within the larger context of the continent. Waberi submits that many contemporary African authors currently living outside the continent

> test their creative machinery in an interstitial space that is always haunted by their experiences in, and on-going relationships with, Africa. It is a space between here and elsewhere, the intimate and the colossal, yesterday and today; a space, finally, that is both foreclosed and open, once improbable, familiar, and strange. This space is in the process of becoming the main scene, if not the *common place* of their enquiry. (2011: 105)

Certainly, writers from the Global South are less and less seen as representatives of the continent and increasingly as 'individual and authentic voices', open toward the rest of the world (De Meyer 2015: 191; my translation). Thus, focusing exclusively on the 'African' elements present in the work of the writers involved in the project would be a gross oversimplification of what they contribute in terms of representation of the genocide. Searching for a type of 'African frame' which guides and underpins the texts might potentially confine one's reading to an essentialist idea of 'Africanness' based on what Waberi has called 'binary oppositions':

In order to understand the turbulence of globalization it is necessary to discard the following binary oppositions: rootedness vs. cosmopolitanism, relativism vs. africanity. The infinite and unpredictable number of possible relations between cultures, places, and temporalities leads us to question the diverse without denying the contours of one's own enclosure, and many African writers sift these enigmas through the sieves of their texts. (2011: 105)

What I hope to do, instead, is to take into account the 'contours' which make up the 'enclosure' of an author growing up with African traditions, while acknowledging that contact with other cultures provides him or her with ways of engaging creatively with, or even problematizing, African culture.

Waberi asserts that 'Francophone African writers, whether or not they work outside of their native countries, remain, as we have seen, ready to make theirs the exploratory power of writing' (ibid.: 110). This interstitial and exploratory space in which African roots dialogue with both its own traditions and other worldviews is inhabited by the majority of the project authors, as is the case with many modern diasporic African writers.[20] The literary contribution of these authors therefore can be better understood within the pluralistic, dynamic, globally connected frame of Afropolitanism.[21]

Ubuntu *and the Oral Tradition*

A critical point of reference for traditional African values is the notion of *ubuntu*, which is present in multiple contexts and forms on the continent and of which I provide only a brief introduction, emphasizing aspects which will be helpful for my analysis.[22]

This worldview is widely accepted as a 'trademark' of African cultures (Gyekye, in Krog 2008: 360) and is found in many African ontologies and in a number African languages, albeit it under a different name (Kamwangamalu 1999: 25). This concept has taken on many forms in discourses on African philosophy and has at times been called 'African humanism' (Gaylard 2004: 267), 'Afro-communitarianism' (Metz and Gaie 2010: 273), or 'interconnectedness-towards-wholeness' (Krog 2008: 355). A Rwandan equivalent of *ubuntu* is the term *ubumuntu*, which is generally accepted as meaning to be human(e), empathetic, and caring. In post-genocide Rwanda, this term has popularly become associated with the notion of peacebuilding and reconciliation facilitated through dialogues called the 'Ubumuntu Conversations' (Musundi 2018).

A variety of sources[23] are available that discuss the meaning of *ubuntu*; in short, it is an indigenous African or sub-Saharan ethical perspective, which 'reflects the African heritage, traditions, culture, customs, beliefs, value systems and the extended family structures' (Kamwangamalu 1999: 26). Scholars of *ubuntu* generally agree that this sense of community represents an alternative voice to individualist-orientated Western discourses, as it evaluates a person's actions in terms of their impact on the harmony and communal relationships in a society (Metz and Gaie 2010: 273).

Some of the fundamental values associated with this notion are 'respect for any human being, for human dignity and for human life, collective sharedness, obedience, humility, solidarity, caring, hospitality, interdependence, communalism' (Kamwangamalu 1999: 26). It plays an important role in community building, as it is associated with the ability to uphold mutual reciprocity, dignity, peace, and harmony; to connect with another in a humane way; and to show compassion, empathy, and solidarity (Gyekye, in Krog 2008: 360; Nussbaum 2003: 21). The South African researcher Pumla Gobodo-Madikizela defines the essence of *ubuntu* as 'that capacity to connect with another human being, to be touched, to be moved by another human being' (in Gade 2012: 489). *Ubuntu* values consensus, a respect for the beliefs of others, communal responsibility toward the ecosystem, co-existence, networks of relationships, brotherhood, kinship, and inclusivity (Botha 2005: 91–2). With its focus on harmony and community, this notion thus has a significant role to play in post-violence contexts, where reconciliation, rehumanization, and restoration are deeply necessary.

Although *ubuntu* is often associated with South Africa and the Truth and Reconciliation Commission (TRC),[24] my use of this term follows Thaddeus Metz's 'normative-theoretical' description which does not limit it to the borders of South Africa or to the way indigenous southern African societies understood it in the past, but includes wider contemporary understandings of this notion (2011: 534–5). In spite of the cultural diversity of the African continent, there are threads of commonality in terms of the values, traditions, and practices present in various African societies, of which the notion of *ubuntu* is an example (Kamwangamalu 1999: 26).

Although different regions have their own taboos, gods, and customs, there are indeed general elements that exist in African tradition, such as the presence of the sacred in everything, the relationship between the visible and the invisible realms and the living and the dead, and a strong sense of community (Hampaté Bâ 1996: 12). One can of course easily be accused of essentialism and homogenization when attempting to ascribe certain values to 'African' culture and tradition; however, there are grounds for 'qualify[ing] a theory as "African" as opposed to Western' (Metz 2007: 333). Furthermore, these recurring elements are present 'not only in the oral traditions of indigenous African societies, but also in the writings of present-day African literati' (ibid.), a view that has directed my analysis of the project. Metz nonetheless prefers to call these elements 'tendencies' and 'intuitions' rather than 'essences' (ibid.).

The transmission of this value system is invariably linked to the oral tradition. Its values are thus not intrinsic, but rather passed on 'by means of oral genres such as fables, proverbs, myths, riddles, and story-telling' (Kamwangamalu 1999: 27). *Ubuntu*, or African humanism, is 'a way of life' which Es'kia Mphahlele claims is 'embedded in our proverbs and aphorisms and oral poetry, and in the way our elders spoke to us' (in Gaylard 2004: 273).

A logical place, then, to start looking at traditional and communal practices in terms of storytelling within the African context would be the oral tradition,[25] a tradition with which the authors from the project are intimately acquainted. Nevertheless, a writer such as Tierno Monénembo, rather than speak of 'oral tradition' or 'African culture' when referring to African literature, labels which suggest a type of rigidity and stagnation, prefers the notion of '*fonds culturel africain*', a cultural collection or stock which acts as a source of inspiration, but is characterized by renewal and invention (Monénembo 2007: 177).

Monénembo poetically admits that he 'entered into the world through the doorway of the tale',[26] that his 'Ariadne's thread' is that of the spoken word, that his 'cradle' was the 'kingdom of words' and that his cultural foundation was that of the grandmother, the sage, and the griot (Monénembo 2007: 174; my translation). For this author, these three elements of his heritage are embodied in three oral forms: the tale (which he characterizes as being supple, exploratory, and open-ended), the proverb (which in contrast is concise ['*lapidaire*'], precise, peremptory, and prescriptive), and finally the griot, that bearer and guardian of the spoken word, who is also a creator, a type of 'writer without a quill' (ibid.: 175, 176).

The African oral narrative serves as a type of bridge-building, unifying device; it is a 'kinship fostering tool' and 'communalizing genre' that has been sorely challenged by the postcolonial and global situation (Opondo 2014: 118). It is compared to an instrument that 'brings together not only the artist and the particular audience, but also the entire community within which the performances are derived and performed' (ibid.).

Oral stories fulfill many roles; because of the cultural and natural objects and social relationships that are present in them, they speak to cultures and contribute to authentic identity formation (ibid.: 119). They are also links between the past and the future that provide continuity and create a sense of community amongst those who 'share these pasts and presents. This sense of community eventually leads to the ownership of the story by the audience. It becomes "our" story, despite the narration by an individual' (ibid.: 119–20). In short, oral culture serves to transmit the past by including those collective characteristics of a specific society which distinguish it from other societies, thus providing continuity (Fiorio 2006: 68). Irene Visser describes oral storytelling as a potential 'ritual means to heal from trauma' when it connects the past to the present and draws upon 'the ancestors and their sacred power to restore harmony' and that oral storytelling can entail a healing and restorative process because it creates a space of 'insight and acceptance' (2015: 259). She concludes that a 'decolonized reading of trauma' requires an acknowledgment of the 'centrality of oral modes of narrative and their ritual function in indigenous communities' (ibid.).

The oral narrative (or even a written narrative based on orality) can become a space in which a 'mental dialogic relationship' can be created between the narrator and the audience, a 'platform' on which ideas can be shared and reacted to (Opondo 2014: 120), thus illustrating why this genre lends itself to situations in which shared stories can be narrated and in which a space for empathetic listening, solidarity, and reciprocity can be nurtured, as is required by *ubuntu*.

It is precisely because genocide is an extreme degree of othering, that listening to another's genocide story is important for restoration and provides those who have not suffered genocide, a way of 'showing *ubuntu*' to those who tell their stories (De Beer 2015: 1).

Solidarity and Participating in Mourning

When I asked Véronique Tadjo how the 'African' composition of the group enhanced the existing body of representation of the genocide, her reaction was that their effort 'intrinsically' added nothing to that of the Western writers, except to redress the imbalance that existed because of the prominent Western media coverage of the event as opposed to the near-silence of the African continent.[27]

I felt, however, that this modest answer did not take into account certain characteristics of their writing, nor the group's desire to demonstrate their 'moral solidarity' with their African brothers and sisters (Djedanoum 1999).[28] This desire is reminiscent of the notions of a shared humanity and the value of community, notions in which *ubuntu* is grounded and which Thaddeus Metz and Joseph Gaie define as the 'combination of identifying with others and exhibiting solidarity with them' (2010: 276).

One of the meaningful ways in which one can demonstrate solidarity with those who have experienced genocide is in somehow participating in the mourning process, especially within the context of Rwandan cultural perspectives on mourning, which I discuss later in this chapter. Translating the experience into words, Boubacar Boris Diop assures us, 'assists the work of mourning'; that was really why the writers were there—to be present for their Rwandan brothers and sisters in their time of mourning: 'That was in a sense the meaning of our presence over there, even beyond literary implication [...] Like in any family, when mourning takes place, the friends and loved ones must be there, so that they can suffer together and turn the page' (in Brezault 2002; my translation).[29]

Thus it seems that the writers did not merely relay and transmit this event, but found themselves in the position of mourners; a literary text can become a type of symbolic reparation, a 'burial rite which removes the individual death from the nothingness of mass death' (Germanotta 2016: 91; my translation).[30] The creation of a communal memory is perceived as a type of 'resurrection' of the dead through the medium of writing (Tadjo, in Hodgkin and Sebag Montefiore 2005: 15), for 'writing is in itself a tremendous battle against the void, against death' (Djedanoum 1999; my translation).[31] Literature goes beyond mere statistics or an impersonal account of the cold facts and nameless and faceless victims, but rather provides a human account with which the reader can identify or which at least enables the reader to seize the enormity and effect of this event (Tadjo, in Hodgkin and Sebag Montefiore 2005: 15). Tadjo explains that they undertook this task as writers and not as historians or journalists, because literature can fulfill this role by addressing the reader on an emotional level and by transforming statistics of victims into names and individual lives (Tadjo 2000).[32] Similarly, Waberi sees the ability to bring the reader to a place of understanding or feeling, even if partially, what the other has gone through, as one of the 'miracles' of literature: 'I do not see my book as a form of testimony [...] I rather place myself in the realm of emotion, of creating understanding: for example make someone experience the last seconds of a dying man' (in Brezault 2000: 1; my translation).[33]

These writers make no claim of actually attempting to ease or understand the pain of the Rwandan people, but rather focus on showing solidarity; offering a shoulder, an ear, a presence; sharing the burden of mourning, a process described by Nocky Djedanoum as a 'powerful encounter' between writer and survivor (2000).[34] However, Djedanoum acknowledges that the baton must necessarily be passed on to the Rwandans themselves so that they can continue by sharing their own stories[35] (in Mongo-Mboussa 2000: 1).[36]

African Enclosures

Apart from the objectives of expressing solidarity and providing a communal response, I identified certain additional features as giving an 'African' frame—or 'enclosure', to use Waberi's expression—to the texts and the project's stated objectives. To my mind, these characteristics, such as allusions to the role of cultural values, the prominence of traditional wisdom in the form of sages and proverbs, and an insistence on the importance of burial customs and the relationship with the dead, added a valuable perspective to the narratives proposed by Western authors. My goal is not to subscribe to some sort of Africanist 'essentialism', but rather to explore some of the 'modalities of African existence in the modern world' and the ways in which the authors engaged with these modalities (Mosima 2018: 23). Many of the above features coincide with characteristics attributed to *ubuntu*, such as the importance of cultural and traditional values, as well as the view that 'a person is a person through other persons', or becomes more human(e) and complete through communal relationships, and its converse, namely that those who do not act in an appropriate manner toward others are likened to animals (Metz 2011: 537).

Another central element is the concept of the 'interconnectedness of human, animal, plant, inanimate environments and the cosmos' (Mphahlele 2002: 137). Tadjo asserts that this notion plays an essential role in West African traditional cultures and can be seen as the 'bedrock of Black Africans' way of being-in-the-world' (2013: 1). She describes this interconnectedness as a form of 'invisibility', which she understands as 'the belief that there is no separation between the spiritual and material worlds' (ibid.: 1, 2).

To my mind, then, the salient aspects of the project linked to the interconnected African worldview are its plurality and multivocality, which open up spaces for the expression of silenced and marginalized voices; its commitment to sharing and solidarity; and, finally, the elements which I identified above as creating an African 'enclosure' in the texts.

RWANDAN CULTURE AND TRADITIONS

In order to show how the narrative of the trauma of genocide can be resituated within a structure that is consistent with African culture and, in particular, with Rwandan values, I now direct my thoughts, at its storytelling traditions, cultural coping strategies, and mourning customs. Upon exploring traditional Rwandan culture and worldview, it becomes clear that certain myths, taboos, rituals, rites, and sacred elements played an integral role in creating a national identity and sense of community.

Traditional Rwandan Myths and Belief Systems

Myths were traditionally highly valued because they had the ability to create a community of shared memory, values, and aspirations and therefore lead to harmonious relations (Kayishema 2009: 12).[37] In oral-based societies, myths, tales, and legends are typically an integral part of individual and communal life and living. Rwandan culture and rituals were traditionally combined with art forms such as dance and music: 'The word "umuco" translated as "culture" means both art and culture. In other words, rituals performed in Rwandan daily practices as well as major life events are both cultural and artistic expressions' (Kalisa 2013: 159).

Jean-Marie Kayishema suggests that the biggest catastrophe that can befall a nation is the destruction of its entire national memory and the consequent removal of its cultural references and cohesion (2009: 28). The myths that are particular to Rwanda, and which traditionally served to affirm the identity of the Rwandan people and to promote unity and stability, are the founding myths of Kigwa and Gihanga (ibid.: 10). The myth of Kigwa is a cosmogonic myth explaining the origin of the Abanyiginya clan. According to this myth, Kigwa (the one who fell from the sky) is a hero (named Sabizeze or Mana) who is born miraculously from the heart of a bull, to his sterile mother Gasani (ibid.: 14–17). To escape from his father's wrath, he falls to the earth, where his name changes to Kigwa and he becomes the ancestor of Gihanga, the founder of the Rwandan monarchy and the sociopolitical order in Rwanda (ibid.: 17). Gihanga in turn receives a 'supernatural mission'. His name signifies 'the one who creates or invents' (ibid.). The two symbols that are linked to this notion of creation are the drum (signifying royalty) and the cow (ibid.). According to the myth, Gihanga is also the symbolic father of Gatwa, Gahutu, and Gatusi. Kayishema suggests that by interpreting these myths in literal and rational, rather than symbolic ways, certain ideological studies subsequently attributed to them a divisionist view of the Rwandan society, in contrast to the unifying intention the myth originally had (ibid.: 18).

Another central figure in the traditional Rwandan belief system, which Kayishema describes as monotheistic, is the figure of Imana (ibid.). This deity is partial to the Rwandan people because, as reflected in the well-known proverb '*Yirirwa ahandi igataha i Rwanda*', Imana spends his days elsewhere but he always comes back to spend the night in Rwanda (ibid.: 19). Many legends exist which demonstrate Imana's interventions in the lives of his people (ibid.). Traditionally, different mediators exist between Imana and his people: the spirits of the ancestors, the king who played an important role in assuring peace and harmony, and Lyangombe, who is the representative of Imana (ibid.: 19–20). In terms of the afterlife, there are specific beliefs: those who die do not go to live with Imana but move on to the peaceful non-active volcano, Mount Karisimbi, while the wicked are cast into the flames of the constantly erupting volcano Nyiragongo (ibid.: 19).

A further important aspect of the traditional Rwandan religious life is the belief in various taboos, which served to maintain social order. They promoted respect for figures of authority and for certain acts, such as sexual relations, which were regarded as being 'sacred'; they included the taboo of blood shedding outside the context of war (ibid.: 21). These taboos were also integrated in the foundation myths, in which their role was to magically protect the authorities and preserve social harmony (ibid.).

Thus, traditional Rwandan culture makes use of taboos and prohibitions which prevent people from behaving in inappropriate ways and which help maintain good relations in society (Bagilishya 2000: 350). These prohibitions and taboos are considered to be 'rules of life', given by God to the ancestors, who in turn passed them on to the next generation as a form of education: 'They are a collection of popular practices respected by all Rwandans and regarded as a kind of social security with magico-religious force. No one knows the origins of these prohibitions and all are content to say that it has always been so' (ibid.: 351). When taboos were transgressed, purification rites were required. Even warriors who returned from war would undergo cleansing rites, because of their contact with blood, before being reintegrated into society (Kayishema 2009: 21). Transgressing these cultural boundaries was seen as rebellion and led to punishment, often by spirits and powers of nature, causing illness and other misfortunes which often befell not only the individual but also the community (Bagilishya 2000: 351). In such cases, it was up to the elders and sages in the community to intervene, to plead with the ancestors and bring about the purification of the victims and the taming of the spirits through traditional rites and the help of a healer (ibid.: 351–2). Although these purification practices are less commonly followed in modern times, after the genocide many Rwandans expressed the need to cleanse the country from the supernatural forces and evil spirits unleashed during the genocide (ibid.: 352).

The combination of the foundation myths, the royal myth, the veneration of the ancestors, the cult of Lyangombe, and the taboos served to maintain peace and harmony, a system which, according to Kayishema, was undermined by the arrival of the colonizers and missionaries (2009: 22). He associates their arrival with a type of 'cultural ethnocide', as the appropriation of the ideologies imported by the foreigners is seen as having destroyed the national solidarity which had been safeguarded by Rwandan culture, myths, rituals, beliefs, and taboos (ibid.: 9). The abolishment of traditional rites and taboos by the Catholic Church, for example, led to the belief that all was now permissible, and replacing Imana with the God of the foreigners led to the Rwandan people having a weaker bond with God than the bond they traditionally had with Imana (ibid.: 26). Kayishema also demonstrates how, in contrast to the racial theories of the colonizers, Rwandan proverbs did not racialize, but suggested, for example, that different groups can be born from the same womb, and that children are all born the same—it is what they eat that differentiates them (ibid.: 25).

If, as Kayishema suggests, the removal or disempowerment of these cultural and religious elements played a nefarious role during the genocide, it would be important to see what space they are given in the novels on the genocide, either in form or in content, and how the novels portray the destruction of cultural and traditional points of reference within the context of the genocide. Integrating artistic, cultural, and ritualistic elements in a genocide narrative that is coherent with the Rwandan context would be a way of writing that takes the Rwandan 'frame' into account and artistically engages with or even restores some of these elements.

Culture and Mourning

A further cultural element which merits discussion is that of mourning customs and burial rites. This aspect is highly relevant to post-genocide Rwanda, where the landscape is littered with unburied and unclaimed bodies. The transcultural psychologist Déogratias Bagilishya speaks of a time, before the genocide, when the death of a community member would automatically bring the community to a standstill out of respect for the dead and in support of the family; 'violating this tradition of honoring the dead and helping the stricken family carried an extreme penalty' (2000: 339). The impossibility of performing all the necessary funerary rites has had—and still has—far-reaching consequences, given the vital role they play in the traditional Rwandan understanding of death.

In Rwandan culture, death does not mean that life is over; rather, it is a form of 'rebirth' or transformation, a phase during which the deceased crosses into the 'invisible world' of the ancestors (ibid.: 343). These ancestors are seen as heroes, saviors, protectors, and 'intermediaries between Imana and their family in the world of the living' (ibid.). Mourning rites and the care that is given to the mortal remains of the deceased symbolize and reflect this belief in the rebirth that is to follow (ibid.: 344).

Before burial, Rwandans traditionally bestow on the body a status similar to that of a fetus. Before the dying person takes his or her last breath, he or she is placed in the fetal position, with hands covering the face. This ritual of posing the body, which symbolizes rebirth, is called '*gupfunya umupfu nkigitebo*', which Bagilishya translates as 'lending to death the form of a basket'; he explains that this metaphor 'conjures the image of a full-term pregnancy' (ibid.). The deceased is then given the necessary for completing the journey toward the ancestors: certain types of food, medicinal plants, and hairs from a sheepskin for clothing. Farewell speeches are offered which refer to the prospect of seeing each other again, and the following words announce the person's death: 'He [or she] has gone to bring help', again emphasizing the fact that the deceased is to return to the living (ibid.).

A mourning period follows, during which friends, neighbors, and family remain with the body and those who have suffered the loss receive special care and cease their activities. The funeral marks the beginning of this period, which is characterized by both intense grief for the loss and enthusiasm for the journey to rebirth (ibid.: 345). A variety of practices are followed during this time, such as throwing away any food found in the house at the moment of death, purifying tools, not having sexual relations, and not cultivating or sowing (ibid.: 345–6). The mourning period is ended with a feast, held to celebrate the reintroduction of the deceased as a 'new and immortal being in the family's daily life', a ritual that is accompanied by an act of physical or symbolic procreation signifying renewed life (ibid.: 346). After this, the deceased remains a real presence in the family in the form of an ancestral protector, and the family continues, ritually, to provide him or her with nourishment and to see to his or her needs (ibid.).

Bagilishya explains that this process helps those who remain behind to process their emotions. However, when a person dies where no one can take appropriate care of the body, or if the body is missing, as was mostly the case during the genocide, the mourning period does not offer the solace that it is traditionally intended to do (ibid.: 346–7). This has further disastrous effects on community life:

> We all fear these deaths for which funeral rites and formal mourning practices are not possible because, in Rwandan tradition, these deaths are to blame for unleashing all sorts of ills, troubles and misfortunes. [...] The intensity of psychological distress (complete loss of control) created by a death that is not associated with any traditional means of protection is so crushing that any Rwandan might well suffer a traumatic reaction. (ibid.: 347)

Bernard Mouralis adds that the practice of making people invisible or disappear (*'la pratique de la disparition'*), which consists of dispossessing victims of their identities and names, makes it impossible for those who stay behind to mourn the dead (2002: 17). Such a society experiences a desperate need to know what happened to their loved ones, to reopen the graves, put names to human remains, and determine the probable dates and places of death (ibid.). Rémi Korman notes that this situation led, for example, to the creation of the notion of 'dignified burial' (*gushyingura mu cyubahiro*) as a response to the cruel and undignified ways in which people had been killed during the genocide (Korman 2015: 57). This 'new funerary ritual', entailed searching for and exhuming the bodies (*gutaburura*), collecting the body parts where possible (*gushyira hamwe umubiri*), and then washing and cleaning the remains (*gukarabya*) (ibid.: 58). He suggests that this process was 'rooted in the way the body is cared for in traditional funeral rites'; therefore, the process of cleaning the body took the place of traditional mourning rites such as posing, embalming, and clothing the body (ibid.).

Once again, the erosion and adaptation of these cultural elements are integral to the genocide story and would be important to include in a narrative on the genocide if it is to be coherent with the Rwandan context. The unburied and unidentified bodies that the genocide has left behind do indeed become a recurring theme in the project.

In Tierno Monénembo's text, a conversation between two children just before the Nyamata massacre alerts us to the significance of the burial rites for this society: 'Look, that's my shroud. My father, Gicari, gave one to each member of the family. [...]. These people are real animals. They know how to kill, but they don't know how to bury. Dying with the shroud in our hand is as good as being buried. That's what my father told us' (Monénembo 2004: 92). The implication is that knowing 'how to bury' someone in a respectful way is an important part of what distinguishes a person from an animal, a value which makes particular sense within the *ubuntu* worldview.

Cultural Taboos and Coping Mechanisms

With regard to trauma and cultural coping mechanisms, Rwandan tradition provides certain approaches to be used in situations of extreme distress. It seems, then, meaningful to deal with 'ideas about grief and trauma in a framework that is coherent with Rwandan culture' (Bagilishya 2000: 337). Doing so is in fact 'essential if one wishes to help Rwandans find words for their fears, hopes and questions about the loss of loved ones in the context of extreme violence' (ibid.). Bagilishya, who lost his own child, uses the example of his mother's intervention during a time of grief to illustrate a traditional approach used in Rwandan culture in times of trauma.[38]

In times of distress, there exists a range of popular beliefs and practices in Rwandan custom to which people can turn, one of which is the use of proverbs. Traditionally, proverbs play a role in both 'representing distress and preventing acts of anger' (ibid.: 341). Proverbs are a part of everyday life in Rwanda, and when people tell their stories, they are often an essential part of the narrative, helping the listener to understand the impact of the story.

Bagilishya confirms the important role of the listener in situations of trauma, aptly illustrating this point with a Rwandan proverb (ibid.).[39] According to him, the word 'proverb' is translated in Kinyarwanda as '*umugani*', a polysemic term implying a situation of dialogue/interaction and which does not simply mean proverb or saying, but can also refer to a tale, myth, legend, parable, or fable (ibid.: 341–2). The use of these creative modes of communication is a strategy which serves to 'symbolize intense distress' and to 'introduce a distance between experience and action, both at the social level and at the level of cognition' (ibid.: 341), as well as functioning as a sign of empathetic listening:

> In Rwandan tradition, the proverb is a mode of communication often used to express what a person has seen, heard and experienced at the level of emotions, feelings and states of mind, as well as to indicate to someone that they have been understood. [...] the proverb is often an appeal to the capacity of each person to give responses or explications through a mode of expression used to recognize, confirm and participate in what the other is living on an emotional level. The proverb creates a bridge between emotions, feelings or states of mind suffered at difficult moments, and the appropriate attitude prescribed by Rwandan tradition, to surmount the difficulties caused by this trying situation. (ibid.)

A proverb (or myth or fable), then, is much more than a form of common wisdom; it is a type of interactive strategy, used to express and acknowledge intense emotions and assist in obtaining some sort of emotional balance and guidance in terms of an appropriate reaction to these emotions. This confirms the notion that 'orality plays the vital role of ensuring continuity' and of 'regulating and organizing societal values' (Obieje 2016: 241). Within the Rwandan context it seems fair to assume that making use of oral modes such as proverbs, fables, and myths to talk of the genocide would imply using a form that is dialogic and interactive. In addition, it would imply a sharing, or at least comprehension, of the other person's experience; it is a type of bridge-building, not only between the one who speaks and the listener, but also between intense emotions and appropriate cultural reactions to such emotions.

Bagilishya notes that, although Rwandan culture had not foreseen the need for creating traditional strategies that would help its people deal with the trauma of genocide, or that could 'serve to create a distance from acting out in response to the extremes of sadness and rage associated with this catastrophe', his own experience showed him how powerful some of the cultural tools were when faced with unbearable suffering (2000: 352). In this context, he cautions that foreign therapeutic models should be adopted judiciously and their appropriateness questioned when dealing with a situation such as the genocide in Rwanda. Here again, the notion of community life and harmony is clearly crucial: 'The mental health and well-being of Rwandans cannot be isolated from that of their families and those who surround them. When working with Rwandans, we must take into account the importance of maintaining harmony within the families and with those who surround them, and the repercussions that may result from interference' (ibid.).

This element is also important in terms of justice, revenge, and reconciliation, because, as Bagilishya concludes, traditional forms of expression such as tales and proverbs, which 'offer the possibility of representing experiences and establishing a certain distance from feelings and acts of revenge, are essential in order to break the cycle of violence which has cast its shadow over Rwanda and its people' (ibid.). It is, however, precisely these cultural and unifying elements which the genocide aimed to destroy, because 'by definition, genocide annihilates everything, including the myths, symbols and language that define a community and its people' (Kalisa 2006: 518).

Homegrown Solutions: Drawing on Tradition in Modern Times

At an international conference on healing and social cohesion held in Kigali, Alfred Ndahiro (2016)[40] spoke on what he defined as Rwandan 'home-grown solutions'.[41] These solutions, drawn from Rwandan culture, traditions, and value systems, seem to reflect both independent and collective thinking and are based on a culture of dialogue, inclusivity, and consensus building, thereby creating a sense of shared responsibility, belonging, and self-reliance. My aim here is not to explain or evaluate the effectiveness of the societal practices described by Ndahiro,[42] but rather to use them as a stimulus to evoke the possibility of similar 'homegrown' recourses to traditional customs and ways of thinking when dealing with testimony and narratives on the genocide.

Ndahiro defines homegrown solutions in post-genocide Rwanda as 'unique' initiatives, drawn from Rwandan culture, which have 'stood the test of time' (ibid.). He posits that these solutions emanate from a traditional culture that is commonly shared by Rwandans and that englobes the 'philosophical' thinking and value system of the Rwandan ancestors, which have been passed on from generation to generation (ibid.). These solutions are deemed to be unique because they are based on both 'independent and collective thinking' and because they are informed by a 'culture of dialogue, consensus building and inclusion'. Furthermore, emphasis is placed on 'shared responsibility and self-reliance' (ibid.). Ndahiro claims that these strategies do not 'borrow from external ideas' nor require 'conventional expert support', and, most importantly, they are aimed at being inclusive of all Rwandans (ibid.). In contemporary Rwanda, these practices are often slightly modified to suit the demands of the current society. Ndahiro provides brief descriptions of a number of such strategies, showing how they link to tradition and how they impact on healing and reconciliation.[43] These initiatives are found in the areas of justice, social welfare, governance, and economic development.

Ndahiro suggests that it is the strong attachment to traditional customs and the value placed on self-worth and dignity amongst Rwandans that have led to the large-scale participation in these strategies and to the 're-emergence of a shared identity, renewed confidence and a positive-thinking mindset' in the aftermath of the genocide (ibid.).

If I draw on these 'homegrown' examples to think about representing the genocide, it would seem that, in comparison to more formal and individual ways of storytelling, a traditional African approach could be described as being community-orientated and informal, as well as 'ritualistic-communal' (Huyse and Salter 2008: 5). I acknowledge that the use of the term 'traditional' may be problematic, as could terms such as 'informal' and 'customary' or 'indigenous': like Lucien Huyse and Mark Salter, I maintain the term 'traditional' while acknowledging the often dynamic and even hybrid nature of the practices and traditions that are discussed (ibid.: 7–8). Their study, which compares traditional mechanisms of justice and reconciliation with other internationally used approaches, speaks of a 'domestic appropriation of previously existing models', suggesting that a number of 'post-conflict societies have now turned their attention to their legacy of indigenous practices of dispute settlement and reconciliation' (ibid.: 3). They also point out that, generally, traditional techniques have been 'greatly altered in form and substance by the impact of colonization, modernization and civil war' (ibid.: 6). These researchers contend that, in fact, it would be naive to view international and traditional approaches as being 'mutually exclusive', arguing rather for a cross-cultural perspective and a 'creative mix' of international and domestic procedures which acknowledge both the limitations and the potential of traditional rituals and beliefs (ibid.: 5, 6, 193).

These various examples, as well as the links to tradition, participatory modes of working and collective goals, were what increasingly started to interest me, as, during visits to the country in 2016 and 2017, I had begun to see similar links in certain forms of informal, collective ways of narrating the genocide. For me, the salient characteristic of these forms of narration is their link to Rwandan culture and tradition, an issue that I explore briefly in the afterword of this book. Furthermore, although I do dwell on the traditional elements of culture and storytelling that structures the project in many ways, it is unarguably characterized by a powerful 'creative mix' of traditional and modern, 'rootedness' and 'cosmopolitanism', universality and Africanity (Waberi 2011: 105).

It would seem, then, that although it would be inappropriate to focus exclusively on the indigenous cultures, value systems, and traditions of the country and continent on which the genocide took place, it would be equally unwise not to take these aspects into account when reading a project such as this one.

If it is true that *ubuntu* symbolizes harmony and connectedness with the other, the cosmos and the Supreme Being, as well as humaneness toward our fellow human beings, it stands to reason that genocide is an extreme example of the violation of the spirit of *ubuntu*. Healing would then, by definition, involve some form of recovery of the harmony and connectedness that had been shattered by the violence. Perhaps this is precisely how indigenous value systems such as *ubuntu*, with its awareness of solidarity, empathy, and hidden spiritual connections, can provide us with pathways to healing and restoration, a way of returning to our personhood. My contention is that the project, with its focus on these aspects, is one such possible pathway to restoration.

In addition, it would seem that the work of the participating writers could potentially act as a type of reconstruction of a 'transcultural' memory of the genocide, a 'new' memory that would take into consideration the foundational myths and cultural values as well as the colonial versions of the history of the Rwandan people (Semujanga 2008: 23). Finally, the writers could bring to the table their own imaginative representation of this historical event in ways which could accommodate conflicting and diverse experiences of trauma.

NOTES

1. An annual festival of African literature and culture based in Lille.
2. Djedanoum (in Mongo-Mboussa 2000) evokes his discussions with other writers during the festival and the role played by the Rwandan journalist and the French radio service (RFI) presenter Théogène Karabayinga, who passed away in 2011.
3. The group had obtained financial support from the Fondation de France, and Djedanoum suggests that the Rwandan authorities feared that the African writers would be manipulated by external powers such as France, ascribing this initial reticence to the strained relationship between France and Rwanda (Mongo-Mboussa 2000). Éloïse Brezault confirms that the Rwandan government may have been suspicious because of the authors' link to France, but also because their texts would be published mainly in Europe and could potentially subvert the official narrative without being subject to censure from the government (Brezault 2016: 235).
4. Bruce Clarke, author of an ongoing memorial sculpture project, 'the Garden of Memory', created for the victims of the genocide of the Tutsis in Rwanda.
5. This comment is based on the following remarks by Diop: « Et nos romans, écrits dans l'urgence du témoignage, ne disent encore rien en profondeur sur le génocide. Cela viendra plus tard et ce sera l'œuvre des victimes elles-mêmes. Ceux qui, à l'âge de quatre ou dix ans, ont vu des inconnus violer leurs mères avant de les tuer à coups de machettes, ceux qui ont vu mourir des êtres chers en parleront demain, car un roman s'élabore plus avec des souvenirs anciens qu'avec de la réalité brute, immédiate. Je suis convaincu que pour pouvoir être dite, la douleur doit traverser des générations, se sublimant ainsi progressivement » (2006).
6. Now Huye.
7. Meja Mwangi from Kenya, for example, was one of the original partici-pants, but as he did not publish a book within the agreed period of time, he is not generally included in discussions on work related to the project.

According to my understanding from an interview with Abdourahman Waberi, the Rwandan writer Tharcisse Kalissa Rugano also intended to participate, but was unable to do so (Waberi, in Brezault 2000). This book also does not consider the contribution of artists such as Bruce Clarke, film makers, and other artistic representations.

8. For a discussion of the unique composition of the participants of this initiative, consult Hitchcott (2009).

9. « En Afrique même, les intellectuels, mal informés ou de plus en plus enclins à l'autodénigrement, ont réagi au génocide par un silence gêné ou par de l'indifférence. [...] En dehors des Rwandais eux-mêmes, la réflexion sur le génocide s'est surtout menée en Europe et en Amérique » (Diop 2005: 83).

10. « Nous sommes venus nous recueillir, écouter, observer, essayer de comprendre et réfléchir ensemble » (Djedanoum 1999).

11. « C'est peut-être là la force de la poésie où on arrive à une espèce non pas d'universalité de la douleur, mais à une espèce de douleur partagée et à un rendu de cette douleur qui soit partageable » (Waberi, in Brezault 2000).

12. « [...] les écouter longuement, les effleurer, les caresser avec des mots maladroits et des silences [...] Que faire encore ? Se tapir modestement. Prêter l'oreille attentive et faire le plus souvent silence tout autour de soi. [...] On se dit que la littérature, cette fabrique d'illusions, avec sa suspension d'incrédulité, reste bien dérisoire. [...] Enfin, de quel droit prendrait-on la parole ? » (Waberi 2004: 15).

13. « Si j'ai un rôle à jouer [...], c'est celui de passeur. Il faut que je puisse être le medium par lequel des mots passent pour pouvoir être utiles, pour changer quelque chose à l'existence, la mienne et celle des autres » (Kalisa 2005: 263). I come back to this notion in my discussion of Lamko's work in Chap. 3.

14. I first started exploring my reading of the project through the lens of *ubuntu* for an article (De Beer 2015), and an edited volume on *ubuntu* and community (De Beer 2019). Some of those preliminary ideas and selected excerpts from these sources have been incorporated in this book with the kind permission of the publishers.

15. Much has been written about the importance of an appropriate listener in the process of verbalizing trauma: see Laub (1992, 1995: 75) and Bal et al. (1999: 7–17).

16. My remarks are based on the following quotation: « Si modeste soit-il, ce voyage des écrivains africains au Rwanda est une première en Afrique. En effet, dans l'histoire de la littérature africaine, jamais un groupe d'écrivains ne s'étaient penchés sur le drame d'un pays donné afin de confronter *ensemble* leurs sensations et réflexions en vue de produire des œuvres de fiction à la fois *individuelles et collectives* » (Djedanoum 1999; my emphasis).

17. Monique Ilboudo confirms, for example, that in Burkina Faso, hers was a single, isolated voice; however, within the larger structure of the project, her voice could at last be heard (Moncel 2000).

18. « Le témoignage est [....] une manière d'inscrire les tragédies africaines dans le champ de la réflexion et de la littérature faite par les Africains eux-mêmes. Notre continent est presque toujours l'objet de l'histoire passée ou présente et donc jamais le sujet de sa propre histoire. Nous avons essayé d'inverser cette tendance [...] » (Hirchi 2006: 601).

19. Some researchers have already shown how the project texts offer a 'restorative and preemptive imagining of postconflict Rwanda' (Montesano 2015: 102).

20. The Franco-Congolese writer Alain Mabanckou is, for example, described as a 'fervent advocate' of the 'littérature-monde movement', whose work moves beyond national borders; however, at the same time, his work also seems to represent a type of 'retour aux sources', a return to Africa, following a voyage to the Congo 23 years after his departure in 1988 (De Meyer 2015: 198–9).

21. Despite the controversy surrounding this term due to criticism of its alleged elitism and commodification, I still prefer to use it in the sense described by Susanne Gehrmann, based on an understanding of the concept as initiated by Achille Mbembe, which 'is relevant for both the diaspora and for Africa. Afropolitanism in this understanding of it decentres, de-essentializes and valorizes the continent' (Gehrmann 2015: 61).

22. Links have already been made by other scholars between *ubuntu* and the traditional Rwandan justice system, *gacaca* (Hinton 2016).

23. For more on the various understandings of this notion, read Christian Gade (2012). John Hailey also provides an in-depth overview, including examples, uses, and critique, of this worldview in his paper entitled *Ubuntu: A Literature Review*. (A paper prepared for the Tutu Foundation, November 2008, London. http://citeseerx.ist.psu.edu/viewdoc/downlo ad?doi=10.1.1.459.6489&rep=rep1&type=pdf. Accessed 6 July 2018.)

24. The TRC was appointed in 1995 and chaired by Archbishop Desmond Tutu. Its main purpose was to promote reconciliation and forgiveness among perpetrators and victims of apartheid in South Africa, primarily through public hearings.

25. I concur with Elisa Fiorio's assertion that the oral tradition does not refer only to stories, but is present in various forms, such as 'historic accounts, myths, tales, poems, proverbs, riddles, enigmas, anecdotes, lullabies, songs, ritual formulas, discourses, customs, biographical accounts, technical explanations, etc.' (2006: 68).

26. « Je suis entré dans la vie par la porte du conte » (Monénembo 2007: 174).

27. Véronique Tadjo, in discussion with the author, July 2010.

28. I base this assertion on the following statement made by Djedanoum: « L'ambition principale de ce projet intitulé 'Rwanda: écrire par devoir de mémoire' est avant tout de témoigner de leur solidarité morale envers le peuple rwandais et de rompre la loi du silence [des intellectuels africains] » (1999).

29. « La fiction, c'est-à-dire la parole, aide, je pense, au travail du deuil. Et c'était un peu ça le sens de notre présence là-bas, au-delà même de l'implication littéraire […] Comme dans toute famille, quand il y a un deuil, il faut que les amis et les proches soient là, pour qu'on souffre ensemble et que la page soit tournée » (Diop, in Brezault 2002).

30. « rite funéraire qui sort la mort individuelle du néant de la disparition de masse » (Germanotta 2016: 91).

31. « Oui, écrire est en soi une rude bataille contre le néant, contre la mort » (Djedanoum 1999).

32. « C'est en tant qu'écrivains et non en tant qu'historiens ou journalistes que nous avons été contactés pour ce projet. La fiction devait être notre matériau puisque c'est celui que nous connaissons le mieux. J'ai tout de suite été d'accord car la littérature a une fonction très spécifique, celle d'aller au-delà des faits et de s'adresser directement à l'émotion du lecteur. Elle présente la réalité sous un jour différent. Sa force, c'est la liberté de création. Ce qui m'intéressait, c'était de redonner aux victimes et aux bourreaux des visages, des noms, des vies. Montrer que ces gens-là étaient bien comme vous et moi » (Tadjo 2000).

33. « Je ne verrais pas mon livre dans l'ordre du témoignage […]. Je me situe plus dans le sentir, dans le faire comprendre: faire sentir par exemple les dernières secondes d'un homme qui va mourir » (Waberi, in Brezault 2000: 1).

34. My translation is taken from the following phrases: « Est-il acceptable de représenter la douleur des Rwandais quand on n'a pas éprouvé soi-même cette douleur ? J'ai des doutes quant à soulager la douleur des Rwandais par nos écrits […] En revanche, ce dont je suis sûr, c'est la force de la rencontre entre les Rwandais et nous, une rencontre qui impose le partage du deuil » (Djedanoum 2000).

35. Koulsy Lamko chose to stay on in Rwanda to work at the Butare Centre for Arts, where he 'experimented with various stage forms' and encouraged participants to 'provide input to the process of reconstruction' (Kalisa 2013: 163). He 'organized several presentations on urgent topics in post-genocide Rwanda such as conflict resolution, AIDS, women's rights and other social issues in post-genocide Rwanda. Lamko has staged conflicting views on what happened in 1994 and on what should happen after the genocide. In performances that lasted hours, he allowed the audience, mostly students, to intervene in case they disagreed or wanted to add to the debate' (ibid.). He ascribes his decision to return to his desire not to

'betray' the confidence that the Rwandans had shown in the writers (Chalaye 2001: 1; Kalisa 2013). Lamko confesses that writing a book—one which he admits is not very widely read—was not enough; it was merely an incomplete tool used for offering a perspective and carrying memory (Chalaye 2001: 1). He speaks of the difficulties he faced in the artistic process and the discouragement prevalent in a country which finds itself in the process of reconstruction, but also of the magnificent texts produced by young Rwandans during writing workshops organized by the Centre.

36. « Et puis, il y a l'acte d'écrire qui est d'une certaine manière un acte contre le négationnisme. Amener les écrivains et les chercheurs africains ici pour qu'ils prennent conscience de ce qui s'est passé, pour qu'ils le fassent partager aux autres, est à mon sens un acte de solidarité avec le peuple rwandais. Nous avons initié un travail, quitte aux Rwandais eux-mêmes à prendre le relais dans la diffusion des livres, des spectacles etc. » (Mongo-Mboussa 2000: 1).

37. Jean-Marie Kayishema also reminds us that the truth represented in a myth is typically symbolic, ontological, and transcendental (2009: 12).

38. It is important to note that Bagilishya is not a Tutsi survivor; he is a Rwandan of Hutu origin and was in Canada at the time of the genocide. His son was killed by a Tutsi soldier and the traumatic event he refers to in his article is the grief and anger that he experienced upon hearing of his son's death when he visited Rwanda a year after the genocide. Upon seeing the powerful emotional reaction of both her son and the young Tutsi survivor who shared the news with him, his mother intervened by using traditional Rwandan responses to trauma, such as non-verbal gestures and the use of proverbs. I refer to his comments purely because his article provides us with many important insights into Rwandan culture in general.

39. 'After many hours confronting and sharing our feelings about what we had experienced, I ended the meeting with my young guest by citing the following Rwandan proverb: Akamarantimba kava mu muntu, which means "the greatest sorrow comes from within" to signify that our ability to survive unusually difficult situations is determined by our inner strength. Without a moment's hesitation, he responded with another Rwandan proverb, Agahinda kinkono kamenywa n'uwayiharuye, which can be translated to mean "the sorrow of a cooking pot is understood by he who has scraped its bottom", signifying that one can only help someone else by genuinely listening to his suffering' (Bagilishya 2000: 341).

40. Dr. Ndahiro is a scholar and educator, and at the time of the conference he was serving as Advisor in the Office of the President of Rwanda. He has published a number of scholarly articles and books and is involved in the rehabilitation of survivors of the genocide against the Tutsis.

41. I do not provide page numbers, as these references are all drawn directly from the paper that he delivered during the conference.
42. Such critical evaluations do exist, such as that found in, amongst other places, Jennie Burnet's (2012) book, the report edited by Lucien Huyse and Mark Salter (2008) on traditional practices, Karen Brounéus's (2008) article on *gacaca* courts and the discussion proposed by Masengesho Kamuzinzi (2016) of the modern-day application of the traditional practice of *imihigo*.
43. One well-documented example of such an initiative in the justice sector is the *gacaca* jurisdictions, or community courts. These were based on an indigenous form of dispute settlement and used to address the immense problem of ensuring justice in the aftermath of the genocide (Ndahiro 2016). Another one of Ndahiro's examples of dispute resolution originating from traditional Rwandan culture is that of the *abunzi*, or community mediators, who are selected from a local community to arbitrate conflicts in the community. Currently, the purpose of the *abunzi* is to 'settle disputes but also to reconcile conflicting members of a local community and restore harmony in the neighborhood' (ibid.). In the social sector, a strategy which is particularly relevant to the most vulnerable members of the society is the practice of *girinka munyarwanda*, or 'one cow per poor family'. Another pertinent example is that of *umuganda*, or community works. Another solution is the *Ubudehe* Program, or the people's participation program, used when identifying problems and solutions in a community.

References

Achariant, Céline. 2002. Entretien de Céline Achariant avec Nocky Djedanoum: Entretien réalisé pour le théâtre international de langue française. Accessed August 2, 2017. http://africultures.com/entretien-de-celine-achariant-avec-nocky-djedanoum-2588/.
Bagilishya, Déogratias. 2000. Mourning and Recovery from Trauma: In Rwanda, Tears flow Within. *Transcultural Psychiatry* 37 (3): 337–353. https://doi.org/10.1177/136346150003700304.
Bal, Mieke, Jonathan V. Crewe, and Leo Spitzer. 1999. *Acts of Memory: Cultural Recall in the Present.* Hanover: Dartmouth College.
Botha, Deonie. 2005. Knowledge Management within the Multinational Organization: The Impact of the African Concept of Ubuntu on Knowledge Processes. *Mousaion* 23 (1): 82–96.
Brezault, Éloïse. 2000. À propos de Moissons de crânes, Textes pour les Rwanda: Entretien d'Eloïse Brezault avec Abdourahman A. Waberi. *Afri-*

cultures. Accessed May 2012. http://www.africultures.com/php/index. php?nav=article&no=1711.

———. 2002. A l'occasion de la sortie du dernier livre de B. B. Diop: Murambi, le livre des ossements. Entretien d'Eloise Brezault avec Boubacar Boris Diop. *Africultures*. Accessed July 6, 2018. http://www.africultures.com/php/index. php?nav=article&no=2577.

———. 2016. Les Œuvres du Fest'Africa: Les enjeux de la trace dans un « lieu de mémoire » déterritorialisé. *Contemporary French and Francophone Studies* 20 (2): 233–242. https://doi.org/10.1080/17409292.2016.1143740.

Brounéus, Karen. 2008. Truth-telling as Talking Cure? Insecurity and Retraumatization in the Rwandan Gacaca Courts. *Security Dialogue* 39 (1): 55–76. https://doi.org/10.1177/0967010607086823.

Burnet, Jennie E. 2012. *Genocide Lives in Us: Women, Memory, and Silence in Rwanda*. Madison: University of Wisconsin Press.

Cazenave, Odile M., and Patricia Célérier. 2011. *Contemporary Francophone African Writers and the Burden of Commitment*. Charlottesville: University of Virginia Press.

Chalaye, Sylvie. 2001. Fest'Africa au Rwanda: un projet artistique qui a fait école: Entretien de Sylvie Chalaye avec Koulsy Lamko. *Africultures*. Accessed July 6, 2018. http://www.africultures.com/php/index.php?nav=article&no=67.

Craps, Stef. 2014. Beyond Eurocentrism: Trauma Theory in the Global Age. In *The Future of Trauma Theory: Contemporary Literary and Cultural Criticism*, ed. Gert Buelens, Sam Durrant, and Robert Eaglestone, 45–61. London: Routledge.

De Beer, Anna-Marie. 2015. Ubuntu and the Journey of Listening to the Rwandan Genocide Story: Original Research. *Verbum et Ecclesia* 36 (2): 1–9.

———. 2019. Ubuntu, Reconciliation in Rwanda and Returning to Personhood through Collective Narrative. In *Ubuntu: The Reconstitution of Community*, ed. James Ogude. Bloomington: Indiana University Press.

De Meyer, Bernard. 2015. Posture et écriture. Le Mabanckou post-Renaudot. *Tydskrif vir letterkunde* 52 (1): 189–200.

Diop, Boubacar Boris. 2003. African Authors in Rwanda: Writing by Duty of Memory. In *Literary Responses to Mass Violence*. Trans. Jane Hale. Brandeis University: International Center for Ethics, Justice and Public Life.

———. 2005. Le génocide et les blessures du silence de Yolande Mukagasana. In *Dix ans après: réflexions sur le génocide rwandais*, ed. Rangira Béatrice Gallimore and Chantal Kalisa, 79–92. Paris: L'Harmattan.

———. 2006. Entretien avec Boubacar Boris Diop par Lanfranco Di Genio. Accessed January 26, 2012. http://www.fieralingue.it/modules.php?name=N ews&file=article&sid=303 (site discontinued).

Djedanoum, Nocky. 1999. Le Rwanda, terre de recueillement de mémoire. Accessed November 1, 2011. http://nocky.fr/ecrits-inedits/ (site discontinued).

———. 2000. Discours d'ouverture de Nocky Djedanoum à l'ouverture du colloque international—Fest'Africa sur le génocide des Tutsi et le massacre des Hutu modérés. Accessed November 2011. http://nocky.fr/ecrits-inedits/ (site discontinued).

Felman, Shoshana, and Dori Laub. 1992. *Testimony: Crises of Witnessing in Literature, Psychoanalysis, and History.* New York: Routledge.

Fiorio, Elisa. 2006. Orality and Cultural Identity: The Oral Tradition in Tupuri (Chad). *Museum International* 58 (1–2): 68–75.

Gade, Christian B.N. 2012. What is Ubuntu? Different Interpretations Among South Africans of African Descent. *South African Journal of Philosophy/Suid-Afrikaanse Tydskrif vir Wysbegeerte* 31 (3): 484–503. https://doi.org/10.108 0/02580136.2012.10751789.

Gaylard, Rob. 2004. 'Welcome to the World of Our Humanity': (African) Humanism, Ubuntu and Black South African Writing. *Journal of Literary Studies* 20 (3/4): 265–282.

Gehrmann, Susanne. 2015. Cosmopolitanism with African Roots: Afropolitanism's Ambivalent Mobilities. *Journal of African Cultural Studies* 28 (1): 61–72.

Germanotta, Maria Angela. 2016. L'écriture de l'inaudible. Les narrations littéraires du génocide au Rwanda, dans Interfrancophonies, n° 7, Nouvelles formes del'engagement dans les littératures francophones, (Alessandro Costantini, éd.), pp. 73–100.

Hampaté Bâ, Amadou. 1996. *Amkoullel, l'enfant peul.* Paris: J'ai lu.

Hartman, Geoffrey. 1998. Shoah and Intellectual Witness. *Partisan Review—New York* 65 (1): 37–48.

Hinton, Samuel. 2016. The Connection Between Ubuntu Indigenous Philosophy and the Gacaca Traditional Judicial Process in Rwanda. *US-China Education Review B* 5. https://doi.org/10.17265/2161-6248/2015.06B.005.

Hirchi, Mohammed. 2006. Entretien avec Abdourahman Waberi. *The French Review.* 79 (3): 598–603.

Hitchcott, Nicki. 2009. A Global African Commemoration—Rwanda: écrire par devoir de mémoire. *Forum for Modern Language Studies* 45 (2): 151–161.

Hodgkin, Marian, and Poppy Sebag Montefiore. 2005. The Rwanda Forum 2004. *History Workshop Journal* 60 (1): 1–24. https://doi.org/10.1093/hwj/dbi033.

Huyse, Lucien, and Mark Salter. 2008. *Traditional Justice and Reconciliation after Violent Conflict: Learning from African Experiences.* Stockholm: International IDEA.

Kalisa, Chantal. 2005. Le gos au Rwanda: entretien avec Koulsy Lamko. In *Dix ans après: réflexions sur le génocide rwandais*, ed. Rangira Béatrice Gallimore and Chantal Kalisa, 259–280. Paris: L'Harmattan.

———. 2006. Theatre and the Rwandan Genocide. *Peace Review* 18 (4): 515–521. https://doi.org/10.1080/10402650601030476.

————. 2013. Theatre and the Rwandan Genocide. *Journal of Dramatic Theory and Criticism* 27 (2): 159–166. https://doi.org/10.1353/dtc.2013.0014.

Kamuzinzi, Masengesho. 2016. Imihigo: A Hybrid Model Associating Traditional and Modern Logics in Public Policy Implementation in Rwanda. *International Journal of African Renaissance Studies* 11 (1): 123–141. https://doi.org/1 0.1080/18186874.2016.1212477.

Kamwangamalu, Nkonko M. 1999. Ubuntu in South Africa: A Sociolinguistic Perspective to a Pan-African concept. *Critical Arts* 13 (2): 24–41.

Kayishema, Jean-Marie. 2009. Aux origines du génocide des Tutsi du Rwanda: l'ethnocide culturel. In *Le génocide des Tutsi: Rwanda, 1994: Lectures et écritures*, Mémoire et survivance, ed. Catalina Sagarra Martin, 9–32. Quebec: Presses de l'Université Laval.

Kopf, Martina. 2012. The Ethics of Fiction. *Journal of Literary Theory* 6 (1): 65–82. https://doi.org/10.1515/jlt-2011-0014.

Korman, Rémi. 2015. Mobilising the Dead? The Place of Bones and Corpses in the Commemoration of the Tutsi Genocide in Rwanda. *Human Remains and Violence: An Interdisciplinary Journal* 1 (2): 56–70.

Krog, Antjie. 2008. "This thing called reconciliation …" Forgiveness as Part of an Interconnectedness-Towards-Wholeness. *South African Journal of Philosophy* 27 (4): 353–366. https://doi.org/10.4314/sajpem.v27i4.31524.

Laub, Dori. 1992. Bearing Witness, or the Vicissitudes of Listening. In *Testimony: Crises of Witnessing in Literature, Psychoanalysis, and History*, ed. Shoshana Felman and Dori Laub, 57–74. New York: Routledge.

————. 1995. Truth and Testimony: The Process and the Struggle. In *Trauma: Explorations in Memory*, ed. Cathy Caruth, 61–75. Baltimore: Johns Hopkins University Press.

Metz, Thaddeus. 2007. The Motivation for "Toward an African moral theory". *South African Journal of Philosophy* 26 (4): 331–335. https://doi.org/10.4314/sajpem.v26i4.31490.

————. 2011. Ubuntu as a Moral Theory and Human Rights in South Africa. *African Human Rights Law Journal* 11 (2): 532–559.

Metz, Thaddeus, and Joseph B.R. Gaie. 2010. The African ethic of "Ubuntu/Botho": Implications for Research on Morality. *Journal of Moral Education* 39 (3): 273–290. https://doi.org/10.1080/03057240.2010.497609.

Moncel, Corinne. 2000. Engagement d'écriture. *Africultures*. Accessed July 6, 2018. http://africultures.com/engagement-decriture-1464/.

Monénembo, Tierno. 2004. *The Oldest Orphan*. Translated by Monique Fleury Nagem. Lincoln: University of Nebraska Press.

————. 2007. Mondialisation, culture métisse, imagination hybride. *Présence Francophone: Revue internationale de langue et de littérature* 69 (1): 173–179.

Mongo-Mboussa, Boniface. 2000. « Nous avions l'obligation morale d'aller jusqu'au bout »: Entretien de Boniface Mongo-Mboussa avec Nocky

Djedanoum et Maïmouna Coulibaly. *Africultures*. Accessed July 6, 2018. http://africultures.com/nous-avions-lobligation-morale-daller-jusquau-bout-1463/.

Montesano, Michael C. 2015. Preemptive Testimony: Literature as Witness to Genocide in Rwanda. *African Conflict & Peacebuilding Review* 5 (1): 88–105. https://doi.org/10.2979/africonfpeacrevi.5.1.88.

Mosima, Pius M. 2018. Francophone African Philosophy: History, Trends and Influences. *Filosofia Theoretica: Journal of African Philosophy, Culture and Religions* 7 (1): 1–33.

Mouralis, Bernard. 2002. Les disparus et les survivants. *Notre librairie : revue des littératures du Sud* 148: 13–18.

Mphahlele, Es'kia. 2002. *Es'kia: Education, African Humanism & Culture, Social Consciousness, Literary Appreciation*. Cape Town: Kwela Books.

Musundi, Sela Muyoka. 2018. How Rwanda is Teaching Peace Education Through Ubumuntu Conversations. *Kujenga Amani*. Accessed August 16, 2018. https://kujenga-amani.ssrc.org/2018/08/14/how-rwanda-is-teaching-peace-education-through-ubumuntu-conversations/.

Ndahiro, Alfred. 2016. Homegrown Solutions, Healing and Reconciliation. Paper presented at the International Conference Healing and Social Cohesion: Understanding Reconciliation Experiences in Post-genocide and Extreme Violent Societies, Kigali, 9–11 November.

Nganang, Patrice. 2007. *Manifeste d'une nouvelle littérature africaine: pour une écriture préemptive*. Paris: Homnispheres.

Nussbaum, Barbara. 2003. Ubuntu: Reflections of a South African on our Common Humanity. *Reflections: The SoL Journal* 4 (4): 21–26. https://doi.org/10.1162/152417303322004175.

Obieje, Doris. 2016. Seasoning the Written: Orality in *Reine Pokou. Concerto pour un sacrifice*. In *Écrire, traduire, peindre—Véronique Tadjo—writing, translating, painting*, ed. Sarah Davies Cordova and Désiré Wa Kabwe-Segatti, 239–252. Paris: Présence africaine.

Opondo, Rose A. 2014. Oral Storytelling and National Kinship: Reflections on the Oral Narrative Performance in the Kenya Schools and Colleges Drama Festivals. *Tydskrif vir letterkunde* 51 (1): 118–131.

Semujanga, Josias. 2008. *Le génocide, sujet de fiction?: Analyse des récits du massacre des Tutsi dans la littérature africaine*. Quebec: Nota bene.

Small, Audrey. 2005. Le projet 'Rwanda: écrire par devoir de mémoire': fiction et génocide dans trois textes. In *Dix ans après: réflexions sur le génocide rwandais*, ed. Rangira Béatrice Gallimore and Chantal Kalisa, 121–141. Paris: L'Harmattan.

———. 2007. The Duty of Memory: A Solidarity of Voices after the Rwandan Genocide. *Paragraph* 30 (1): 85–100. https://doi.org/10.3366/prg.2007.0016.

Tadjo, Véronique. 2000. Réponses de Véronique Tadjo aux questions de Eloïse Brezault à propos de *L'ombre d'Imana, voyages jusqu'au bout du Rwanda*

(Fest'Africa, Lille, le 11/11/2000). Accessed October 24, 2017. https://veroniquetadjo.com/fr/entretiens/.

———. 2013. Lifting the Cloak of (in)visibility: A Writer's Perspective. *Research in African Literatures* 44 (2): 1–7. https://doi.org/10.2979/reseafrilite.44.2.1.

Visser, Irene. 2015. Decolonizing Trauma Theory: Retrospect and Prospects. *Humanities* 4 (2): 250–265. https://doi.org/10.3390/h4020250.

Waberi, Abdourahman A. 2004. *Moisson de crânes: textes pour le Rwanda*. Paris: Serpent à plumes.

———. 2011. Fragments of an African Discourse: Elements for a New Literary Ecosystem. *Yale French Studies* 120: 100–110.

CHAPTER 3

Journeys and Fables: Koulsy Lamko and Véronique Tadjo

This chapter investigates two texts produced for the project, namely Véronique Tadjo's *L'ombre d'Imana: voyages jusqu'au bout du Rwanda* (published in English as *The Shadow of Imana: Travels in the Heart of Rwanda*) and Koulsy Lamko's *La phalène des collines* (The Butterfly of the Hills).[1] Both of these are hybrid, polyphonic texts. Lamko interlaces three stories, which include a fable-type narrative of a nocturnal butterfly roaming the hills.[2] Tadjo's contribution is a travel account which at times adopts other generic forms and slightly subverts the genre of the classical travel diary.[3]

These two literary works provide examples of value systems, approaches to storytelling, and attitudes to trauma that are particular to African contexts. Although I have chosen their texts to investigate these elements, the references to African tradition are in fact present throughout the project and many of my observations are equally applicable to the other works.

When analyzing African literature, it does not suffice to simply identify oral markers and conclude that a text is therefore authentically African. A more meaningful approach is to consider the writer's intent and the creative reappropriation of the oral narrative genre—in other words how the writer may have transformed certain oral traditions in meaningful ways and how this speaks to the sociopolitical context of the text (Julien 1992).[4] In my discussion, I consider how elements such as the use of oral forms, the acknowledgment of traditional customs as well as of the invisible world, shared listening and interaction—all important elements in

© The Author(s) 2020
A.-M. de Beer, *Sharing the Burden of Stories from the Tutsi Genocide*, Palgrave Studies in Cultural Heritage and Conflict,
https://doi.org/10.1007/978-3-030-42093-2_3

traditional Rwandan (and 'African') culture—are creatively embedded in these narratives. Irene Visser remarks on indigenous literatures that 'situate trauma in the context of ritual and ceremony', and the limitations of secular, Eurocentric frameworks that 'impose Western notions of religion-as-superstition on non-Western literary texts' (2015: 260). She advocates the acknowledgment of the validity of certain 'religious and spiritual modes of addressing trauma' and for the importance of minority cultures to have knowledge of their own indigenous culture and heritage (ibid.). Both Lamko and Tadjo weave the traditional African worldview, indigenous spiritual elements, and rituals into their stories in imaginative ways. Tadjo does so in the form of certain oral elements and a chapter on mourning and the anger of the dead; Lamko in the interaction between his characters and their relation to nature and the immaterial world as well as in his use of mythical elements and references to burial customs and the notion of initiation. Both these writers make use of tropes such as masks and shells that are not only sacred objects but speak metaphorically of what is hidden behind the surface and that make the uninitiated reader more aware of the invisible world.

I also use the metaphor of the journey as a mode of analysis, not only because of the obvious link to the cultural notion of a voyage of initiation, but because that is indeed an element that these two texts have in common. In fact Tadjo confirms her particular interest in the notion of initiation which is an important element in many traditional tales (in Anyinefa and Rice-Maximin 2008: 371).[5] Her text takes on the form of a travel account, whereas the thread that binds together the three narratives in Lamko's story is that of someone undertaking a journey, whether it is the wandering soldier, the mythical Butterfly or the returning refugee. Due to the trope of travel that structures the narrative, both works offer a plurality of voices,[6] with each text creating a range of characters or narrators that provide (often conflicting) perspectives on the genocide, as they are confronted with their journey through history and the genocide sites.[7]

Audrey Small notes that the physical journey the authors undertook to post-genocide Rwanda changed them in various ways, an observation that has been confirmed by the writers in interviews (2007: 86). The parallel between the unsettling process that they went through and similar quests that the characters or narrators in their texts embark on is embodied in the travel analogy, or the initiation quest, an obvious choice through which to analyze these texts. Various critics[8] have already read selected texts from the project from this perspective, so although I will be using it here, this is not the main focus or contribution of my analysis.[9]

The characteristic associated with travel that is central to my reading is the possibility of being transformed and unsettled, especially by participating in the listening process—which implies values strongly associated with *ubuntu*, such as solidarity, sharing, hospitality, and showing empathy. This is the writer's obligation that Tadjo speaks of and that she defines as 'keeping one's eyes open to society and the world' (2009: 53; my translation).[10] The type of travel in question is not dark or shallow tourism, but a journey which Tadjo's subtitle qualifies as traveling '*jusqu'au bout*', into the very heart or to the very end of Rwanda, a type of traveling that Pramod Nayar calls 'affective travel'[11] (2009) and which implies being 'implicated *in* and *through* the act of listening' (Dauge-Roth 2009: 168).

Tadjo's journey to Rwanda seems to have taught her that writing is, first of all, listening, and she thanks those who were willing to let her 'hear their voices' (2002: 119).[12] Her first objective, it would seem, was not to speak for the other, but to listen to their stories and enable others to do so.[13] In this regard, she is a '*porte-voix*' (megaphone or amplifier of voices) rather than a '*porte-parole*' (spokesperson), an important distinction that points to her focus on making the Rwandans' voices heard rather than speaking on their behalf (Fonkoua 2016: 107).

Like Tadjo, Lamko embraces his role as a listener and hopes to be transformed and to transform others through his writing (Lamko in Kalisa 2005: 263). He calls himself a go-between; the French term that he uses is '*passeur*', a polysemic word which refers literally to a ferryman who moves between two shores, or one that helps someone to cross a border, but also to one that transmits knowledge, a type of intermediary between two cultures or eras (ibid.; my translation). This notion is, as we will see later on, significant when read in conjunction with Lamko's text and its allusions to the Butterfly's desire to be allowed to cross over to the other world as well as her mission of transmitting cultural knowledge to her niece, who is not initiated into her country's culture.

KOULSY LAMKO AND THE WANDERING RWANDAN

The editor's note in *La phalène des collines* describes Lamko as a 'cultural entrepreneur' (Lamko 2002: 7), pointing to the value this author attaches to the cultural nature of the contexts he writes about. When describing 'African' theater, Lamko evokes elements such as funeral rites, traditional songs and tales, onomatopoeias, and nursery rhymes; he also advocates the use of collective creations and gives preference to local languages (Lamko in Lavoie & Camerlain 1994: 96). At the same time, he warns of the danger of idealizing traditions and of the need to move beyond clichés associated with artistic creation in Africa (ibid.: 98, 100–1). Lamko's own text is highly original and simultaneously integrated into the oral and written African tradition (Coquio 2004: 147). It would be helpful then to look at how he creatively reappropriates (borrowing from Eileen Julien's [1992] argument) the oral genre in his fable-type text in order to write about the genocide.

Although the back cover of the book calls it a 'lyrical novel' (*roman chanté*), Lamko himself remains ambiguous about the genre of his text: 'I think it's a novel,' he says, 'a novelistic form. Some say it's more of a long poem, but I am not quite sure what it is' (Chalaye 2001; my translation).[14] Éloïse Brezault (2002) calls it an allegorical tale, and it is indeed metaphorical, a fable in which names and places are imbued with figurative value. It is also theatrical, lyrical, and fantastic, while being rooted in reality (Coquio 2004: 146).

His response to the task of expressing the unspeakable is a 'kaleidoscope' of generic and stylistic approaches—ranging from the fantastic to the allegoric, the poetic, and the epic—interspersed with songs, poetry, parodies, metaphors, hyperboles, tales, symbols, apocalyptic references, and monstrous comparisons (Amougou Ndi 2010: 259–87). The text even includes the absurd 'story board' of a proposed film, which we are told is merely a 'digression', but which is nevertheless filled with significant references to the rest of the text (Lamko 2002: 152). We also find the Ten Commandments; the gifts of metamorphosis, invisibility and of being in different locations at the same time; ritual dances; initiation rites; the learning of new languages; and unforeseen rainstorms (ibid.).

The story unfolds five years after the genocide and the main narrative is that of the Butterfly, the incarnated dead Queen, who was repeatedly raped and impaled with a wooden crucifix by a Catholic priest. Lamko interweaves her tale with that of her niece, Pelouse, and with Fred R., an exiled soldier. Each of these stories represents a different journey, with its own objective. The Butterfly roams the hills furiously, waiting for someone to take pity on her soul and bury her remains according to the customs, so that she can undertake her final journey and be reborn into the invisible realm. Pelouse grew up in exile in Paris and has never seen her Rwandan homeland. She travels to Rwanda with a delegation of French researchers who are investigating the role of France in the genocide. Her trip is transformed into a quest to learn more about her country and its history than first impressions offer. Fred R. is searching for his roots and the Rwandan motherland he has never known.

All three stories are narrated by the Butterfly, and typographic elements announce the change in focus each time the text shifts to a different main character. Each character has his or her own distinctive ambiance, tone, and motifs. The notions of restlessness and metamorphosis are associated with the Butterfly. Her life is continuous uncertainty and change; she flies and soars, moving constantly between the spiritual and physical realm: 'Come to think of it. The life of a butterfly is nothing other than the fate of a perpetual emigrant, made up of a string of hazards, a whirlwind of metamorphoses' (ibid.: 20).[15] Pelouse, who until this point has never 'known the smell of the motherland', is associated with her 'monstrous' Canon camera, the lens through which she approaches the genocide, and which initially defines her (ibid.: 24). Fred R. is a stranger who has no surname and whose motif is that of fleeing: 'Fred R. is forever running his marathon of exile. He cannot grow roots anywhere'; he travels 'down all the paths of discontent, the dead-ends, the boulevards lined with intolerant, selfish, frightened faces' (ibid.: 20).[16] His restless, nomadic drifting links him to the Butterfly.

Various parallels between the three characters are established and we come to feel that they are in fact three faces of the same person: the wandering, exiled Rwandan. Thus, Lamko's focus is on the plight of the dead who have not been buried according to the rites, those who have been unable to bury their loved ones, and the diaspora who roam the continent and elsewhere, searching for their roots.

At times the text can be overwhelming in its uninterrupted flow of brutal words and nauseating images but Lamko's exordium alerts us to his narrative strategy and how to read this 'uninterrupted verbal logorrhea' (ibid.: 9). A mathematician, he explains, uses proof, formulas, calculations, and statistics, and the same applies to the historian, who simply summarizes the events, provides figures, facts, and estimates (ibid.: 11–12). However, this approach will not suffice when one is confronted with death: one cannot simply 'abbreviate' or summarize the death of humankind because, as Lamko so eloquently writes: 'encompassed in Man, there is also woman, old man, infant, man, life, hope, eternity' (ibid.: 12). This is where a poet is needed: not to summarize or enumerate, but to somehow bring the statistics to life. Lamko warns us, therefore, that his text is not a neat formula, but rather 'a polyphonic work of painful cacophonic arpeggios', which will unsettle rather than appease (ibid.). On the other hand, he remains aware of the danger of embellishing and distorting and so, paradoxically, he notes that his only right is to 'paraphrase' the events (ibid.).

Butterfly of the Night: Blurring Boundaries

The protean narrator of Lamko's text speaks with and for many voices, some real, others mythical and symbolic: she is a 60-year-old woman who seeks refuge in a church in Gikongoro and is raped and killed by a Catholic priest. She is also the Butterfly, the incarnation of the queen's spirit. She is a historical reference to the former Tutsi queen, Queen Gicanda, assassinated in Butare during the genocide (Cazenave and Célérier 2011: 93).[17] At the same time, it seems to be an attempt by Lamko to exorcise the haunting image of Mukandori/Mukandoli,[18] a Tutsi girl who was bound, raped, and impaled at Nyamata church and whose body was on display when the authors visited Rwanda (Lamko, in Kalisa 2005: 273).[19] It is interesting to note that Mukandori's story is one of the 'iconic stories' discussed by Erin Jessee to warn researchers of the risks of thoughtlessly reproducing 'single' narratives that have the potential of promoting dangerous political agendas, thus confirming the importance of remembering that stories are plural and should be told in context (2017: 144, 150). As we will come to see, Mukandori's story is present throughout the project and indeed interpreted in multiple ways by the authors.[20]

Lamko's approach to representing the complexity of the genocide, through the character of the Butterfly, is unexpected. His subversion of the conventional connotations of a butterfly shocks and unsettles expectations we may have, alienating and disorientating us. Her character is paradoxical: she is terrified of flying into something and yet she flies around 'fearlessly' (Lamko 2002: 14–15). She is characterized by a range of visceral emotions: fear, vertigo, anger, violent nausea, and a bitter, cynical tone: 'I was born neither of man, nor of woman, but of anger,' she says (ibid.: 13). This graceful, mythical 'enormous butterfly of the night with the colors of the burnt earth' is also flippant, erratic, and crude (ibid.).[21] The term which she chooses to associate herself with is 'heretic', because of her transgression in terms of space and boundaries (ibid.: 54). Although this fragile insect is traditionally associated with grace and beauty, Lamko transmits the abnormal cruelty of the genocide through her transgressive and crude tone and graphic descriptions (De Beer 2015: 5).[22]

Lamko's Butterfly embodies the traditional notion of interconnectedness by blurring the boundaries between the physical and the spiritual world. At the most unbearable moment of being raped in the church, the Queen departs from her physical body—her 'shell'—and crosses 'the border between being and nothingness' into the 'unlimited territory' where one becomes part of the 'non-visible realities' (Lamko 2002: 46).[23] She calls herself the 'Queen's *muzimu*' (ibid.: 111), a Kinyarwanda word that means a ghost or a spirit returned from the dead, or the spirit of an ancestor; she adds that a '*muzimu* knows neither obstacles nor limits' (ibid.: 29) and is not limited by the 'tyranny' of time or the world's rules and regulations (ibid.: 14). Thus she moves around freely, sometimes inhabiting her own remains, at other times living in the bodies of animals, birds or insects, or in the breeze or the rain (ibid.: 29), a spirit being who metamorphoses into a fish, a grain of light, a thorn, a frog, or a mongoose—whatever form will enable her to survive (ibid.: 162–3). When she feels the urgent need to tell her own story, she is again reincarnated into a physical being, a Butterfly which can interact with the material world: 'I emerged from the nothingness of a ghost and from the dried-out remains of an anonymous woman [...] Simple process of metamorphosis that would allow me to move from the invisible to the visible, from the nonphysical body to the incarnated' (ibid.: 13, 28–9).[24] It is the combination of the fantastical and the first-person narration that allows Lamko to obscure these boundaries: the fact that the fantastical narration of the Queen's metamorphosis is presented through the first person suggests that although the story seems impossible, it was nevertheless a lived reality (Amougou Ndi 2010: 260–1).

If Lamko is wary of the danger of embellishing and distorting, this sentiment is echoed by the spirit of the dead queen, who has been hovering around the church where the rape took place. She listens to a guide misrepresenting the story of her death, a narrative which visibly frustrates her, especially when she hears the visitors making inane comments and expressing doubts. She hastens to tell the story herself, silencing the guide with an epileptic fit:

I had decided to tear away the Word and to imprint it directly on the consciousness of these two unusual visitors in its unabridged, integral, uncensored version [...]: you alone are a true witness of your tale and you alone a true reflection of your face, because you alone know from what weariness is born the shadow beneath your eyes. My story is well and truly mine, the story of a queen, and, above all, the story of a vagina: a vagina with a tree thrust up into it. (Lamko 2002: 31)[25]

Thus she reappropriates the right to tell her own story, in her own way. The Butterfly incarnates in various ways the traditional belief that death is not the end of life, but rather an altered state of existing, and that the dead are still present and can still intervene and interact with the living, albeit in a different form or through dreams and visitations.

Pelouse and the Double Gaze: A New Way of Seeing

The second journey belongs to Pelouse, who is herself a tourist but also a guide, an interpreter, a 'perfect script-girl', and a photographer for her French colleagues. She travels to various genocide sites with the team, where they expect her to take copious notes and photos, thus providing the 'backbone' of their findings (ibid.: 140). She is not only the 'eyes' of the delegation but also their 'memory' (ibid.: 93).

As Nicki Hitchcott (2015: 63) points out, the head of the delegation seems to think that Pelouse's gaze is more 'authentic' because of her Rwandan origins: 'we need your eyes, as you are from this country' (Lamko 2002: 94). She is expected to 'grip the camera lens in order to fix and express the nausea, the absurd, the inexpressible, the violence and all this with that authenticity that can only be arrived at through the truth of a double lens' (ibid.: 140).[26] And yet, like most of the writers participating in the project, Pelouse is the absent witness, the outsider who arrives after the genocide and tries to capture it belatedly and 'vicariously' (*par procuration*) through the 'double' gaze of her camera and her notes (ibid.: 25, 140). This meticulous note taking and capturing of information mirrors Lamko's initial reference to the mathematician and the historian, for whom accurate facts and figures are all that matter.

This superficial approach to the genocide sites makes the Butterfly furious: she wonders what this 'Negro lady with a camera' is doing there and rants about the 'thirst for sensationalism' of those who 'gorge' themselves on images and virtual reality. It is 'unconfessed cannibalism', wails the Butterfly, when the bodies of those that are photographed are 'consumed' by the camera (ibid.: 24–5).[27] This comparison of dark tourism to a type of cannibalism is a comment on the transformation of genocide sites into tourism sites, where people attempt to 'savor' life through their screens and camera lenses (ibid.). This points to the process that Pelouse will need to undergo in terms of how she sees and interprets the landscapes, people, and history of her country; she arrives with what Lamko calls her 'double gaze' (ibid.: 140) and Dauge-Roth (2010: 142) calls her 'inherited gaze'.

It becomes clear that Pelouse, who experiences love for the motherland of which she is a descendant, will need to pass through a process that will prepare and qualify her for telling its painful story. It is her aunt, whose tomb she is looking for, who will lead her to see differently and become more sensitive to the invisible world.

Fred with No Surname: Exile and Identity

The third character, Fred R.,[28] appears in almost every chapter of the text. Although Pelouse and the Butterfly meet, their paths never cross that of Fred R., so that even in the narrative, he remains distant and 'in exile'. His story is the background ambiance, filled with the despair that accompanies the lives of those who have lost all points of reference. He is the Tutsi diaspora, the exile without roots. His perpetual refrain is 'Where am I going? What am I doing?' (Lamko 2002: 20). He never really belongs and has little contact with his own cultural roots and myths; he spends his whole life trying to gain access to those of the countries he lives in, 'begging for the land of his neighbors, seeking their ancestors, simulating their laughter and inhaling their smells' (ibid.: 20). His character is also a constant reminder of the power of the word and the propaganda based on myths of ethnic belonging and exclusion.

In their country of exile, his parents obtain a 'true false identity' for him so that he can be integrated into the society (ibid.: 49). This will be his 'second birth' and the continuation of an identity crisis which follows him wherever he goes (ibid.). Given the importance of child naming in Rwandan culture, and the fact that names often indicate roots and context, and are seen to have an influence over a child's future,[29] the fact that Lamko chooses to endow Fred with only an initial for a surname is highly significant. At the age of ten, a schoolmate calls Fred a 'filthy little Rwandan' (ibid.: 51), which leads him to ask his mother what it means to be a Rwandan. She responds by singing him a Kinyarwanda song about his country of birth, the legendary Nyabarongo River, and Lyangombe. Thus he learns that only the 'true' motherland 'knows better than sorghum beer' how to comfort you (ibid.: 53).

Later he remembers this, throws his false passport into the lake and leaves, swearing that no one will ever ridicule him again. Fred compares himself to a mullet, 'that migratory fish who is never satisfied in any water' (ibid.: 61). His travel companion is his shadow, with whom he reflects on the difference between a wasp and a bee—both are insects, and both are necessary in nature; the difference between them is but a 'nuance' (ibid.: 62). He thus constantly questions the notion of alterity and reflects on the effects of ideologies that shape the way people act. His meandering thoughts are triggered by what he sees on his journeys: a child's game, an object or creature in nature which he imbues with symbolic and allegorical value. A dung beetle, a bird, a fish, a wasp, and a pebble—all lead him to reflect on exile, the war, xenophobia, and freedom.

Fred becomes a guerrilla fighter, championing whatever cause for freedom comes his way. This endless quest for liberty becomes his new internal homeland (ibid.: 82). When he tries to settle down and find a job, he is criticized for not being 'intellectual' enough, a comment which leads him to vehemently condemn those 'intellect-tuels'[30] who use their intelligence to manipulate others through the power of their words—an oblique criticism of genocide ideology and propaganda (ibid.: 145, 147–8). He lashes out at those who are 'initiated' in the art of using language to manipulate others, and whose journeys consist of writing—journeys which stretch over 'miles of parchment' (ibid.: 146), a reference to the danger of writing about an event that one has not personally experienced and the power of the written word.

Lamko imbues Fred with the secret knowledge and way of interpreting nature and the physical world that is characteristic of one who has grown up within a traditional African framework. The bush 'holds no secrets from him' (ibid.: 103), and having grown up on the continent, he displays that hidden connection with nature and the invisible world that the Butterfly endeavors to impart to Pelouse, who has grown up in Europe—the ability to hear and see what cannot be heard and seen in the physical, rational realm (ibid.: 127). His parents' death is communicated to him through the animal world. One day, a cat crosses the road where he is walking and Fred, who 'understands the language of animals' ever since his wanderings have started, divines that his mother R. and his father R. have been killed in their adopted country, into which they had tried to 'graft themselves like mushrooms' (ibid.: 180).

This exacerbates his situation of non-belonging; not only is he a refugee, but henceforth he is also an orphan. This somehow makes him stronger; he has become a mythical creature, metamorphosed into a salamander who can 'cross through fire without burning', another trait that he has in common with the Butterfly (ibid.). He seems to be preoccupied with the same concern that the Butterfly has, namely that of crossing into the next world. Significantly, Fred's conclusions about this are based on three things; a child telling him how to 'reach paradise' by avoiding all obstacles when playing hopscotch (ibid.: 208), a myth about the origin of death that his mother told him as a child (ibid.: 209), and the 'rosary of proverbs' he has learned during his life's travels (ibid.: 201). The myth about death reminds us of Tadjo's myth of the monster who consumed himself,[31] as in both stories, destruction comes because of greediness and the characters devouring everything within reach (ibid.: 209). Given the role played by proverbs in traditional society and the guiding role of the Christocentric rosary, Lamko's rosary metaphor is significant, reminding us that in many ways the rosary had come to replace the proverbs in this society.

Wherever Fred goes, he is an outsider who uses a 'barbarian language' and claims his territory to be the 'unlimited' realm of dreams and nightmares (ibid.: 126). Fred's life embodies the life of exile led by many Tutsis, and the way they were treated at various moments in the history of Rwanda, so that they fled the country in huge numbers. It is a state of endless non-belonging, displacement, and transit. Here too, the parallel between Fred R. and the Butterfly is significant. Both in the visible and the invisible realm there is no peace for those who are away from family, roots, and homeland, or those who have not been buried according to the customs.

The Journey of Initiation

Whereas Fred R. remains in exile throughout, Pelouse, though born in exile, will be initiated into the Rwandan culture. This is not a journey she will make on her own and maybe this is what distinguishes her from Fred; he is a solitary traveler, whereas Pelouse is accompanied on her journey by various people who assist her, the first of which is her deceased aunt.

When their paths first cross, while Pelouse is visiting a genocide site church with her camera and the delegation, she is scared off by the Butterfly. Later, Pelouse does not recognize her when she enters through a window of their vehicle; she panics and admits that she has a butterfly phobia and is 'allergic' to them (ibid.: 60). The symbolic meaning of this reaction is clear; Pelouse is not yet ready to be confronted with the reality of genocide that the Butterfly carries with her, and the invisible realm and cultural knowledge into which her journey will initiate her.

Pelouse does, however, gradually open herself up to this possibility. Her first step is to isolate herself from the other foreign delegates, who are staying at the luxurious Hotel Mille Collines. She chooses a small hotel in a less affluent area in Kigali, a place that her fellow travelers will not deign to visit: they do not find it necessary to mix with the 'foul-smelling' locals in order to obtain the information they have come to find (ibid.: 94). When they visit the sites, they focus on statistics and demand proof, treating the remains of the victims as 'museum pieces' (ibid.: 22–3). They will not look beyond the surface of the country, while Pelouse will, and will thus be transformed. The officer in charge of the investigation, the 'musungu[32] with opulent jowls' (ibid.: 93) will deny the role that France played in the genocide: 'It's also true that we provided a few firearms, a few machetes and trained the killers ... we have to be objective! But we were not at the barricades. We like all the Africans' (ibid.: 95).[33] When the musungu tries to convince Pelouse of France's innocence while they eat a meal, she starts feeling progressively more nauseous. Eventually, she vomits on him, an act which clearly symbolizes her rejection of the conclusions he has already come to at this early stage of the inquiry.

Pelouse's official mission as photographer and translator for the delegation is gradually subsumed by her personal quest to find the body of her aunt, of whom she still has a photo. She also becomes less efficient in her work as photographer and note taker: when, after their visit to the church, she develops the photos of the raped woman's body, they all mysteriously come out blank. We are told that the queen's spirit is behind this—she refuses to let herself be imprisoned in a 'black box' and thus rejects the distant and clinical gaze of a camera (ibid.: 111).[34] In a sense, her aunt's mission is to transform Pelouse—from a 'mathematician' who crunches numbers to a 'poet'—and to replace the second lens of the camera with the ability to see beyond the surface. When the group stops to take photos of the Nyabarongo River, she is the one who makes Pelouse see beyond its surface and become aware of 'all the bitterness that the river struggles to vomit up' and the horrific memories it carries (ibid.: 64).

The Butterfly, who describes herself as a 'regardant' (one who watches and sees), appears to Pelouse in a series of recurring dreams and visitations, sharing with her what she calls the 'philopoetry of the art of seeing', foregrounding the motif of the poet's gaze/perspective on life (ibid.: 88–9).[35] She encourages Pelouse to stop limiting herself to the negative restrictions of her current way of thinking; these are linked either to fear and mere survival ('one should'), or even to 'you have to', which is more personal and at least implies an individual choice according to the conscience (ibid.). It is necessary to move beyond these first two options. Her aunt suggests that 'you can' offers a choice which opens one up to the possibility of 'miracles' and to the infinite (ibid.: 89). She explains, in a type of prophetic message, what this initiation process of blurring and crossing boundaries will entail: 'If you push back the limitations imposed by *one should* and *you have to* you will discover in that effort the strength you need to act. Once you have escaped from the fetters of your body, then you will enter into the valley of timelessness ... where you will sow a seed' (ibid.: 90). In fact, this change in perspective is a necessity for the type of journey that Pelouse (and by implication the writers participating in the project) has undertaken: '[I]f you can't push back the boundaries,' she says to her niece, 'pack up your bags and go back to where you came from' (ibid.). This time, when Pelouse wakes up to find the Butterfly in her room, she merely crosses to the other side of the room, not fleeing as she would have done before.

The unsettling journey to each of the sites, alternated with disturbing visitations by her aunt, multiple visions, and discussions with other survivors that she meets, is what will guide Pelouse's process of initiation (Amougou Ndi 2010: 297). She has, in fact, been prepared for this even before coming to Rwanda, because of her 'initiatory journey' while shooting a film elsewhere in Africa (Lamko 2002: 158). There (in Mali) she discovered the same idyllic landscapes, poetry, smells, and pastoral scenes that her aunt had always described to her when talking of her motherland (ibid.: 158). As she now travels through Rwanda, Pelouse discovers a love for this enchanting country which she has never known except through 'the pictures that her aunt had painted for her during her brief visits to Paris' (ibid.: 143).[36] She becomes aware of the 'hidden mystery' under the feigned indifference of the inhabitants, the masks offered by the country to those who do not see beneath the surface (ibid.).

Her aunt encourages this awakening that is taking place within Pelouse by revealing herself to her, not in the form of a Butterfly this time, but in her own body, impaled with a crucifix: 'If you really are looking for me, if you are looking for my tomb, if you want to be freed from all fears, you will need to learn to understand the hidden things of life, those which exist beyond the physical world. Do not fear obstacles. The boundary only exists in the minds of those who confine life to watertight compartments' (ibid.: 144).[37]

She tells Pelouse about the million wandering souls who wait, like her, for the funeral rites to be performed so that they can embark on the final journey in the woven papyrus boat that will take them there (ibid.). The

Butterfly remarks that the land has become arid and that weeds have started invading it; this persuades her of the urgency of convincing Pelouse to start acting. Thus, she suggests that there is a link between the fact that the rites have not been observed and the disasters that befall the country. The implication is that the state in which the country finds itself can be improved if these cultural rites are followed and the delicate balance restored (ibid.: 182).

Pelouse's initiation quest then involves two main tasks: getting to know the history of the genocide on more than a superficial level and symbolically performing the burial rites for her aunt and other unburied dead (Amougou Ndi 2010: 309). Indeed, the process of initiation encompasses not only a series of rites, but also oral instruction and, eventually, a change in the status of the novice undergoing the process (ibid.: 291).[38] Pelouse will be transformed from a detached outsider to someone who understands her deep connection with her homeland and thus is willing to take on the pain of her compatriots (Germanotta 2016: 84).

It is the mentoring relationship between Pelouse and her deceased aunt which most vividly embodies some of the elements that Es'kia Mphahlele has identified as the 'traditional values' inherent to African humanism, namely 'respect for elders, sense of community, neighbourly attachments, sense of ancestral presence, the appropriate funeral rites, solid social relationships' (2002: 284). The Butterfly endows Pelouse with the ability to see and hear on a different level—not enough to belong to the 'invisible world of the spirits', but the ability to have 'double vision' and 'double hearing', a gift which will sensitize her to that world (Lamko 2002: 102).

The process of initiation is equally helped along by two survivors whom she meets at the small hotel that she has moved to, and where the restaurant has become the gathering place for all those who are trying to forget (ibid.: 66). Muyango-le-crâne-fêlé (Muyango-the-cracked-skull) is a poet, one of the main 'pillars' of the bar and the 'Circle of the Muse', which is made up of the regular drinking clients. Épiphanie, the other 'pillar', is a survivor marked by the death of her husband and children (ibid.: 70).

Like the Butterfly, Muyango does not allow himself to be limited; he claims that he constantly enlarges the borders of his own kingdom, even beyond the realm of the volcanoes (ibid.: 76). This is significant in terms of his relationship with the invisible world for in the traditional Rwandan imaginary, the realm of the volcanoes is connected to the next world, because these mountains are where Rwandan people spend the afterlife (Kayishema 2009: 19).

Muyango, who not only is open to the invisible world but also possesses cultural knowledge and personal memory of the genocide, is equipped to accompany Pelouse on her quest. He already sees beyond the surface, the 'exterior', and he realizes that she has no 'landmarks', no 'memory of the places, the times, the smells, the colors and the sounds' that she will need to guide her; he knows that the Rwanda that she now faces is no longer coherent and its memory is an 'abyss', an 'empty' ocean (Lamko 2002: 76–7). Like the Butterfly, Muyango the poet embodies the notion of the transmission of cultural knowledge and memory to the uninitiated. He encourages Pelouse to revisit her way of seeing and writing, but also to connect on a profound level with nature. He advises her to take notes differently, to take photos differently, drawing her inspiration from the country, its landscapes, and the culture that she is now discovering for herself:

> Your photos will be charged with rhythms and emotions and will implicitly celebrate the new humanity to be brought about beyond the lakes, the hills, the volcanoes, the flight of the weavers or the smoke from the banana fields ... (ibid.: 113)[39]

Muyango proposes an approach that has been touched by emotions and the 'rhythms' of all Pelouse has seen; the gaze which he offers her is in fact like his own poetry, which in the first place is not a way of writing but a way of looking; he calls it a '*regard*' (ibid.: 79).

Muyango knows that when an outsider truly wishes to communicate and connect with Rwandans, it is important to move beyond the polite 'shell' behind which they often hide: 'We are welcoming, we laugh with the visitor, we're considerate and friendly, but this is only the surface. If you want to know what we really think, you have to go deeper than the shell' (ibid.: 106).[40] However, Épiphanie, the other survivor that accompanies Pelouse on this path, warns her that embracing the approach advocated by her aunt and Muyango does not come without a price: 'Little mother, you are a daughter of this country of hills; but you have known only the smell of its womb. Me, I've experienced this country smack in the face! It's not the same thing! Exile shaped you; the country destroyed me. Be careful that this country doesn't destroy you as well' (ibid.: 174).[41] Épiphanie senses that the initiation process will entail some sort of 'destruction' or breaking down (Amougou Ndi 2010: 305).

In fact, Pelouse soon starts to experience what it really means to be armed with a 'double' eye and a 'double' ear (Lamko 2002: 102). When the French delegation visits the site of Bisesero, Muyango insists on accompanying them to tell them the famous epic of the courageous Tutsi resistance in the hills of Bisesero.[42]

Muyango ends the detailed heroic saga with the story of a man who loses his mother, wife, and child, and who mourns them by covering his hair, chest, and limbs with the blood and fat dripping from their bodies (ibid.: 124). He tries in vain to bury them before leaving with the basket in which his wife had carried their child. Like the Butterfly, he underlines the importance of telling the story correctly and expresses his frustration at those who distort it to suit their own needs: 'History/The story loses nothing through repetition when one tells it accurately' (ibid.: 113).[43] We learn much later that this is his own story; he alone could have told it accurately.

Muyango's narrative and the moving atmosphere of Bisesero touch Pelouse profoundly. She feels completely alone, and it is as if she herself experiences the heat, anguish, hunger, and thirst that Muyango speaks of. Given her aunt's aversion to the camera, it is significant that Pelouse is so disturbed that she is no longer able to take photos or notes. She starts sweating and trembling and a fainting spell—a type of trance brought on by the Butterfly—renders her helpless. This moment is a significant stage of her initiation process, a type of 'ritual death' (Amougou Ndi 2010: 305).

Pelouse's process of initiation will involve not only emotional and physical unsettlement, but also a stripping of that which is familiar and comfortable and which serves as points of reference. During a violent storm, she loses both her camera and rolls of film as well as all the notes she made for the delegation. Pelouse will thus be obliged to reconsider her strategy of recording the genocide. It is in fact Épiphanie who will accompany Pelouse on this 'learn[ing] to listen' part of her quest (De Beer 2015: 7). When Pelouse decides to leave the security of the Hôtel de la Muse, in order to get to know 'the real country', it is Épiphanie who invites her to share her home (Lamko 2002: 171). Épiphanie's life is a vicious suicidal circle of drinking and insomnia (ibid.: 69). She fruitlessly tries to pick her life up again and find some sense in living after the genocide, but is haunted by the loss of her family; she was the only one who saw their cruel death, perpetrated by her own cousin, and has not shared this with anyone else. Her life reminds us of the circle of non-verbalized trauma that survivors often get caught up in: 'Long identical days: cheap wine, pee, slices of grilled banana, chicken gizzards pinched left, right and center from clients' plates … cheap wine, pee, gossip, bouts of crying … Today like yesterday and like tomorrow. A life going round in circles' (ibid.: 67).[44]

However, the act of finally sharing her story with Pelouse, who listens attentively to all her memories, will provide a way out of the circle of trauma. At the same time, it will take Pelouse a step further on her own journey, transforming her into a maternal figure in spite of the fact that she is no older than Épiphanie (De Beer 2015: 7). Thus Lamko has created, through Pelouse and Épiphanie, a relationship that embodies the process of active and appropriate listening and showing solidarity, and the possibility of healing this holds. For Pelouse, not only does traveling become a mode of listening, but listening becomes a form of traveling, of displacing oneself into the journey that the other has made.

After telling her story to Pelouse, Épiphanie realizes that for the first time in five years, she has slept well and not been filled with fear. Lamko seems to suggest that through listening to her, Pelouse has helped her to begin her own journey of working through. This provides her with new hope and determination; although her brother-in-law, who has returned from exile, threatens to take her home, she and Pelouse vigorously start planting flowers and vegetables in her garden, where she vows to 'cultivate' her husband's memory (Lamko 2002: 192). This is an almost joyous act of remembering and speaks of faith in the future; it echoes the words Lamko has dedicated to Alice Karekezi[45] in the preface of his text. Lamko describes Alice planting flowers in the muddy soil of Butare, and he says: 'Let us plant, my sister, the rain and the sun will make hope grow' (ibid.: 10).[46] In this way he refers to the natural cycle of nature, which renews itself, to evoke the possibility of personal healing and renewal. Through Épiphanie's act of planting flowers while thinking of her husband, the act of remembering is linked to the process of growth, and the process of mourning is imbued with a positive connotation. This notion of hope and restoration is evoked in three different ways in Lamko's dedication, where he speaks first of shared laughter and hope, then of dreams that are true and just, and concluding with the affirmation 'I believe in LIFE' (ibid.). Through the journey of restoration embodied in several of Lamko's characters, this author in fact confirms the notion that 'trauma victims may find in their belief systems pathways to resilience and recovery' (Visser 2015: 261).

Pelouse, who recognizes all the 'miracles' of healing that are happening around her, decides to open a beauty salon with Épiphanie, a place surrounded with flowers that they will call 'The clinic of hope'. Here they plan to help women cut off the hair they have grown in mourning and also exorcise the despair that has been growing in their souls: 'It will be aesthetic surgery of the soul [...]; we will be mirrors that will give them back their reflections, concave or convex for those filled with despair, but harmonious and balanced when they want to move beyond the signs of chaos' (ibid.: 195–6).[47] As with various examples from the texts produced for the project, this comment can also be read as a subtle reference to the writers participating in the project, whose task was to reflect—as lucidly as possible—the contradictory images they were faced with in post-genocide Rwanda, whether concave, convex, or harmonious.

It seems that, in spite of the challenges faced by survivors, Lamko's text is a call to embrace life again, and as Josias Semujanga points out, the ethical position taken throughout the novel is that of confidence in and love for life and beauty (2008: 220). Muyango's advice to Pelouse is to remember that 'every quest is like a cheerful piece of music that one composes' (Lamko 2002: 113). It is 'not a requiem', he says, an affirmation which clearly points to Lamko's preference for working through the period of mourning in order to move beyond it to a time of new life (ibid.). On a deeper level, this echoes the Rwandan tradition of viewing death as a time of rebirth into a new dimension, and therefore something to be mourned with a requiem, but even more so, to be celebrated with a cheerful song. This is especially significant as the context of the quest that he evokes is that of Pelouse mourning her aunt and finding her remains. It would seem that, on various levels, Lamko's text portrays the traditional view of death, as explained by Déogratias Bagilishya (2000), namely that it ideally ends in rebirth and renewal.

As noted above, Pelouse's journey of initiation involves getting to know the history of the genocide and symbolically performing the necessary burial rites for the unburied dead (Amougou Ndi 2010: 309). It is this second aspect that is illustrated in the text, not only through the Butterfly's anger at not been buried in a dignified manner, but also through the process of mourning that Muyango goes through. The work of mourning/remembering is a theme that dominates Lamko's text, a task which, as Paul Ricœur tells us, can paradoxically lead to a time of active forgetting and even potentially forgiving (1995: 81). One day, Muyango arrives at the door of their salon and asks Pelouse to shave off his hair of mourning and to cut his nails, which he has allowed to grow into 'claws' (Lamko 2002: 198). This is the moment that Muyango admits to Pelouse that the

man from Bisesero who had coated his body with the fat from his murdered loved ones was indeed him, and that he had been telling his own
story. In this way, Lamko expresses the desire to see survivors work
through the mourning process and embrace life again:

> I understand Muyango! The field of the memory of the dead, one has to
> trim it, cut back the lies that have grown so that the truth can blossom. I am
> going to cut your hair, I am going to cut your nails, destroy all the lies that
> have grown on your body. Because the lie is refusing to live. And then you
> will go and wash yourself in the Nyabarongo ... the river that flows.
> (ibid.: 199)[48]

The reference to the cleansing power of the Nyabarongo[49] is significant,
because it is a way of textually restoring and renewing the bloody image of
this river that has been strongly associated with the genocide. This site is
intimately connected to the history and myths of the country. In the royal
mythology, the Nyabarongo held a specific status and was considered by
the Tutsi monarch and his subjects to be a symbol of 'sacred time and
space' and connected with certain kingship rituals related to the deceased
kings (Meierhenrich 2009: 17–18). In light of this history, the act of
throwing bodies into the river was not only a physical but also a symbolic
act of defiling this sacred space (ibid.: 18). Furthermore, the Nyabarongo
was historically linked to purification: 'The notion of purity and the related
metaphors of flow/blockage have historically been of great significance in
Rwanda' (Meierhenrich 2009: 16). The use of the Nyabarongo to 'rid'
the country of the Tutsis was in fact a subversion of the traditional notion
of purification associated with this river (Meierhenrich 2009: 16).[50]

The conflicting and gradual change in Pelouse's way of looking at the
Nyabarongo reflects the different roles played by this river in the history
of the country. It also demonstrates how she has learned to look differently and beyond what is immediately visible. As her insight increases, she
becomes aware of the contradictory meanings attached to the river. When
she first sees it and tries to take a photo of it, she is struck by its magical
appeal, its beauty, its life-giving qualities (Lamko 2002: 63). However, the
driver and the Butterfly in turn both remind her that this river has carried
streams of blood and bodies, bits of flesh and skin (ibid.: 63–4). A chilling
metaphor is used, of a woman menstruating streams of blood and her
ovaries being torn out (ibid.: 64); thus the image of life is transformed
into one of horror and destruction (ibid.). The trope of purification is

introduced here when the guide says to Pelouse: 'Never stare too long at the rippling water. Water is life when it doesn't carry along human carcasses, scraps of rib, stumps of arm, intertwined bowels. Here, she [the water] is impure' (ibid.: 65).[51] Pelouse (and the reader) learns once again that appearances are misleading, even when it comes to a beautiful, magical river. At the end of the journey, however, Lamko's text reinvests the river with its healing role. Pelouse again attributes a purifying, life-giving quality to this river by encouraging Muyango to go and wash away his pain in it. Thus Lamko's notion of celebrating life and moving beyond the confines of death is also demonstrated in his textual treatment of the Nyabarongo River. Furthermore, he engages with the mythical historiography, the symbolism, the oral history, and the use of propaganda which an uninitiated visitor may not be familiar with but which Rwandans are acutely aware of.

Through both Muyango's mourning process and Pelouse's search for her aunt's tomb, Lamko grapples with the reality of the thousands of unburied victims and the consequences for both them and the living. His text demonstrates a profound awareness of the traditions surrounding death as a form of 'crossing over/passage' (*passage*), which include highly dramatized rituals, poetry, and praises to honor the deceased, who is moving on to the 'village of the dead' (Marcelli 2011).[52] The Butterfly reminds us that since the beginning of time, black people have buried their brothers (and sisters), entrusting them to the earth or the river, thus fertilizing the earth and the water and returning both childhood and 'the seed of origins' to them (Lamko 2002: 54–5). However, if for some reason a 'black brother' was not 'buried under a fist of soil or in a drop of water', he would refuse to enter into the 'City of Time'; he would roam the hill until someone performed the correct rituals (ibid.: 55–6).[53] Since the Butterfly's death, she has waited for someone to show her the way to the 'river on which the papyrus boat floats', but it seems that the living are too busy with everyday survival and pleasure to tend to the needs of the dead: 'They were all too preoccupied by their tiny slices of life, champagne and Coca-Cola' (ibid.: 58).[54]

The notion of *passage* is, again, reminiscent of Lamko's desire to act as *passeur* or go-between. This can be interpreted on more than one level. Lamko's role is to 'take the reader with him, from a position of possible ignorance or disinterest to "the other side", where he "knows" and is changed by that knowledge' (De Beer 2015: 6). Pelouse, similarly, is a type of interpreter or intermediary between her homeland and the foreign visitors (ibid.: 6). Both Lamko and Pelouse have to undergo a process of initiation into the rites and customs of the country in which they are themselves foreigners. And yet, they are not the only *passeurs* in this story; this role is in fact ascribed to various actors. Muyango will initiate Pelouse into seeing beyond the surface and writing with her heart as well as her mind. The deceased aunt presents another type of *passeur*—she will be the one who mediates between two cultures and passes on cultural and hidden knowledge to her niece. In telling Pelouse her story, she is following the traditional forms of the rites, in which the ancestor tells his or her descendants the story of how the deceased moved from the world of the living to that of the dead (Semujanga 2008: 243–4).

Pelouse, who has now learned about the burial rites, will be the one who performs them for the Butterfly's wandering soul and who accompanies her to the border between the visible and the invisible realm, thus in turn becoming a *passeur* for her aunt. One day at sunset, she follows a bird to a cemetery, where her aunt 'imprints' in her a vision of a dance performed by the spirits of the dead.[55] Muyango, who has had the same vision, also follows the bird to the cemetery. They have both brought the prescribed food for the dead, which will help them on their journey to the new world. It is in this burial rite that the visible and the invisible world meet, both on an individual and community level (Semujanga 2009: 52). A magnificent butterfly joins them and Pelouse and Muyango make love there, in a symbolic gesture that reminds us of the traditional ritual of procreation that ends the mourning period and that points to renewed life (Lamko 2002: 203).

The notion of initiation includes not only the possibility of ritual death, but also of a potential rebirth (Amougou Ndi 2010: 291). This is another element that Pelouse and her aunt—who, after all, are not completely separate entities, as the aunt claims that she has been in Pelouse from the beginning—have in common (Lamko 2002: 207). The Butterfly, according to Rwandan tradition, will move on to be rebirthed, and Pelouse will obtain a new status—she will become a different person through her journey and the teaching of her aunt and the rites that she goes through.

When the rest of the team leaves Rwanda, Pelouse decides to stay behind,[56] setting herself the task of finding out 'the number of victims that no-one could ever exactly determine with certitude' (ibid.: 205).[57] Now that the rites have been performed, the Butterfly is free to leave the physical world, to leave behind time and age and any other limits imposed by it:

> I float towards the City of Time. During the crossing, in the boat on the great river, I am jubilant. All around me, birds chirp freedom. [...] They also tell of the victory of the women walking in a single file, the women who bend down to pick up bricks, who build the irrigation channel on the shoulder of the road they are tarring. To drain the streams of water. (ibid.: 216)[58]

It is significant that Lamko's novel concludes with the same image that it opened with: a group of women carrying bricks and working on the roadside. Thus he honors the strength and resilience of the women we meet in the pages of his book. The concluding part ends with the celebration of the victory of these women and an ambiance of new life suggested by this image of rebuilding, working together, overcoming, moving on, and the renewal that streams of water bring.

An integral thread of this narrative is the blurring of the two realms that is such a central part of Rwandan tradition. Through the recurring intertextual references, Lamko's text evokes the story of the Rwandan 'cosmogony': that of the ancestor sharing wisdom with his or her descendants during the rites of *guterekera* (communion with the ancestors) and *kubandwa* (being possessed by a spirit, or higher initiation into the cult of Lyangombe) (Semujanga 2008: 235–6). In these ceremonies, the dead and the living exchange words, food and drink, thus embodying the ancient myth according to which life flows from the ancestors to their descendants; to live, says Semujanga, is to be initiated into the signs which demonstrate the link between the worlds of the living and that of the dead (ibid.). The existence and nature of this link with the supernatural is part of the knowledge which Pelouse must acquire and it is at the moment of sharing this secret knowledge with her, Semujanga points out, that the spirit of the queen reincarnates herself in the form of a nocturnal butterfly (ibid.: 237).

This theme of the transmission of tradition, and initiation into secret knowledge and the invisible realm is reflected in the book's cover image, title, and Lamko's choice of characters, genre, and physical settings. One of the central visual images that speaks of tradition is that of the woven basketwork[59] that decorates the second edition (published in 2002).[60] It is up to the reader to imagine the nature of the item, but there are multiple possibilities provided by the narrative itself. Lamko himself evokes an image of baskets filled with bricks, carried by the women in his opening lines: the long row of women, building an irrigation channel, and carrying in their baskets not only bricks, but ideas (Lamko 2002: 13). This image highlights the tradition of passing on the art of weaving from mother to daughter as a type of rite of passage and reminds us of the passing on of cultural knowledge that takes place in the text, especially from the aunt to her niece.

The cover image could also refer to the burial rites; the basket in which Muyango's wife carried their baby before his wife and baby died, and which becomes for him a symbol of their burial (ibid.: 124). Furthermore, it evokes the image of the papyrus-woven barque which carries the Butterfly toward the City of Time (ibid.: 213). Finally, when read in the light of Rwandan tradition, there is a link to the burial ritual, '*gupfunya umupfu nkigitebo*', which Bagilishya has taught us is the act of placing the remains in the form of a fetal position, thus 'lending to death the form of a basket' (2000: 344). Whichever interpretation is given to the weaving, they point back to traditional culture and burial rites.[61]

The title, *The Butterfly on the Hills*, similarly evokes the mythical world of traditional Rwandan belief. The Butterfly speaks of metamorphosis and is a link between the two worlds. The image of the hills also invokes a meeting of the two realms. The hills are emblematic of community life and an undeniable physical part of the Rwandan landscape and history but they are also a reference to the invisible world: the 'Hill of the Dead', or the volcanic mountains where the deceased go to in the afterlife. Thus both the hills and the Butterfly belong to the physical and the invisible realms.

Almost all the sites that Lamko chooses to evoke in his text are connected somehow to the cultural rape of Rwanda and the 'ethnocide' that Kayishema refers to (2009: 9). The respective church sites remind us of the role of the missionaries and the church in eroding traditional belief systems, and the conflict between 'Black Imana' and 'White Imana' (*Imana Lenoir* and *Imana Leblanc*).[62] Nyanza speaks of the royal and foundation myths that the colonizers undermined, and the Nyabarongo River of the subverted myths and historiography connected to the site and the origin of the Tutsis.

Furthermore, Lamko's choice of narrator in the form of a metamorphosed and reincarnated Butterfly speaks of the vital role of ancestral presence and border crossing. Like Muyango, this enigmatic narrator constantly brings us back to tradition, but also to a celebration of new life: as she leaves this world, she says: 'Strike up a dance song, fist raised to the sky. Tra la la. Hold on tight, very tight' (Lamko 2002: 216).[63]

Lamko's choice of style and genre too is significant: Mphahlele has upheld the myth as a form of narrative which enriches us, due to its 'compelling poetry', its allegory and its 'symbolism', suggesting that the myth is a vehicle which 'promotes harmony between humans and nature in a triumphant, inviolable, pantheistic union that negates death' (2002: 135). Through the use of traditional storytelling techniques such as fable, myth, poetry, song, symbolism, and supernatural elements, Lamko's tale embraces the role of the oral tradition. It is precisely this quality of his writing—his use of allegory and the symbolic, his focus on ritual and his voluntary journey into a place where boundaries between death and life, between the survivors and the dead, between myth and reality, between the natural and the supernatural collapse—that in my view positions him as an authentic listener and narrator of the story of those who embrace this worldview.

This clearly points to a desire to write in a way that is both dialogic and builds bridges between the witness, writer, and listener/reader, but also respects the way in which traditional elements such as the myth and the proverb speak to powerful emotions and culturally appropriate reactions to intense trauma.

Thus Lamko's choice of textual and paratextual elements all speak of his aspiration to integrate the traditional values of African humanism in his narrative, and of the importance of burial customs, relationships, and respect for the elders, the 'connectedness with the higher spiritual realm and the integral role played by the spiritual and religious in traditional African humanism' (ibid.: 151).

Véronique Tadjo and the 'Cloak of Invisibility'[64]

Véronique Tadjo is known for her creative exploration of ancient cultures and rituals and for drawing from the mythological and poetic wealth of the African oral tradition:

> I follow the African tradition of storytelling which gives me a great freedom of interpretation of our myths and legends. I am interested in preserving the richness of our cultural heritage for the generations to come. Many of us live in big African urban centres or in the diaspora and are increasingly losing contact with oral traditions. One after the other, our stories and mythical characters are disappearing. Instead of lamenting this phenomenon, I feel it is my role as a writer and as an artist to fight against alienation and amnesia. (Tadjo 2013b)

This Ivoirian author has acknowledged that writing about the genocide was a 'turning point' for her, because it strengthened her interest in myths and legends (Tadjo 2013a: 5). Her work on Rwanda has been described as a 'distinctively African attempt' to grapple with the genocide and with 'issues of sovereignty and violence' (West-Pavlov 2014: 115). She submits that elements of her writing that are often termed as 'avant-garde', such as the mixture of genres, are in fact largely due to her African oral heritage (Dahouda and Tadjo 2007: 184).[65] The influence of this tradition is clear, not only through the 'dialogical', participatory nature of her writing, but also in its 'open-ended', innovative character (West-Pavlov 2014: 123). Her oeuvre represents an intersection between tradition and modernity, between Africa and the world, and has been described as a type of 'trans-African poetics'; it is anchored in Africa, while constantly reinventing and looking outward and she seems to conceive of this continent as an organic whole while appreciating its multiplicities and plurality (Mazauric 2016: 91–2).

Tadjo constantly questions univocal narratives; she renews, creates alternative histories, rewrites, and subverts; she engages in new ways with traditional art, myths, legends, symbols, and the notion of invisibility by placing them in contemporary contexts. Thus her engagement with African literature and culture is multiple and constantly evolving (Cazenave 2016: 175–82; Davies Cordova and Wa Kabwe-Segatti 2016: 13; Imorou 2016: 148). Romuald Fonkoua suggests that the novelty of her work consists in reappropriating ancient words, symbols, and masks, and using them, not simply as a form of popular wisdom, but as a form of African art in her writing (2016: 118). Therefore, when I speak of an African or Afropolitan frame to her work, it is with the awareness of the dialogue that she creates between Africa and the world outside this continent, between tradition and modernity. Perhaps her own words best metaphorically describe Tadjo's self-assigned role as a writer and her engagement with history, tradition, and modernity:

> I, the sorcerer, the man with clay hands and a red heart, I command you to get impregnated by a man who will know how to reconcile concrete and earth; a man whose soul will feed on the soil and on ideas; a man who will come to see many things at once, from high and from below; see the yeas and the nays, the past and the present. A man who will know how to rethink our traditions without negating them; how to understand the world without becoming alienated. (2008: 61)

Tadjo's 'mosaic' of stories in her travelogue presents us with the diverse voices of those who have been mutilated, orphaned, murdered, and bereft as well as those who have betrayed, murdered, raped, and maimed, or witnessed all of this (Tadjo 2009: 53).[66] Mirroring the meanderings of remembering, her text alternates between past and present, narrating stories that are linked, not necessarily by chronology or a narrative thread, but by their common experience of evil and the observations of the writer-traveler on that experience. Like Lamko, Tadjo blurs generic and narrative boundaries as she positions herself as 'an ambiguous tourist' (Hitchcott 2009: 149).[67] She recalls being extremely aware of her position as a non-witness, as a foreign writer, and as an outsider[68] who had not witnessed the genocide.[69] She acknowledges that her text is a subjective interpretation of the story of the genocide seen through her own eyes.[70] It is no testimony, she says, 'for I was not there; I do not possess the truth' and 'like everyone else, I am trying to understand', 'my book tells of a personal journey and I am part of it' (Tadjo 2000b; my translation).[71]

Among the texts produced for the project, Tadjo's has received the most critical attention in the form of journal articles and book chapters. Her text has been read from perspectives as diverse as 'affirmative biopolitics' and questions about futurity on the African continent in the face of prevailing Afro-pessimism (West-Pavlov 2014), to ecocriticism—in which her account is seen as a 'vernacular mourning ecology for post-genocide Rwanda' (Hemsley 2016: 226)—and described as a form of 'preemptive testimony' (Montesano 2015) or a 'human rights narrative' which creates a form of 'affective literacy' (Nayar 2009: 35, 36). My goal in this section is therefore not to offer a comprehensive analysis of her text,[72] as a large body of critical work already exists.[73] I will, instead, attempt to provide a fresh insight by looking at her text through the lens of *ubuntu* and the various elements of the 'African' frame present in it.[74]

A Death-Bound Journey

Tadjo's text speaks of her own journey of initiation into not only Rwandan culture and historiography, but also into the dark recesses of human nature (Tadjo 2000a: 1).[75] The subtitle, *Travels in the Heart of Rwanda*, with its evocation of multiple journeys, establishes her commitment to creating a plural narrative. It invites different interpretations and intertextual links have been made to Joseph Conrad's *Heart of Darkness* and Louis-Ferdinand Céline's *Voyage au bout de la nuit*.[76] Thus, a dialogue is established between the local and the universal; evoking not only Rwanda, but the African content and its colonial history, and the universal notions of journey and evil are inscribed in her subtitle and text. Traveling to the 'heart' of Rwanda, says Tadjo, also takes place when we are confronted with its refugees scattered all over the world, even in our own countries (Tadjo 2000a: 1).[77] Her 'internal journey' was a profound voyage to the 'very core of death'; she undertook it not only as a writer but as a fellow African and, ultimately, as a human being (Tadjo 2000b; my translation).[78] It was a journey that would require of her to listen, reflect, and be changed by it. It was akin to what Abdourahman Waberi calls a 'journey without stopovers to the furthest depths of inhumanity' (2016: 436–40).

Tadjo was unable to participate in the initial trip to Rwanda and therefore undertook her first visit alone in 1998, after which she joined a small group of the authors on a later occasion in 1999. Her 'jumping-off point' and unexpected 'first encounter' with Rwanda is South Africa, where she spent a few days before her journey to Rwanda (Tadjo 2002: 3–4). This symbolic point of departure provides her with the occasion to evoke the parallel histories of Rwanda and South Africa, with their concomitant reconciliation processes and the monumental events that were taking place almost simultaneously in these two countries in 1994.

Tadjo provides a detailed account of the detour she has to take and the obstacles she must overcome in order to arrive in Kigali. There is no direct flight from Johannesburg and she is obliged to travel via Paris and Brussels, cities representing two countries that are both heavily implicated in Rwanda's history. This detour indicates that the story she tells will be neither simple not direct, and although it both starts and ends in Africa, it will have to include the colonial history of the country and the role of these powers in the genocide, as 'France and Belgium continued until the very end to support a genocidal regime' (ibid.: 33). She is disorientated by having to run to catch her connecting flight and not being able to check her luggage through to her final destination. She is 'beside[s] herself' when she loses track of her suitcase in Brussels, luggage for which she has no baggage insurance (ibid.: 6). Her growing sense of unease and disorientation, of being 'stripped' of what is known and comfortable is heightened by the awareness that traveling can be a dangerous enterprise (De Beer 2015: 7). She highlights this through comments on eight foreigners murdered in the Ugandan jungle, the realization that 'there are risks attached to travelling' and that 'you can get yourself killed' just about anywhere (Tadjo 2002: 7–8).

By the time she is on the plane, her 'mind is spinning' (ibid.: 8). She knows that on this journey she will inevitably 'meet death' and that she will have to 'work out what to do when [she] gets there'—regarding not only her lost luggage, but also the unknown experience that lies ahead (ibid.: 6–7). However, from the very first lines, Tadjo inserts the invisible, strangely comforting presence of the dead into her narrative; she senses that her departed mother is undertaking this unsettling journey with her, holding her hand, encouraging her (ibid.: 6). In the end, Tadjo's encounter with death will confirm what traditional African ontology has already told us: 'Death is natural. *It is the other side of life* and we should not be afraid of it' (ibid.: 118; my emphasis).

Drums, Masks, Shadows, and Cycles

Tadjo is visibly disorientated by what she finds upon her arrival in Rwanda, and one of her first responses seems to be to turn to an appreciation of the land and its traditional cultural elements (Nichols 2016: 69). She incorporates these into her narrative: objects, symbols, and figures of cultural importance such as the sacred drums, the cows, the royal city of Nyanza, Imana (the creator), the *mwami* ('half-man, half-god'), and the 'all-powerful queen mother', 'man as warrior', the stars, the moon, and the fertile green hills (Tadjo 2002: 18–19). She cites a proverb that teaches us that the 'royal drums were venerated like gods', tells us that they were decorated with trophies of war and that these 'ritual objects', once sprinkled with calves' blood, were used for divination (ibid.: 18–19). She also notes, however, that of all this, 'almost nothing remains' (ibid.: 18). This is the 'cultural ethnocide' that Kayishema evokes, and Tadjo's sad conclusion is that it has stripped the nation of their inner compass: 'the wide streets of beaten earth seems to lead nowhere,' she laments (ibid.).

What is interesting, however, is her nuancing of what the interference of colonial powers was able to achieve in Rwanda; there is the acknowledgment that within these age-old cultural traditions, the 'seeds of violence' always existed, 'buried in the ancestral land' (ibid.: 19). By juxtaposing her discussion on these cultural practices and beliefs with a paragraph on the warrior kingdoms—in which '[h]eroic violence' and the practice of measuring courage by the 'number of enemies killed in battle' reigned—she suggests that the traditional celebration of 'man as warrior' might also have contributed to the violence of the genocide and that we can never know exactly how the memory of a nation is formed or what age-old images of 'slaughter' shape its future (ibid.). To my mind, this entering into dialogue with certain accepted beliefs is Tadjo's way of inhabiting that 'interstitial' and exploratory space that Waberi speaks of, a space where African roots dialogue with other worldviews (Waberi 2011: 105).[79]

Another cultural object which Tadjo includes and develops into a subversive trope is that of the African mask,[80] examples of which she comes across in the house of the 'Man with the masks':

> There were masks everywhere: round masks, square masks, serene masks, frightening masks, with huge teeth, with closed mouth, with bulbous eyes, with eyes shut. Laughing masks, sacred masks, struck with astonishment. Terror masks, masks of the banned, masks of violence.
>
> At the end of the corridor he opened the door to his bedroom. Sacred masks trained their powerful gaze in the direction of his bed. [...] Lying in his bed, he was nothing more than a body over which the masks mounted guard and whom they surrounded with their breath. (ibid.: 31)

The reference to the 'breath' of the masks is significant when read in the light of Tadjo's following remarks:

> Those who live in the 'visible' world have the duty to keep the communication open and to nurture the 'invisible' world in the same way as the 'body' is animated by an invisible 'breath' coming out of its mouth. In some African languages, the same term is used when talking about the *soul*, the *act of breathing*, and the ability to think. It is said that the dead keep living, going about their business and interfering in real life. The power of the dead and all spirits can be invoked to bring strength. Even sacred objects like masks and statues are vivified by an invisible force. (Tadjo 2013a: 2; my emphasis)

The 'breath' then not only imbues the masks with life, but also emphasizes the presence of the spirit world and its life force that integrates itself constantly into the physical realm. By investing the masks with 'breath' and portraying them as guardians, she underlines their traditional role in African ceremonies, rituals, and celebrations, namely to represent the spirits of the ancestors or deities or certain animals and to control good and evil forces in the community or bring about appeasement. The motif of the mask then also speaks of the interaction between the physical and spiritual realm, because in African tradition, the bearer of the mask provides a connection between the human and the spirit world.[81]

Pamela Nichols interprets Tadjo's fragmentary style, and the ensuing spaces between the fragments which invite the reader to fill them, as a type of 'speaking masks', an 'African literary strategy' for talking about the genocide and for evoking (invoking?) the 'presence of invisible others, dead and alive': 'Tadjo's search for understanding is transnational. The mask as a motif is African but is viewed from a moving cosmopolitan diaspora. This is not a Jungian sense of mask as persona and archetype but rather of the mask as an African ritual practice and aesthetic connecting to what Kwame Anthony Appiah has termed "the ontology of the invisible"' (Nichols 2016: 67).

As Nichols points out, the mask is not only an African motif, and Tadjo, while imbuing the mask with its traditional African connotations and functions, moves beyond this and uses it as a type of investigative technique which extends beyond its African borders. It becomes a polysemous metaphor throughout her text for the façade that Rwandans are obliged to live with in post-genocide Rwanda and for the writing process which Tadjo undertakes as a type of unveiling or unmasking of this façade, as well as for the deconstruction of the misconceptions that people have on the origins of the genocide (Semujanga 2008: 178).

When the writers arrive in Rwanda, they are confronted with a country bearing a mask; it 'seems to have forgotten everything, digested everything, swallowed everything'—the streets are tranquil, filled with people with polite smiles who carry on with daily life (Tadjo 2002: 9–10). However, they soon realize that appearances are deceptive, that 'people's memories are teeming with poisoned images' and that they 'carry their pain silently in their souls' (ibid.: 10).

The different characters that we meet represent an array of masks, providing different 'glimpses of human experience' of the genocide (Nichols 2016: 71–4). Indeed, Tadjo narrates a whole range of stories, 'which allows readers, in Tadjo's words, to "get under people's skins", look into their eyes and "see what is inside" (11)' (De Beer 2016: 47). Thus, a skin is also a mask and according to Nichols, Tadjo's text 'resonate[s]' with the ancient traditional Rwandan ritual of *gusasa inzobe*, which can be described as a form of truth-telling:

> Gusasa Inzobe means literally to take off your skin, lay it down on the grass so as to make a communal place for sitting, so as to hold discussions. Metaphorically it means for all people to sit down together, discard social distinctions and see and hear each other. [...] Remove all masks and sit and talk as equals. When the masks are put aside, collectively, it is said to be pos-

sible to become more human again. And so Ubumuntu can grow, 'Ubumuntu' the Kinyarwanda word for 'ubuntu', or the becoming more human. (Nichols 2016: 75)

Masks abound and change form, both in the country and in Tadjo's narrative. Not only do the eyes, 'blinded by darkness and emptiness', the skins and the silence of the people she meets need to be unveiled, the geographical sites also present their façades to the world (Tadjo 2002: 5). When Tadjo first sees Kigali, she notices only that which is achingly familiar to her: stalls selling bananas, people strolling around and laughing, buying newspapers and Coca-Cola; even the moon and the stars seem 'impenetrable' and Kigali is 'donning the raiment of a new existence' (ibid.: 9, 10). However, she soon starts to sense the unease behind the seeming normalcy and Edenic image that the country offers and she starts revising her description of the city and landscapes.[82]

Finally, Tadjo comes full circle in reminding us that it is not only the Rwandans and their genocidal landscape who carry masks, but that we too arrive on our journey of discovery with masks that need to be unveiled; the old guide at Ntarama church observes the visitors, studies them, weighs them up, and finally 'strip[s] them of their masks' (ibid.: 14). Throughout the text Tadjo constantly urges us to move beyond masks and veiled eyes, no matter what the cost: 'We can shut our eyes to the ugliness of the world. But we must open our pupils to see the truth,' she writes (ibid.: 102).

Another crucial image that Tadjo engages with is the subtle but ubiquitous motif of the shadow, which evokes the interconnectedness of natural phenomena, the cosmos, and human beings. The polysemic title of her text links the image of the shadow to Imana and the traditional proverb associated with his presence (or absence) in Rwanda, pointing to the metaphysical crisis in which post-genocide Rwanda finds itself.[83] In her text, shadows take on a variety of forms and are 'endowed with both positive and negative functions' (De Beer 2016: 57).[84]

Another almost invisible motif that is threaded through Tadjo's text and that hints at her awareness of the connection between humans and nature and her appreciation of nature—similar to the awareness we find in Lamko's text in the Butterfly and Fred R.—is the motif of the seed embedded in an ongoing cycle. At times, the seed is a metaphor for the dead, who are 'buried in the earth' and then reborn; at other times it is something that one needs to invest in which will then bear fruit, like the 'tree of suffering' that she hopes will bear 'fruits of peace' (Tadjo 2002: 27).

Seeds are not always beneficial—they can be the seeds of violence, buried in the 'ancestral lands' and 'germinated' over time to become 'poison grass' (ibid.: 19) or belonging to the perpetual 'cycle of violence' which we need to 'dismantle' (ibid.: 34), or the 'seeds of hatred' that caused the 'spiralling violence' (ibid.: 37), or the 'unpunished crimes' which 'engender' other crimes in turn (ibid.: 27).

However, whether these seeds bring forth destruction or hope, they always belong to a cycle, and in Tadjo's text, cycles abound: a newly born litter of kittens brings hope to Consolate, who has given up on the future (ibid.: 29); in the genocide, dogs fed on the rabid bodies and birds 'fed on the eyes of corpses'(ibid.: 27). There is also the enigmatic cycle that Tadjo evokes in the alleged story of the widow-survivor who fell in love with her son's murderer: 'This love was born of death. Death is its beginning and its end. Death is love, the connection' (ibid.: 37). And, of course, there is the all-encompassing cycle of life and death which Rwanda reminds Tadjo of: 'Rwanda [...] is despair and the desire to come alive again. It is death which haunts our life. It is life which overcomes death' (ibid.: 38). It is also the cycle of the dead who return to 'float' among the living (ibid.: 41). Even Isaro's tale is built around the notion of her deceased husband's 'voice' and essence, which seems to partly return to her through the presence of Nkuranya (ibid.: 51).

It is in the tale of the wrath of the dead (discussed below) that this cycle is probably most eloquently expressed:

> The dead will be reborn in every fragment of life, however small [...] They will be reborn in the dust, in the dancing water, in the children who laugh and play as they clap their hands, in every seed hidden beneath the black earth [...] May they remain the stars of our firmament, those we see in the dark night and which will still be shining for generations to come. (ibid.: 46–7)

It is then through the imaginative use of these cultural, natural, and religious symbols that Tadjo enters into dialogue with the challenges that post-genocide Rwanda faces.

Interconnectedness, Border-Blurring, and the Third Journey

In multiple ways, Tadjo's text engages with values that can be directly associated with an interdependent, communitarian worldview. A first obvious presence in her text of this type of ethics is the notion of interconnectedness: an awareness of the unseen connection between humans, but also between the material and spiritual world and between humans and the cosmos. Her dedication, which seems to have been omitted in the English translation, is to 'all those who have departed but still *remain in us*' (Tadjo 2000c: 8; my translation, my emphasis),[85] hinting at a sensitivity to the cohabitation of the living and the dead.

Tadjo celebrates this connectedness firstly through her 'constant reminder that we are all part of a shared humanity' (De Beer 2019: 198). One of the ways in which she accomplishes this is to engage in 'border-blurring' as opposed to the 'border-drawing' that genocide discourse relied on (West-Pavlov 2014: 118). This approach can be linked to a 'particular African tradition of deconstructive thought', which she pursues in unexpected ways (ibid.: 118) The voices from her text do not fit the homogenized classifications that are frequently associated with the account of the genocide; 'they are often at once perpetrator and victim, wounded human being rather than Hutu, Tutsi or even foreigner', demonstrating how suffering is 'essentially a human experience' (De Beer 2019: 194–6).

Not only does she foreground the interconnectedness between Rwandans, she also maintains that what happened in Rwanda 'concerned us all'—it is also our 'nightmare, and our 'primal fear', not just that of a single nation 'lost in the dark heart of Africa' (Tadjo 2002: 3). Throughout the text, this stance is maintained: 'We must all bear responsibility for this humanitarian failure' (ibid.: 34). Even in her own country and all over the world, there is no escape from the consequences of the genocide: 'Yes, I went to Rwanda but Rwanda is also here in my country. The refugees are scattered all over the world, carrying within themselves the blood and fury of the abandoned dead' (ibid.: 37). Even the prisoner whose hearing she attends feels strangely familiar: 'I have the impression that I know him, that I have seen him at home, in one of the streets of the capital' (ibid.: 93). This inclusion of her native Côte d'Ivoire, and her references to post-apartheid South Africa, is a further form of border-blurring in which the problems of non-belonging move beyond the borders of Rwanda. Tadjo insists on illustrating the links between what had happened in Rwanda and the rest of the world, thus focusing on the universality of evil and inhumanity and calling on us to acknowledge our own responsibility.

The reader is invited to participate in the dialogue initiated by the author, and in her journey, in which she is bound to encounter death. She reminds us that it is not 'natural death' as we know it, but death made 'cruel' and 'hideous' because of the violence of the genocide (ibid.: 118):

'Are your fears more terrifying than mine? Do you fall deeper into your abyss than I into mine? What sacrifice would you be willing to make to preserve your humanity? Are you prepared for this incredible encounter with death distorted by cruelty?' (ibid.: 10). She places herself in the shoes of the Rwandans and asks the reader to engage in a similar act of solidarity and empathetic listening:

> In the dark night of absolute blindness, what would I have done if I had been caught up in the spiralling violence of the massacre? Would I have resisted betrayal? Would I have been cowardly or brave, would I have killed or would I have let myself be killed? Rwanda is inside me, in you, in all of us. Rwanda is under our skin, in our blood, in our guts. In the very depths of our slumber, in our waking hearts. (ibid.: 37–8)

In our shared humanity, the task of remembering, reconstruction, and prevention that lies ahead is never just the Rwandans', it is also always *ours*:

> [...] he guards the evidence of *our* inhumanity.
> *We* have to dismantle the cycle of violence [...]
> *We* must never cut off the way back. *We* must understand, like a song to be hummed, that the world is still standing and that the picture *we* have of ourselves is absolutely real [...]
> [...] *we* must recognise within ourselves the fears that drive *us* [...]
> *We* must lay down arms and let the wounds heal [...]
> *We* need to understand. *Our* humanity is in peril. (ibid.: 15, 34, 38, 116, 118; my emphasis)

Like the participants of the project, the reader is confronted with the knowledge of the genocide and called upon to react: 'Occasionally, someone will reveal a secret to you that you have not asked to know. Then you are crushed under a burden of knowledge too heavy to bear' (Tadjo 2002: 3). We can no longer remain mere observers of this journey of reconstruction, which is as 'affective' as it is spiritual or physical (Nayar 2009).

A further strategy used by Tadjo to oblige the reader, who finds himself or herself in a 'hermeneutical darkness', to become implicated in the journey is by 'gradually eclipsing herself' as she 'transfers the responsibility of interpretation to her readers': 'It is ultimately our role to connect the fragmented snapshots and heterogeneous voices Tadjo stages [...] she functions more and more like an archivist or *une passeuse de paroles* (a messenger) who limits her role within the process of writing history to the selection of what she sees as worthy of memory [...]' (Dauge-Roth 2010: 116). Tadjo suggests that this type of approach is not merely a tool she uses to write about the genocide, but a heritage which flows from her cultural background and which permeates her oeuvre. In this way she reminds us of the call for participation traditionally required by the griot from the audience: 'Oral literature greatly influences my work! I love its coded language filled with imagery. Its suggestive power. I also like the idea that the audience is expected to participate in the narrative and to interpret the messages' (Dahouda and Tadjo 2007: 184; my translation).[86]

A notion that stands in opposition to the principles of interconnectedness and communitarianism is the 'physical fear of the Other' (Tadjo 2002: 10).[87] Once again, this problem is not unique to Rwanda; Tadjo calls it an 'obscure fear' of the human race which had its origin in a time when humans 'had not yet discovered their humanity' (ibid.: 9, 10). The writers participating in the project constantly reflect on this aspect, which became embodied in the Rwandan context through the harmful opposition between Hutu, Tutsi, and Twa identities.

Tadjo insists on overturning these imposed identity boundaries, as she clothes the people in her text with hybrid or complex identities, often refusing to assign them to any of the categories that played such an important role in the genocide.[88] She also lays bare the role played by colonial discourse and genocidal propaganda in fostering and exploiting this opposition. This reaction toward the Other, Tadjo seems to say, is not automatic; it is created, invented, and learned: 'And I am afraid when, in my country, I hear people talk of who belongs there and who doesn't. Creating division. Creating foreigners. Inventing the idea of rejection. How is ethnic identity learned? Where does this fear of the Other come from, bringing violence in its wake?' (ibid.: 37). She shows how the fear of the Other—or what Russell West-Pavlov has called the 'language of biopolitics, with its inner/outer border demarcations constituting community, immunity and threat' (2014: 117)—was incited during the training of young militia: 'They gave us clubs and told us where to strike; it was them or us and there was no greater fear than that, that they were the ones wanting to kill us, who would one day kill us if any of them survived' (Tadjo 2002: 103).

She points out that the 'theories' on the alleged 'foreign' origin of the Tutsis, propagated by European historians, were not underpinned by historical proof. However, sadly, the Rwandans seemed to have appropriated them, to their own detriment (ibid.: 22). Tadjo demonstrates how even the theories on the alleged physical characteristics pertaining to each group was 'interiorised' (Semujanga 2008: 166) by the Rwandans. She does so by relating an incident where Thérèse Kubwimana claims that the author, due to her particular skin color, hair, and 'black gums', which are a 'sign of beauty in the Tutsi culture', looks like a Rwandan (Tadjo 2002: 22). Not only does this forge an even stronger bond between Tadjo and the people whose stories she has come to listen to—and in whose country she recognizes the 'familiar' faces from home (ibid.: 9)—it also reminds us of the price paid by Tutsis for the imposed colonial hypothesis about their origins and physical traits. These assertions about 'tall and slender' Tutsi 'shepherds' may have been 'made in the form of flattery', but this discourse was subverted during the genocide when their bodies were sent 'back' to Ethiopia in the Kagera river (Tadjo 2002: 22).

The validity of these ethnic categorizations is interrogated by demonstrating how random and unstable they were. Tadjo tells, for example, of a Zaïrean woman who is raped by the Interahamwe because she has the physical features typically identified with Tutsi women (ibid.: 90), thus reflecting on all the different types of victims that suffered as a result of the genocide against the Tutsis. Thus we see how the fear of the Other, in its many forms, contributed to genocidal acts, but also how the author in various ways deconstructs the notion of Otherness.

Another example of border-blurring that we have already discussed when analyzing Lamko's book, and which an author or reader uninitiated into the local culture might not be as sensitive to, is the porous boundaries between the dead and the living, and between the human and the natural world. When drawing from her titles and subtitles, one easily arrives at the conclusion that Tadjo is dealing with two types of journeys: one physical (traveling to the sites and through the country) and the other affective and philosophical (dealing with human nature, inhumanity and evil), or two physical journeys, namely her first and second journey to Rwanda. This assumption is only partially correct; for it fails to include a vital aspect which Tadjo points out in a later article. There are, in fact, three types of journeys. The third one is a metaphysical journey: the journey into the 'invisibility' of parts of the story she was telling and listening to, a notion which she considers to be an extremely relevant source of inspiration for her and other African writers (Tadjo 2013a: 3, 6). It is this third journey that I believe merits further critical attention.

The concept of 'invisibility', which refers to 'the belief that there is no separation between the spiritual and material worlds', is explored in the section in her travel account which Tadjo herself describes as a 'purely imaginative' part (ibid.: 1–3). This section is situated between the 'first' and 'second' journey and comprises four subsections, of which 'The wrath of the dead' is the first. In sections leading up to this part of her text, Tadjo gradually initiates the reader into this aspect of African ontology by juxtaposing two opposing ways of perceiving the remains of a victim. This implied comparison takes place during the very first site visits she narrates, namely the churches at Nyamata and Ntarama, an account which unfolds over several micro-narratives. Her initial description of Nyamata reads like an inventory, and this reminds us of Pelouse's initial approach to the genocide (in Lamko's text, discussed above). Tadjo starts by providing statistics, facts, a graphical image (almost like Pelouse's photos), a detailed description of Mukandori's mutilated corpse, and a scathing remark on the fact that she is used as an 'example', put 'on show' (Tadjo 2002: 11). No reference is made to the invisible world, to the spirit of the deceased that we are looking at.

It is at these sites that the authors become aware of the dehumanization of the victims, both during and after the genocide. On a cultural level, this is significant, for respect for the deceased is a key traditional value. At Nyamata, Tadjo remarks on the objectification and impersonal display of the bodies in the church: 'They look like things destined for the scrapyard. Skulls are piled on top of each other, torn and mouldy clothes mingle with the scarcely recognisable remains' (ibid.: 13). She talks about the blackened or white skulls and the bones of unidentified victims, not buried according to the rites. Their purpose is mainly to bear witness, and she notes that such a pile of disintegrating bones, skulls, and 'broken objects'— and the all-pervasive stench that rises from them—cannot be called a 'memorial'; it is 'death laid bare, exposed in all its rawness' (ibid.: 12, 13). One senses the author's revolt against this treatment of the dead, for she sees and hears beyond the physical remains that lie before her, and she warns us that 'these dead are screaming still' (ibid.: 12).

At the nearby church of Ntarama, Tadjo describes a similar intrusion of the dead into the world of the living. They are not only a physical presence through the stench of death and visual images, but also a metaphysical presence: 'Particles from the massacre are floating in the air. The dead point an accusing figure at the living who are still making use of them. The dead want to return to the earth. They rise up in protest. They want to melt into the earth' (ibid.: 16).

Tadjo's reaction when faced with this dilemma of the unburied deceased being treated like statistics and proof, and the memorial acting as a type of 'museum' with bodies on 'display', with no regard for the peace of their souls, really comes at the end of her visit to Nyamata (ibid.: 15). Here, she textually demonstrates how the process of depersonalization and dehumanization can and must be reversed. When a guide invites her to write in the register, she too is given a number, but she rehabilitates the number by investing it with humanity, with a name, a home, and a unique identity, similar to what she will attempt throughout her text to do for those whom she meets on her journey, both those who are still in the visible world and those who have moved on:

> I am number 7317
> I write my surname and my first name.
> My address in Rwanda.
> My address abroad. (ibid.: 13)

This revolt against the dehumanization of the dead is a central theme in the project. Abdourahman Waberi confirms that for every body that has become a statistic, there exists a name and a surname, a home address, friends and loved ones, a whole life. He protests against the 'spreadsheets' and 'columns' to which the dead are relegated:

> The nature of our humanity calls on us to give, if only momentarily, a face, a name, a voice and leaving a living memory to the hundreds of thousands of victims so that they don't end up as mere numbers. Or worse even, stored away in the vault of memory or at best abandoned dormant in the columns of a spreadsheet more or less officially recognised by our so-called collective conscience […]. (Waberi 2016: 100–2)

Boubacar Boris Diop concurs that the deceased are not mere statistics. When his main protagonist, Cornelius, visits Murambi, Gérard, who is guiding him, says, 'You'll see the same bodies everywhere', to which he replies dryly: 'I don't think so' (Diop 2006: 1398), for he knows that amongst those bodies are individuals, people with separate lives, dreams, and stories.

Tadjo would later accentuate that these African writers found it 'impossible' to talk about Rwanda without referring to 'the presence of the dead and their continuous impact on the memory of the living' (2013a: 3). She also admits that her rendition of the journey to the invisible world of the dead, which includes the chapter titled 'The wrath of the dead', was motivated by her personal experience of burial customs from her native culture, a belief system which is prevalent in almost all African countries (Tadjo 2000a). The section in her text that is largely allegorical and imaginative is not purely a symbolic tale, but based on the very real presence of the dead permeating the lives of the living. This is a spiritual reality which haunts the inhabitants of post-genocide Rwanda.

It is significant that the vehicle she uses to talk about this unseen world comes in the form of an imaginative tale. Tadjo admits that this genre, which allows for different levels of reading and gives much freedom to an author in terms of time, space, and inclusion/exclusion of details, is one of her favorites, and that using it sets her at ease because it 'corresponds' to something real in her native West African culture (in Anyinefa and Rice-Maximin 2008: 371).[89] This author does warn of the danger of entrusting history uniquely to the oral tradition: 'Is Africa's orality a handicap to the collective memory? We must write to give information some permanence' (2002: 27). Yet this does not prevent her from drawing from the oral tradition when writing both this imaginative part of her text and an allegorical tale of the monster who consumed himself, which appears in the closing pages of her 'Second Journey'.[90]

Let us return now to the tale about the 'wrath of the dead', which is reminiscent of the oral tradition (Tadjo 2013a: 3). In between the two rather realistic sections of the text (filled with travel details, interviews, documents, and descriptions of places and of her own physical and affective reactions), the author unexpectedly inserts this tale which speaks of the haunting presence of the deceased:

The dead were paying regular visits to the living [...] The town streets were filled with spirits moving around, whirling in the stifling air. They jostled the living, clambered on their backs, walked alongside them, danced around them, followed them through the crowded alleyways. [...] They were in every neighbourhood. You could feel them as they scurried past people.

The spirits were hurrying home to visit everyone they had known, in the places that they had loved and which were still their own [...] They floated among the living [...] (Tadjo 2002: 41)

By embedding this image-filled, highly poetic tale within the realistic travelogue, and thus interweaving these two forms of apparently conflicting genres in such a seemingly natural manner, Tadjo suggests that for the Rwandans, the presence of the dead is a natural part of everyday life and that the invisible world seamlessly intrudes into the rational, physical, and scientific world (De Beer 2019: 199–200). The dead reprimand the living, who are starting to forget them. Their presence is untimely and unsettling, and they have the power to bring everything 'to a halt', 'making the days and nights unbearable' for those who have remained behind (Tadjo 2002: 42, 43).

An aspect of the traditional African way of being in the world that is sharply foregrounded in this tale is the belief that Bagilishya (2000: 351) refers to, namely that when certain cultural taboos are transgressed, punishment by spirits and powers of nature often follows and affects the whole community, a situation which requires the sages and elders to intervene by pleading with the ancestors and performing the necessary rites. This speaks then of the connection that exists between human beings, the spirit world, and nature. In Tadjo's tale, it is suggested by the presence of a violent wind that carries the rage of the deceased and 'pierce[s] the eardrums of the survivors' and an 'angry rain' which hammers out the refusal of one of the spirits to accept his untimely death:

> Some of the dead were so enraged that they refused to go when the time came to quit the earth. There was one in particular whose head had been cut off and who was angry with everyone. His ally was a torrential downpour.
>
> ◆
>
> The rain fell furiously. An angry rain shrieking its refusal to open the gates to the other world. And it hammered the earth with great strokes in order to say: 'No!' (Tadjo 2002: 42)

The punishment that they fear from the dead is that a 'swirling horde of demons' will be unleashed, or a 'terrible drought' will torment them, that their entrails will be devoured, their eyes torn out and their hearts burnt (ibid.: 46–7).

A wise man is sent for, not only to listen to the angered spirit, but also to 'offer words of appeasement' to the dead and perform ritual offerings (ibid.: 43–4). Only then does the rain subside and nature become calm again. In this chapter, the soothsayer plays an intermediary role between the dead and the living, between human beings and nature and between the physical and spiritual realm.[91] He seems to embody the bridge between the two worlds that Tadjo evokes in a later article: 'There is a bridge between life and death thanks to which the two remain connected' (2013a: 2). He pleads for ritual and respectful burying of the 'desiccated bodies', an act that would 'hide their decay and their blinding nakedness' (Tadjo 2002: 44, 45). He evokes the life–death mirror image that forms such an important thread in Tadjo's narrative by calling the dead the 'images of life', saying that such rites would again give them the right to 'assert' themselves in the lives of the living and return to them in a harmonious way instead of haunting them (ibid.: 45). The words of the diviner articulate the interdependence between the dead and the living: 'We must ask them to yield up to us the secrets of life, which becomes triumphant once more, since only the living can bring the dead back to life. Without us, they no longer exist. Without them, we fall into emptiness' (ibid.). In Tadjo's tale, death then is not the end; 'it is the "connection" which allows futurity to flourish' (West-Pavlov 2014: 127). Death 'is not stronger than life, for life always regains the upper hand in the end' (Tadjo 2002: 118).

Tadjo also incorporates the belief that the deceased return and are to be welcomed as guests in their former homes: 'We must open the door to them, let them settle in, show them how we are living […]' (ibid.: 45). Tadjo's understanding of invisibility as 'the belief in vital forces animating all earthly creations, alive or dead' and that there is therefore a 'hidden world' that interpenetrates the living one (Tadjo 2013a: 1–2) is made visible through this tale. In writing it, the author is performing an act of unveiling, of 'lifting the cloak of (in)visibility' (Tadjo 2013a: 1) on this 'hidden world' inhabited by the dead but which constantly reintroduces itself into the world of the living (ibid.: 12).

It is not only in 'The wrath of the dead' that we see this; in all four of the micro-narratives which make up this 'third journey',[92] situated between Tadjo's two physical journeys, death, mourning and the invisible are central themes. Sometimes death is physical, for example, in the case of Isaro's husband, and at other times it is symbolic or emotional, for example, in the case of Anastasie and Annonciata, who are raped. In this sense, the focus is not only on the unseen spiritual world described above, but also on the invisible pain that widows, rape victims, and the family of victims experience. What is relevant here is the importance of seeing these stories through the lens of the invisible pain that they carry within them and the theme of death, loss, and mourning which connects them. In all the stories in this section following that on the wrath of the dead (those of

Romain and Isaro, Anastase and Anastasie, Karl and Annonciata, and Seth and Valentine) Tadjo depicts different forms of mourning and the pain of those who stay behind or who were not there to protect their loved ones. She thereby links these accounts with the introductory tale on the disharmony between the dead and the living.

Another example in this series that speaks of the constant presence of the dead is a narrative entitled 'His voice', which Tadjo recounts immediately after the tale of the soothsayer. Years after her husband's suicide, Isaro has not been able to get rid of his possessions because 'things have a soul', and she thinks that Romain might show himself through them (Tadjo 2002: 56). She has erected a small altar in his memory and has been 'expecting his return for a long time' (ibid.: 56). When Nkuranya phones her to make an appointment, she believes that she recognizes Romain's voice and is convinced that it is Romain's spirit who has come back to her (ibid.: 51). However, their first meeting is inexplicably interrupted by a bee that seems to be especially attracted to Isaro. Is it perhaps Romain's spirit that hovers close to them and disrupts their conversation? Or is it his voice and spirit that have returned through Nkuranya? Tadjo leaves these questions open, but what is significant is the haunting presence of the dead and the way in which Isaro expects her deceased husband to reintroduce himself into her life. Another interesting point is that in this particular story, the deceased is not a Tutsi victim, but a man accused of participating in the genocide. Once again, Tadjo resists facile categorization. Her narrative suggests that this type of relationship with the dead is not reserved for certain groups; it is a common element of Rwandan traditional thought.

Anastase and Anastasie's story, as well as that of Karl's family (entitled 'Those who were not there'), speaks of a different kind of death—this time through rape, which I discuss in greater depth in Chap. 5, when I analyze Monique Ilboudo's text. What I will say at this point is that in the story of Anastasie's rape by her brother, one easily focuses on her—and rightly so, as she is the victim of this narrative and Tadjo's portrayal of her experience is so unsettling. However, we should also stop for a moment to think about the brother and perpetrator, Anastase, to whom Tadjo has also given a voice, one which is probably more difficult to listen to. The story in fact starts with his experience of confusion and mourning when Anastasie dies. Tadjo's description of his struggle with his sister's death, 'the woman he had loved', but raped, is imbued with multiple images connected with the circle of death and rebirth and linked to nature: he thinks about 'descending into the bowels of the earth', sees the clouds 'sliding to infinity', and feels himself drawn to the 'moment of the sun's rebirth' as daylight arrives, wondering whether this 'fusion' and energy is where all souls vanish to when they die (ibid.: 61). 'I must learn to live without her,' he says, 'on the other side of time' (ibid.: 62). Through this character, with whom the reader struggles to be comfortable because of his status as perpetrator, Tadjo again demonstrates that certain experiences, such as mourning, is common to the human being, be that person a perpetrator, survivor, or onlooker.

In the subsection 'Those who were not there', two stories are narrated: that of Karl and Annonciata and that of Seth and Valentine. Both speak of the experience of those who were absent. In the aftermath of the genocide, Karl, a foreigner, is haunted with regret. Although he is able to find his Rwandan partner and their children, it becomes clear that Annonciata has been so marked by her experiences that she has 'withdrawn from the world' and he has lost 'the woman who had seduced him with her energy and high spirits' (ibid.: 74). The invisible that Tadjo seeks to show here is of a different nature: it is when the living—who have survived the worst possible experiences, such as Anastasie, raped by her own kin, and Annonciata, who was raped repeatedly and now has acquired immunodeficiency syndrome (AIDS)—become the walking dead, death, and shadow lurking inside their souls. It also the invisible pain of Karl, who failed to protect his partner and now lives in the 'chains' of perpetual mourning and grief; he wants to 'punish himself, to sentence himself to extended suffering' (ibid.: 75). How does one mourn a loved one who survived physically but has become 'only the shadow of her former self' (ibid.: 74)?

The link between the invisible or death and mourning, and Seth and Valentine's story, is more difficult to make. However, one possible way of looking at it is through the theme of the 'impossibility of mourning' due to displacement and absence; those who have been exiled have not been able to bury or mourn their dead. They do not have access to the sites of mourning, a reality which interferes with their mourning process because, as Nayar (citing Derrida and Dufourmantelle) notes, 'mourning must have an identifiable body, remains or topos'—thus an identifiable 'resting place' for the dead (2009: 39). Those in exile have access to none of those three necessary elements: 'If, as Derrida proposes (2000, p. 111), a mourning that occurs without a place (topos) is interminable, Rwandans in exile (such as the attendant Tadjo meets in Durban) do not have a place to mourn: their dead lie interred in a "foreign" land, so to speak (they, the

survivors have since left). Hence, their mourning never ends [...]'
(ibid.: 45).

This is possibly why the 'call of the country' that Tadjo talks about is so
strong upon the exiled, the 'life-blood' that connects Seth to his native
country where his parents were assassinated in the 1963 massacres (Tadjo
2002: 76). Thus, throughout this 'in-between' section that Tadjo has
inserted between her two more obvious and realistic travel narratives, the
story of the invisible world of the dead, the mourning and the exiled is
depicted.

Like Lamko's novel, Tadjo's text is structured by the age-old motif of
the journey of initiation. However, reading these two texts through the
metaphor of the journey demonstrates how two authors can use the same
trope and yet approach it in essentially different ways. The allegorical journey of transformation evoked by Lamko encompasses not only the experience of the foreign visitor; it merges the story of three main characters
who represent different voices and different modes of traveling (De Beer
2015: 5). Although we can easily draw certain parallels between Lamko
and Pelouse, he is not a character in his own book; he rarely (if at all)
inserts himself as writer directly into the journey(s) he is describing.
Elements of orality are pervasive throughout his text, and the cultural and
traditional aspects that he includes are guiding principles for his characters
on their respective journeys.

Tadjo, on the other hand, is an integral part of her own story; it is her
journey that we are reading about, her discovery of the stories of genocide. Her text, although it contains some symbolic, oral, and allegorical
elements, reads essentially like a genuine travel diary, grounded in real life
experiences; true or imagined discussions with Rwandans; realistic descriptions of prisons, genocide sites, and orphanages; and evocations of newspaper extracts and other documents; as well as the author's reflections on
human beings' relation to violence and evil.

Like Lamko, Tadjo engages with the intersection of the two realms that
is such a central part of Rwandan (African) tradition and she too grounds
her text with cultural symbols, motifs, and a title that refers to traditional
values. It is when she inserts her tale on the invisible world that her travel
diary opens up, that we understand that we are to read beyond the surface
of the physical realities the text confronts us with.

She not only draws from but also renews and reappropriates cultural
objects, symbols, and customs and invests them with new possibilities.
Even the traditional notion of invisibility is applied in different contexts,

and the creative writing process, through its ability to create images, becomes a 'bridge' between the visible and the invisible (Cazenave 2016: 180). In Tadjo's work, writing is an act of making visible, of building a 'greater awareness', and of 'attempting to "lift the cloak" of their invisibility' (Tadjo 2013a: 4).

NOTES

1. For Tadjo's text I have used the published English translation, but all English citations from Lamko's texts are my translations from the original, published in French. Where deemed necessary, I provide the original French in footnotes or brackets.
2. The French word used in the title is '*phalène*', which can also be translated as 'night moth' or 'night butterfly'.
3. Josias Semujanga (2007) provides an in-depth analysis of Tadjo's 'subversive' use of the classical travel diary genre combined with a mixture of other genres, including testimony and reporting.
4. Eileen Julien demonstrates this principle through examples of the epic, the initiation story, and the fable as three narrative genres that are present in many oral traditions, and she looks at how these forms have been reappropriated in certain novels (1992: 47).
5. « Tout le côté initiatique des contes est très important pour moi » (Tadjo, in Anyinefa and Rice-Maximin 2008: 371).
6. As Stéphane Amougou Ndi (quoting Joëlle Gardes-Tamine) reminds us, when recounting the unspeakable, it is meaningful to use a narrative form that offers various perspectives as this allows us to constantly pluralize and question the story that we are creating (2010: 259).
7. One sees, for example, the varying reactions and discourses offered by different characters in Lamko's novel as they are confronted with the Nyamata genocide memorial: Védaste, the guide, who 'embodies' the view of the survivors as well as the politically correct, official government view; the Butterfly, who represents the voice of the deceased; the head of the French delegation who is there to exonerate the French; and Pelouse, who is the voice of the diaspora (Dauge-Roth 2010: 137–9).
8. See De Beer (2015), Fonkoua (2003), Germanotta (2016), Hitchcott (2009, 2015), Nayar (2009), and Semujanga (2007).
9. I have used this trope in a previous article to analyze Lamko's work, and therefore, parts of this section include an adaptation of this article (De Beer 2015).
10. « Mais chacune de mes œuvres m'a amenée à prendre conscience de plus en plus profondément de la responsabilité de l'écrivain. Garder les yeux

ouverts sur la société et sur le monde » (Tadjo 2009: 53). According to Tadjo, her text on Rwanda would become the first of a trilogy on those unacceptable acts that should not be tolerated in society (in a discussion with the author in 2010).

11. Pramod Nayar suggests that Tadjo uses two modes of witnessing in her text: the first one is collective and comprises observing and documenting what is visible in terms of facts and statistics, and the second is more subjective and affective and entails 'delving beneath the placid surfaces to discover the horror buried beneath' (2009: 38).

12. *L'ombre d'Imana: voyages jusqu'au bout du Rwanda* was translated by Véronique Wakerley in 2002 as *The Shadow of Imana: Travels in the Heart of Rwanda*. I will be using Wakerley's translation throughout unless otherwise stipulated.

13. For a discussion of Tadjo's text as a shared form of witnessing and listening, a 'call to dialogue', read Griffin (2008).

14. « Je pense. Une forme romanesque. D'aucuns disent que c'est plutôt un long poème. Moi-même, je ne sais pas trop ce que c'est » (Chalaye 2001).

15. « Maintenant que j'y pense. La vie d'une phalène est rien d'autre qu'un destin d'émigré perpétuel, confectionné d'un chapelet d'aléas, un tourbillon de métamorphoses » (Lamko 2002: 20).

16. « Fred R. court encore. Fred R. court toujours son marathon d'exilé. Il ne peut pousser racine nulle part [...] parcourt toutes les pistes du mépris, les impasses, les boulevards au bord desquels se dressent des visages intolérants, égoïstes et apeurés » (Lamko 2002: 20).

17. Odile Cazenave and Patricia Célérier point out that her death was 'emblematic' of the 'will to eradicate the royal Tutsi lineage' (2011: 93).

18. Both these versions of her name are used by the authors.

19. Alexandre Dauge-Roth suggests that it is through the 'regenerating power' of the metaphor, that Lamko 'literally brings Mukandori back to life' and thus frees her silenced voice to enable her to tell her own story (Dauge-Roth 2010: 135).

20. Mukandori is discussed in more detail in Chap. 5.

21. « Moi, je suis désormais une phalène, un énorme papillon de nuit aux couleurs de sol brûlé » (Lamko 2002: 13).

22. Amougou Ndi provides a helpful analysis of the brutal, allegorical narration of the rape of the queen and the symbolism and literary devices employed by Lamko to do so (2010: 272–7).

23. « Me voici partie! Hors de ma coquille. Je passe la frontière entre l'être et le néant, pour ce territoire de l'illimité où l'on participe immédiatement à des réalités non visibles » (Lamko 2002: 46).

24. « J'ai surgi d'un néant de fantôme et d'une dépouille sèche de femme anonyme au milieu d'autres cadavres amoncelés dans une église-musée-site du

génocide. [...] Simple opération de métamorphose pour passer de l'invisible au visible, du corps aphysique à l'incarné » (Lamko 2002: 13, 28–9).

25. « J'avais décidé d'arracher le verbe et de l'imprimer directement à la conscience de ces deux visiteurs hors du commun: version originale et intégrale dans une édition non-expurgée. [...]: l'on est seul vrai témoin de son histoire et seul véritable miroir de son visage, puisqu'on sait de quelle fatigue est née le cerne sous l'œil. Mon histoire est belle et bien mienne, une histoire de reine, et, surtout, celle de mon sexe: un vagin rempli d'arbre » (Lamko 2002: 31).

26. « saisir l'objectif de l'appareil pour fixer et dire la nausée, l'absurde, l'ineffable, la violence et cela avec cette authenticité qui seule apporte la vérité d'œil double » (Lamko 2002: 140).

27. « Que diable pouvait venir glaner une Négresse avec un appareil photo ? [...] Ah ! le siècle cul-de-jatte, irrésistiblement avide de sensationnel et qui adore se gaver de virtualité; le siècle friand des misères d'homme à déguster par procuration d'écrans et d'objectifs de caméras. Cannibalisme non-avoué ! » (Lamko 2002: 24–5).

28. This emblematic character refers to Major General Fred Rwigema, who was the military leader of the Rwandan Patriotic Front (RPF) and who died mysteriously in 1990. Born in Rwanda in 1957, he had lived in exile from 1960.

29. Alexandre Kimenyi notes that in Rwandan culture, names 'are not drawn arbitrarily from concrete nouns or just made up by general rules of Kinyarwanda syntax. Naming is a matter of great importance and the namer is very careful in choosing or giving a name to a child. All the names have a significant meaning implied in them by the namers. Names have a spatio-temporal character in the sense that they indicate the conditions and circumstances—political, social, atmospheric, and economic—in which the baby was born or that the namer has experienced' (Kimenyi 1978: 268).

30. This can be read as a play on the French word '*tuer*' (to kill): they kill with their intellect and their words incite others to either kill or be killed: « 'Fuis parce que les hommes qui arrivent sont des cancrelats avec des cornes de buffle et des crocs de lion, ils te boufferont !' Et le peuple tue pour ne pas être bouffé. [...] Ce sont des 'intellect-tuels' qui tuent! » (Lamko 2002: 147).

31. This is discussed in the section on Tadjo's work later in this chapter.

32. A Kinyarwanda word meaning 'foreigner/white person'.

33. « C'est aussi vrai que nous avons fourni quelques armes à feu, quelques machettes et entraîné les tueurs ... Il faut être objectif ! Mais nous n'étions pas sur les barricades. Nous aimons bien tous les Africains [...] » (Lamko 2002: 93, 95).

34. « Coup classique de fantôme ! Moi, *muzimu* de Reine, je ne pouvais évidemment pas laisser enfermer ma carcasse dans une boîte noire—fut-elle celle de l'appareil photo Canon de ma nièce » (Lamko 2002: 111).
35. « [...] la philopoésie de la regardance » (Lamko 2002: 89).
36. « [...] qui était le sien mais qu'elle ne connaissait que par la peinture que lui en avait fait sa tante pendant ses brefs séjours à Paris [...] » (Lamko 2002: 143).
37. « Si tu me cherches vraiment, si tu cherches ma tombe, si tu veux être affranchie de toutes les hantises, il faut que tu apprennes à saisir les choses cachées de la vie, celles grouillantes au-delà du sensible. N'aie pas peur des obstacles. La frontière n'existe que dans l'esprit de ceux qui bornent la vie en compartiments étanches » (Lamko 2002: 144).
38. Amougou Ndi (2010: 292–315) provides an in-depth analysis of the initiation process that Pelouse undergoes and its different stages.
39. « Tes photos seront chargées de rythmes et d'émotions et célébreront, en filigrane, la nouvelle humanité à engendrer par-delà les lacs, les collines, les massifs volcaniques, le vol des tisserins ou les fumées des champs de bananiers ... » (Lamko 2002: 113).
40. « Nous sommes accueillants, nous rions avec le visiteur, nous sommes prévenants, accortes, mais cela n'est que la surface de la croûte. Pour savoir ce que nous pensons réellement, il fait aller au-delà de la coquille » (Lamko 2002: 106).
41. « Petite maman, tu es fille de ce pays de collines; mais tu n'en as connu que l'odeur du sein maternel. Moi le pays je l'ai eu en plein dans la figure ! Ce n'est pas la même chose ! L'exil t'a construite; le pays m'a détruite. Fais attention à ce que le pays ne te détruise pas à ton tour [...] » (Lamko 2002: 174).
42. Through Muyango's voice, Lamko subtly subverts the epic in terms of hero and victim, because as Lamko points out, the real heroes in his narrative were those who had died fighting, whereas the losers were those who had killed them (Lamko, in Marcelli 2011). This can be seen as an example of the way in which the authors participating in the project use traditional genres creatively, but also destabilize them in order to engage with certain complex issues in post-genocide Rwanda. Determining who are heroes, who are victims, and who are perpetrators is indeed a controversial issue in the aftermath of the genocide.
43. « L'histoire ne souffre jamais de redites lorsqu'on la délivre avec fidélité » (Lamko 2002: 113).
44. « Longues journées identiques: bibine, pipi, tranches de banane grillée, gésier de poulet piqué à gauche à droite dans les assiettes des clients ... bibine, pipi, ragots, crises de larmes ... Aujourd'hui pareil à la veille et au lendemain. Une vie en rond » (Lamko 2002: 67).

45. This presumably refers to Alice Karekezi, the lawyer and human rights activist who worked extensively in Rwanda with the rights of women and the role of women in peace-building and transitional justice.

46. « À Alice KAREKEZI, 'Ngonkom', qui plante du jasmin, des belles d'aube, des flammes de bois et des trompettes d'or dans le sol limoneux de Butare, je dis par ces mots: 'Plantons, ma sœur, et la pluie et le soleil feront croître l'espérance' » (Lamko 2002: 10).

47. « On y coiffera toutes les femmes qui voudront bien se débarrasser de leurs cheveux de deuil, on y coiffera aussi les âmes qui ont poussé de denses broussailles de désespérance. Ce sera de la chirurgie esthétique des âmes […]; nous serons miroirs pour rendre aux gens leur image, concave ou convexe lorsqu'ils sont désespérés, mais harmonieux et équilibrés lorsqu'ils ont envie de dépasser les marques du chaos » (Lamko 2002: 195–6).

48. «—J'ai compris Muyango ! Le champ de la mémoire des morts, il faut le débroussailler, tondre les pousses mensongères pour laisser fleurir la vérité. Je vais te coiffer, je vais te couper les ongles, détruire tous les mensonges qui ont poussé sur ton corps. Parce que le mensonge, c'est le refus de la vie. Et puis tu iras te laver dans le Nyabarongo … le fleuve qui coule » (Lamko 2002: 199).

49. Sometimes referred to as the Kagera or the Akagera. The Nyabarongo flows into the Kagera river. Consult Meierhenrich (2009).

50. Apart from the link to precolonial myths, mention of Nyabarongo also immediately brings to mind the Hamitic myth/hypothesis and its notorious link with the genocide: 'This largely discredited theory of the separate origins of Hutu and Tutsi (which has survived in practice) revolved around the latter's "foreignness"' (Meierhenrich 2009: 15). The Hamitic hypothesis, which was not in line with the traditional myths, but rather a European myth on the origin of the Tutsis, suggested that they had descended from Ethiopia via this river, thus making them foreigners and outsiders in Rwanda. During the genocide, this same river was used to carry these 'foreign' bodies back to where they allegedly had come from centuries before. Léon Mugesera's 1992 anti-Tutsi discourse, in which he promised to send the Tutsis back to Ethiopia via the Nyabarongo River was a way of reinforcing the Hamitic myth, which had been embraced and internalized by many Rwandans (ibid.: 15).

51. « Ne laisse jamais ton regard se perdre sur les rides de l'eau. L'eau c'est la vie quand elle ne charrie pas des carcasses d'hommes, des lambeaux de côtes, des moignons de bras, des trognons de jambes, des lianes d'entrailles entrelacées. Ici, elle st impure » (Lamko 2002: 65).

52. « […] il me semble que nos traditions profondes envisagent la mort comme un passage et souvent elle donnait lieu à un rituel très théâtralisé où la souffrance s'exprimait en vers poétiques, mêlant récits de hauts faits de celui qui

quittait le monde des vivants avec l'espoir qu'il vivra en paix dans le village des morts » (Marcelli 2011).

53. « Depuis que la terre est terre, le Nègre a toujours enseveli son frère Nègre mort, l'a confié aux entrailles de la terre ou à l'eau du fleuve. Il faut refertiliser la terre et l'eau, leur rendre l'enfance, le grain des origines. Mais quand le frère nègre […] n'avait pas été inhumé sous une poignée de terre ou dans une goutte d'eau, il refusait d'entrer dans la Cité du Temps. Il continuait de vagabonder sur la colline » (Lamko 2002: 55–6).

54. « Mais moi, Celle du milieu des vies, j'avais toujours attendu, planant invisible au-dessus de ma carcasse séchée et exposée pour le regard des curieux. […] j'attendais depuis des dizaines de lunes qu'un Nègre vaillant et viril daignât m'appeler, héler la Négresse morte mais qui continue de rôder, me suggérer de l'index le chemin du fleuve sur lequel flotte la barque en papyrus […] Rien à l'horizon ! […] Ils étaient tous trop préoccupés par leurs minuscules tranches de vie, champagne et Coca-Cola » (Lamko 2002: 58).

55. Semujanga suggests that the text evokes in various ways the theme of the dance of death (*danse macabre*), a dance which symbolizes the allegorical notion of the all-conquering and equalizing power of death (2008: 235).

56. Here again, Pelouse is like Lamko, who decided that his work was not finished once he had completed his book, but who came back to Rwanda to undertake and initiate further projects in the post-genocide community life.

57. « être sûre du nombre de victimes qu'on n'a jamais réussi à déterminer avec certitude et exactitude » (Lamko 2002: 205).

58. « Je vogue vers la Cité du Temps. Dans la traversée, sur le grand fleuve, en pirogue, je jubile. Tout autour de moi, les oiseaux pépient liberté. […] Ils racontent aussi la victoire des femmes qui se courbent et ramassent des briques, confectionnent la rigole sur le bas-côté de la voie que l'on bitume. Pour drainer le ruissellement des pluies » (Lamko 2002: 216).

59. The image brings to mind the traditional hand-woven baskets for which Rwanda is famous, and in which women carry all sorts of goods, also for ceremonial purposes.

60. The first edition was published in 2000 and the cover resembles the texts published by Monique Ilboudo and Nocky Djedanoum, who used artwork by Bruce Clarke on the covers of their books.

61. Although it was not completed at the time of their first visit to Rwanda, and this connotation may not have been intended by the author, the motif of the woven item also reminds us of the traditional symbolism used at the Bisesero site. One of the main symbols of this memorial site is the *agaseke* basket. This type of basket traditionally has a lid, because what is held inside is usually secret. At the Bisesero site the basket is symbolized through a building without the top part (the lid). It allegedly serves as a symbol of

intimacy and the unity of Rwanda that was broken during the genocide. Portrayed without the lid, which traditionally covers the secret gifts that it contains, this basket becomes a symbol of the desecration of everything that Rwandan society held sacred and which the genocide destroyed. (This information was given to me by the guide at the memorial site, but I was not able to verify it in written documents on the memorial.)

62. This conflict is discussed in greater detail in my final chapter.

63. « Entonner la ronde, le poing au ciel. Tra la la. Serrer fort, très fort » (Lamko 2002: 216).

64. I borrow this from the title of her article (Tadjo 2013a).

65. « Le mélange des genres (poésie, musique, récit historique et autres) est vu comme quelque chose de très avant-garde dans la littérature écrite contemporaine, alors que la tradition orale fonctionne ainsi depuis toujours » (Tadjo in Dahouda and Tadjo 2007: 184).

> Dans la tradition orale, on s'aperçoit qu'il y a un mélange de genres incroyable. Il y a la narration, l'histoire, la poésie, la musique… Q: … le conte, les proverbes… R: Voilà! Il existe une liberté extraordinaire et c'est cette liberté selon la tradition orale que j'ai voulu adopter. (Tadjo in Anyinefa and Rice-Maximin 2008: 373)

66. For more on the use of the 'multiplicity of narrative voices', divided into the autobiographical, testimonial, and fictional voices, in Tadjo's text, consult Griffin (2008). See also Glover's (2011) reading of the use of polyphony in Tadjo's text as compared to, for example, Diop's use of polyphony.

67. Nicki Hitchcott (2009) analyzes Tadjo's text as a travel narrative, and looks at the 'shifting positionalities' that Tadjo assumes.

68. Zakaria Soumaré makes a useful distinction between 'inside witnesses' (*témoins du dedans*), 'context witnesses' (*témoins de contexte*), and 'outside witnesses' (*témoins du dehors*). The first group are those who experienced the genocide, the second are those who were in exile at the time, and the third category are those, such as the non-Rwandan authors, who were not directly involved (Soumaré 2013: 124–8). The last group is what Hartman would call the 'intellectual witness' (1998).

69. Véronique Tadjo, in discussion with the author, July 2010.

70. Véronique Tadjo, in discussion with the author, July 2010.

71. « C'est pour cela que ça ne m'a pas gêné de me mettre en scène et de dire dès le départ que c'est un voyage personnel: je n'ai pas vécu les événements, je ne suis pas là pour témoigner, je ne détiens pas une vérité […] Comme tout le monde, j'essaie de comprendre […] » (Tadjo 2000b).

72. An important theme, for example, that I do not address in this chapter is that of sexual violence. I do, however, include a detailed, comparative analysis of it in Chap. 5 when I discuss Monique Ilboudo's work.

73. Consult, for example, the following works: Bazié (2004), Cazenave (2004), Coquio (2004), Dauge-Roth (2010), Davies Cordova and Wa Kabwe-Segatti (2016), Germanotta (2016), Griffin (2008), Hemsley (2016), Hitchcott (2009, 2015), Mizouni (2015), Nayar (2009), Semujanga (2007, 2008), Small (2005, 2007), and West-Pavlov (2014).

74. For the following discussion on Tadjo's text as read in the light of the principles of *ubuntu*, I have reworked and integrated certain ideas and quotations from an existing chapter with the kind permission of the publishers; see De Beer (2019).

75. « Aller au Rwanda, c'était pour moi faire un voyage intérieur, entrer dans un questionnement sur la vie et la mort, sur la nature humaine et sur le Bien et le Mal » (Tadjo 2000a: 1).

76. « Une ironie renforcée par le sous-titre du livre: *voyages au bout du Rwanda* qui évoque le célèbre roman de Céline, *Voyage au bout de la nuit*—une parenté paratextuelle qui renvoie aussi à une identification thématique car, de même que Céline fustige la déshumanisation de l'être dans la grande boucherie de la première guerre mondiale, Véronique Tadjo décrit ici le degré zéro de l'humain » (Mongo-Mboussa 2000).

> If the title of the presently reviewed English translation of Véronique Tadjo's text recalls Joseph Conrad's *Heart of Darkness*, the French original—*L'ombre d'Imana: voyages jusqu'au bout du Rwanda* (Paris: Actes Sud, 2000)—inevitably evokes Céline's *Voyage au bout de la nuit*. A coincidence? In any case, even without wanting to find any ideological affinity between Tadjo's text and these others, one cannot fail to notice the theme of the journey into horror or abjection that they share. (Anyinefa 2005: 137)

77. « J'ai voulu aussi montrer par ce sous-titre, qu'il y a plusieurs façons de voyager au Rwanda. Les réfugiés rwandais sont disséminés dans le monde entier. […] Le Rwanda est partout et on peut le rencontrer même chez soi » (Tadjo 2000a: 1).

78. « 'jusqu'au bout du Rwanda' comportait cette idée: 'jusqu'au bout de la mort'. C'était un voyage dans la mort. [...] Car souvent, tu peux prendre l'avion et repartir sans avoir rien vu. Tout glisse sur toi, mais là, au Rwanda, il fallait aller jusqu'au bout, il fallait faire tout un voyage intérieur » (Tadjo 2000b).

79. She takes a similar stance when she is confronted with issues of justice in post-genocide Rwanda. She cites the *gacaca*, the traditional and by now well-known justice system, established in the face of the incapacity to deal with the overwhelming number of cases, but instead of blindly condoning this measure, she immediately questions whether it will be able to deal with the enormity of genocide injustices, and whether it is still relevant in mod-

ern times: 'How did the ancestors judge? How did they mete out punishment? Traditional customs are being revived in the face of this emergency. Solutions for the present must be sought in the past. [...] But who will be the judged and who will be the accused? [...] Did the ancestors know the crime of genocide?' (ibid.: 97).

80. The following discussion on the motifs of the masks and shadows is an adaptation of a section from a previously published book chapter; for a more detailed discussion of these motifs, consult De Beer (2016: 52–60).

81. This is a recurring motif in her oeuvre, also found, for example, in her children's books (Cazenave 2016: 182–3).

82. For a detailed discussion on geographical locations such as Kigali, the Nyabarongo River and the hills, seen as a form of mask, consult De Beer (2016: 51–7).

83. Discussed in greater depth in my concluding chapter.

84. For a discussion on how Tadjo 'extends the shadow's metaphorical figuration by associating various characters with one of its forms and then linking it to the masks that are present in the eyes of the Rwandans', consult De Beer (2016: 57–9).

85. « À tous ceux qui sont partis mais qui restent encore en nous » (Tadjo 2000c: 8).

86. « La littérature orale a une grande influence sur mon travail! J'aime son langage codé et très imagé. Sa force de suggestion. J'aime aussi l'idée qu'il est demandé à l'auditoire de participer à la narration et d'interpréter les messages » (Dahouda and Tadjo 2007: 184).

87. Parts of the following paragraphs on the fear of the Other is a summary of a section from a published chapter (De Beer 2019).

88. For detailed examples, consult De Beer (2016) and Semujanga (2008: 177).

89. « Je ne sais vraiment pas pourquoi j'aime tant la forme du conte. Peut-être tout simplement parce que j'ai vécu la plupart de mon temps en Afrique de l'Ouest où le conte reste encore un genre privilégié. C'est la tradition du conte. Peut-être que l'explication vient de là. Et puis, ce que j'aime dans le conte, ce sont ses différents niveaux de compréhension. On peut comprendre un conte d'une certaine façon à tel âge, ensuite en grandissant et en le relisant, on le comprend un peu plus et puis on arrive finalement à un niveau de compréhension assez élevé. Cela m'intéresse. Par ailleurs, je crois que c'est une forme qui donne beaucoup de liberté. Effectivement, dans le monde du conte, on a le droit de faire tout ce que l'on veut, ce qui permet de sauter les étapes, d'éviter les détails ennuyeux, d'enjamber le temps, les espaces … Je trouve que cela donne beaucoup de liberté et je suis sereine parce que je sais que cela correspond à quelque chose de vrai dans ma culture. Bien sûr, je sais qu'il y a des contes pour enfants et des contes pour adultes. Mais certains contes n'ont pas d'âge. Et il y a même des contes

modernes. Tout le côté initiatique des contes est très important pour moi » (Tadjo, in Anyinefa and Rice-Maximin 2008: 371).

90. This apologue, which suggests that greediness leads to self-destruction, is a well-known children's tale (Tadjo 2000a). The narrative style, with its repetitions, rhythm, listing, exaggeration, and griot-like exhortation to 'Listen to this tale of a monster which was always hungry', imitates the oral tradition and creates the impression of an audience listening to an age-old story: 'He devoured the earth, the sun, the moon, the stars, but, he was still hungry [...] He ate one of his fingers, then two, then three and so on [...]' (Tadjo 2002: 115).

91. The figure of the sage is in fact present in many of the texts from the project and they either embody or subvert traditional belief systems. I discuss this in greater depth in my concluding chapter.

92. These are: 'The wrath of the dead', 'His voice', 'Anastase and Anastasie', and 'Those who were not there'.

References

Amougou Ndi, Stéphane. 2010. *La représentation littéraire de la brutalité: le géno-cide rwandais dans quelques romans africains francophones.* Saarbrücken: Poitiers University.

Anyinefa, Koffi. 2005. *The Shadow of Imana: Travels in the Heart of Rwanda* (review). *Research in African Literatures* 36 (1): 137–138. https://doi.org/10.1353/ral.2005.0004.

Anyinefa, Koffi, and Micheline Rice-Maximin. 2008. Entretien avec Veronique Tadjo, ecrivaine ivoirienne. *The French Review* 82 (2): 368–382.

Bagilishya, Deogratias. 2000. Mourning and Recovery from Trauma: In Rwanda, Tears Flow Within. *Transcultural Psychiatry* 37 (3): 337–353. https://doi.org/10.1177/136346150003700304.

Bazié, Isaac. 2004. Au seuil du chaos: devoir de mémoire, indicible et piège du devoir dire. *Présence Francophone* 63: 29–45.

Brezault, Éloïse. 2002. *La Phalène des collines* de Koulsy Lamko: Koulsy Lamko a participé à 'Rwanda: écrire par devoir de mémoire. *Africultures.* Accessed July 9, 2018. http://africultures.com/la-phalene-des-collines-2576/.

Cazenave, Odile M. 2004. Writing the Rwandan Genocide: African Literature and the Duty of Memory. In *Reconstructing Societies in the Aftermath of War: Memory, Identity and Reconciliation*, ed. Flavia Brizio-Skov, 70–84. New York: Bordighera.

———. 2016. Des mots à l'image, de l'écriture à la peinture: une praxis du renou-vellement dans l'oeuvre de Véronique Tadjo. In *Écrire, traduire, peindre— Véronique Tadjo—Writing, Translating, Painting*, ed. Sarah Davies Cordova and Désiré Wa Kabwe-Segatti, 175–189. Paris: Présence africaine.

Cazenave, Odile M., and Patricia Célérier. 2011. *Contemporary Francophone African Writers and the Burden of Commitment*. Charlottesville: University of Virginia Press.

Chalaye, Sylvie. 2001. Fest'Africa au Rwanda: un projet artistique qui a fait école: Entretien de Sylvie Chalaye avec Koulsy Lamko. *Africultures*. Accessed July 9, 2018. http://www.africultures.com/php/index.php?nav=article&no=67.

Coquio, Catherine. 2004. *Rwanda: le réel et les récits*. Littérature et politique, 0985-9632. Paris: Belin.

Dahouda, Kanaté, and Véronique Tadjo. 2007. « Rendre hommage à la vie. » Entretien avec Véronique Tadjo, écrivaine ivoirienne. *Nouvelles Études Francophones* 22 (2): 179–186.

Dauge-Roth, Alexandre. 2009. Testimonial Encounter. *French Cultural Studies* 20 (2): 165–180. https://doi.org/10.1177/0957155809102632.

———. 2010. *Writing and Filming the Genocide of the Tutsis in Rwanda: Dismembering and Remembering Traumatic History*, After the Empire: The Francophone World and Postcolonial France. Lanham, MD: Lexington Books.

Davies Cordova, Sarah, and Désiré Wa Kabwe-Segatti. 2016. *Écrire, traduire, peindre—Véronique Tadjo—Writing, Translating, Painting*. Paris: Présence africaine.

De Beer, Anna-Marie. 2015. Ubuntu and the Journey of Listening to the Rwandan Genocide Story: Original Research. *Verbum et Ecclesia* 36 (2): 1–9.

———. 2016. Véronique Tadjo and the Masks and Shadows of Rwanda. In *Écrire, traduire, peindre—Véronique Tadjo—Writing, Translating, Painting*, ed. Sarah Davies Cordova and Désiré Wa Kabwe-Segatti, 43–63. Paris: Présence africaine.

———. 2019. Ubuntu, Reconciliation in Rwanda and Returning to Personhood Through Collective Narrative. In *Ubuntu: The Reconstitution of Community*, ed. James Ogude. Bloomington: Indiana University Press.

De Beer, Anna-Marie, and Elisabeth Snyman. 2015. Shadows of Life, Death and Survival in the Aftermath of the Rwandan Genocide. *Tydskrif vir letterkunde* 52 (1): 113–130. https://doi.org/10.4314/tvl.v52i1.8.

Derrida Jacques and Anne Dufourmantelle. 2000. Of Hospitality, Trans. Rachel Bowlby, Stanford University Press, Stanford, USA.

Diop, Boubacar Boris. 2006. *Murambi: The Book of Bones* (Kindle edition). Translated by Fiona McLaughlin. Bloomington: Indiana University Press.

Fonkoua, Romuald. 2003. A propos de l'initiative du Fest'Africa: « Témoignage du dedans », 'témoignage du dehors ». *Lendemains: Etudes Comparées sur la France/Vergleichende Frankreichforschung* 112:67–72.

———. 2016. Politiques de l'histoire chez Véronique Tadjo. In *Écrire, traduire, peindre—Véronique Tadjo—Writing, Translating, Painting*, ed. Sarah Davies Cordova and Désiré Wa Kabwe-Segatti, 105–118. Paris Présence africaine.

Germanotta, Maria Angela. 2016. L'écriture de l'inaudible. Les narrations littéraires du génocide au Rwanda, *Interfrancophonies*, Nouvelles formes de l'engagement dans les littératures francophones, ed. Alessandro Crostantini. 7: 73–100. https://doi.org/10.17457/IF7_2016/GER.

Glover, Jonathan D. 2011. *Narrating Crisis: Rwanda, Haiti, and the Politics of Commemoration.* Gainesville: University of Florida.

Griffin, Jenelle. 2008. Responding to the Shadows: Reimagining Subjectivity in Tadjo's *L'Ombre d'Imana.* *Women in French Studies* 16: 113–126. https://doi.org/10.1353/wfs.2008.0004.

Hartman, Geoffrey. 1998. Shoah and Intellectual Witness. *Partisan Review—New York* 65 (1): 37–48.

Hemsley, Frances. 2016. Non-mourning and Ecocritical Ethics in Véronique Tadjo's *The Shadow of Imana: Travels in the Heart of Rwanda. Journal of Commonwealth Literature* 51 (2): 226–239. https://doi.org/10.1177/0021989415628029.

Hitchcott, Nicki. 2009. Travels in Inhumanity: Véronique Tadjo's Tourism in Rwanda. *French Cultural Studies* 20 (2): 149–164. https://doi.org/10.1177/0957155809102630.

———. 2015. *Rwanda Genocide Stories: Fiction after 1994.* Liverpool: Liverpool University Press.

Ilboudo, Monique. 2000. *Murekatete: Roman.* Bamako, Mali and Lille, France: Le Figuier Fest'Africa.

Imorou, Abdoulaye. 2016. La littérature d'énfance et de jeunesse chez Véronique Tadjo: un cas de contre-littérature. In *Écrire, traduire, paindre—Véronique Tadjo—writing, translating, painting,* ed. Sarah Davies Cordova and Désiré Wa Kabwe-Segatti, 139–155. Paris: Présence africaine.

Jessee, Erin. 2017. The Danger of a Single Story: Iconic Stories in the Aftermath of the 1994 Rwandan Genocide. *Memory Studies* 10 (2): 144–163. https://doi.org/10.1177/1750698016673236.

Julien, Eileen. 1992. *African Novels and the Question of Orality.* Bloomington: Indiana University Press.

Kalisa, Chantal. 2005. Le gos au Rwanda: entretien avec Koulsy Lamko. In *Dix ans après: réflexions sur le génocide rwandais,* ed. Rangira Béatrice Gallimore and Chantal Kalisa, 259–280. Paris: Harmattan.

Kayishema, Jean-Marie. 2009. Aux origines du génocide des Tutsi du Rwanda: l'ethnocide culturel. In *Le génocide des Tutsi: Rwanda, 1994: Lectures et écritures,* Mémoire et survivance, ed. Catalina Sagarra Martin, 9–32. Quebec: Presses de l'Université Laval.

Kimenyi, Alexandre. 1978. Aspects of Naming in Kinyarwanda. *Anthropological Linguistics* 20 (6): 258–271.

Lamko, Koulsy. 2002. *La phalène des collines.* Paris: Le Serpent à Plumes.

Lavoie, Pierre and Lorraine Camerlain. 1994. Chemin faisant : Entretien avec Koulsy Lamko. *Jeu* 73: 94–102.

Marcelli, Sylvain. 2011. Rwanda, mémoire d'un génocide—La parole des fantômes. Accessed September 13, 2017. http://interdits.net/interdits/index.php/Rwanda-memoire-d-un-genocide-La-parole-des-fantomes.html.

Mazauric, Catherine. 2016. Véronique Tadjo ou l'écart transafricain. In *Écrire, traduire, peindre—Véronique Tadjo—Writing, Translating, Painting*, ed. Sarah Davies Cordova and Désiré Wa Kabwe-Segatti, 89–102. Paris: Présence africaine.

Meierhenrich, Jens. 2009. The Transformation of *lieux de mémoire*: The Nyabarongo River in Rwanda, 1992–2009. *Anthropology Today* 25 (5): 13–19. https://doi.org/10.1111/j.1467-8322.2009.00687.x.

Mizouni, Sophia. 2015. Triple posture testimoniale de Véronique Tadjo dans *L'Ombre d'Imana: Voyages jusqu'au bout du Rwanda*. *Nouvelles Études Francophones* 30 (1): 66–78. https://doi.org/10.1353/nef.2015.0031.

Mongo-Mboussa, Boniface. 2000. *L'Ombre d'Imana* de Véronique Tadjo. *Africultures*. Accessed July 9, 2018. http://africultures.com/lombre-dimana-1616/.

Montesano, Michael C. 2015. Preemptive Testimony: Literature as Witness to Genocide in Rwanda. *African Conflict & Peacebuilding Review* 5 (1): 88–105. https://doi.org/10.2979/africonfpeacrevi.5.1.88.

Mphahlele, Es'kia. 2002. *Es'kia: Education, African Humanism & Culture, Social Consciousness, Literary Appreciation*. Cape Town: Kwela Books.

Nayar, Pramod K. 2009. Affective Travel: Terror and the Human Rights Narrative in Véronique Tadjo's *The Shadow of Imana*. *IUP Journal of English Studies* 4 (3–4): 35–48.

Nichols, Pamela. 2016. Whispering of the Masks: Véronique Tadjo's Writing of Genocide. In *Écrire, traduire, peindre—Véronique Tadjo—writing, translating, painting*, ed. Sarah Davies Cordova and Désiré Wa Kabwe-Segatti, 65–76. Paris: Présence africaine.

Ricœur, Paul. 1995. Le pardon peut-il guérir? *Esprit (1940–)* 210 (3/4): 77–82.

Semujanga, Josias. 2007. Le témoignage de l'*Itsembabwoko* par la fiction. *L'ombre d'Imana*. *Présence Francophone* 69: 106–135.

———. 2008. *Le génocide, sujet de fiction?: Analyse des récits du massacre des Tutsi dans la littérature africaine*. Quebec: Nota bene.

———. 2009. Par-delà l'innommable, la littérature. *La phalène des collines* de Koulsy Lamko. In *Le génocide des Tutsi: Rwanda, 1994: Lectures et écritures*, ed. Catalina Sagarra Martin, 35–69. Quebec: Presses de l'Université Laval.

Small, Audrey. 2005. Le projet « Rwanda: écrire par devoir de mémoire »: fiction et génocide dans trois textes. In *Dix ans après: réflexions sur le génocide rwandais*, ed. Rangira Béatrice Gallimore and Chantal Kalisa, 121–141. Paris: Harmattan.

———. 2007. The Duty of memory: A Solidarity of Voices after the Rwandan Genocide. *Paragraph* 30 (1): 85–100. https://doi.org/10.3366/prg.2007.0016.

Soumaré, Zakaria. 2013. *Le génocide rwandais dans la littérature africaine franco-phone*. Paris: Harmattan.

Tadjo, Véronique. 2000a. 'Le pardon ne veut pas dire l'oubli': entretien de Boniface Mongo-Mboussa avec Véronique Tadjo. Accessed July 9, 2018. http://www.africultures.com/php/index.php?nav=article&no=1611.

———. 2000b. Réponses de Véronique Tadjo aux questions de Eloïse Brezault à propos de *L'ombre d'Imana, voyages jusqu'au bout du Rwanda* (Fest'Africa, Lille, le 11/11/2000). Accessed October 24, 2017. https://veroniquetadjo.com/fr/entretiens/.

———. 2000c. *L'ombre d'Imana: voyages jusqu'au bout du Rwanda*. Babel; 677. Arles, France: Actes sud.

———. 2002. *The Shadow of Imana: Travels in the Heart of Rwanda*. Translated by Véronique Wakerley. Oxford: Heinemann.

———. 2008. *The Blind Kingdom*. Translated by Janis A Mayes. Oxford: Ayebia Clarke.

———. 2009. Chemin d'écriture. *Cultures Sud* 172: 53–56.

———. 2013a. Lifting the Cloak of (in)visibility: A Writer's Perspective. *Research in African Literatures* 44 (2): 1–7.

———. 2013b. Biography. Accessed June 24, 2018. https://veroniquetadjo.com/en/biography/.

Visser, Irene. 2015. Decolonizing Trauma Theory: Retrospect and Prospects. *Humanities* 4 (2): 250–265. https://doi.org/10.3390/h4020250.

Waberi, Abdourahman A. 2011. Fragments of an African Discourse: Elements for a New Literary Ecosystem. *Yale French Studies* 120: 100–110.

———. 2016. *Harvest of Skulls* (Kindle edition). Translated by Dominic Thomas. Bloomington: Indiana University Press.

West-Pavlov, Russell. 2014. "Regardez la vie reprendre": Futurity in Véronique Tadjo's L'Ombre d'Imana/The Shadow of Imana. *Tydskrif vir letterkunde* 51 (2): 114–129. https://doi.org/10.4314/tvl.v51i2.9.

CHAPTER 4

Harvests and Bones: Abdourahman A. Waberi and Boubacar Boris Diop

This chapter deals with Abdourahman Waberi's *Moisson de crânes: textes pour le Rwanda* (2004) (translated in 2016 as *Harvest of Skulls*), and Boubacar Boris Diop's *Murambi: le livre des ossements* (2000) (translated in 2006 as *Murambi: The Book of Bones*).[1] The main concerns that structure my reading of these two texts are the social and historical dynamics that led to mass participation in the genocide and in particular the 'power that language has garnered in our chaotic world', as well as the culture of submission to figures of authority (Waberi 2016: 77). This approach is aligned to the ongoing attempt to decolonize trauma theory because of its focus on the specific 'historical and political processes' that led to the genocide (Visser 2015: 251).

In the previous chapter, I emphasized the potential reconstructive power of the community and *ubuntu*—through solidarity and listening as well as the African ontologies which are a significant presence in the project. In this chapter, I investigate another type of power which is also linked to and driven by a sense of community, but which divides rather than creates harmony.[2]

The power exerted by the community is demonstrated through the pernicious impact of disinformation, indoctrination, rationalization, conformism, and authoritarianism. The creators of propaganda relentlessly pursued the polarization and stigmatization of identities, and the political abuse and misrepresentation of foundation and identity myths and migration theories. One of the main strategies of this rhetoric of discrimination

© The Author(s) 2020

A.-M. de Beer, *Sharing the Burden of Stories from the Tutsi Genocide*, Palgrave Studies in Cultural Heritage and Conflict, https://doi.org/10.1007/978-3-030-42093-2_4

was depicting the Tutsi as cockroaches or snakes, 'as vermin to be extermi-nated' (Fletcher 2014: 1). Words, and images created through words, were used to dehumanize and objectify.

The 'foreign invader' (Tutsi) was depicted not only as an enemy, but also a threat to the unity of the society, and it was the obligation of each 'true' citizen toward the community to eradicate this threat.[3] Furthermore, the genocidal language and physical weapons used to perpetrate the geno-cide were intimately linked to the cultural heritage of compulsory com-munal tasks, such as clearing and working the land.[4] Genocide ideology appropriated the notion of collective, communal service and the vocabu-lary related to it in order to promote 'cleansing' the land of those who were seen to have 'invaded' it; thus, 'working' (killing) constituted ren-dering a service to the community. With regard to this euphemistic use of certain terms, which in this society was linked to implicit connotations, Narelle Fletcher makes the important point that

> although the manipulative purpose of genocidal discourse may well be expressed in many instances by very direct and brutal language, it can also be formulated in more subtle and insidious ways through the implicit connotations of the terminology used. In fact, the use of polyvalent or euphemistic language can be a very effective strategy for minimising sponta-neous resistance to concepts that are naturally abhorrent. (2014: 3)

Although written forms of propaganda like the *Kangura* magazine,[5] the Bahutu Ten Commandments,[6] political tracts, and the Bahutu Manifesto[7] formed a part of this, the focus was on oral forms of persuasion like songs, discourses like the infamous Léon Mugesera speech,[8] and broadcasts by Radio Télévision Libre des Mille Collines or RTLM 'hate radio' station.[9] These discourses not only encouraged participation; they often provided instructions on how to participate. Fletcher (quoting Hintjens and Des Forges) notes, for example, that Mugesera's speech, which is known for its vigorous, inflammatory style, is often considered as a '"blueprint" for the practical implementation of the genocide' (2014: 2).

Apart from the power of language, a further contributing factor to the mass participation was the strong traditional culture of conformism and blind submission to authority.[10] The society that participated in the geno-cide is described by a Rwandan lawyer as one riddled with conformism and characterized by a reverence for those in position of power and authority:

'Conformity is very deep, very developed here,' he told me. 'In Rwandan history, everyone obeys authority. People revere power, and there isn't enough education [...] So the people of influence, or the big financiers, are often the big men in the genocide [...] the people were looking to them for their orders. And, in Rwanda, an order can be given very quietly.' (in Gourevitch 2000: 23)

In the discussion of Diop's text, it becomes clear that submission to figures of authority began at home, as part of a traditional sociocultural upbringing. This was easily transposed into the religious and political spheres. Another body of power that played a nefarious role before and during the genocide was the international community—in particular the French authorities—an aspect which Waberi touches on and Diop explores extensively in his text. These political and societal influences are some of the lenses through which I analyze these texts and where meaningful, I include examples from the other texts that form part of the project.

Before considering these two texts in detail, I look at the theme of dehumanization through propaganda, as well as the creative use of proverbs and other forms of traditional oral wisdom as presented throughout the project.

Umugani, Proverbs, and Wisdom

The power of language is a theme that is present throughout the project and the authors creatively insert the use of proverbs, inflammatory statements, and other forms of oral guidance or persuasion in their narratives. These elements are so pervasive that they create a type of background refrain to the project. As shown in Chap. 2, these oral forms are intimately linked to traditional beliefs, taboos, coping mechanisms, and behavior that is deemed to be appropriate according to customs. Proverbs and *umugani* (tales, myths, legends, and fables) are a cultural mode of communication, a bridge between the narrator and listener, between emotion and response (Bagilishya 2000: 341).

They are also an integral part of the language and culture. Claudine, for example, an exiled returnee in Monénembo's novel, tries to prove her Rwandan cultural knowledge and heritage, and that her 'soul is from' Rwanda, by proudly boasting that she knows the *intore* dance and the game of *igisoro*, and that she not only speaks Kinyarwanda fluently but also knows its proverbs (Monénembo 2004: 16, 35).

Proverbs are lessons, truths, reflections, and rules of moral behavior (Ahimana 2009: 302, 310).[11] This connection with wisdom is not only applicable in Rwandan culture. The proverb is widely considered as the 'anonymous expression of everyday wisdom', and because it is a shared wisdom, it refers to the moral system and cohesion of the specific social community to which it belongs (ibid.: 300; my translation).[12]

The use of proverbs in the project serves to remind and inform us of the implicit rules that govern Rwandan society, and the authors use them as ways of demonstrating or even problematizing existing systems of thought. They belong to tradition and originally functioned for the good of society, but they become dangerous weapons in the hands of the propagandists, who appropriated and abused them, using them to manipulate, inventing new slogans and metaphors, in full knowledge of the power wielded by the communal word in their society.

Many examples of oral sayings that rule and direct society structure the project narratives. The connection between proverbs and wisdom is clearly demonstrated through the two figures of 'wisdom' in Tierno Monénembo's text: the witch doctor and Faustin's father. Both of them teach Faustin about life through their constant use of proverbs, and when they are gone, he remembers them by their words of wisdom or warnings. The epigraph of Monénembo's novel reads: 'The pain of others is bearable' (2004: 2). This is presented as a Rwandan proverb and reflects the attitude that allowed so many people to participate in the genocide. Waberi similarly evokes Wole Soyinka's appropriation of an infamous statement which takes on the form of a proverb and which reminds us how, ironically, millions of people became mere statistics during the genocide: 'A single death is a tragedy, a million deaths a statistic' (ibid.: 96).

The most widely quoted Rwandan proverb, integrated by the writers, concerns the Rwandan deity, and the popular belief that, although Imana might spend his days elsewhere, he comes back to spend his nights in Rwanda ('*Imana yilirwa ahandi ikarara i Rwanda*'). Through this proverb that speaks of Imana's preference for and protection of Rwanda, the authors explore the theme of Imana's perceived abandonment of his people during the genocide.

In Diop's novel, for example, we learn that Simeon, Cornelius's uncle and a sage figure, feels that Imana has betrayed them; he insists that there were no supernatural signs warning them of what was to come and this omission is interpreted as a broken 'pact' between Imana and his people (Diop 2006b: 1584). Simeon, who has lost his faith in Imana and the ancestral beliefs, engages with this proverb by ridiculing it: '"What do you mean? Djibouti schoolchildren don't know that God finds our Rwanda so pleasant that he never spends the night elsewhere?" asked Simeon, mockingly' (ibid.: 1343–4). Simeon's struggle reflects the implicit question of Imana's absence and abandonment, also found in Tadjo's title.[13] He sings to Imana of his bewilderment:

> Ah! Imana, you astonish me, tell me what has made you so angry, Imana! You let all this blood pour out on the hills where you used to come to rest at night. Where do you spend your nights now? Ah! Imana, you amaze me! Tell me then what I have done to you, I do not understand your anger! (ibid.: 1728–31)

Monique Ilboudo's protagonist evokes the same proverb by wondering if Imana even exists and, if he does, what power he could possibly have— that's to say if he hasn't abandoned them: 'Maybe He forgot to come back? Maybe He grew tired of our gentle country?' (Ilboudo 2000: 41). Waberi incorporates this proverb in his chapter (discussed above) devoted to the use of extremist propaganda. Here, the orator's voice suggests that tradition should be questioned and the status quo changed. Imana may have been happy with the state of affairs in Rwanda, but extremists weren't; their oral traditions had told them to live in peace, but now things needed to change and God would be on their side:

> Harmony and peace. That's how things used to be. God was happy on this earth, but we weren't. For centuries that's the way things were. That's how the world was transmitted to us orally, but henceforth, with the help of the Most High and all our sons and daughters, a few adjustments will need to be made, by any means necessary. (Waberi 2016: 348)

In a later chapter in which the narrator is no longer the perpetrator, but someone who observes the aftermath of the genocide, Waberi again hints at this proverb. Evoking the 'wasteland' in which the survivors find themselves, he sarcastically compares the Tutsis who have been killed to Imana by saying that they are 'as happy as God in Rwanda': 'Well-meaning men and women, the most compassionate and the most inspiring, but also the most fragile, were the first to be killed. As happy as God in Rwanda' (ibid.: 444–9). Thus, Imana's 'happiness' in Rwanda is questioned and the age-old proverb can no longer be seen as an infallible truth. Through these new ways of questioning and subverting the proverb, a form of communication which is familiar to Rwandan society, the authors express the complex consequences of the genocide and of the people's sense of betrayal by their God.

Personhood and Dehumanization

Ubuntu requires of us to develop our '(moral) personhood' and to 'exhibit humanness' toward the Other; this is what makes of us a 'true' or 'complete' person or a 'genuine' human being (Metz 2011: 537). We can in fact become 'more or less of a person', depending on our relationships with others (ibid.). According to this worldview, then, personhood is something to be acquired and that can be lost; it is not an automatic function of being human (Krog 2008: 360). Conversely, someone who 'does not relate communally' is described as not being a person, and 'those without much *ubuntu*, roughly those who exhibit discordant or indifferent behavior with regard to others, are often labelled "animals"' (ibid.).

This is a powerful theme that is introduced in most of the project texts, presumably because of the inhumanity and cruelty of the genocide as well as the all-pervasive animal trope associated with the propaganda and dehumanization of the genocide discourse. This trope, consisting of a host of comparisons to not only animals (cows, dogs, hens, and gorillas) but also sub-animal creatures and insects (two-headed serpents, vampires, cockroaches, and caterpillars), suggests that during the genocide, the community descended into the 'less-than-human' realm (Hemsley 2016: 227).

The irony is that genocide transforms both perpetrator and victim into the non-human. The militia are often portrayed as having behaved like inhuman creatures. Even worse, they convinced themselves to participate in the massacres by reducing their fellow humans to the status of subhuman and inanimate objects—'a heap of flesh', a skull, a creature without a human gaze (Tadjo 2002: 117)—thus elevating themselves to a position of power and impunity[14]:

> To erase all humanity. To look no more into the face of others. Above all, to exchange no more glances. An animal, a heap of flesh. A skull cracking like a dry branch.
> [...] so that the act is nothing more than a gesture of unbelievable power. To be master of the slave kneeling at one's feet. God made man. (ibid.)

In Diop's novel, a *génocidaire* describes the distribution of victims' belongings among them after a massacre as follows:

> Among other groups of Interahamwe the fellows are already getting into fights: one of them wants to kill a girl and another wants to keep her for his nights, or vice versa. That's just human nature. I'd be happy to, but when you start to let emotions enter into the picture you just can't stop, and it's the work that suffers. Once we were outside we saw a pack of dogs roaming around Nyamata. Gangs of children were waiting for us to leave so they could get into the church. There were so many cadavers that there was always a chance that the little ones would find something. I've even been told that they play football with the skulls, but I haven't seen that with my own eyes yet. (Diop 2006b: 878–83)

By juxtaposing these four remarks—on the militia's fight about the girls who have become objects, loot to squabble over; on dogs prowling around the church, lying in wait for what they can get from the massacre; on children who hope to also get their share; and finally on skulls being used as footballs—the author places human and animal on the same level; all rushing to the scene to see how they can profit from it. What further saddens in this extract is the implication that not only the men but also the women and children sacrifice their humanity as they get caught up in the frenzy of genocide.

Tadjo sadly admits that the women were the ones who 'helped men to rape, who sang to give them the courage to massacre, who betrayed, who pillaged, who decided to join in the act of cruelty. With machetes, they killed other women, mutilated children, finished off men' (Tadjo 2002: 101). Thus, the author overturns the supposition that women were merely passive bystanders. Tadjo knows that the price that these women have paid for their lack of moral personhood is to lose their traditional identity as nurturers and bearers of life: 'Educated women, agitators, officials, accusers, organizers. These women killed their own destiny as women' (ibid.: 102).

This is what Djedanoum describes as an 'ocean of inhumanity' (2000: 47) and Waberi calls the 'desert of inhumanity' (2016: 603). In his text, Waberi describes the killers as 'bovine militias pushing their way through the entangled stalks' and invading the hills, arriving by foot, 'the way animals do' (ibid.: 296, 334). He articulates the dehumanizing rhetoric which reduces the Tutsis to snakes and contagious outcasts: '[W]e gnawed away at our nails waiting to be unleashed on those two-headed serpents, those lepers to be banished forever' (ibid.: 303–12). The Tutsis are no longer humans; in his text they are reduced to mere 'skull bearers', waiting to be harvested (ibid.: 269–71).

In Lamko's text, this motif is just as prevalent: he conjures up mythical creatures that are half-man and half-beast that devour and destroy, images that remind us of the lengths to which human beings will go in their cruel and voracious pursuit of their prey:

> It's the animal that we have to study in order to uncover man's limits. Caterpillar man, let loose on the green grasslands and leaves, devours unrestrained all but the veins of the leaves. Grasshopper man strips the leaves of the thorn trees, [...] Boa-man swallows the buffalo [...] Elephant man with its mortar-hoof crushes all the anthills in its path [...] Owl-man detests the light. (Lamko 2002: 48–9)[15,16]

In each image he creates, it is the animal part of the creature that represents danger and a destructive appetite. The Interahamwe are described as 'a horde of barbarians starving for treasures [...] like a pack of wild dogs, barking with rage, tongues hanging out, sharp fangs' (ibid.: 118). A perpetrator voice in his text scornfully depicts this descent into the non-humane of both victim and perpetrator when he explains in detail how to kill a Tutsi. They are 'cockroaches' who do not die easily, he says. You need to 'crush' them and 'stamp on them'; you need a 'strategy' to kill them (ibid.: 175): pretend they are chickens; imitate the clucking of the mother hen until they come to you; tempt them with sorghum; kill the strongest, biggest one first, creating fear and panic:

> You have to treat them like chickens! Get it! The strategy?
> [...]. You call the hens and the cocks. Cluck cluck cluck! Prehistoric man's age-old trick when he invented theatre; imitate the animal in order to get closer to him, [...]
> That's a recipe of how to do it, and get it done fast ... (ibid.: 175–8)[17]

The notion of having a 'strategy' or 'blueprint' for treating another human being like an insect or an animal to be slaughtered or harvested, is not only humiliating, it immediately makes it more acceptable to participate in the killing, for one is offered a simple 'recipe' to follow.

In discussing this trope of dehumanization, Frances Hemsley's cautionary comments are pertinent. She posits that when we compare humans to animals, we fail to acknowledge the plurality and 'humaneness' of the animal world:

> Genocide is conceptualised here as a process of rendering other humans as animal [...] where the racial or ethnic other is conceived of as animal, and the animal is conceived of as less-than-human. What remains unthought is how our humanity is a naturalised assumption: how the multiplicity of animal beings radically complicates divisions between 'the human' and 'the animal'. (2016: 227)

In light of Hemsley's comments, Tadjo offers a valuable angle on the representation of the motif of dehumanization. Her text, through its engagement with the non-human, does demonstrate an awareness that the animal kingdom is indeed more valuable and dignified than is often implied. Her references to the Rwandan gorillas problematizes the 'position of mastery' traditionally assigned to the human race (Hemsley 2016: 227). It is not clear whether she does this because she holds the same view as Hemsley and endeavors to question the assumption that animals are less than human or whether she intends to show how, in Rwanda, the value of human life had been devalued.

What is important, however, is that, like many other elements in her text, Tadjo slightly subverts this concept. It is her discussion on the gorillas that 'prefigures' her preoccupation with the 'non-human environment' (ibid.: 227). This is not a frame to be taken lightly, as Tadjo chooses to introduce both her journeys to Rwanda with references to the gorillas: the first time sparked by a newspaper article on tourists coming to see the gorillas and allegedly murdered by Hutu rebels in Uganda (Tadjo 2002: 7), and the second time by a conversation on the plane with a woman from the Dian Fossey Foundation (ibid.: 81).

Tadjo notes that the presence of the gorillas has turned Rwanda and its neighboring countries into popular tourism destinations. Her gorillas have an almost mythical quality, and Tadjo describes them as unsettlingly human. They are neither cruel nor subhuman; these 'majestic' 'totem-animals' inhabit a 'kingdom', a reserve has been dedicated to their use (ibid.). The gorillas seem to be beyond the reach of human harm, and their kingdom is likened by Tadjo to a sort of secluded paradise, enveloped in mist, surrounded by age-old trees who watch over them. Here, they are 'outside of time' and 'space is silent' (ibid.); Hemsley describes it as a type of 'echo-archaic enclave' (2016: 229). One cannot help but compare this to the exposed and dangerous situations in which the Tutsis found themselves during the genocide, and Tadjo subtly emphasizes this contrast by stating that Dian Fossey 'loved animals more than the human race' (Tadjo 2002: 82).

In this way, the author interrogates the established human–animal borders that we often take for granted. In the final lines of her discussion on the gorillas, she subverts the existing order of human beings as the master over the animal kingdom by foregrounding not the human gaze, but that of the gorilla: 'Do the great apes know what happened at the foot of the mountains? Were they aware of the carnage, did they sense death as it spread across the territory of humans?' (ibid.: 83).

Tadjo's implied comparison between the humans and gorillas is bitterly ironic, because the reader knows that since the genocide, the gorillas, the country's 'principal tourist attraction', have had to compete with dark tourism and the genocide sites (ibid.: 81). However, this seems to be precisely what Tadjo is driving at: the race for survival between humans and animals. She shows how the gorillas compete with the inhabitants of the country in terms of their value, and implies that this value estimation comes from outside, from the 'foreigners' who arrive in the country, ignoring the villagers and engaging in expensive projects related to the gorillas:

> Yes, it is true that once upon a time, the villagers used to hunt the gorillas, but what did they know then of the terrifying creatures with their frighteningly human appearance? It took the establishment of the research station for them to understand that these creatures were Rwanda's most precious possession. More precious than themselves? The competition was on. (ibid.: 82)

Sadly though, akin to the ethical binaries imposed on the Rwandans and which they internalized, many of them seem to have embraced this notion that the lives of their fellow citizens were less 'precious' than those of the gorillas so carefully conserved by the foreigners.

Monénembo's text provides yet another perspective on the issue of dehumanization. The three traumatized child victims whom we meet in his text regress into what seems to be a decidedly less-than-human condition. We are never told what exactly they experienced and witnessed, only that they were found 'wandering through the brush among the wild cats and the monkeys' (Monénembo 2004: 39). The descriptions that characterize them, however, suggest some sort of traumatic experience which has caused them to 'shr[i]nk' back into a state of early childhood (ibid.: 43). This in turn takes Faustin (their older brother) back in time to when he had to look after them while his parents were working. They emit 'inhuman cries' and have to be 'bottle-fed' and locked away so that they don't 'set fire to the dormitories' or 'eat the Hirish woman alive' (ibid.: 39). The director of the orphanage describes them as 'three little devils', 'wild' children who seem to have 'gone mad' (ibid.: 40). When Faustin goes to them he has to step over 'traces of excrement' while they avert their 'bulging and bloodshot eyes' and carry on with their 'horrible wails', and when he sings his mother's lullaby, Ambroise curls up in a 'ball like a kitten' and begins to sob (ibid.: 44). They have to then relearn how to stop soiling themselves and after a while they start 'emitting human language sounds' again (ibid.). In this way, Monénembo depicts the dehumanizing effects of extreme trauma.

These authors then creatively demonstrate how the victim, survivor, and *génocidaire* are reduced to something less than human through genocide. In so doing, they remind us of the restoration that is needed in the aftermath of the genocide, not only of the victims, but also of the perpetrators and bystanders, who have all forfeited a part of their personhood and need to be 'allowed back into humanity' (Krog 2008: 362) and 'reincluded in the moral community' (Staub 2006: 873).[18]

Abdourahman Waberi and the Harvest of Death

Waberi's contribution to the project is a collection of texts which wavers between personal travel diary, reportage, poetic citations, embodiment of propaganda discourse, and philosophical reflection. As this author is widely associated with the notions of nomadism, exile, and mobility, it is no wonder that he opted to use the genre of travel writing.

He ascribes his preference for merging travel account and fiction to the flexibility offered by combining the external perspective of a 'writer-traveler' who listens with the internal focalization that a fictional novel offers (Waberi, in Brezault 2000). Thus, including the writer's perspective enabled him to have a 'dialogue' or confrontation with himself as the writing subject, a type of mirror of what he heard and understood on his journey (ibid.).

As with Lamko and Tadjo, Waberi's text is multiple, hybrid, and fragmentary in form: the plural forms in his subtitle (*Texts for Rwanda*)[19] and section titles (*Fictions* and *Stories*) already alert us to this fact. The gaze and the voice presented by the text are also multiple: sometimes intimate and at other times distant. The narrator adopts the voices of perpetrator, propagandist, genocide site guide, prisoner, victim, and traveling writer, vacillating between personal and impersonal, singular and plural pronouns, making it difficult to distinguish between his voice and the many other narrative voices he introduces. His 'impressionistic patchwork' offers a collection of snapshots and impressions rather than the unfolding of a coherent story (Hitchcott 2015: 57).

This fragmentary and multivocal approach, vis-à-vis the linear and flowing novels associated with previous generations of African writers, characterizes the work of the postcolonial Francophone African writers of Waberi and Tadjo's generation (Gbanou 2004: 83; Soumaré 2013: 128). It is a subversive shift, prompted by a range of issues which these writers face as they come into contact with situations of migration and exile, postcolonial ideologies, cultural hybridity, and the uncertainty of the postmodern world (Gbanou 2004: 83).[20]

Indeed, Waberi attributes the fragmentary nature, the multiplicity of voices, and the disrupted chronology of his text to the complexity of the world he writes about (Brezault 2000). Throughout the text, he questions the role and limits of writing and language, and scoffs at the naivety of attempting to construct a classical narrative about the genocide based on coherence and chronology. The genocide brings an end to continuity, cutting short the life stories and legends of a people: 'Never again will we hear stories about yesterday, of bygone days, or of tomorrow. Never again will we have to listen to someone spinning a yarn that opens with the naïve or arrogant words "Once upon a time",' say the perpetrators to encourage each other to kill the Tutsis (Waberi 2016: 314).

As we have seen, contemporary African writers such as Waberi constantly renew traditional attitudes about being African. They perform a 'transnational turn' in which they interpret Africa in new ways that differ from existing postcolonial literary approaches and 'the more essentialist-based, literary-philosophical movements such as Negritude and pan-Africanism' (Orlando 2016: 1). Valérie Orlando reads Waberi's oeuvre through the lens of Achille Mbembe's notion of the Afropolitan worldview, noting that Afropolitan authors defy and interrogate 'nativist' notions of culture and the 'stereotypes associated with the continent as defined by the West, while also defining identity not as insularly nationalist and tribal but rather global and transnational' (ibid.: 3). Waberi's text indeed establishes multidirectional links between the genocide in Rwanda and similar events from other cultures and contexts, a process which creates a 'transnational and transhistorical web of memories' (Hitchcott 2015: 152).

Like Tadjo, Waberi constantly moves between Rwanda and the continent to which it belongs, or even wider, universal contexts. The text contains references to African history, rulers, and political events. It cites renowned, international writers, creating a type of 'intertextual dialogue', in particular with authors who have written on violence elsewhere, such as Aimé Césaire, Paul Celan, and Primo Levi (Soumaré 2013: 128–32).[21] Thabo Mbeki and the dream of the African Renaissance, Wole Soyinka, Antjie Krog, Mia Couto, Meja Mwangi, and Ngũgĩ wa Thiong'o are all present, as if to confirm the African context of the genocide, and the solidarity that the rest of the continent should be demonstrating with the Rwandan people.

In a country such as Rwanda, a writer can still be seen as a 'bearer' of collective memory (Waberi, in Brezault 2000), and throughout the text Waberi seems overwhelmed by the enormity of this responsibility: 'One almost feels like opening with an apology for the very existence of this work' (Waberi 2016: 64). It is a grueling task that he would not have managed to complete had it not been for his sense of moral duty toward his Rwandan and African friends (ibid.: 65). The humility and the discomfort of the author, who would have preferred to 'simply vanish, to be forgotten, to refrain from adding to the general pessimism' and to 'play dead', can be sensed throughout (ibid.: 69).

Ironically, although Waberi's text deals extensively with the power of the word (both good and bad), it is ultimately a reflection on the incapacity of language to express evil (Mongo-Mboussa 2000). In spite of its unthinkable 'symbolic power' (Waberi 2016: 95), language 'remains inadequate' and words are mere 'unstable crutches' in assisting us on this journey (ibid.: 81). One can but acknowledge that the power of literature is 'negligible' and that fiction has little power to 'remedy' any situation (ibid.: 92). Nevertheless, Waberi hails the therapeutic properties of language and the power of the pen (ibid.: 98). Language and literature may have their shortcomings, and yet they remain 'miraculous weapons' that can offer hope to the world (ibid.: 83).

The epigraph cites Joel, the prophet who encourages the Judean elders to transmit the history of the devastation of their land to the next generations (ibid.: 61–3).[22] By starting off his text with this forceful admonition, he makes it clear that narrating the story of the genocide is an imperative that cannot be ignored by the writer who listens to his conscience.

This Biblical quote starts with the call to 'Hear', 'give ear', and finally 'tell' the next generations, thus foregrounding the process of listening that Waberi has assigned to himself: it is his duty to hear and repeat in order to transmit a message to the next generations. He uses a series of metaphoric images to compare the task of writing to the construction of a 'pantheon of ink and paper' in memory of the victims (ibid.: 87). Through the use of the term 'pantheon', he places the dead on the level of the gods, or at least of heroes of the country, thus confirming the traditional Rwandan view of the deceased ancestors as heroes. Writing their story is compared to transforming oneself into a receiver and transmitter of stories, a 'chamber of echoes' (ibid.). The writer becomes a 'crucible', a melting pot filled with the stories of survivors (ibid.: 90).

These analogies all demonstrate a desire to retreat into the background in order to make the survivors' voices known, and to share the work of mourning by listening actively and appropriately to their stories. Both the echo and the crucible metaphors imply receiving and repeating the story of another, but at the same time configuring and reconfiguring it (according to the process of mimesis proposed by Paul Ricœur [1983]), referring to the creative and selective process of writing, but also to the receptive stance of the listener.

Caroline Laurent notes that this text, which is characterized by its orality, constitutes a type of 'methexis', a form of theater in which there is a sharing and participation, a 'polyphonic' echo of a multiplicity of voices (2015: 80–1). In addition, the fragmentary nature of Waberi's text creates the impression of a 'progressive composition' in which the meaning gradually emerges from the different parts (Laurent 2015: 83–4). This construction foregrounds the process Waberi is engaged in, namely the act of listening, which gradually transforms itself into writing (ibid.). Waberi's role is that of '*auctor*', a term that encompasses the dual notion of being both an outside witness ('*tiers*') and a co-creator who listens and links the oral and the written (ibid.: 83).[23]

In the English translation of Waberi's text, a section[24] has been added to the preface in which the author argues that the role of witness is being passed on from Europeans to Africans (Waberi 2016: 110–14). In the face of the disasters that have befallen the African continent, he sees this task that has been bequeathed to them as finding that 'possible opening', the 'fertile' space between 'reality and imagination' to create testimony, an approach which he clearly followed in his text (ibid.: 127). As we read, we ask ourselves: are we reading real stories based on testimonies or fictions created by the author? Even Waberi is not clear on that: he assures us that in his text 'the leading role is given to fiction', but then adds that 'imagination and subjectivity are there merely to nourish the book's nervous system' (ibid.: 70). The author admits that, due to the difficult nature of the stories, and his own inability to fully understand and transmit the event through fiction, he ended up with a type of '*bricolage*', constantly struggling to find a balance between factually transcribing the stories he had listened to and transforming some of them into fiction (Brezault 2000).

The author's tendency to use real life references, press articles, and some seemingly arbitrary, everyday objects and incidents as an entry point into profound reflections—the way a traveler would do when confronted with scenes, objects, and daily life during the course of a journey—is present throughout. Violin gut strings that produce beautiful music, originally made from animal tendons, lead him to reflect on the Achilles tendons of the Tutsis that were cut during the genocide. The scars on the neck of a taxi driver in Bujumbura serve as an implicit reminder of the ties of violence between Burundi and Rwanda. A newspaper article on Rwandan women who allegedly wanted to sell skeletal remains as souvenirs in Dar es Salaam provokes a discussion on rumors, fabrication, and refugee communities. An old dog named Minuar provides an occasion to reflect on the role of the international peacekeeping mission, and on the dogs who started eating corpses during the genocide. A blood-stained bandana becomes a symbol for the militiamen 'smoking weed' and 'dispensing death' (Waberi 2016: 453). The World Cup that France has just won only serves to underline the anger of the Rwandans because of the 'disgrace[ful]' way in which the French army and authorities behaved during the genocide (ibid.: 480). All these items seem mundane and insignificant, but they are anchored in the reality of the genocide. This approach of drawing creatively from real life objects and images is in fact one that Waberi admits to using often in his writing process, stating that one can invent a whole world from a sensual look, an old book, a photo, or postcard, a Bedouin song or a citation from the Koran, the Bible or Goethe's work (Waberi 2003: 936; my translation).[25] Thus Waberi moves freely 'between reality and imagination' (Waberi 2016: 127).

The text is divided into two sections, the titles of which reflect this ambiguous position between reality and imagination. The original French titles were *Fictions* and *Récits*. *Fictions*, which is at times disjointed yet imaginative, is followed by a second, more personal type of travelogue, entitled *Stories*. Although the title has been translated as *Stories*, it could perhaps be more accurately translated as *Accounts*, as the focus here is not on an invented story, but rather on the accounts or testimonies of what the author saw and heard as he traveled through Rwanda. Although Waberi ends off with this more 'realistic' section named *Stories*, I only briefly look at it before analyzing the first more imaginative part titled *Fictions* because of its focus on the power of language.

Accounts from Kigali

The second part of the text, *Stories*, creates less the impression of fiction and more of a travel account, with dates, place names, a mention of the author's birthday, and a World Cup game won by the French. Here, the presence of the author is strongly felt in the descriptions of his own journeys to Rwanda, his hotel in Nyamirambo, bus ride, and impressions of the country and it is in this part that several parallels can be drawn between Tadjo and Waberi's texts.[26]

He limits the description of this journey mainly to Kigali and neighboring Burundi (Bujumbura). Twice he visits Kigali (*No, Kigali is not sad* and *Return to Kigali*).[27] His first visit leads to reflections, not unlike those of Tadjo, on the idyllic appearance of the green hills and trees and the 'enchantment' and 'magical' qualities of this 'paradise', this land of milk and honey which is Rwanda, and the quarter of Nyamirambo in which the authors stayed during their residency (ibid.: 467, 469, 470). In spite of this Edenic appearance, however, there has been no rain for months and the inhabitants wonder openly if it might be some divine retribution for what the country has been through.

Like Tadjo, the author is struck by the frenzied way in which Rwandans have thrown themselves into reconstructing the country, and the hunger for education and knowledge amongst them: 'The sons and daughters of this country are working tirelessly to rebuild it. In every office you step into there's a civil servant eager to assist you […]' (ibid.: 485–6). It is a city in which the 'scent of blood has vanished', a city 'buzzing' with activity, energy, enthusiasm, and 'fresh ideas' that presents a thriving face to the world, but hides much pain, unresolved issues, and burning memories beneath the surface: 'One refrains from awakening the still waters of memory, sheathing wounded hearts in leather' (ibid.: 499, 501, 502).

In his account of his *Return to Kigali*, which he describes as a journey undertaken with Tadjo and others, there are once again many parallels between Tadjo and Waberi's texts: references to the unsettling nature of their personal journey and the Paris–Brussels–Nairobi–Kigali flight, comments on the gorillas for which Rwanda is famous, as well as comparisons between the disaster in Rwanda and the inspiring democratization of South Africa, and finally, reflections on the prisons they visit and the prisoners they meet there. The topic of gorillas lead both Tadjo and Waberi to reflect on the value of human and animal lives in Rwanda and their comments suggest that at times, the lives of the country's prize 'tourist attraction' (Tadjo 2002: 81) was deemed to be more valuable than that of the human beings and that in fact it was the Tutsis who had become the 'endangered species' (Waberi 2016: 516). Both make observations about interactions between Africans and Westerners on the flights between Brussels and Africa, subtly foregrounding the tension created between African and Western notions of public traveling. Both these authors refer to the abuse and misrepresentation of history as well as the harmful influence of the European colonizers on the relationship between Hutus and Tutsis.

Both Waberi and Tadjo, who traveled together to the prisons on their follow-up visit, seem to be struck by the surprisingly strong sense of rank and order of this system. Their descriptions of Rilima prison[28] foreground the 'rigid hierarchy' (Waberi 2016: 561) which seems to organize community life in prison in which 'prisoners police themselves' (Tadjo 2002: 98). The existence of these hierarchies and categories is an important aspect which I highlight here, not only because it could be seen as way in which Rwandans restructure community life after the destruction and chaos of the genocide. It also ties in with the way in which the collective society was organized before the genocide and explains the influence that authoritarian figures and leaders held over members of the community: 'Rank, authority, the old scheme of things is being set up again' (Tadjo 2002: 98). This is the 'censorship' and 'prohibitions' that Waberi evokes and that society passes down and imposes on its members (2016: 290).

Fictions: *Language and Its Power to Mobilize and Dehumanize*

Waberi's focus on the (destructive or creative) power of language—and especially of the spoken word—is a key theme in *Fictions*. In this first section of the text, the author addresses three main themes; the process of extermination ('Terminus'), propaganda ('The Cavalcade'), and dehumanization ('And the dogs feasted'). In these three subsections, he engages with the types of rhetoric used to manipulate the masses and problematizes the popular myths, proverbs, and slogans used in genocidal logic to convince them to participate in the genocide. To my mind, the strongest trace of the oral culture present in Waberi's contribution, and arguably one of the most powerful elements, is the inclusion of different types of oral discourse, his 'interaction with the social discourse of the time' and in particular various forms of anti-Tutsi propaganda (Semujanga 2009: 114). His text is filled with references to well-known songs, speeches, proverbs, myths, rumors, and oral history and how these were incorporated by those who engineered the genocide. He demonstrates how the reinterpretation of myths and traditions contributed to this process. In this sense, the section title *Fictions* is less a reference to the genre of the text than to the notion of playing with words in order to manipulate—using existing oral discourse and twisting them in an effort to convey the desired message.

In 'Terminus', the focus is on the attitude and mentality required to execute a genocide. Waberi demonstrates the necessary mechanics of exterminating an entire people and reflects on the 'radical' nature of this process (Coquio 2004: 152). This entails creating propaganda, slogans, and pogroms; denigrating and dehumanizing a group of people; transforming the genocide into a collective crime in which individual responsibility disappears; installing a culture of obeying authoritarian figures; providing the participants with practical guidelines of how to achieve this almost impossible task; and, finally, knowing how to placate or even make accomplices of a passive, uninvolved international community.

'Terminus', Waberi tells us, refers to the notion of driving out, banishing, and annihilating (2016: 220). This concept of complete extermination is compared to a macabre 'harvest of skulls', a grotesque metaphor used as his title and repeated in this subsection (ibid.: 282). The author juxtaposes two highly symbolic and contradictory notions. A harvest is normally associated with life and abundance, but here it becomes a euphemistic metaphor for collective killing. The title is an implicit reference to the way in which the authors of the genocide appropriated with great ease the traditional vocabulary of communal cleaning and working to create a psychological link between these tasks, intended to improve the environment, and the task of killing the Tutsi 'invaders'.

To this image, he links that symbol of death, the skull, and notes that the rest of the world—the 'missionaries of powerlessness'—failed the Rwandans, arriving too late, 'long after the harvest' and then often 'like flies swarming a butcher's block' hoping to make some sort of profit from it (ibid.: 269–70). He comments on the international community, the Church and the government in a bitter tone: 'In the meantime, no ripples, dead calm, the UN couldn't give a damn; faced with warmongers, Kofi Annan merely shrugs' (ibid.: 301–02).

'Terminus' often reads like a calculated prescription of procedures, a practical 'script', designed for those who follow orders:

> The *script* is pretty much the same everywhere. The local civilian population gathers in an administrative building, usually in a school or a church, in response to an *official announcement* made by the *mayor* of the municipality or on the *national radio*. Then, a triage process *is carried out*, separating longtime neighbors, parishioners, childhood friends, inhabitants of the same compound. Hutus *are asked* to vacate the premises immediately. Grenades *are tossed* haphazardly into the assembly. Machine guns open fire. The Rwandan house *is given* a thorough cleaning. (ibid.: 238–42; my emphasis)[29]

The impersonal mode and passive voice (which is more strongly emphasized in the original French through the use of the impersonal pronoun '*on*') are used when coldly narrating the atrocities of the genocide. This extract emphasizes the way in which the genocide was meticulously planned and executed. It also shows the role of official bodies and authoritarian figures, and that it was a mass effort in which the individual could anonymously participate without assuming individual blame for it. Furthermore, positive notions of purification of the community are attached to the slaughter.

The words of the 'giggling and trumpeting' Hutu prisoners after the genocide reflect this same impassive, detached tone, and in the original French text, the impersonal third-person is once again used to deflect blame and guilt.[30] They cleverly use a proverb, 'Calamities are best when not shared', to support the point that it is best not to get mixed up in other people's business and that they were therefore not responsible, again presenting themselves collectively as a 'we' who could not prevent the genocide: '"We weren't there when the crime occurred!" Calamities are best when not shared. We are just poor peasants. We didn't see it coming. Hear anything. [...] We didn't see it coming. We couldn't do anything. We were worried they would kill us too. You can't revive the dead' (ibid.: 285–9).[31] No one seems inclined to take responsibility or show remorse, as 'either no one was to blame or [...] everyone was at fault' (ibid.: 289).[32]

Waberi shows how anecdotes, proverbs, myths, and the way in which they are used to serve ideological purposes need to be questioned. He demonstrates how public opinion, attitudes, and taboos govern a society and how these are reflected in the oral sayings embraced by that society. He paints a portrait of a society where mutual silence and censorship are imposed instead of individuals assuming responsibility for their deeds: 'Our lips are sealed, just like they were yesterday. Even when censorship is not handed down, society finds a way to get organized and impose its own prohibitions' (ibid.: 289–90). Waberi expresses the terrible impact of this attitude on the society by quoting a few disjointed lines from a work by Aimé Césaire, lines which speak of destruction and depravity: 'World, beware, there is a beautiful country that they have spoilt with dissolute unreasonable larvae a world shattered flowers dirtied with old posters a house of broken tiles of leaves torn apart without a tempest' (Césaire, in Waberi 2016: 287–95).

Thus Waberi demonstrates his interest in how a genocide vocabulary comes into being and genocidal attitudes are reflected in language. Terms and slogans become deadly weapons: the machete was not the only instrument in the hands of the torturers; it was in fact the power of 'writings' of intellectuals such as Ferdinand Nahimana[33] and Léon Mugesera[34] that mobilized the people (ibid.: 95). He illustrates how discord was already sown back in 1962 during independence, mainly through the word: 'Already people fantasized about genocide—the word as much as the deed' (ibid.: 248); new slogans promoting 'work' were quickly integrated into society: 'Work will set you free' (ibid.: 249), and it became clear that 'pogroms would soon follow' (ibid.: 251). Even those who kept quiet in those times demonstrated their consent (ibid.: 295). Leading up to the genocide, patriotic songs, like those sung by Simon Bikindi,[35] played their role in motivating the 'receptive hearts' (ibid.: 305) of those who were unloading the shipments of machetes arriving from China, and the 'enthusiastic' voices of Kantano Habimana and Valérie Bemeriki on the hate radio encouraged them (ibid.: 323).

He provides us with insight into the rhetoric that the young *génocid-aires* were constantly subjected to by their superiors and which they internalized; this included references to purifying the country of the 'lepers'(ibid.: 308), of protecting themselves against the 'enemy' that would exterminate them if they didn't act first: '[W]e made a covenant with the cleansing fires from the depths [...] the cockroaches were armed, and we were afraid of their gunfire [...] we had to fight back' (ibid.: 318–20). He includes the propagandist appropriation of the Hamitic myth in the mouths of the killers, who gloat that their victims will not have the 'luxury of heading back to Ethiopia along the Nyabarongo River' (ibid.: 313).

From the first lines, he engages with the received notions surrounding Tutsi identity and the use of dehumanization in propaganda, showing how harmful the consequences were of identity classifications. Tutsis were categorized as cattle keepers but in his text he shows that this ironically lead to them being slaughtered like mooing cattle. They are described as 'ruminants' with 'confused' looks on their faces (ibid.: 370). Tutsi tendons that were cut during the genocide are compared to cow tendons used for fabricating violin strings (ibid.: 232–3). A Tutsi victim twists and writhes 'like an earthworm chopped in half' (ibid.: 243). This trope of dehumanization is continued in a subsection, written in a passive, detached tone and entitled 'The hunting season is open'. Children 'born into the wrong families' are locked away in cells with rats, subjected to laboratory tests and finally openly terrorized while the international community turns a blind eye (ibid.: 252).

Waberi devotes a whole chapter, entitled 'The cavalcade' (The stampede) (ibid.: 337), to a propaganda speech. This chapter essentially represents the voice of the instigator. It certainly conjures up the infamous speech by the skilled orator Léon Mugesera and the 'rhetorical strategies' he used, including 'lexical and syntactical repetitions, inclusive terminology ("we," "us"), and instructional language ("we must not let ourselves be invaded!"/"unite!"), humour in the form of mockery of political opponents, rhetorical question', and so forth (Fletcher 2014: 4). It describes the so-called invasion of Rwanda by the Tutsis descending from Abyssinia and is delivered in seductive, inflammatory language. It is a 'reconstitution' of the political discourse that was used in the media leading up to and during the genocide, and as Audrey Small points out, more 'coherent', 'lyrical', and 'eloquent' than the other parts of the text, suggesting that 'the power of language is relegated to Evil whereas the victims are left with confusion and distress' (Small 2005: 126; my translation).[36]

The Hutus are depicted as victims of a dangerous, barbaric invasion and thus a violent reaction is justified through tropes of dehumanizing the Other, and the promise of divine approbation if they rid their country of these 'vermin' (ibid.: 380). As in Mugesera's speech, this act becomes a moral obligation, their 'job' (ibid.: 39). The Hamitic myth is interweaved with references to Ethiopia, and the Tutsis described as 'nomads' thus confirming the notion that they came from elsewhere (Waberi 2016: 343). We are reminded of the foundation myths and the contesting versions of migration theories and theories on identity formation which form part of Rwanda's complex historiography.[37]

In contrast to the 'disease'-carrying invaders, the native inhabitants are described as 'brothers of the hoe' (ibid.: 340), 'sons of the earth' (ibid.: 360), 'children of humus and clay' (ibid.: 364), and 'children of the cultivators' (ibid.: 380), clearly illustrating humility and brotherhood among the Hutu who, in their 'inferior' position as crop farmers, are depicted as mistreated victims, 'trampled' by the enemy (ibid.: 378). In this way the author incorporates a range of stereotypical ideas and terminology widely used by propagandists to demonize and objectify the Tutsis.

Here Waberi also evokes the role of rumor in propaganda, calling it 'Queen Rumor' (*La reine Rumeur*) (2004: 36; my translation) who mobilizes everyone. Those who know how to manipulate with words are venerated as bards and 'great poets' and become 'prestigious figureheads' (Waberi 2016: 388–9). Those who promote violence are encouraged to make use of the power of rumors and, when inciting others in public, to hide under the 'protective mantle' of their eloquent forebears and leaders (ibid.: 388). References to these powerful rumors (usually in the form of persuasive anecdotes) is in fact one of the oral textual elements that Waberi refers to and, as Homi Bhabha has taught us, the influence of this type of social discourse lies in its 'enunciative aspect', its 'performative power of circulation', and its ability to create panic (2004: 286).

Waberi's propaganda speech contains an example of a well-known anecdote about a Tutsi child who was spared by a group of perpetrators and who, decades later, became the leader of the Tutsi guerrilla army. This anecdote, evoked by Waberi, Diop, and Tadjo, was told and retold by the Hutu power extremists, and the RTLM propaganda to justify the murder of children during the genocide (Jessee 2017: 115). In Diop's novel, the story is attributed to an influential senior Hutu officer and the narrator suggests that the anecdote has not only been repeated many times but that it has 'numerous variations', placing it in the category of persuasive rumor rather than fact (Diop 2006b: 232–40). Waberi, in turn, imbues this anecdote with a higher authority—that of the sacred forest. The orator warns that if even one Tutsi child is spared, the sacred Byumba Forest will 'never forgive' them (2016: 370–4).

Waberi also incorporates a powerful metaphoric title from a 1993 article in the *Kangura* magazine to persuade his listeners:

> With one cockroach for every eight or nine of us, no, what am I thinking, for every twelve of us, the harvest should take only a few days, wouldn't you say? As the old saying goes, "A cockroach will never become [give birth to] a butterfly." Once completely cleansed, Rwanda will once again be pure and virginal as in the early days of creation. (Waberi 2016: 338–405)

The origin of this saying—whether it is indeed an 'old saying', appropriated by the author of the article, or a newly invented piece of anti-Tutsi propaganda—is not revealed to us, but it is clear how powerful such a metaphorical statement can be.[38]

An aspect in Waberi's text that is strongly linked to the erosion of the moral community is the devaluation of traditional and cultural values and the harmful influence of this devaluation on the relationship between Hutus and Tutsis. We have seen that traditional African worldviews favor solidarity and sharing. However, in the time leading up to the genocide, the ancient values which encouraged reciprocity and brotherhood were progressively replaced with new, more 'modern' discourses and codes of behavior (Semujanga 2008: 102). Waberi reminds us that the missionaries first taught the Rwandan children to reject the ancestral values of their forebears. Josias Semujanga (ibid.: 101–2) suggests that Waberi shows how these children, who in time became adults, learned to scorn the traditional myths and ancient memory of the Rwandan people, and the old ways of living together. This process of rejection would eventually influence the gradually increasing polarization between Hutus and Tutsis, leading to a 'deeply entrenched hatred between Tutsis and Hutus' (Waberi 2016: 549).[39]

In demonizing the Tutsis, the propaganda served to remove the moral and social obligations linked to the traditional principle of reciprocity and brotherhood which had always existed in the society (Semujanga 2008: 69). It undermined the wisdom of the elders and destroyed the principle of mutual integration of the three original groups which assured the unity of the Rwandan nation (ibid.: 69). Waberi's orator subverts traditional sayings by claiming that the well-known dictum of three ethnic groups that have been 'woven into one braid' is a 'fable', a 'machination' (2016: 395–6). Whereas Rwandans are known to share the same language, traditional culture, and beliefs, the orator suggests that the Tutsi invaders had none of these elements and appropriated these customs for themselves upon arrival: 'Without place, gods or fire, the nomads ransacked, killed, scorched the earth and the people on their way through' (ibid.: 342–3).

Waberi's orator also undermines oral and cultural tradition and myths by saying that the 'Most High' will help them to make some 'adjustments' to the way in which the 'world was transmitted to [them] orally' (ibid.: 350), suggesting that God is on their side, that the 'secular wisdom of [their] fathers has its limits' (ibid.: 353), and that new values are needed to cope with modern life. The way in which the orator incorporates the Bahutu Ten Commandments suggests that this new way of living is more acceptable than the old codes of behavior. Instead of simply citing them, the orator describes and endorses the new set of values promoted by this document. To do so, he uses a prescriptive tone, reminiscent of a pastor preaching the gospel: 'Marriage outside of one's ethnic group must be prohibited. This makes perfect sense and is in accordance with the Scriptures and in keeping with the guidelines promulgated by our social revolution' (ibid.: 354–6).

These commandments become a weapon to incite Hutus to participate in denigrating the Tutsis. By including the Bible and the 'White Fathers' in the argument, the orator foregrounds the status and influence of the Bahutu Ten Commandments; they are in line with and endorsed by the Holy Scriptures and therefore must be obeyed: 'I can see from your reaction that you think I am exaggerating—go ahead and seek advice from our friends the White Fathers, dive back into your Bible […]' (ibid.: 357–8). The orator links these Commandments to the Church and therefore to acts of obedience. By blurring the lines between this document and the Bible, the Commandments are elevated to the status of Holy Scriptures and thus become sacred.

Waberi furthermore demonstrates how propaganda discourse skillfully drew on existing allegiances to the traditional deities, as the orator notes that the troubled 'wandering spirits' of the sacred Byumba Forest will only be appeased and assuaged through the spilling of blood; in short, cleansing the country of the foreigners is divinely sanctioned and even required by the spirit world (ibid.: 373). Thus, acts of murder are linked to bloody sacrifices performed for traditional deities, suggesting that the authority behind these orders is not only the Christian God, but also the sacred authority of the traditional Rwandan religion. In this way, the speech contains key elements from Rwandan belief and which would speak to the masses that grew up in this culture. Here too, the tactics used by Waberi's orator are eerily similar to those of Mugesera. Fletcher argues, for example, that Mugesera does not rely on blind submission by his listeners, but rather constructs a clever argument that appears to be grounded in Rwandan law and traditions and furthermore cites authoritative texts like the gospel to support his argument (2014: 6). In a similar vein, Waberi's orator uses traditional tropes and refers to authoritative texts like the Bible and the Bahutu Ten Commandments. He claims that even the gods and ancestors 'sought refuge on the peaks of volcanoes' in order to escape from these enemies (ibid.: 366).

He also casts them in the role as victims suggesting that if they consider the 'evidence', they will realize how they are blamed for everything, from the 'the mutilated nose of Queen Hatshepsut's Sphinx' to the 'drought in East Africa', and this gives them the right to defend themselves (ibid.: 359–61). Indeed, in every sense, the Hutus are led to see themselves as victims acting in self-defense, not only against the invading Tutsis—who stole their land, their language, their gods, and their rites—or against the bloodthirsty spirits of the forest who seek to be avenged, but also against the 'foreign devils', the colonizers who were instrumental in destroying their culture and history: 'our heroes, buried, decapitated; our history, falsified, distorted, dismantled and rewritten with help of foreign devils [...] they've taken our language, our gods, and gone so far as to imitate our funerary rites' (ibid.: 392–4).

Finally, in the third part of this section, Waberi focuses on the theme of dehumanization through the trope of a dog in a chapter entitled 'And the dogs feasted'. Throughout his text the image of dogs feasting on corpses is a metaphor for human beings' descent into barbarism on this 'journey without stopovers to the furthest depths of inhumanity' (2016: 436, 441). This phrase, which he repeats twice, is reminiscent of Tadjo's subtitle (*Travels in the Heart of Rwanda*), both cases evoking the journey into the dark heart of the genocide. In this chapter, Waberi moves freely between the narrative of a wounded victim fleeing from the dogs during the genocide and an old woman, the sole survivor of an entire family, who has kept a dog who came back to her after the genocide. She has named him Minuar, and he is a symbol of the genocide on various levels; like those perpetrators who killed their friends and neighbors, he allegedly ate some of her family members. Like the old woman who survived, he miraculously escaped being killed by the soldiers. Because of his name, he is also a constant reminder to her of the betrayal of the international community, the MINUAR, or United Nations peacekeeping mission (UNAMIR), who failed them (ibid.: 429–35)[40].

Although this motif is the focus of this chapter, Waberi evokes it throughout his text. Twice, he quotes Aimé Césaire's work *And the Dogs Were Silent* (ibid.: 281, 293), which speaks of murder and destruction, and later on he presents the discourse of the perpetrator who claims that the dogs, the 'carrion', and the 'rodents' will assist them in tracking down their victims (ibid.: 387).

In addition to the metaphorical comparison of humans to animals, Waberi provides descriptions of real dogs, attracted by blood and corpses. They undergo a macabre transformation and become savage beasts who start eating the dead, reminding us that genocide not only corrupts and dehumanizes humans, but also depraves and unbalances the natural and animal world. Waberi offers us a grotesque image of dogs losing all their 'former canine grace' and degenerating into wild animals (ibid.: 409–15). They become 'wild donkeys, lunatics', that run around 'braying and bleating', 'body snatchers', and 'scavengers' who carry diseases and wait with the locusts and birds of prey for new bodies to arrive (ibid.: 410, 413, 420). They are transformed into voracious 'mad dogs', 'coyotes', and 'jackals' in whom the pack mentality has been stirred up (ibid.: 411–2). In this ambiance of growing bestiality, the border between human and animal becomes blurred and hybrid creatures are engendered. We no longer know whether Waberi is talking of dogs or humans, because 'men have become dogs who roam around in packs and the dogs have turned into mad monsters' (Delas 2002: 46; my translation).[41]

Waberi's intricate and fragmented text reflects the complexity of the genocide and its logic. It has a specific focus on language and the way it can be abused by those in power, in the form of propaganda, rhetoric, and the misrepresentation, falsification, and distortion of history, myths, and proverbs—all in the service of the devaluation of personhood. Conversely, it reflects on and even mirrors the struggle and powerlessness of both the survivor and the intellectual witness to effectively narrate the trauma of genocide, and this is perhaps why Mongo-Mboussa describes Waberi's text as a 'noble failure' (2000; my translation). Waberi's contribution seems to suggest that the story can never be fully told, and especially not in a linear fashion; we can merely provide impressions and glimpses of it.

Boubacar Boris Diop and Barebone Writing

Like Waberi, Diop engages with the role of language, not only in promoting genocide, but also, in narrating it and expressing its consequences. Diop indicates that, after hearing testimony upon testimony, he realized that the only way in which he could write about the genocide was to do so with great 'simplicity' and 'modesty', rather than trying to impress others with 'metaphors and verbal pirouettes' (Diop 2003: 118). Thus, he made a deliberate choice to write in a way that would be lucid and clear, creating simple characters who would be accessible to young people and with whom they could identify—a novel which, in his own words, would be 'easy to read' and which young people would have the courage to complete (Diop 2006a).[42] Like the bones he was writing about, his words would be stripped of embellishments.

Diop speaks of the creative tension he experienced between the real stories he heard and the imaginative world of the fictional novel, expressing his fear that his imagination would be limited by reality. In his earlier works, he had felt free to 'proudly manipulate' reality whereas, in this case, the people whose testimonies they were writing had begged them not to write creative fiction, but to 'report' their words 'faithfully' (Diop 2003: 115).

In the end, he did write a fictional novel, but the style in which he chose to do so has been described as 'raw stripped narrative' (Montesano 2015: 93). The unambiguous approach and the clarity provided by facts, dates, historical figures, real sites, and places add a dimension of journalistic reportage to the novel. This conforms to the desire to inform, and to be 'faithful' to the 'truth' of the stories the authors had heard, in spite of making use of fiction and literature to do so. In this regard, Diop's contribution is seen as a demonstration that fiction is able to 'turn official reportage inside out to expose the motivating ideological fantasies articulated both within Rwanda and from without' (Kroll 2007: 657).[43] Even so, in spite of his uncomplicated, almost simplified style, it remains significant that this author, who is also a journalist and social scientist, chose fiction as a vehicle to write about the genocide.

Much like Cornelius, his writer-protagonist, Diop seems to increasingly question symbolic interpretations of the genocide and progressively moves away from 'specialized language (particularly that of symbols) towards the nakedness of the document' (Arnould-Bloomfield 2010: 508). This becomes clear, for example, when Diop narrates scenes from Murambi where the dogs came to feast on the blood of the victims. When Cornelius wants to interpret this in a symbolic way—as 'monsters drinking the blood of Rwanda'—another character stops him by insisting that it is not a symbol, but something they literally saw with their own eyes, and that it should therefore not be reduced and sublimated into something less horrifying than it really was (Diop 2006b: 1460–1).

Elisabeth Arnould-Bloomfield interprets Diop's esthetic choices, not as a mere refusal to write symbolic literature in the face of the reality of the genocide (although this interpretation is valid), but qualifies it as a type of 'concrete literature' in which 'words do not merely mirror genocide but act as sublimation of its inter-subjective violence' (ibid.: 506, 507). In Diop's text, words are 'quite literally, fighting words' which not only represent but which 'act' (ibid.: 506).[44]

Furthermore, Diop's use of the form of first-person testimony creates a 'zone of sharing' in which the experience becomes a tellable story that can be actively received; thus a social link is re-established between the narrator and listener and art becomes a form of 'vital mediation' of the testimony of the survivors (Semujanga 2008: 127–8).[45]

Such a reading of the novel confirms the importance of providing a space of appropriate listening to the survivor because, in the encounters that Diop's novel enacts, the victim is offered a space to be seen and heard so that his or her violent experience is 'sublimate[d]' into words (Arnould-Bloomfield 2010: 511). Words then become active expressions of the violence experienced by victims.

Diop's title prefigures his realistic and concrete approach to writing about the genocide, for Murambi, Bisesero, Ntarama, and Nyamata are not imaginary or symbolic places, but rather physical genocide sites, confirming the authenticity of the narrative and the historic reality it deals with. The notorious site of Murambi is the place 'of bones', the corporeal proof of what some have tried repeatedly to deny. It is fitting then that Diop writes his 'book of bones' in an effort to counter this attempt at denial and erasure.

The title of the novel summons two essential principles on writing about the genocide: that of returning to the site of the event, and the inevitable presence of the remains of those who have been slaughtered (Bazié 2004: 43). Both these elements are key to Diop's novel, for it is at the sites that his protagonist, Cornelius, encounters not only the survivors, but also the stark, physical reality of the event through the remains that confront him. Isaac Bazié makes a meaningful link between the subtitle, 'the book of bones', and the biblical prophecy in Ezekiel on the Valley of Dry Bones, because of the desire that exists in both cases to somehow 'reawaken' and bring back life to the dry bones:

> Prophesy to these bones and say to them, 'Dry bones, hear the word of the Lord! This is what the Sovereign Lord says to these bones: I will make breath enter you, and you will come to life. I will attach tendons to you and make flesh come upon you and cover you with skin; I will put breath in you, and you will come to life. Then you will know that I am the Lord.' (Ezekiel 37:4–6)

Tadjo may imbue her masks with breath and Waberi might call language a 'miraculous' weapon (2016: 83), but it was never possible for the authors to physically resurrect the bones of the dead. Rather, they contributed to a type of communal memory, thus attempting to 'resurrect' the dead through the imaginative medium of writing (Tadjo, in Hodgkin and Montefiore 2005: 15). Diop ascribes this type of restorative potential to the literary text; it becomes a 'funerary monument' during the ritual of mourning because, in contrast to a journalist or a historian who focuses on providing statistics, the novelist attempts to reanimate those he or she writes about (Diop 2003: 120). Journalists and historians, faced with multitudes of massacres and atrocities, have no choice but 'to let the dead bury the dead', whereas the novelist 'tries to bring them back to life', and this is perhaps one of the reasons for Diop's insistence on writing fiction (ibid.: 119).

Diop does not engage with the invisible world in the way Tadjo and Lamko do but he confirms that his title implies, foremost, that his text had been written for the dead (in Bénard 2001), and Bazié's (2004) assertion that his aim is a type of resurrection seems to be confirmed in the concluding paragraphs of Diop's novel. The ending suggests that it is not only the dead who are in need of a type of resurrection, for the 'living dead' who have survived often need it as desperately. At Murambi, Cornelius meets a young woman, dressed in black, who regularly returns to the site to bring homage to her departed loved ones. She haunts the final pages of the text—this woman who is described as a mere silent 'form', a flitting 'shadow' who 'obviously' doesn't 'want to be seen' (Diop 2006b: 1749, 1750, 1756). She thus becomes the embodiment of those who have been relegated to the shadows and the silence, and Cornelius, like the project authors, makes the choice 'to wait for her' and listen to her: 'He had to see her face, listen to her voice. She had no reason to hide, and it was his duty to get as close as he could to all suffering' (ibid.: 1757–8). This desire to see and listen, to give back a voice and a face to one who has become a shadow, remains the author's desire throughout. His novel closes with the wish to tell the 'woman in black' that the 'dead of Murambi, too, had dreams, and that their most ardent desire was for the resurrection of the living' (Diop 2006b: 1756, 1759). Such a restoration, says Diop, is possible when we at least acknowledge what they have gone through (in Brezault 2002).[46]

Exile and Identity

Diop narrates the causes and consequences of the genocide through a multivocal novel that unfolds as a journey undertaken by Cornelius, a Rwandan whose sense of identity is precarious and undermined by his life narrative. Born to a Hutu father and Tutsi mother, living in exile from a young age, Cornelius returns from Djibouti four years after the genocide, scared that he may not even 'look like a Rwandan anymore' (Diop 2006b: 423). He is there to learn the 'truth' about the genocide and he is accompanied on his quest by his childhood friends, Jessica Kamanzi and Stanley Ntaramira. Diop creates a protagonist who, like the author, did not experience the genocide, but journeys to Rwanda after the fact in order to write about it, and ends up constantly questioning his ability to do so.

Juxtaposed with Cornelius's itinerary are other fragmented and incomplete stories,[47] encompassing different positions in which people found themselves during the genocide: perpetrator, victim, bystander, moderate Hutu, and Rwandan Patriotic Front (RPF) infiltrator. Thus Diop creates what Kroll has called a 'multiple, decentred narrative' (2007: 655). Various chapters carry the names of their fictitious first-person narrator-protagonists, who tell their stories in the mode of eyewitness testimony: victim-eyewitness, perpetrator-eyewitness, and spectator-eyewitness.

By using a range of subjective, flawed voices, Diop invites the reader to reflect on the 'instability of historical discourse' (Hitchcott 2009: 54) on the country and exposes the reader to a an interesting 'mix of knowledge and ignorance' on the genocide itself (Arnould-Bloomfield 2010: 506–7). Characters who narrate their own stories do not have access to the privileged position of the 'all-knowing, external and rational perspective' normally associated with a third-person narrator, but tell the 'truth' of the event from their personal and often contradictory positions (ibid.).

This choice of narrative voice not only allows the reader to become aware of the plurality of lived realities of the genocide, but also speaks to the issue of the witness position. Those whom he presents as eyewitnesses tell their stories in the first person and the perfect tense, but Cornelius, who is in many ways an absent or intellectual witness, is characterized by a third-person narrative and the past historic tense, thus suggesting the distance felt by those who did not personally experience the genocide.

Little by little, Cornelius comes to see that, in the eyes of the survivors, he is not the innocent victim he thought himself to be, but rather the outsider: '"He looks as if he's insinuating that I wasn't there when people were being killed and now I've come to bother the hell out of everyone with my pain," Cornelius thought bitterly' (Diop 2006b: 599–600). At Murambi, Gérard will confirm this to him: 'I wanted you dead. It's your father who did it. And you, you weren't there when we were suffering' (ibid.: 1432). This revelation will only serve to make Cornelius even more aware of his position as outsider, a type of impostor among the survivors: 'For himself, everything had been so easy: he felt that he would never be able to understand the pain that had not been his. His return was almost becoming another exile' (ibid.: 1435–6).

Thus, a parallel is created between the 'outsider' author and his 'absent' protagonist and the distance which they both try to overcome in their quest for the truth and for continuing to write about it. On a structural level, the novel moves constantly between these two positions. Chapters 1 and 3 take place immediately before and during the genocide and contain first-person narratives of those who have ostensibly witnessed it. These are alternated with Chaps. 2 and 4, which take place after the genocide, depicting the 'return' of Cornelius. Jessica Kamanzi is the one character who moves between these two worlds and the only character to have a voice in all four parts of the novel: as first-person narrator in parts 1 and 3 and as a character in Cornelius's return journey in parts 2 and 4. Thus, in Diop's novel, Jessica assumes the role of the *passeur*[48] who connects these worlds of before, during and after the genocide and who accompanies Cornelius on his quest to discover important parts of his family's truth. She is the one who narrates the experience of the girl who was raped by a Hutu priest as well as the death of a Hutu nun who refused to kill Tutsis and attempted to help them to escape. Jessica is portrayed as a thin, 'graceless' girl (Diop 2006b: 663) with a 'bony body' and 'sad eyes' who seems to be in 'bad health' (ibid.: 404, 405). She has been marked by her experiences: she has 'learned to lie' and 'lead a double life' in order to survive (ibid.: 309).

Cornelius's quest will culminate, as is suggested by the title, in his return to his place of birth, Murambi. This is also the site of his father's betrayal, the school in which his family was massacred, and his father's house. It is here where he will acknowledge that 'every Rwandan should have the courage to look reality in the eye', an act for which he will need the guidance of his uncle, Simeon Habineza (ibid.: 1404).

It is also here where he will again meet Gérard Nayinzira, the 'Skipper', who has been haunting him since his revelation in a bar in Kigali that he has drunk blood and that his 'blood is full of blood' (ibid.: 567). Gérard demonstrates the malaise that at times exists between survivors and returned exiles: since meeting him, Cornelius is aware of his animosity, his 'enigmatic reproaches' (Diop 2006b: 564), and his 'absent and vaguely hostile air' (ibid.: 570). Cornelius has the impression that Gérard stares at him 'with a special intensity' (ibid.: 571). However, it is only at Murambi that Gérard will reveal that he is one of the few survivors from this site, for which Cornelius's father was largely responsible, and that he survived by lying under a pile of bodies and was thus forced to swallow their blood.

It is perhaps in the character of Gérard that we most clearly see the signs of trauma in Diop's novel: he is obsessed with his experience of having drunk blood and speaks of it all the time and seems to be plagued by turmoil and isolation (Germanotta 2016: 82). Like many in his situation, he suffers from survivor guilt: 'Sometimes I go back to Murambi. I look at the place where my remains would have been and I tell myself that something's wrong, I move my hands and my feet because it seems strange to me that they're still there, and my entire body seems like a hallucination to me' (Diop 2006b: 1700–2). Furthermore, he demonstrates another form of tension often found among survivors: the desire not only to be listened to, but to be believed, for they have experienced the 'unbelievable':

> I saw that with my own eyes. Do you believe me, Cornelius? It's important that you believe me. I'm not making it up, for once that's not necessary. If you prefer to think that I imagined these horrors your mind will be at peace and that's not good. This pain will get lost in opaque words and everything will be forgotten until the next massacre. They really did all these incredible things. (ibid.: 1698–1700).

As Nicki Hitchcott notes, 'Cornelius must not only believe the story but he must be troubled by it and so remember it. In this way, the text affirms the need for the horror of the Rwandan genocide to be recounted and acknowledged' (2009: 53). This is then the path that Cornelius must take, as a character embodying the task that the project participants assigned to themselves and as a role that we as readers are in turn invited to take up.

Like Lamko, Diop portrays Cornelius's gradually growing knowledge of the genocide as a journey of initiation, a quest which involves painful discoveries, disillusionment and, ultimately, the power of transformative travel. Like Tadjo, Cornelius is disorientated by the journey and his itinerary to Kigali is no more direct than hers. He travels through Abidjan, Kinshasa, Nairobi, Dar es Salaam, Addis Ababa, and Entebbe. By evoking all these countries from the African continent, Diop too situates the genocide beyond the borders of Rwanda, underlining its African and universal origin and nature. No one can remain uninvolved; we are all implicated somehow; and Cornelius will soon become horribly aware of this when he discovers that his own father was a notorious perpetrator, the Butcher of Murambi, who orchestrated the death of his own Tutsi wife and children. This reality, of a father arranging the demise of his own family, again reminds us of Tadjo's monster who ended up eating his own flesh.

At first, Jessica and Stanley hide this terrible knowledge from Cornelius, but discovering the truth is in fact the purpose of his journey: 'He wasn't afraid of the truth, he had also come back to learn it' (Diop 2006b: 715). This process is of course not straightforward and will challenge his assumptions. Upon arrival he finds that when he wants to write a letter to his girlfriend, his ideas are 'no longer clear' (ibid.: 466) and his first evening out with Stanley to a restaurant in a city 'that he hardly knew' includes a host of undercurrents and a feeling of general 'malaise' that he struggles to understand, a further part of his general sense of disorientation (ibid.: 578).

Stanley warns Cornelius that initial appearances are not to be trusted. When he arrives, he stares at the city, 'trying to fathom intuitively the secret relationship between the trees standing still on the side of the road and the barbarous scenes that had stupefied the entire world during the genocide' (ibid.: 420–1). In the streets of Nyamirambo, where he stays with Stanley, there are no remaining signs of the genocide. There are no barricades, corpses, dogs, or vultures: 'Banal scenes in a city like any other. It was astounding to Cornelius to note that the events of 1994 had left no visible traces anywhere'; the 'city refused to show her wounds' (ibid.:

539–40, 542). Initially, from a distance, the hills of Kigali are 'sublimely beautiful', but later on he will discover 'her hidden side' (ibid.: 647), her 'nauseating fumes' (ibid.: 641), poverty, and open gutters, filling him with a sense of betrayal.

Diop traces Cornelius's itinerary, which is above all a physical discovery of real sites and people connected to the genocide and of his own place in this history. During a visit to a genocide site one is faced with physical proof of the atrocities committed, and feels most keenly the inability to write the genocide story, and one is easily overcome with silence in the face of the horror (Germanotta 2016: 89). This sense of inadequacy is echoed by Diop's remark when narrating the story of a girl raped by a priest: 'All that is absolutely unbelievable. Even words aren't enough. Even words don't know any more what to say' (Diop 2006b: 957–8).

Cornelius too is confronted with the inability to find the appropriate words. He is filled with rage because, while living in exile, it was 'as if he'd never been aware of the atrocities committed in the country' (ibid.: 783). Like in Tadjo's travel diary, the trope of luggage is significantly integrated. Jessica's playful remark about his meager amount of luggage is a jarring reminder of the way in which exile strips people, and the implication is that Cornelius may not have much to offer them: '"Well, here's someone who's coming back to us from a lifetime of exile with almost nothing," said Jessica, laughing' (Diop 2006b: 424). Cornelius describes his own life in exile as a 'long series of ruptures' (ibid.: 473). His birth country, which should fill him with a sense of longing and comfort, in fact fills him with dread: 'ever since his childhood, Rwanda frightened him' and he cannot forget the terror he experienced there before fleeing to Burundi (ibid.: 480).

His journey is not only intended to help him find the truth about the genocide, but to discover who he really is; it is intimately related to his sense of self. Jessica unwittingly asks him the question that so plagues him: 'So who is this person who's come back home to us?' (ibid.: 407). This makes him realize that all his experiences in exile, 'away from Rwanda, would only find its true meaning in what had happened four years earlier. In a certain way, his life was just beginning' (ibid.: 408–9). Cornelius's need to understand the genocide is driven by his need to know himself:

> He sensed how difficult it was going to be for him to put some order into his life and he didn't like the idea. To come back to one's country—to be happy there or to suffer—was a rebirth, but he didn't want to become

someone without a past. He was the sum of everything he had experienced. His faults. His cowardliness. His hopes. He wanted to know, down to the very last detail, how his family had been massacred. (ibid.: 486–9)

The project that Cornelius has embarked upon is in fact defined for him by Stanley, who has himself discovered that 'no-one one is born a Rwandan. You learn to become one. […] It's a very slow project that each one of us takes upon himself' (ibid.: 528–9).

It is on the day of their visit to the sites of Nyamata and Ntarama that Jessica tells him about his father's role at Murambi. Like Pelouse in Lamko's text, Cornelius will discover that deeper knowledge comes at a price: 'You have a long path to take in your heart and in your mind. You're going to suffer a lot, and that might be good for you' (ibid.: 841–2). He realizes that he will ultimately have to make this journey alone and that it will involve going back to the origin of his existence, the house in which he was born, and the village in which he grew up.

In fact, Cornelius's journey has a lot to do with returning from exile and facing everything one has missed out on. He realizes that 'one doesn't emerge from exile without becoming a child again' (ibid.: 1317). We learn that he hardly knew his own mother and never met his siblings, who were born after he left at the age of 12. He will need to rely on some of his mother's belongings, which he finds in her home, to learn more about her and thus 'do up the loose and frayed threads of his existence' (ibid.: 1571). His uncle Simeon teaches him that memory is necessary and that we need to know where we come from. If Cornelius wants to understand and come home to Rwanda after the genocide, he also needs to go back to its roots, its history, and its culture—the 'place where Rwanda was born', the 'world that nothing could destroy' (ibid.: 1334, 1361). Simeon is the one who points him to Rwanda's cultural and traditional memory: his childhood impressions of the child playing flute on the shores of Lake Mohazi, the shepherd, the bull with the 'pointed horns' (ibid.: 1336). This is the Rwanda that should inform Cornelius's knowledge and his memory and which will give him strength to face the terrible truth. It will also give him the courage to accept and claim the Rwandan identity that is his: 'I am Cornelius Uvimana. I am the son of Doctor Karekezi', he will say to the survivor at Murambi, and again to the shopkeeper (ibid.: 1376, 1511). He will have to accept his past in order to 'begin to recover his serenity and a sense of the future' (ibid.: 1571). Initiation, then in Diop's novel is different from initiation in Lamko's, it is less about discovering the traditional culture and customs, and more about Cornelius's discovery of his own identity and roots, and what it means to be Rwandan.

In Cornelius's character, Diop emphasizes the profound unease of many of the inhabitants of post-genocide Rwanda: 'He had suddenly discovered that he had become the perfect Rwandan: both guilty and a victim' (ibid.: 833). Jessica teaches him that being the child of a perpetrator is a terrible legacy that many Rwandans will have to face in the years to come and that, in that sense, he too is a 'perfect Rwandan': 'There were tens or hundreds of thousands of killers. Many of them were fathers. And you, you're just the son of one of them' (ibid.: 840). Her revelation profoundly changes everything for Cornelius, imbuing his return from exile with new meaning. When he still considered himself 'innocent' in terms of the genocide, his intention was to write an absurd play about it, but this was before he discovered that 'he was the son of a monster' (ibid.: 831). He now realizes that this idea was completely 'out of place' and that 'the only story he had to tell was his own: the story of his family' (ibid.: 833).

He also comes to know that the genocide is not one of those 'action films' where the weak is saved by a 'strong and brave young hero' (ibid.: 1704–5). Simeon, a 'storyteller' (ibid.: 1735) in his own right, teaches him that 'a genocide is not just any kind of story, with a beginning and an end between which more or less ordinary events take place' (ibid.: 1733). Cornelius is now embarrassed by his initial idea of writing a play, and yet, faced with this knowledge, he chooses, like Diop, not to remain silent but to find the words to tell the story: 'But he wasn't giving up his enthusiasm for words, dictated by despair, helplessness before the sheer immensity of evil, and no doubt a nagging conscience. He did not intend to resign himself to the definitive victory of the murderers through silence' (ibid.: 1735–7).

Authoritarian Figures and Systems

When Aloys Ndasingwa from Diop's text tells of the massacre at Nyamata, his narrative depicts not only the perverted sense of morality among the *génocidaires*, but also the stature of those in positions of authority. When they take the loot from the victims' bodies, their leader forces them to share it 'fairly' among them, an act which earns him the respect of his Hutu subordinates. Ironically, Aloys does not consider it 'unfair' to kill the Tutsis and steal their belongings: 'We put everything together to divvy up among ourselves at the end of the day. That was a good idea our commander had; it's good for a commander to be fair, that way they respect you and there's no fighting' (Diop 2006b: 877–8).

As discussed in the introduction, the act of killing was sanctified by referring to the Tutsis as the 'sub-citizens' in the community in comparison to the Interahamwe, who were seen as the 'ultra-citizens' defending their own country (Semujanga 2008: 134).

Faustin Gasana, a Hutu soldier in Diop's text, provides us with an example of the sense of false heroism attached to being part of this elite group of 'ultra-citizens'. His family and neighbors treat him like a hero. By comparing the militia to brave 'warriors' and heroes from 'ancient times', Diop demonstrates how deep-seated cultural tropes, as well as the fear of being defeated, were drawn upon by propaganda: 'I have the sensation of reliving a scene from ancient times, from times when the bravery of warriors was exalted before battle' (Diop 2006: 275–6). Faustin, however, is astute enough to see that they are not heroes, but citizens slaughtering fellow citizens—neighbors, friends, and family: 'To be frank, I am by nature rather reserved, and all of that rather bothers me. I am not going to war. I am not running any risk. In Kibungo, like in the rest of Rwanda, we're just going to line the Tutsis up along the barricades and kill them. Each one in turn' (Diop 2006: 276–7).

Through Faustin, Diop provides us with what Sadibou Sow calls a 'perfect illustration' of the culture of submission to authority (Sow 2009: 103). His authoritarian, extremist father clearly represents those figures who encouraged genocide; his room is filled with official photos of the first president of Rwanda, Grégoire Kayibanda, and President Juvénal Habyarimana, and he quotes the same propaganda to his son that the militia feed the young recruits. Whereas his son still speaks of 'Tutsis', the older man insists on calling them '*inyenzi*' (cockroaches), demonstrating that he has completely embraced and internalized the process of dehumanization, in contrast to his son who merely seems to act out of a sense of duty (Diop 2006b: 219). He also displays a sense of superiority toward the women that surround him, sending his wife out so that the 'real men' can talk (ibid.: 217).

We learn that it is not the way his father treats Faustin that makes him defer him and love him, but merely his position of parental authority: 'I'm fond of the old man. He's my father' (ibid.: 257). Faustin is expected to obey him, even though he senses that his controlling and abusive father seems to have lost his 'sense of reality' and that his father underestimates the complexity of what they are planning to do (ibid.: 247). The relationship between them is not one of mutual love and acceptance; rather, they tolerate each other: the father is never satisfied with Faustin's efforts and the son is constantly trying to please his father. In his mind, Faustin calls his father 'the old man' (ibid.: 196), describing him as spiteful, demanding, and difficult, whereas the father, although he has had reports on his son's good work for the cause, thinks of him as a 'bad son' (ibid.: 203), belonging to a 'generation of incompetents' (ibid.: 206), and doubts his 'commitment' to the cause (ibid.: 228).

Faustin's father allows no space for his opinion. When he tries to openly voice his doubts to his father, the father reacts by patronizing him: 'I feel a bit annoyed. I've never liked his odd habit of asking questions that, in many cases, he often already knows the answers to' (ibid.: 251–2). When Faustin wants to avoid conflict and leave because his father starts to insult him the old man shouts and shows that he thinks it his right to dictate even his son's emotions: 'You're mad aren't you? How dare you get mad at your father?' (ibid.: 255–6).

Diop stages the inner conflict that Faustin experiences in an interesting way; however hard Faustin tries to respect his father, the narrative is filled with disparaging comments on the older man's repulsive physical state of 'decrepitude' (ibid.: 223); his wound oozes a smelly yellow liquid and his breath smells badly enough that Faustin 'recoil[s]' from it (ibid.: 232).

Despite his father's aggressive insults, Faustin continues to make an effort to humor him and remain submissive. However, as soon as he leaves his presence, Diop tells us that Faustin starts to 'think the unthinkable', namely to entertain thoughts about his father's 'fetid' breath, the fact that he is constantly on the verge of dying, but never finally gets round to doing so, and his insulting behavior toward others (ibid.: 265–6). Thus 'strange ideas begin to assail' him (ibid.: 262). Diop clearly hints at the degree of submission demanded from Faustin; he may not even think negative things about his father, for those are 'the unthinkable'.

What is more, Faustin's timid attempt to stand up to his father by thinking bad thoughts about him leads him directly to thoughts about the Tutsis, and how difficult it is going to be to actually kill all of them. In this way, Diop creates a direct link between the father's authority and that of the official authorities, who expect the soldiers to exterminate the entire Tutsi population. We see then how the culture of submission that already existed in people's homes, and which included controlling others' thoughts and emotions, could easily be abused to manipulate people to participate in the genocide.[49]

However, Diop seems to suggest that blind submission to authority is not the only possible way. He does this through the juxtapositioning of Simeon, the substitute/adopted father figure in Cornelius's life, and Cornelius's real father, an authoritarian 'monster', who is an embodiment of the propaganda that fed the genocide (ibid.: 831). Simeon is the antithesis of authoritarian characters such as Faustin Gasana's father and Cornelius's father, Dr. Joseph Karekezi, who explains his actions through a sense of 'duty' toward the community: 'Come what may, I'll have done my duty. Duty. A simple word that I'm fond of' (Diop 2006b: 978). In Karekezi, Diop provides us with a complex, paradoxical perpetrator. He is married to a Tutsi woman whom he appears to love deeply, together with their children, yet whose death he arranges during the Murambi massacre. In his early career, he publicly stood against the violation of Tutsi rights and was even tortured for it, yet he eventually becomes the fearsome 'butcher of Murambi' (ibid.: 113). Simeon describes him as a 'cold-blooded, resolute killer', motivated by a desire for power and by greed (ibid.: 1469). He ends up doing what he seems to think is his duty because he truly comes to see the Tutsis as the 'enemies' and to believe that there are 'two bloods': one belonging to the Hutus and the other to the Tutsis (ibid.: 1009, 1490). He comes to consider the blood of the Tutsis as 'rotten', even that of his wife and children: 'At the last minute she'll curse me, thinking that I never loved her. That isn't true. It's just history that wants blood. And why would I only spill other people's? Theirs is just as rotten' (ibid.: 1052–4). He describes his marriage to her as a 'youthful mistake that destroyed [his] entire life', noting that he will 'never forgive anyone again for spoiling our blood' (ibid.: 1057–8). However, he claims that he himself has 'never spilled a drop of blood' (ibid.: 1238); he doesn't get his own hands dirty by killing anyone and doesn't see himself as a monster, but rather as someone who is 'determined' to get the job done (ibid.: 998). This character is the embodiment of what the Rwandan lawyer in Gourevitch's text described as the 'big men' in the genocide, to whom the uneducated looked for orders (2000: 23).

Karekezi completely identifies with the 'cause' of the genocide, talking of the militia as 'our men' (Diop 2006b.: 1031). He is a respected figure of authority amongst the perpetrators, is hailed by them as 'Papa', the benefactor and leader of the Interahamwe (ibid.: 1428). In this case, according to him, the job of eliminating the Tutsis is what will bring justice and truth (ibid.: 1070, 1071). He treats the Interahamwe with 'a mixture of affection and contempt' (ibid.: 1148). Colonel Perrin describes him as someone who is 'used to being obeyed' (ibid.: 1114), who seems 'like a normal man' (ibid.: 1123) but 'carries his head haughtily and has a mistrustful look' (ibid.: 1124). Perrin describes the contradictory feelings that Karekezi inspires in him: 'He awoke in me the sort of repugnance and fascination one feels in the presence of sadistic murderers they talk about in the newspaper. But on the other hand, I had some respect for his courage, which came very close to recklessness' (ibid.: 1131–2). He seems to have 'a touch of the heroic captain who refuses to abandon the deck during the shipwreck' and yet, when the colonel arrives to evacuate him, he anxiously runs to the car that will take him to safety (ibid.: 1137–8).

Simeon, on the other hand, criticizes the tendency of displaying absolute obedience to authoritarian bodies, be they religious or political, local or foreign. He points out to Cornelius that the damage done by foreign authorities in the country 'was only possible because we [the Rwandans] were not free people' and then asks him: 'Have we ever been bothered by our chains? Sometimes I think not. We can't hold our own lack of pride against anyone else. […] if the master is a slave, we shouldn't obey him. We have to fight him' (ibid.: 1644–7). Simeon also knows that one cannot simply blame colonialism for what happened in Rwanda, but that the perpetrators have to shoulder the blame for their own actions. Rwandans have to take responsibility for allowing themselves to be duped by the lies told to them: 'What should we be more amazed at? The audacity of the foreigners, or the incredible stupidity of people back then?' (ibid.: 1640).

Through the figure of Simeon, Diop engages with what Irene Visser (quoting Achille Mbembe) calls the 'sensitive issue of complicity', in other words, the acknowledgment of the complexity of the process of colonization and the ways in which colonized people have allowed themselves to be manipulated and misled and their subsequent feelings of guilt and shame (2015: 258). Complicity is in fact dealt with extensively throughout the project; in Waberi's text, for example, it is demonstrated through how Rwandans progressively embraced Western notions of religion and values. But complicity is also a central theme in the genocide itself; this is where the project pays attention to the complexity of choices made by ordinary Hutu citizens to either comply with the orders of those in positions of authority and become complicit in genocidal logic or choose to resist it.

Simeon presents us with a different type of authority: one who refuses to dictate or prescribe, who constantly urges Cornelius to find his own path and discover his own answers, who reminds Cornelius that no one person is to blame. Perhaps the most powerful lesson that Simeon teaches Cornelius is that there are times where no one can help you, and where language fails you: '"There are no words to speak to the dead," said Simeon in a tense voice' (Diop 2006b: 1607).

Simeon appears to have much wisdom, which he transmits to his nephew during their conversations on memory, regrets, and respect, while admitting that he does not have all the answers. When Cornelius asks Simeon for advice, he compares himself to a path—not one that can show Cornelius the way, but rather one that encourages him to find his own path and his own truth:

> You must be like the solitary traveler, Cornelius. If he gets lost, he looks up at the sky and the trees, he looks all around him. But the traveler could have said to himself, bending down toward the ground: 'I'm going to ask the path, who has been here for such a long time, he'll surely be able to help me.' Now, the path will never show him the way to go. The path does not know the way. (ibid.: 1604–6)

Diop's novel constantly attempts to suggest that life must triumph over death and destruction, and it is in the person of someone such as Simeon, who fills the streets of Murambi with his powerful presence, that Cornelius most sees this possibility: 'Thus, in the very country where death had worked away at destroying all energy, the force of life remained intact' (ibid.: 1597).

Through embodying the strong culture of submission to figures of authority within major relationships portrayed in Diop's text, plural perspectives on how Rwandans were possibly influenced by this culture are provided. Some of these narratives confirm its immense hold over the people of Rwanda by showing how it functioned in society, both at home and within social and religious structures. Others invite us to question the power of the culture of submission by demonstrating that some had the courage to stand up for their convictions, despite the price they knew they would pay.

Diop briefly explores another form of authoritarian influence in his novel, namely that of the media. This author-journalist is well aware of the versatile power of the media; that it can be used as propaganda, to raise awareness, but also to desensitize. The Tutsi narrator in his text muses on this process of desensitization:

> I've seen lots of scenes on television myself that were hard to take. [...]
> Newborns they toss, laughing, into bread ovens. Young women who coat
> their throats with oil before going to bed. [...] I suffered from these things
> without really feeling involved. [...] It always happened so far away, in coun-
> tries on the other side of the world. (ibid.: 182–7)

When the president's plane has been shot down, the radio quickly becomes
a tool used to order everyone to stay at home. It is not only an actor in the
genocide, but also a sign and barometer of people's loyalties. The neighbors, who secretly used to listen to the propaganda of Radio Mille Collines,
now suddenly start to do so openly and in the streets; everyone has a radio
'glued to his ear' (ibid.: 340).

In her foreword, Fiona Mc Laughlin remarks that, as a journalist, 'Diop
is both fascinated and horrified by the role that the media played in the
Rwandan genocide' (in Diop 2006: 89). This becomes a clear thread in
the novel, in which there are constant references to radio and television
broadcasts, announcements, and shows:

> While soccer matches keep the rest of the world entertained, in Rwanda the
> radio takes on a most sinister role. The infamous Radio Mille Collines punc-
> tuates the novel with incendiary messages of hatred, goading people to mur-
> der. [...] What is truly horrifying here is the way in which the genocide is
> rendered banal and packaged within the norms of the medium as entertain-
> ment, until its seduction gives way to the sobering realization that genocide
> ought not to be the stuff of game shows, and that the disembodied voice of
> Radio Mille Collines is itself an actor in the genocide. (McLaughlin, in Diop
> 2006: 89–94)

Diop demonstrates this eerie cohabitation of hate speech and entertain-
ment when, after joking about how to recognize a Tutsi, the radio host
urges listeners to participate in the genocide: 'Have fun, my friends, but
don't forget the work that's waiting for you!' (ibid.: 343). The author
shows how, as the *génocidaires* started fleeing, this radio station urged
Hutu women to enjoy the attention of their allies, the French military
who arrived in the country to manage Operation Turquoise: 'My Hutu
sisters, make yourselves pretty, the French soldiers are here, now's our
chance, because all the Tutsi girls are dead!' (ibid.: 1282).

Another form of authority that hugely influenced the unfolding of the
genocide is the international community, and in particular the French
government. Diop explores this by depicting the stereotypical attitudes

toward Rwanda that were prevalent in the international community. He constantly alludes to the close relationship between the Rwandan and French authorities, representing the *génocidaires* as 'straw' puppets in the hands of the French (Diop 2006b: 345).[50]

When the Rwandan president's plane is shot down, someone remarks that those who did it were jealous because he was favored by the French president: 'President Mitterrand gave him a plane as a gift and those who shot it down said: "Since we can't have one of our own, we're going to destroy it!"' (ibid.: 152–3). When the barricades go up, Jessica cynically notes that '[s]omewhere in Paris some sinister civil servants are rubbing their hands together: the situation is under control in Kigali, the RPF won't get in. Their straw men got the army generals and commanders together' (ibid.: 344–5). The French are seen by the *génocidaires* as their 'foreign friends' who 'supported [them] against the whole world in this business' and from whom they expect intervention when the RPF starts gaining the upper hand (ibid.: 1033, 1036).

The most powerful depiction of the relationship between the French and Rwandan authorities is the absurd play that Cornelius invents one night in a drunken state, and which illustrates the implicit derision with which many in Europe regard the African continent. These attitudes are embodied in the caricatures of the French General Perrichon, Captain Régnier and his two local 'assistants' (ibid.: 622), Pierre Intera, and Jacques Hamwe, who 'go everywhere together' (ibid.: 628):

> 'Yes. At the beginning of the play there's this French general who strides across the stage with an enormous cigar in his hand. […] A pudgy guy with a mustache, wearing silk pyjamas. Want me to tell you what the general's worried about? Well, here goes: he's upset, he says they might have killed his cat during the genocides.' 'The genocides?' 'Yes, the general has this damned theory about reciprocal genocides. Everyone tries to kill everyone else, and afterwards there's no one left to kill anyone. Are you following me?' […] 'The perfect asshole, this general. […] He has nothing against blacks, but aren't they exaggerating a bit? They get up to their tricks and instead of facing up to things, they say it's the whites' fault, that it's the cats' fault, and when they start eating each other, the good souls say, "Yes, but you have to understand, there's famine." He'll state it bluntly: "Blame it on the famine!" […] Are you still following me, my dear Roger?' (ibid.: 601–14)

This scathingly absurd and exaggerated play, filled with criticism and mockery, can of course be interpreted on various levels. On the one hand, it is a creation that Cornelius will come to regret and be ashamed of once he learns that the 'truth' of the genocide is more complex than he thought, and that he and his family are not as 'innocent' as he had assumed. On the other hand, it does raise issues with which many in post-genocide Rwanda grapple: the role of colonialism and the continued involvement and interference by Western powers. The two local recruits, representing the *Interahamwe* as their surnames (Intera and Hamwe) suggest, are the henchmen of the French, and they are available for the captain when he needs them to 'work': at his command, they 'torture, rape, and kill' (ibid.: 625).

Cornelius's play also speaks to deeply troubling Afro-pessimistic views on the continent. These views portray the genocide as merely the consequences of ancestral interethnic 'hatred from time immemorial' (ibid.: 760) and as savage Africans killing each other on a dark, uncivilized continent. As Michel Seremundo says: '[W]hatever happened in Rwanda, it would always be the same old story of blacks beating up on each other. Even Africans would say, during half-time of every match, "They're embarrassing us, they should stop killing each other like that"' (ibid.: 179–81).[51]

Furthermore, the play evokes denialist theories of so-called double genocides or interethnic massacres, in which 'Hutus kill Tutsis and Tutsis kill Hutus' (ibid.: 759), discourses which fail to acknowledge that what happened in Rwanda was a genocide against the Tutsis. The play also reminds us of a society in which the lives of human beings were reduced to being worth less than the lives of animals, and where, when faced with the choice of evacuating, foreigners chose to take their pets with them rather than attempting to save fellow human beings. Finally, it reveals the stereotypes attributed to people from designated groups by casting the characters as types or caricatures and lumping them into opposing categories: the Blacks and the Whites.

Another occasion for reflecting on the controversial role played by the French-led military operation, which was widely condemned after the genocide, is provided by the cynical narrative of Colonel Perrin, a French soldier who was tasked to evacuate highly placed officials like Cornelius's father, Karekezi, when the RPF started getting the upper hand:

> As of a few days ago my job has been primarily to evacuate ministers, prefects, and superior officers to Bukavu. These gentlemen have only one thing in mind: not to be here when the RPF arrives. They helped themselves to

the reserves in the Central Bank and carried away or destroyed the adminis-
tration's documents and possessions. (ibid.: 1134–5)

Karekezi astutely guesses that the French may not be willing to take their
support of the Hutu radicals to its logical conclusion: 'Perfect. You're
walking out on us because we've gone a bit too far?' (ibid.: 1167–8). As
Jessica notes during the final days of the genocide, France is abandoning
her 'friends in difficulty', because 'those allies [the *Interahamwe*] have, so
to speak, raised the bar too high. They haven't realized that their spectacu-
lar barbarity was in fact a political liability' (ibid.: 1275–6). Indeed,
although he does not acknowledge this to Karekezi, Perrin knows that the
behavior of the *génocidaires* has put the French in a difficult position.
When the RPF arrive, the French no longer know who to back: 'In Paris,
confusion had reached a peak. Certain enthusiasts already saw us going at
it with the RPF resistance fighters in the streets of Kigali, to sort this business out one on one. Others were saying: "We've messed around enough,
that does it"' (ibid.: 1159–61).

Through exposing Perrin's private thoughts, Diop bitterly accuses the
French and clearly portray the self-serving and hypocritical role they
played in what they called the 'Rwandan case' (ibid.: 1171, as well as the
way in which they manipulated and used their Hutu 'assistants' (ibid.:
622): 'Doctor Karekezi's Parisian partisans were fully aware of his secret
activities. They knew what dubious trafficking went on in his tea factory.
But he was all the more attractive to them because of it: the man could
advance concealed for a long time' (ibid.: 1177–8).

Perrin himself claims to merely follow orders, and prefers to be at a
distance from his own 'crazy' French superiors, 'these men with a one-
track mind' who refuse to give up control of Africa: 'Africa is ours, we're
not going to let it go' (ibid.: 1188–9). In the end, Perrin knows that the
French will regret their role in the 'Rwandan affair' (ibid.: 1199), the 'sinister farce' they played out (ibid.: 1280), and they will have lost much
credibility: 'an Operation Turquoise that lots of people are laughing at. To
play the kind soul after letting our protégés commit all these stupid atrocities! No one's been fooled' (ibid.: 1200).

Ultimately, Karekezi accuses the French of not having the 'balls' to
'carry their plan through to its logical conclusion' (ibid.: 1205, 1210). He
also does not allow them to plead ignorance: 'You had this country under
your control, Colonel. You knew every nut and bolt of the killing machine
and you looked away because it suited you' (ibid.: 1213–4). Perrin

acknowledges that, although the Rwandans made their own choices, and the genocide was their own 'fault', the French cannot pretend to be innocent, and he says to his idealistic friend: '[W]e did nothing to prevent the massacres. We were the only ones in the world who could have done it [...] My dear Jean-Marc, we're in blood up to here in all of this' (ibid.: 1121–2). Finally, Cornelius reminds us of the infamous statement made by the 'Old Man',[52] President Mitterrand, who had continued to support the interim government and who had said, 'In those countries a genocide doesn't mean much' (ibid.: 1712). In the end, history would not be kind to him for uttering those careless words; it would 'bring him down a peg or two' (ibid.: 1714).

Diop, then, through Cornelius's absurd play, the thoughts of a French colonel, and the interaction between an infamous perpetrator and the French colonel, addresses the French intervention in the genocide, again demonstrating that the weapons of literature can provide perspectives in ways that history and journalism are unable to do.

In different ways, Waberi and Diop show how mass participation was encouraged through propaganda, the legitimization of violence, the culture of submission to authority, the fear of becoming a victim oneself, and the creation of the perception that the Tutsi was a subhuman.

Although both Waberi and Diop are concerned with the power of language, and both deal with the issues of submission to authority and the role of those that are in positions of power, their approaches are very different. Where Waberi's text embodies and demonstrates propaganda discourse, its rhetoric and distortions, Diop's text embodies violent encounters between the victim and listener, but this is also linked to an attempt at literary restoration/restitution of those he is writing about. Diop demonstrates the fluidity of historiography and the way in which it has become unreliable by using a series of subjective voices who tell incomplete stories. Waberi, on the other hand, demonstrates in his powerful chapter on propaganda how myths were reinterpreted and authoritarian bodies and documents used to influence the masses.

These two authors also deal in different ways with the relationship between reality and imagination. Both texts are based on real stories that the authors listened to and people whom they met, but Waberi chose to present the story as part of a hybrid travel diary in which he is often physically present—as a reluctant, tentative transmitter of stories, constantly doubting the power of the word. Diop, on the other hand, creates a novel, with fictional characters and a storyline, and does not speak of his own experience as a writer, except perhaps implicitly and metaphorically though the character of Cornelius.

In these texts we see how literature, through its own engagement with language, can become a way to understand and even subvert the work of propaganda. While propaganda claims that there is a single truth, and is coercive, literature constantly points us to the multiple truths, perspectives, and realities that make up our society. Literature, we are again reminded, can be the opposite of propaganda; propaganda sets a fixed meaning while literature, at least the type that we are dealing with here, renders those fixed meanings unstable. And, like Simeon the sage, such literature ultimately places the responsibility and authority on the shoulders of the individual, the reader who has to find his or her own way through the narrative and the language in which it is written or spoken.

NOTES

1. Unless otherwise indicated, all citations from Waberi's text are taken from the Kindle edition of the 2016 English translation by Dominic Thomas and all citations from Diop's novel are taken from the Kindle Edition of the text translated in 2006 by Fiona McLaughlin. In both cases, Kindle Locations replace conventional page numbers in the references indicated.

2. Some of the key ideas and examples used in this chapter will also be discussed in a chapter from a forthcoming edited volume on the aftermath of the genocide (in *In the Shadow of Genocide: Memory, Justice, and Transformation Within Rwanda*, eds. Stephanie Wolfe, Tawia Ansah and Matt Kane).

3. Mamdani (2002) discusses the tension between 'citizen' and 'foreigner' extensively in his text on the genocide.

4. For a discussion on customary obligations and communal work such as bush clearing and 'coerced labour' in the Rwandan community, see Mahmood Mamdani (2002: 194).

5. Established in 1990, *Kangura* was published in French and Kinyarwanda, and promoted ethnic hatred.

6. 'The Hutu Ten Commandments' was a document that was published in the pro-Hutu, anti-Tutsi newspaper *Kangura* in December 1990, almost four years before the genocide. The document was published in Kinyarwandan and has also been translated as 'The Ten Commandments of the Bahutu'.

7. The Bahutu Manifesto, drafted by nine Rwandan Hutu intellectuals in 1957, was a political document that called for Hutu ethnic and political solidarity, as well as the political disfranchisement of the Tutsi people.

8. Read Narelle Fletcher's article on this speech and the role of propaganda (2014).
9. Radio Télévision Libre des Mille Collines, established in 1993.
10. For more on the influence of the culture of submission to authority, read Philip Gourevitch (2000). Sadibou Sow also discusses this phenomenon in detail in his chapter entitled 'Poétique de la soumission à l'autorité' (2009: 99–124).
11. « à la fois, des leçons, des vérités, des réflexions, des pensées, des règles de conduite et de morale » (Ahimana 2009: 302).
12. I only include a few examples, but Emmanuel Ahimana presents a detailed study of the use of proverbs, which he considers to be markers of orality in the three novels that he analyzes, namely that of Lamko, Monénembo, and Diop.
13. I have discussed Tadjo's polysemic title and the motif of the shadow in detail in a previously published chapter (De Beer 2016: 57–9).
14. For more on how this process enables the perpetrator to justify killing another, consult Hemsley (2016).
15. All quotations of Koulsy Lamko's (2002) text are my translations, as no formal translation has been published.
16. « C'est dans l'animal qu'il faut creuser pour déterrer les limites de l'homme. L'homme chenille, lâché sur la toison verte des pâturages et des feuillages, dévore sans retenue jusqu'aux nervures. L'homme criquet effeuille les épineux, [..]. L'homme-boa avale le buffle [...]. L'homme éléphant à la patte-mortier écrase toutes les termitières sur son passage [...] L'homme-hibou a horreur de la lumière » (Lamko 2002: 48–9).
17. « 'Le cafard, ça meurt difficilement. L'on a beau le piétiner, l'écraser du talon, lui répandre toute sa substance blanche et graisseuse par terre, tant qu'il garde ses élytres, il se relève et s'en va, vous échappe. Il a la coque dure. Il faut que vous ayez à faire à des poulets ! Compris ! La stratégie ?

    Facile ! Vous vous levez le matin, vous bouchez hermétiquement toutes les moindres issues de l'*urugo*. [...] Vous appelez les poules et les coqs. Cot cot cot ! La vieille recette de l'homme préhistorique lorsqu'il inventait le théâtre: imiter l'animal pour mieux l'approcher, [...] Voilà une recette pour faire comme il faut, pour aller vite.... (Lamko 2002: 175–8)

18. For a discussion of the psychological effects of group violence on the perpetrator, bystander, and victim, consult Staub (2006).
19. This subtitle was omitted in the English translation.
20. Sélom Gbanou's (2004) article provides a valuable discussion of fragmentation as found in several of Waberi's texts as well as in the work of other African writers of his generation.

21. Zakaria Soumaré provides an in-depth analysis of the use of citations in the epigraph and elsewhere in the text (2013: 128–32).

22. 'Hear this, you elders; give ear, all inhabitants of the land! Has such a thing happened in your days, or in the days of your fathers? Tell your children of it, and let your children tell their children, and their children to another generation' (Joel 1:2–3). This reference to Israel creates a link between the suffering of the Tutsis and the Shoah, a 'metaphor for absolute violence' which is again referred to in Waberi's preface and later on in the text (Semujanga 2008: 100).

23. Caroline Laurent (2015) also provides a meaningful discussion on the potential plurality of art, in terms of both writing and eventually reading, which is facilitated through the act of listening performed by the artist/writer.

24. Originally written in 2009 and entitled *The Sunny Side of Life*.

25. « On peut inventer d'un regard empathique et sensuel tout un monde, et ce à partir d'un vieux livre, une carte postale tout droit sortie de la Quinzaine coloniale des années 1930, d'un chant bédouin, d'une photo sépia et racornie, d'un verset du Coran ou de la Bible, d'une citation tirée du sommeil d'un grand livre de la Weltliteratur dont rêvait Goethe » (Waberi 2003: 936).

26. As only two authors participating in the project chose the genre of travelogue, it is worthwhile to note that several significant parallels can be drawn between their texts (both first published in 2000). Both Waberi and Tadjo subvert the travel diary in generic and metaphoric ways. Both evoke two separate journeys in which they physically participated, and which lends a specific structure to their texts in terms of form as well as content.

27. Years later, after the publication of the travelogues, both Tadjo and Waberi returned to Rwanda and reflected on the changes they saw. In 2010, Tadjo revisits and reflects on 'the changing landscape of memory in Kigali' (Tadjo 2010) and Waberi speaks of Kigali '15 years later' (in a section that was added to the later English translation of his text) and how it has become unrecognizable to him in the nine years since he last visited it (2016: 127–31). Waberi tells of the progress and the striking National Memorial in Kigali but also of the 'silent minority'—the survivors, the 'forgotten people of Bisesero' (ibid.: 182, 184). He speaks of the determination of the post-genocide society to revive 'traditional, often subversive cultural practices' such as black humor in music and theater, the 'ironic use of figures' in the traditional *intore* dance and the 'feudal art of the drum now appropriated by women' (ibid.: 203–4).

28. Tadjo (2002: 96) speaks of a prison visit to *Rilissa*, while Waberi (2016: 554) cites *Rilima*, stating that Tadjo was with him on this visit. It seems probable then that in spite of the different names used, they are both refer-

ring to their visit to Rilima prison, or at least used it as a point of departure for this part of their narrative on prison life after the genocide with Tadjo simply masking the name slightly.

29. « *On* regroupe la population civile dans un bâtiment administratif, une école ou une église à la suite d'une annonce officielle faite directement par le bourgmestre de la commune ou par la radio nationale. Ensuite *on* procède au tri. *On* sépare les voisins de toujours, les ouailles de la paroisse, les amis d'enfance, les habitants de la même parcelle. Les Hutus sont priés de vider les lieux sur-le-champ. *On* lance des grenades en veux-tu en voilà dans la foule agglutinée. *On* mitraille. *On* procède au nettoyage de la maison rwandaise de fond en comble » (Waberi 2004: 24; my emphasis).

30. The use of the pronoun '*on*' rather than '*nous*' lends a more oral feel to the text.

31. « 'On n'était pas là au moment des faits !' On ne mélange pas ses malheurs à ceux d'autrui. Nous ne sommes que de pauvres paysans. On n'a rien vu venir. Rien entendu […] On n'a rien vu venir. On n'a rien pu faire. On ne voulait pas mourir avec eux, non. On ne peut plus rien pour les morts » (Waberi 2004: 34).

32. This notion of collective responsibility is also foregrounded in Tadjo's text. She cites a report in which a participant declares that 'No person killed another person single-handed' (Tadjo 2002: 84).

33. Co-founder of the hate radio station, Radio Télévision Libre des Mille Collines (RTLM), which broadcast anti-Tutsi propaganda and information that helped coordinate the killings.

34. Mugesera is considered to be one of the senior politicians responsible for planning the genocide. On 22 November 1992, he gave a speech in which he threatened that the Tutsi would be forcefully returned to Ethiopia which, according to Hutu propaganda, is the country of origin of the Tutsi.

35. The RTLM frequently played songs like Bikindi's 'Father of the Cultivators'.

36. « Ce chapitre montre que le pouvoir du langage est relégué au Mal, tandis que pour les victimes, il ne le leur reste plus que confusion et détresse » (Small 2005: 126).

37. For a discussion on the various narratives and counter-narratives that exist with regard to Rwanda's history, see Harrow (2005). Semujanga (2005) also provides a helpful description of these myths.

38. Alexandre Dauge-Roth points out that is precisely this demeaning metaphor which Lamko engages with in his novel by symbolically negating it through the resurrection of Mukandori in the form of a Butterfly (2010: 136).

39. Waberi's original text reads: « La trop usitée haine ethnique entre Tutsis et Hutus n'existait pour ainsi dire pas avant 1959, et jamais de manière récur-

rente dans l'histoire de la contrée. Pourtant, l'histoire de ce peuple a été touchée en son nerf sensitif quelques décennies auparavant, lorsque les missionnaires ont réussi à pervertir irrémédiablement la pensée religieuse ancestrale et l'équilibre des pouvoirs temporels et éternels » (Waberi 2004: 77).

40. MINUAR stands for: *Mission des Nations Unies pour l'assistance au Rwanda*. It refers to the The United Nations Assistance Mission for Rwanda (UNAMIR) which was established by the United Nations Security Council Resolution 872 on 5 October 1993.

41. It is not only in Waberi's text that the figure of the dog is present; the whole project is permeated with real dogs, as well as 'rhetorical' and 'symbolic' dogs (Delas 2002: 48). Daniel Delas provides an in-depth description of the various ways in which the authors deal with this motif (2002).

42. « Voilà, mon but en écrivant [*Murambi*], c'était d'amener chaque lecteur à se mettre à la place des victimes, au lieu de penser que tout cela était trop horrible pour être réel ou trop lointain pour le concerner. J'ai pensé que le dépouillement des personnages allait leur donner de la force. J'ai constamment pensé aux jeunes de tous les pays en écrivant ce livre. C'est d'ailleurs une des raisons pour lesquelles il est, de tous mes romans, le plus facile à lire » (Diop 2006a).

> J'ai écrit ce livre dans un rythme assez rapide contrairement à ma manière d'écrire jusqu'à présent où je prenais mon temps. Là, j'ai essayé d'aller vraiment à l'essentiel, d'être efficace. Je voulais qu'un jeune homme de vingt ans, qui n'a pas beaucoup l'habitude de lire et qui ne s'intéresse pas beaucoup aux massacres à travers le monde, ait le courage de lire ce livre jusqu'au bout et qu'un jour je puisse discuter avec lui ou avec les autres générations. (Brezault 2002)

43. Catherine Kroll provides an analysis of Diop's novel in terms of the uses of fiction, in demonstrating the interconnectedness between the different role players and in the questioning of accepted binaries. She also looks at his exposure of the role of propaganda and rationalization of actions. Finally, she shows how, through literature, he examines the many fictions that are created around Rwanda's history, both from inside and outside its borders, and the complexity and at times multiple and fluid identities of the various characters he creates.

44. Arnould-Bloomfield demonstrates how Diop uses language, not merely to reflect, but to concretely and actively express and fight against the violence experienced. This process involves more than moving from symbolic to literal/realistic writing. It makes of the text an interactive space in which a 'verbal encounter between victims and writer (and writer and readers)' is facilitated and enacted (2010: 509). Diop's novel, when viewed in this way,

has 'performative' value, because in its staging of these interactions, 'acting and speaking' are foregrounded rather than mere 'seeing' (ibid.: 510).

45. « La narration à la première personne, authentifiée par le je qui raconte, semble constituer le témoin et l'existence même de l'événement raconté comme témoignage. Car depuis la fin de la guerre mondiale [...] le récit du témoin est devenu consubstantiel à la survie même de la victime de massacres. L'écriture façonne une zone de partage de l'événement dans la mesure où elle se fond sur l'idée selon laquelle celui qui se propose comme récepteur d'un récit, crée la possibilité du témoignage, et réinvente de fait, un lien social » (Semujanga 2008: 127–8).

46. « Et cette résurrection des vivants passe au moins par la reconnaissance par le monde. Par vous, par moi. Le fait que le monde ait découvert et accepté l'Holocauste a beaucoup fait pour aider les Juifs dans leur travail de deuil » (Diop, in Brezault 2002).

47. Semujanga (2008: 132) suggests that the fragmentary and incomplete nature of these stories corresponds to the disrupted society that Diop is attempting to write about.

48. Koulsy Lamko's term, as discussed in Chap. 2.

49. This theme is also present in the other texts: Koulsy Lamko, for example, scathingly engages with the role of the Catholic Church as a key body of authority that had a huge societal impact on the mass participation.

50. Hitchcott suggests that although Diop has long been known for his outspoken criticism of President Mitterrand and France's role in the genocide, his fictional novel 'with a wider readership' would probably end up more effectively 'drawing attention to France's guilt' (Hitchcott 2009: 56).

51. Also see Small (2005: 122–3).

52. The term 'old man' is used a great number of times in Diop's novel and refers to three different people, all three of whom represent different figures of authority in Diop's novel. One is Faustin Gasana's authoritarian, extremist father; the second is Simeon, the wise uncle; and the third is President Mitterrand.

REFERENCES

Ahimana, Emmanuel. 2009. Les violences extrêmes dans le roman négro-africain francophone: le cas du Rwanda: étude de langue et de style. PhD dissertation, University of Bordeaux 3.

Arnould-Bloomfield, Elisabeth. 2010. Commitment and Genocide Literature: Boubacar Diop's *Murambi, The Book of Bones. Contemporary French and Francophone Studies* 14 (5): 505–513. https://doi.org/10.1080/1740929 2.2010.525126.

Bagilishya, Deogratias. 2000. Mourning and Recovery from Trauma: In Rwanda, Tears Flow Within. *Transcultural Psychiatry* 37 (3): 337–353.

Bazié, Isaac. 2004. Au seuil du chaos: devoir de mémoire, indicible et piège du devoir dire. *Présence Francophone* 63: 29–45.

Bénard, Marie. 2001. Entretien avec Boubacar Boris Diop. Accessed July 13, 2018. http://aircrigeweb.free.fr/ressources/rwanda/RwandaDiop1.html.

Bhabha, Homi K. 2004. *The Location of Culture*. London: Routledge.

Brezault, Éloïse. 2000. À propos de Moissons de crânes, Textes pour les Rwanda: Entretien d'Eloïse Brezault avec Abdourahman A. Waberi. *Africultures*. Accessed July 13, 2018. http://www.africultures.com/php/index.php?nav=article&no=1711.

———. 2002. A l'occasion de la sortie du dernier livre de B. B. Diop: Murambi, le livre des ossements. Entretien d'Eloise Brezault avec Boubacar Boris Diop. *Africultures*. Accessed July 13, 2018. http://www.africultures.com/php/index.php?nav=article&no=2577.

Coquio, Catherine. 2004. *Rwanda: le réel et les récits*. Littérature et politique, 0985-9632. Paris: Belin.

Dauge-Roth, Alexandre. 2010. *Writing and Filming the Genocide of the Tutsis in Rwanda: Dismembering and Remembering Traumatic History*, After the Empire: The Francophone World and Postcolonial France. Lanham, MD: Lexington Books.

De Beer, Anna-Marie. 2016. Véronique Tadjo and the masks and shadows of Rwanda In Écrire, traduire, peindre - Véronique Tadjo - writing, translating, painting, eds. Sarah Davies Cordova, and Désiré Wa Kabwe-Segatti, 43–63. vol. Les cahiers. Paris: Présence africaine.

Delas, Daniel. 2002. Entre fiction et témoignage: les chiens du génocide rwandais. *Notre librairie: revue des littératures du Sud* 148: 44–50.

Diop, Boubacar Boris. 2000. *Murambi: le livre des ossements*. Paris: Stock.

———. 2003. African Authors in Rwanda: Writing by Duty of Memory. In *Literary Responses to Mass Violence*. Brandeis University: International Center for Ethics, Justice and Public Life, Brandeis University.

———. 2006a. Entretien avec Boubacar Boris Diop par Lanfranco Di Genio. Accessed January 26, 2012. http://www.fieralingue.it/modules.php?name=News&file=article&sid=303 (site discontinued).

———. 2006b. *Murambi: The Book of Bones* (Kindle edition). Translated by Fiona McLaughlin. Bloomington: Indiana University Press.

Djedanoum, Nocky. 2000. Nyamirambo! : recueil de poésies. Bamako, Lille: Le Figuier, Fest'Africa.

Fletcher, Narelle. 2014. Words that Can Kill: The Mugesera Speech and the 1994 Tutsi Genocide in Rwanda. *Portal: Journal of Multidisciplinary International Studies* 11 (1): 1–15. https://doi.org/10.5130/portal.v11i1.3293.

Gbanou, Sélom Komlan. 2004. Le fragmentaire dans le roman francophone africain. *Tangence* 75: 83–105. https://doi.org/10.7202/010785ar.

Germanotta, Maria Angela. 2016. L'écriture de l'inaudible. Les narrations littéraires du génocide au Rwanda, *Interfrancophonies*, Nouvelles formes de l'engagement dans les littératures francophones, ed. Alessandro Crostantini. 70: 73–100. https://doi.org/10.17457/IF7_2016/GER.

Gourevitch, Philip. 2000. *We Wish to Inform You that Tomorrow We Will be Killed with Our Families: Stories from Rwanda*. London: Picador.

Harrow, Kenneth W. 2005. "Ancient tribal warfare": Foundational Fantasies of Ethnicity and History. *Research in African Literatures* 36 (2): 34–45. https://doi.org/10.2979/RAL.2005.36.2.34.

Hemsley, Frances. 2016. Non-mourning and Ecocritical Ethics in Véronique Tadjo's *The Shadow of Imana: Travels in the Heart of Rwanda*. *Journal of Commonwealth Literature* 51 (2): 226–239. https://doi.org/10.1177/0021989415628029.

Hitchcott, Nicki. 2009. Writing on Bones: Commemorating Genocide in Boubacar Boris Diop's *Murambi*. *Research in African Literatures* 40 (3): 48–61. https://doi.org/10.2979/RAL.2009.40.3.48.

———. 2015. *Rwanda Genocide Stories: Fiction after 1994*. Liverpool: Liverpool University Press.

Hodgkin, Marian, and Poppy Sebag Montefiore. 2005. The Rwanda Forum 2004. *History Workshop Journal* 60 (1): 1–24.

Ilboudo, Monique. 2000. *Murekatete: Roman*. Bamako: Le Figuier; Lille: Fest'Africa.

Jessee, Erin. 2017. The Danger of a Single Story: Iconic Stories in the Aftermath of the 1994 Rwandan Genocide. *Memory Studies* 10 (2): 144–163. https://doi.org/10.1177/1750698016673236.

Krog, Antjie. 2008. "This thing called reconciliation" … Forgiveness as Part of an Interconnectedness-Towards-Wholeness. *South African Journal of Philosophy* 27 (4): 353–366. https://doi.org/10.4314/sajpem.v27i4.31524.

Kroll, Catherine. 2007. Rwanda's Speaking Subjects: The Inescapable Affiliations of Boubacar Boris Diop's *Murambi*. *Third World Quarterly* 28 (3): 655–663. https://doi.org/10.1080/01436590701193072.

Lamko, Koulsy. 2002. *La phalène des collines*. Paris: Le Serpent à Plumes.

Laurent, Caroline D. 2015. Le Génocide rwandais: L'Écrivain-témoin indirect comme « donneur d'échos » dans Moisson de crânes de Waberi. *Nouvelles Études Francophones* 30 (1): 79–90. https://doi.org/10.1353/nef.2015.0035.

Mamdani, Mahmood. 2002. *When Victims Become Killers: Colonialism, Nativism and the Genocide in Rwanda*. Princeton: Princeton University Press.

Metz, Thaddeus. 2011. Ubuntu as a Moral Theory and Human Rights in South Africa. *African Human Rights Law Journal* 11 (2): 532–559.

Monénembo, Tierno. 2004. *The Oldest Orphan*. Translated by Monique Fleury Nagem. Lincoln: University of Nebraska Press.

Mongo-Mboussa, Boniface. 2000. *Moisson de crânes, textes pour la Rwanda* d'Abdourahman A. Waberi. *Africultures.* Accessed July 13, 2018. http://africultures.com/moisson-de-cranes-textes-pour-la-rwanda-1712/.

Montesano, Michael C. 2015. Preemptive Testimony: Literature as Witness to Genocide in Rwanda. *African Conflict & Peacebuilding Review* 5 (1): 88–105. https://doi.org/10.2979/africonfpeacrevi.5.1.88.

Orlando, Valérie K. 2016. The Transnational Turn in African Literature of French Expression: Imagining Other Utopic Spaces in the Globalized Age. *Humanities* 5 (30): 1–12.

Ricœur, Paul. 1983. *Temps et récit.* L'Ordre philosophique. Paris: Seuil.

Semujanga, Josias. 2005. Rwanda: Des récits coloniaux aux mots du génocide. In *Dix ans après: réflexions sur le génocide rwandais,* ed. Rangira Béatrice Gallimore and Chantal Kalisa, 31–59. Paris: Harmattan.

———. 2008. *Le génocide, sujet de fiction?: Analyse des récits du massacre des Tutsi dans la littérature africaine.* Quebec: Nota bene.

———. 2009. Le génocide des Tutsi dans la fiction narrative. *French Cultural Studies* 20 (2): 111–132. https://doi.org/10.1177/0957155809102628.

Small, Audrey. 2005. Le projet « Rwanda: écrire par devoir de mémoire »: fiction et génocide dans trois textes. In *Dix ans après: réflexions sur le génocide rwandais,* ed. Rangira Béatrice Gallimore and Chantal Kalisa, 121–141. Paris: Harmattan.

Soumaré, Zakaria. 2013. *Le génocide rwandais dans la littérature africaine francophone.* Paris: Harmattan.

Sow, Sadibou. 2009. *Esthétique de l'horreur: le génocide rwandais dans la littérature africaine.* Houston: Rice University.

Staub, Ervin. 2006. Reconciliation after Genocide, Mass Killing, or Intractable Conflict: Understanding the Roots of Violence, Psychological Recovery, and Steps Toward a General Theory. *Political Psychology* 27 (6): 867–894. https://doi.org/10.1111/j.1467-9221.2006.00541.x.

Tadjo, Véronique. 2002. *The Shadow of Imana: Travels in the Heart of Rwanda.* Translated by Véronique Wakerley. Oxford: Heinemann.

———. 2010. Genocide: The Changing Landscape of Memory in Kigali. *African Identities* 8 (4): 379–388. https://doi.org/10.1080/14725843.2010.513252.

Visser, Irene. 2015. Decolonizing Trauma Theory: Retrospect and Prospects. *Humanities* 4 (2): 250–265. https://doi.org/10.3390/h4020250.

Waberi, Abdourahman A. 2003. Comment j'ai ecrit mes livres (et autres considerations sommaires). *Modern Language Notes* 118 (4): 933–938. https://doi.org/10.1353/mln.2003.0083.

———. 2004. *Moisson de crânes: textes pour le Rwanda.* Paris: Serpent à plumes.

———. 2016. *Harvest of Skulls* (Kindle edition). Translated by Dominic Thomas. Bloomington: Indiana University Press.

CHAPTER 5

Living in Shadows: Monique Ilboudo and Tierno Monénembo

The portrayal of the aftermath of genocide is the perspective that I have adopted for this chapter, in which I analyze the novels *Murekatete* by Monique Ilboudo (2000)[1] and *L'aîné des orphelins* (2000) by Tierno Monénembo (translated in 2004 as *The Oldest Orphan*). Both create protagonists who embody post-genocide realities and are marked by the traces of traumatic memory. I explore in greater depth the role of the authors in the presence of trauma, not only as writers but as confirming intellectual witnesses and appropriate listeners in the process of transforming traumatic memory into narrative memory (or stories).

As we have seen in the previous chapter, effectively depicting the origin and causes of the genocide was a major concern for the authors of the commemorative project. Another key refrain that characterizes their work is the difficult cohabitation that is the aftermath of genocide. Rwanda today is a society inhabited by orphans, widows, prisoners, perpetrators, and returnees, all living in close proximity in a country characterized by sites of violence, haunting memories, daily fears, and recurring nightmares. It is clear that writing what Dominick LaCapra would call a 'redemptive narrative' with a comforting ending (2001: 98–9, 154) is not particularly appropriate for representing this type of daily struggle.

In Ilboudo's text, the act of rape is a pivotal moment, and in Monénembo's text, the focus is on the plight of the orphans left behind by the genocide. Before analyzing these two texts in detail, I first present

© The Author(s) 2020   159
A.-M. de Beer, *Sharing the Burden of Stories from the Tutsi Genocide*, Palgrave Studies in Cultural Heritage and Conflict,
https://doi.org/10.1007/978-3-030-42093-2_5

a general discussion on the aftermath of the genocide, with a specific focus on survivor guilt and genocide rape.

LIMBO, RAPE, AND SURVIVAL

Those who have been 'lucky' enough to survive a genocide are often tormented by guilt and questions typical of what has been referred to as survivor guilt. They may feel guilty for trying to move on with their lives, or for thinking less frequently of those they have lost, or even for failing to embrace life fully (McNee 2004: 3). This state of existence is a form of limbo in which the survivor is 'caught between worlds; unable to return fully to the world of the living because she/he has not been able to mourn those lost to the genocide. Caught in a half-life that cannot be called death, the survivor tries to straddle both worlds' (ibid.).

Furthermore, because we would rather forget than constantly be reminded of humankind's atrocities, society often places the survivor in an unbearable position. They are expected to carry a 'double burden'—that of the haunting memories as well as that of bearing testimony: 'The victim must relive the events of his/her torture, and face the disbelieving faces of those who do not want to believe, or the taunts of those who wish to scapegoat him/her and escape condemnation' (ibid.: 5).

Murekatete, the narrator in Ilboudo's text, clearly suffers from survivor guilt. Through juxtaposing various terms associated with life and death (*vie, vivre, vivant, mort,* and *mourir*), the author evokes the impasse, the limbo in which she lives, constantly vacillating between these two realities: 'I never understood why I had escaped. Why me? Why not the others? Why not my children, two little innocent ones so full of *life*? Why not my mother, my sisters, my father, all the others? They all deserve to *live*. They are all *dead*. I am *alive*. Yet, I deserved to *die*' (Ilboudo 2000: 22; my translation, my emphasis).[2]

Survivor and author, Esther Mujawayo, says that her only way of taking revenge on her tormentors is to embrace life, to choose to be '*vivante-vivante*' (fully alive) rather than to be a mere '*survivante*' (survivor) (Mujawayo and Belhaddad 2004: 5). For various reasons, Mujawayo seems to have been able to make this choice, but there are many for whom this does not seem possible. They realize that having survived is only a first step. What now seems to be required of them—in a world where they are constantly haunted by unthinkable memories, recurring nightmares, hatred, regret, suicidal thoughts, physical pain, and other difficulties—is, like Mujawayo, to move on from being 'survivors', to *choose* to stay alive, and possibly *embrace* life again. However, even before the genocide, they had been led to believe that they had no right to be alive:

> Worn down by decades of bullying, humiliations and terror, the Tutsi people, riddled with guilt and complexes, had for the most part resigned themselves. These members accepted their condition as subhuman, second rate citizens. Most of us barely counted ourselves lucky that we had been allowed at least to live. (Kayimahe 2001: 44; my translation)[3]

Philip Gourevitch cites a survivor who describes having to face this psychological challenge:

> I had accepted death. At a certain moment this happens. [...] Death was more or less normal, a resignation. [...] When you are that resigned and oppressed, you're already dead. [...] These victims of genocide had been psychologically prepared to expect death just for being a Tutsi. They were being killed for so long that they were already dead. (2000, 22–3)

The project contains an interminable list of such victim-survivors, who are caught between life and death, the 'living dead'[4] who walk around with a destructive burden of guilt. This is an issue clearly portrayed in Diop's novel: 'we suffer a lot, even if we don't show it. Some feel guilty for not having been killed. They wonder what fault they committed to still be alive' (Diop 2006: 1359–60). Jessica asserts that this emotional destruction is in fact part of what the perpetrators had envisaged: 'Their new credo seems to be reduced to this: we can't eliminate all of them, but the survivors can at least be dead with sorrow for the rest of their lives' (ibid.: 1098–9).

Survivors are tormented by their memories in the dead of the night, while the rest of the world sleeps:

> Cornelius knew from experience that it was the most difficult time of day for the Murambi townspeople, the moment when bitter memories resurfaced. [...] A mere suggestion was enough to bring the torment back to life: the color or cut of a dress, a melody, or the sound of a voice. (Diop 2006: 1662–5)

In conversation with Cornelius, Gérard poignantly and accusingly describes the difference between those who have been physically marked by the genocide and those such as Cornelius, who have escaped this ordeal:

'You were making big gestures, your entire body was getting away from you, while we, because of circumstances, we've learned to draw in our bodies, we've received so many blows, right?' (ibid.: 1443–4). When Cornelius meets a young woman dressed in black at Murambi, he wonders whether she is dead or alive, as sometimes those who had survived seemed less alive than those who had died: 'She herself, was she dead or alive? [...] after such an ordeal, there was a little bit of death in everyone. Maybe there was less life left in the veins of that unknown woman than among the remains of Murambi' (2006: 1752–6).

Diop also narrates the story of a young girl, raped by a priest, for whom death has become such a reality that she integrates it as part of her name and identity; dying is what she has become:

> 'What's your name?' 'I have no name. *I'm the one who's going to die.*' 'But you're telling me intimate details, it's not worth going into every detail.' 'Oh yes it is!' she said vehemently. 'Oh yes it is! I don't want to die with that secret.' 'People usually say, "I don't want to live with that secret," I thought again'. (Diop 2006: 937–9, my emphasis)

Waberi notes that, for the survivors, 'life as it was once has vanished' and their joy of living is 'stillborn' (2016: 448). He demonstrates how even dawn, normally associated with new beginnings and life, brings nothing but 'ashes' to those families who have experienced genocide: 'All that remains of these exterminated families are hints of a skeleton in what is left of a peasant dress, a jaw or a fragment of a skull—by no means enough to ignite the spark that lies in each of us. Only the stench of gangrenous death lingers. Too weak to face the ashes at dawn' (ibid.: 444–7).[5]

Anastasie, a character in Tadjo's text, experiences a similar kind of living death. When her brother rapes her, she experiences what Tadjo calls 'her first death':

> She was ashamed. She felt dirty, repulsive. She no longer existed. [...]
> Her mind detached itself from her body, floated in the room and hit the ceiling. That was her first death. [...]
> Officially she died several years later [...]. (2002: 66–7)

Épiphanie, the survivor in Lamko's novel, leads a different type of living death, characterized by reckless and despondent behavior. The only life that seems possible to her now is one which does not conform and which follows neither faith nor law, a way of coping which Lamko describes as a 'philosophy of survival' (2002: 69). Her self-destructive behavior brings to mind other characters from the texts produced for the project: Venant, a character in Ilboudo's novel, who destroys his own marriage after experiencing the genocide sites, and Faustin, Tierno Monénembo's teenage survivor, the anti-hero who mocks all convention and who, when the judge asks him what it means to live, answers flippantly: 'Eating a good dish of *umushagoro*, getting drunk when you please, and screwing the woman you love without the law meddling' (Monénembo 2004: 84).

In the aftermath of genocide, it is not only the victims who are accompanied by the specter of death; those who had participated or are accused of participating in the killings, as well as their families, also constantly face it. Diop suggests that the souls of many of the ordinary citizens who had been forced to participate in the killings were destroyed in the process:

> Not having succeeded in getting rid of all the Tutsis, now they're saying that every Hutu must kill. It's a second genocide, through the destruction of souls this time. Lots of ordinary citizens went to it joyfully. It makes for a more lively and colorful infamy, but not more tolerable. And it's not easy for everyone. You should see these decent family men at work. They were not at all prepared for what was expected of them. If they don't yell out they'll never succeed. (2006: 1099–101)

The suffering of those who were not perpetrators but who were intimately connected to them, and who now live in a state of perpetual mourning, such as Isaro or Consolate, characters in Tadjo's text, is another theme addressed by the project. Years after the genocide, Isaro discovers the body of her husband. They had tried to 'resume a normal life' after the genocide, but his unemployment and the constant accusations regarding his role in the genocide led him to take his own life, leaving Isaro with questions, doubts about his innocence, and grief. Her life is marked by the expectation that he will somehow return to her (Tadjo 2002: 56).

Consolate, who has lost her father and whose mother and brothers are in prison (are they *génocidaires?*), is described as a graceful woman with a sweet face, but Tadjo notes that she has given up on embracing life in any type of meaningful manner:

> For her the country is an interminable exile. She is here, but she has left long ago [...]. She does not recognise the land which has betrayed her and which

continues to reject her, for she can find nothing to hang on to any more. She has resumed her everyday activities, making those daily gestures of a life which is beginning again but which no longer has any savour. You feel that she is alone and that she will remain alone for a long, long time. [....] So Consolate has mourned the future. The future no longer exists for her. Her days are nothing but a long, anguished wait, a desire to leave for another place. The world stretches beyond the other side of those hills, far from death, far from this prison, from her captive memory, fixed, frozen in time. (ibid.: 28–9)

Thus, this state of living death, or mere physical survival, comes in many forms and these are presented to us through the people we meet in the texts. Many of them seem incapable of facing or planning for the future: 'As for me, the future consists of one day just following another. How can you envisage the future here? What future? Tomorrow seems a long way off to me. Plan what?' (Tadjo 2002: 110).

Among the voices who carry the double burden of both haunting memories and testimony is that of the raped woman, a voice that has largely remained silent, for various reasons.[6] As Eleni Coundouriotis notes, 'you only have your word', for physical wounds related to sexual violence eventually heal and often the only proof that a rape victim has is their testimony (2013: 365).

Karen Brounéus has underlined the importance of questioning assumptions about the possible healing ability of 'truth-telling' about sexual violence in public contexts such as truth commissions (2008: 55). She evokes the probability that such forms of witnessing will retraumatize victims and open them up to intimidation, harassment, increased vulnerability, isolation, and insecurity. She also acknowledges, however, that although public hearings may not be the ideal place for these women's voices to be heard, the fact remains that their stories must somehow be told. It is with this in mind that I look in this section at the rape narratives that are presented to us through the project and the concerns they raise about the consequences of sexual violence in post-genocide society.[7]

In this particular society, gender classification 'makes certain Rwandan women invisible' and they are particularly vulnerable to stigmatization and marginalization (Burnet 2012: 129–30). As virginity was traditionally seen to be one of the main requirements for a bride to be considered desirable in Rwanda, unmarried women who were raped needed to remain silent about this in order to at least maintain the 'public illusion of virginity' (ibid.: 135). In many cases, however, pregnancies and HIV made it impossible to keep the experience secret (ibid.). Indeed, empirical studies show that genocide rape survivors suffer from unwanted pregnancies, sexually transmitted infections, sleeping and mental disorders, HIV infection, and suicidal behavior as well as being ostracized from their families (Brounéus 2008: 66; Zraly and Nyirazinyoye 2010: 1657). Investigators have identified psychological and physical symptoms endemic to rape survivors, such as tremendous fatigue, constant backache and headaches, memory loss, incessant anguish, hallucinations, and, for a large number of survivors, the impression of being insane (Mujawayo and Belhaddad 2004: 203, 207). During a study performed by an association for women in Rwanda focusing on the taboo topic of rape, it was found that 80 percent of female survivors had been raped and more than half of them infected with human immunodeficiency virus (HIV)/acquired immunodeficiency syndrome (AIDS) (ibid.: 196–7). Women were often gang-raped or raped multiple times. Although a word for rape had allegedly not existed in this society before the genocide, the term '*kubohoza*', meaning 'to help liberate' through violence, became a common word for it, because of its use by perpetrators: 'We have liberated those Tutsi women, we have liberated those arrogant ones ...' (ibid.: 196).[8] Burnet explains that this term was used as a 'euphemism for rape' and implied liberating Tutsi women 'from their Tutsiness' (2012: 63). The term 'evolved' and was used for various purposes during different times in history and also applied to the forcible taking (confiscating) of land and other resources, reinforcing the notion that women were seen as property (Temple-Raston 2005: 154).

Sexual violence has long been acknowledged as one of the weapons of the genocide, 'systematically used by Hutu extremists towards Tutsi women and girls as a method of war, not only to inflict pain and humiliation but also to spread HIV' (Brounéus 2008: 55). In spite of this, Diop's novel reminds us how radical the use of rape was in a society where sexual relationships are regulated by certain taboos:

> She just alludes to the stories of rape. It's true that they're talking a lot about it. The youngest ones are very excited by the idea that they'll be able to have sex with young women any time they want, just like that. They've always been told that the path to intimacy with a woman is long, complex, and often discouraging. They're discovering with pleasure that times can change very quickly. (2006: 300–2)

Mujawayo points out that, although being raped had often paradoxically saved these women from being killed, they emerged from the horrors of the experience reluctantly, because they now had to live through a 'hell worse than death' (Mujawayo and Belhaddad 2004: 197). They had been left alive by the perpetrators 'so that there would be no point in surviving', because they would be living a 'continual death' (ibid.). In her narrative, Mujawayo's description of this 'continual death' encompasses both its psychological and physical manifestations.

The experience of being raped is often portrayed as a form of dying. Severe trauma such as rape can be described as a type of 'death' experience, not in the sense of physical death, but of a 'lived experience' of 'dying permeating life' (Tidd 2005: 408). This takes on various guises: one of its manifestations is the fracturing or multiplication of the self, during which a victim 'creates a second "self" due to conflict in the "original self"' (Tidd 2005: 408, 412).

What is equally of interest is the reaction of rape victims to this experience and the elements that have the potential to enable them to demonstrate resilience and agency in its aftermath.[9] During an ethnographical study conducted among survivors of genocide rape in southern Rwanda, researchers established that resilience among survivors was often determined by certain sociocultural elements and processes. It was shaped by 'the cultural-linguistic specific concepts of *kwihangana* (withstanding), *kwongera kubaho* (living again), and *gukomeza ubuzima* (continuing life/health)' (Zraly and Nyirazinyoye 2010: 1656). *Kwihangana* is defined as 'an intrapsychic creative process of drawing strength from within the self in order to withstand suffering'; *kwongera kubaho* refers to 'the re-establishment of the fundamental existential conditions of being; in other words, that living life is still possible after many terrorizing experiences of rape and torture'; *gukomeza ubuzima* denotes a 'sense of moving forward in life and living on despite the ongoing struggles of accepting myriad problems and fighting for survival' (ibid.: 1662).

The researchers drew up a list of resilience processes they identified among these women. From these, the following were found among 90 percent of the resilience narratives they listened to: being with, caring, connecting, imparting or receiving advice, expressing problems, fortifying positive affect, incorporation, meaning making, acknowledging oneself as a human being, sharing the same problem, and thought control (ibid.: 1661). These suggested an 'orientation to the world that involved being socially connected to like others in order to make meaning, establish normalcy, and endure suffering in daily life', reflecting an attitude to life that certainly echoes the sense of community that is often associated with traditional African communitarian worldviews (ibid.: 1662). Indeed, their investigations suggest that establishing situations in which sexual violence survivors could 'safely socially connect around their shared experiences of rape' might have contributed to increasing their resiliency (ibid.: 1656). The social and community aspect becomes especially important in the context of mass rape, as this destroys and damages 'multiple aspects of human life including social bonds [and] cultural practices' (Robben and Suarez-Orozco, 2000 quoted in Zraly and Nyirazinyoye 2010: 1656).

When reading narratives of genocide rape, it is first of all helpful to establish how the authors choose to represent both the victim and the perpetrator, and secondly to ascertain whether resilience, as described above, is evident in the lives of the victims, enabling them (or not) to embrace life instead of merely surviving their trauma. What many of these narratives have in common is their concern with quality of life after the genocide. Mujawayo explains that the true violence of genocide is 'not only the violence of death or physical torture', but the destructive violence that is internalized, and that 'makes of you what others want you to be: nothing, even less than nothing. Even while alive, you cease to exist' (Mujawayo and Belhaddad 2004: 152). It is this tension between survival, obliteration, and embracing life that provides a helpful focus in the rape accounts offered by these texts.

Rape is, in fact, a recurring element in survivor testimonies: either experiencing it or witnessing it. It is therefore no wonder that it is also a ubiquitous presence in the project. Although rape is ostensibly not one of the main themes in Diop's novel, he in fact makes various allusions to it—some detailed, others merely mentioning incidents. We learn, for example, that Siméon's wife was raped and we read Jessica's description of the rape of a young Tutsi girl by a priest (Diop 2006: 910–73).[10] She is filled with beauty and light and reminds Jessica of the sun, but it is precisely this light and charm that represents her biggest danger:

> 'I'm too beautiful to survive. I'm as beautiful as the sun, and like the sun there's nowhere for me to hide. They won't believe their eyes when they see me walking peacefully down the street.' Yes, that young woman had an almost supernatural beauty. It took away any chance she had of escaping the killers. They were going to rape her a thousand times before they killed her. She knew it, and she was going out of her mind. (ibid.: 913–7)

Her narrative in fact speaks of the physical traits and beauty that were ste-reotypically attributed to Tutsi women and of how the process of raping them was related to the implied power of desecrating the beauty that they were renowned for. It also depicts the type of unbearable choices that Tutsi women were forced to make. In order to save herself from being handed over to the Interahamwe, who would gang rape her; 'Twenty or thirty guys on a bench. Some of them old enough to know better', she gives in to the perverse rape of a depraved priest, who bursts into tears and pretends that he loves her (ibid.: 926).

In another narrative of a militia raping a woman at Murambi, rather than focusing on the reaction of the victim, Diop insists on showing the inhuman brutality of the man who commits this act and thus transgresses the taboos of society. His graphic description illustrates his protagonist's undertaking to 'tirelessly recount the horror' with 'words covered with blood and shit' (ibid.: 1738–9). It is Gérard, the survivor who witnessed the event, who gives this description:

> I saw an Interahamwe rape a young woman under a tree. His boss came by and shouted at him: 'Hey, Simba, everywhere we go it's always the same story, first the women, the women, the women! Hurry up and finish your push-ups, we promised Papa we'd do a good job!' The boss took a couple of steps, then, changing his mind, came back to crush the young woman's head with a big stone, and in a single blow there was just this red and white pulp in place of the skull. That didn't stop the Interahamwe who kept work-ing away at the twitching body. His eyes were popping out of his head, raised upwards, I think he was even more excited than before. (ibid.: 1693–7)

As if Gérard (and Diop) fears that a listener/reader might prefer to tune out or gloss over such a graphic description, thinking that it might be exaggerated or overdramatized, he desperately adds: 'I saw that with my own eyes. Do you believe me, Cornelius? It's important that you believe me. I'm not making it up, for once that's not necessary' (ibid.: 1697–8). This plea engages with the difficulty that many rape victims encounter in trying to prove their story or making others believe and acknowledge what they have gone through.

Vénuste Kayimahe's rape narrative of the daughter of a dear friend is particularly striking; in contrast to the rest of his testimony, the narration of this family's fate is one of the few instances where trauma becomes evi-dent through textual signs. When telling of their humiliation, the narrator zooms in and switches to the present tense, lending a surreal sense of being present to the narrative. This is even more interesting because Kayimahe was not there himself, he had been told this by someone else.

The family is found to be hiding in the CECFR (the former Franco-Rwandan Cultural Center in Kigali, 'Centre D'Echanges Culturel Franco-Rwandais) and are chased out and taken to the basement of a house opposite the center, where they are tortured by *génocidaires* and their daughter raped after being crucified against a wall:

> Over there, the torture session continues, more mechanical, more methodi-cal. First, all of them are asked to lean against the wall, head down and feet in the air, and to remain in this uncomfortable and unseemly position until given permission to rest. […] Everybody is bleeding, nobody is crying any-more and the torturers themselves seem to be tiring. This is when the most terrible thing happens.
>
> Suddenly catching sight of one of the young girls, the filthy animals decide to rape her. […] But she carries on struggling, crying, refusing and pushing away these hideous bodies which are crowding up against her […]
>
> The rest of the family became quiet. In the face of the horror, the unspeakable, they modestly looked away. (ibid.: 203–4)[11]

As is shown here, the narration then suddenly retreats back to the more distant past tense when he speaks of the families shocked silence and averted gaze.

Those who visited Nyamata church were confronted with the remains of Theresa Mukandori.[12] The visual shock of this image of a woman, cru-elly tied up, raped, and impaled, ostensibly deeply troubled and enraged the project participants, because Mukandori is referenced in most of the texts. Diop notes that, although they changed many of the names of the people whose stories they were writing about, not one of the authors wanted to change her name; they all refer to her as Mukandori or Mukandoli (because in Kinyarwanda the letters l and r are equivalent) (Bénard 2001).[13]

Due to the enormity of the symbolic transgression that she represents, she becomes a shared intertextual reference to inhumanity. Each author inserts this emblematic figure into his or her text in a unique, creative way, whether through graphical images, symbolic evocations, or hints at that which is being left unsaid. Some imagine her life before the genocide, the incident of her rape, and death. Some describe the effect that this image has on them (or on their protagonists). To others she serves as metaphoric inspiration for a character in their texts and a way of embodying the question of God's apparent absence during the genocide. Some refer to her as a way of commenting on the ongoing conflict related to the choice of burying the bodies or exposing them as an example for all to see. Mukandori's recurring appearance in the texts produced for the project demonstrates the enormous impact of such a collaborative approach (Bénard 2001)[14] and it is through a figure such as this that we can, in fact, most clearly see the rich possibilities offered to us by the imaginative and polyphonic narrative that the project has created.

Lamko's description of the rape of his narrator, the Tutsi Queen whose character is inspired by Mukandori's story, is detailed, angry, and extremely graphic: 'Furious, he runs dragging along the enormous cross in solid ebony, reserved for Easter High Mass [...]. He throws himself on me with the crucifix, violently spreads my limp legs, and shoves it hard into my vagina, [...]' (2002: 46, 109).[15] As we have already seen, Lamko transforms this character into a mythical and highly symbolic figure which allows him to demonstrate the destructive role of the Catholic Church (Kalisa 2005: 275).

Another significant aspect of Lamko's representation is that he insists on giving ownership of the narrative back to the victim, the spirit of the raped woman who has returned in the form of a butterfly (2002: 31). This is an interesting notion when taking into account the importance of verbalizing trauma, and Lamko's work opens up new possibilities by giving this type of agency to a deceased person. Alexandre Dauge-Roth interprets this 'posthumous ability' of the victim to narrate her own death, conferred on her by Lamko, as a symbolic gesture through which his writing 'emancipates' her memory from the 'horrific sexual and ideological violence' to which she has been subjected, while freeing herself from the position of passive victim (2010: 140-1).

When Tadjo visits Nyamata, she is met with the remains of this woman whose 'wrists are bound, and tied to her ankles'. Tadjo describes her as an 'enormous fossilized foetus' with 'legs spread apart', who has been displayed on a 'dirty blanket' together with other skulls and bones (2002: 11). The style chosen by the author to speak of her is stripped and austere, providing us only with the most essential information, and it is the unsaid that is probably the most powerful part of her description: 'She has been raped. A pickaxe has been forced into her vagina. She died from a machete blow to the nape of her neck. You can see the groove left by the impact' (ibid.: 11).[16] The image of a fetus with legs spread apart is powerful,

linking the strongest possible image of innocence to that of extreme violation and desecration. Furthermore, it speaks not only of the incongruity
and sacrilege of the acts of genocide but also of the cultural Rwandan
concept of death as a type of rebirth.

Ilboudo's representation of Mukandori reminds us that this author is
known for her relentless battle for women's rights. She insists on the victim's femininity, destroyed by the act of rape, as well as on the bonds of
solidarity and sisterhood among women:

> I came face to face with Mukandori, my beloved sister. Bound, raped, mur-
> dered. Mukandori, brought out from the cesspit, frozen in a posture of
> prayer, of futile supplication. Four years after her death, I heard her cries of
> distress, her groans. 'Have mercy!' she begged. How could they? This stake
> in her aching womanhood, in her tarnished womanhood! How could they
> dare? I saw her exposed, her modesty desecrated. (Ilboudo 2000: 65; my
> translation)[17]

By emphasizing her posture as being 'frozen' in prayer, she evokes the
'absence' of Imana in the face of a victim whose last act seems to have been
that of praying.

Diop's text also picks up on this theme. Mukandori is introduced as
Jessica's naive and trusting friend who believes that no harm will come to
them. Before the genocide, Theresa (Mukandori) had confidently declared
to Jessie that the perpetrators will 'never be able to do anything, knowing
that God can see them' (Diop 2006: 784–5). After her death, Jessica
remembers her words and responds: 'In those days, Theresa, God was
looking elsewhere …' (ibid.: 785–6). Diop transmits the paralyzing and
unsettling impact of seeing her corpse through the eyes of Cornelius, who
visits Nyamata, as the author did and as others would do in turn:

> The young woman had her head pushed back and the scream extracted from
> her by the pain had been frozen on her still grimacing face. Her magnificent
> tresses were disheveled, and her legs wide apart. A stake—of wood or of
> iron, Cornelius didn't know, he was too shocked to notice—had remained
> lodged in her vagina.
>   All that he could do was to shake his head nervously. (ibid.: 778–80)

The author also emphasizes the stereotypical notion of the beauty and
femininity of Tutsi women by endowing Theresa with magnificent braids.

Faustin, the orphan in Monénembo's text, was present at the Nyamata massacre, and so, technically, is the only one among all the narrators/ characters in the texts produced for the project who could possibly have witnessed Mukandori's rape. However, he suffers from repressed memory and Monénembo does not provide us with a description of the rape or confirm whether Faustin was indeed a witness. Rather, his reference to Mukandori comes through an irreverent, crass, and rather exaggerated remark, so typical of his cynical young protagonist. Faustin cites her death, not as a way of empathizing or mourning, but as a way of proving that he will again be blamed for everything that goes wrong. For him, her death is just another example of all these things for which he has no desire to be held responsible: 'The famine, the cholera, the boiling lava flow in Karisimbi's crater, they were all my fault! I might as well be the one who moved the rock of Kagera, thrust a stake up Mrs Mukandori's vagina (whose impaled mummy image went around the world), stirred up the demons, and unleashed the elements!' (Monénembo 2004: 43).

Funga, the witch doctor, claims early in Monénembo's text that the sacrilegious and deliberate moving of the 'sacred rock of Kagera' by the white people has led to the 'catastrophes' that have befallen Rwanda (ibid.: 9). Here, Monénembo reinforces this notion in linking Mukandori's rape to all the other cataclysmic events, and especially the moving of the rock, pointing to the role of colonialism and the Catholic religion in the history of the country. Furthermore, he places her death on the same level as the other devastating events that have occurred in the country, thus elevating it to something more than the cruel rape of a Tutsi girl—it is the rape of the country, the destruction of its moral and social fiber. It is then this cynical character that reveals to us the enormity of this sexual and symbolic transgression.

Thus Mukandori becomes a figure that inhabits the world of the project, a shared reference to inhumanity made visible through her remains. Diop argues that the authors were, in a sense, addressing the killers, saying, 'You wanted to kill her, but we are going to bring her to life again' (Bénard 2001). It is, however, more than saving her from the oblivion of forgetfulness that the authors attempt to do. Literature is also their way of mourning this woman, who had not been properly buried at the time of their visit and whose spirit they sensed was waiting for the final rites. And so each author participates in this process in his or her own unique way.

Although it is referenced throughout the project, it is the two female authors, Tadjo and Ilboudo, who write most extensively on the issue of sexual violence. In this introductory section, I briefly consider Tadjo's contribution but will focus on Ilboudo's rape narrative in the next section where I analyze her novel.

Tadjo's text contains several micro-narratives which speak of sexual violence experienced by women during the genocide. Her propensity for including marginalized voices is illustrated by the fact that, together with the by now well-known account of Mukandori, she narrates the fate of the Zairean woman who was raped and her child killed before her eyes, simply because she resembled a Tutsi.

Her story is configured in terms of an uninterrupted, fragmented interior monologue which respects neither the conventions of punctuation nor the sequence of tenses, a textual strategy which transmits signs of trauma in the character's soul and her narration. The reader senses that she does not pause for breath and her words flow like water through a broken dam wall:

> Back home with my parents they gave me a lot of sympathy, I sleep in the same bed as my mum, and she holds me tight in her arms to help me to sleep, I told her I want to go back to bury my baby properly, at night I am always afraid, I dream of the child's corpse swollen like a pig on the road and all his clothes were torn but still he looked at me, even today I can't forget that body, even now I can't be alone in the house, if someone knocks on the door, I have to listen quickly and stop what I am doing because I am so frightened by everything I've seen. (Tadjo 2002: 92)

Although she survives and returns to her parents' home, where they comfort her, her rambling narrative clearly points to symptoms associated with trauma: nightmares and flashbacks of her baby's corpse, and regression into safe childhood memories and behavior. She seems to experience a state of hyperarousal, a persistent expectation of danger, triggered by situations that remind her of the original trauma. In her case the trigger is a seemingly innocuous knock at the door. The author does not endow her with any of the processes of resilience that have been identified in my earlier discussion on recovery after rape.

Another rape narrative, one that is only included through suggestion and by focusing on the devastating consequences of this weapon of war, is that of Nelly and her daughter. Tadjo describes her awkward encounter with Nelly, presumably a Tutsi survivor, an emaciated woman whose face is covered with patches from some disease, probably AIDS. Nelly speaks incoherently, laughs loudly, and screams at the visitors not to forget her. She shows them her daughter and two children—a boy, whom she describes as 'a gift from God', and another baby, a product of the war: 'I don't want this one. He was born of the war. What are we to do with him?' (ibid.: 35). In a few short sentences, Tadjo depicts the consequences of the genocide: AIDS, unwanted children, the erosion of appropriate social behavior, and society's discomfort with survivors' needs. The narrator's reaction to Nelly's unsettling comments and gestures confirms that society is disturbed by survivors and their stories: she feels contaminated by her contact with Nelly, and she wants to wash her face, which Nelly has touched and kissed. Is it Nelly she does not want to have contact with or the horror of genocide? We are not told whether it is Nelly or her daughter who was raped. What is most disturbing is that Nelly is clearly conflicted in her feelings toward the 'unwanted' child: first she 'slaps his bottom' and looks as if she wants to hit him, and then, seemingly admonished by her daughter, she 'plants a smacking kiss on his head' (ibid.).

Another victim that haunts the pages of Tadjo's travel account is Anastasie, the young girl who was raped, not by the *génocidaires*, but before the genocide by her brother, in an act that seemingly has nothing to do with ethnic violence. The author's choice to include this narrative may shock, but it is effective in transmitting the sense of betrayal experienced by those who were harmed by the people closest to them, as was often the case during the genocide: 'He had lost Anastasie at the very moment when he had hoped to bring her back, not only as his sister, but as the woman he had loved and with whom he had so much in common' (ibid.: 63). The author subtly accentuates this closeness by her choice of mirror names for brother and sister, Anastase and Anastasie. This incident also seems to be a mutation of the tale that Tadjo tells of the monster who consumes himself (ibid.: 16).

Being raped transforms Anastasie's flesh into a 'prison' (ibid.: 63). She is filled with a 'complete and irresistible emptiness' and her body is henceforth 'inhabited by Evil' (ibid.: 65). She feels 'invaded by the memory' and longs only to sleep, to 'disappear into oblivion', to close the door to the sounds of life and let herself be 'carried away by the underground stream'—in short, she wishes to die or at least retreat into a safe childhood past in which she is still a 'little girl with no cares or responsibilities' (ibid.: 63). Yet her sleep is plagued with 'hostile dreams' (ibid.).

At the moment of rape, Anastasie dissociates herself from her body, but instead of protecting her, this becomes a self-destructive experience: 'She no longer existed [...]. Her mind detached itself from her body, floated in the room and hit the ceiling. That was her first death' (ibid.: 66).

Anastasie's physical death takes place a few years later, during the genocide. Her story leaves us with two interesting points. The first is that she dies bravely, belonging, 'despite her youth', to a resistance group which fought day and night to prevent the militia from entering the neighborhood. This seems to suggest that through her social connection with a group, Anastasie found some form of resilience despite her difficult history. The second is that Tadjo makes the deliberate choice to never explicitly confirm her ethnicity, only stating that when the killing began, she died among the 'Tutsis and those who had tried to defend them' (ibid.: 67).

These diverse rape narratives underline the symptoms of traumatic memory and the death experience as they manifest not only in the victims' physical bodies, but also in their relationships and their minds. These symptoms are transmitted through interior monologue, fragmentation, elliptical phrases, and euphemisms, all of which suggest the victims' struggle to articulate their experiences.

Monique Ilboudo and the Stillborn Child

Monique Ilboudo, who hails from Burkina Faso, writes her novel from the point of view of her eponymous narrator, Murekatete, a woman born from a Hutu father and Tutsi mother.[18] This choice is significant because as discussed in the next section, like many of the other texts from the project, it prompts the reader to reflect on the polarization of identities.[19] Furthermore, her victim-protagonist is not a Tutsi survivor, but a Hutu[20] woman who loses her Tutsi husband and children to the genocide. The Interahamwe mistake her for a Tutsi woman and attack her because she is fleeing and therefore seems guilty to them. Venant, an exiled Rwandan Patriotic Front (RPF) soldier, saves her, nurses her back to life, and becomes her husband. The novel then deals with their attempt to lead a meaningful life as a couple after the genocide. However, visiting the genocide sites unhinges their marriage and their story ends in 'ruin and desolation' (Ilboudo 2000: 66).

Although Ilboudo's novel is fictional, it contains many elements typically included in autobiographical writing, such as the choosing of a name, the character's circumstances of birth, education, faith, relationships with parents, and first love—all of which creates the sense that one is reading testimonial literature.

The events, which are not related in a chronological fashion, can be grouped, like many genocide narratives, according to whether they happened before, during, or after the genocide. The chronological distortions and the fragmentary, cyclical structure of the text illustrate the non-linear and associative functioning of traumatic memory and, in the words of Ursula Tidd, 'bear witness to the unexperienced experience of death' (2005: 413).[21] Ilboudo's use of tense suggests that Murekatete's rape by her own husband, although it takes place after the genocide, is in fact a defining moment of trauma for her. Life before the genocide is narrated mainly in the literary past tense (past historic and imperfect), alternated with scenes from the present, told in the present and perfect tense, but when Murekatete narrates the moment of the rape, she makes use of an unusual mixture of the past and present, a device which points to the effect of trauma on a victim's sense of time[22]: 'Head spinning, I lose control completely. A choking sensation. I can't breathe. I start panting like a drowned person, saved at the last moment. [...] I was paralyzed. I wasn't crying anymore, I was no longer moving' (Ilboudo 2000: 69).[23] In the same way, the period of the genocide is emphasized through the use of tense and chronology: the only time when the chronological order is not subverted is during the five consecutive chapters, in the middle of the text, which describe the genocide. This section is chronological and detailed, as if in suspended time.

Unnatural Death and Painful Survival

The title, *Murekatete*, announces the main theme of this novel,[24] namely death and the attempt to embrace life after the genocide which is also, understandably, a recurring theme in the project.[25] Murekatete seems to be destined to die before her time, and even after miraculously surviving the genocide, the shadow of death constantly hovers over her. In the opening chapters of the text, we learn that from the very beginning death has haunted Murekatete, for she was not 'born to live': 'I died at birth. The small grave was already dug. Everybody was ready for my funeral. Only my mother clung to the crumpled little corpse, refusing to let it be buried' (ibid.: 11).[26] Instead of the usual terms associated with life and birth, her arrival in the world is announced in funerary terms—'corpse', 'funeral', 'grave', and 'burial'—and her mother is accused of 'playing with a cadaver' (ibid.). Even her conception took unexpectedly long, making her mother's in-laws impatient and suspicious, so that in the end, no one but her mother is surprised when the child is 'stillborn' (ibid.). Urged by her mother's milk, pleas, and lullabies, she nevertheless decides to live, a choice that she questions afterward: 'I was alive. First resurrection. "Thank-you God", prayed my mother. But was I right to have stayed? I still wonder' (ibid.: 12).

Her father, however, who treats her like a 'princess', is determined to protect her and demonstrate his belief in her capacity to survive, thus giving her a name to 'dream' of: 'Murekatete' (ibid.). This life-endowing name which means 'May she live! May she be happy/have a comfortable life!' is the one that she adopts, quickly abandoning her unsuitable Catholic name, Primitive (ibid.).

Ironically, however, life becomes a struggle against death: the untimely death of her beloved Hutu father, which appears to be a politically motivated murder of a man who refuses to give in to identity politics, and subsequently the deaths of her mother, Tutsi husband, children, and other family members.

This text traces the protagonist's failed attempt to embrace life after the genocide and to be '*vivante-vivante*' (fully alive) instead of '*mort-vivant*' (half-dead, half-alive) (Mujawayo and Belhaddad 2004: 223). Murekatete seems doomed to remain caught up in her own failed narrative,[27] as one who has survived and yet cannot integrate her traumatic past into her life story.

Death is a motif associated not only with her but also with her nation, and when the three-month 'eclipse' of the genocide comes upon them, she remarks that 'Death was everywhere' (Ilboudo: 2000: 34). Like Tadjo, Murekatete observes that, from an African perspective, death is a natural part of our existence; however, when it comes unexpectedly and on an abnormally large scale it shocks, it is unnatural: 'Unnatural death. There is nothing more natural than death. All who live must one day die. So, dying is normal and when we are born we accept that it is so. [...] Death is not natural when it collectively strikes those who yearn for nothing but to live' (ibid.).[28]

Her narrative on life and death reflects the unsettling experience, described by Jorge Semprun, of passing through death.[29] Her life, after the genocide, closely resembles that of a '*revenant*', one who has returned from the dead (Semprun 1996: 121; my translation). It seems then that Murekatete's 'stillborn' birth foreshadows this living through or passing through death that she will experience. Her name might prophesy a fulfilling and comfortable life, but the unwelcome and inopportune presence of death continues to haunt her, like a jealous, rejected lover: 'I chose life, and death jealously follows me everywhere. Death is breathing down my neck. It lurks around, destroying everything I love. Will I manage to shake it off one day? [...] Was I right to have chosen life? What was the point of surviving at my birth just to experience this apocalypse?' (Ilboudo 2000: 22).

Her incredible resilience and 'capacity to regenerate' herself leads to her 'rebirth' on two occasions in her life: at birth, after her family had already dug her grave, and again during the genocide, when she is attacked and her mutilated body left for dead (ibid.: 12, 15–16). She is 'brought back to life' by Venant (ibid.: 47): 'It was my second resurrection, Venant was the architect. Like my mother once, he performed a miracle' (ibid.: 16).[30] However, this miracle seems to be limited to the physical domain: 'what should have been a *second life*, had until now been nothing more than *painful survival*' (ibid.: 22; my emphasis).[31]

The ubiquitous themes of death, loss, lurking madness, and 'painful survival' permeate her narrative. Murekatete is portrayed as being unable to resume her life after the genocide:

> Because I am not dead, I must live. Upon waking up, I find that I am as distraught as I was the night before. I cannot find the necessary energy to become part of the frenetic activity that is surrounding me; that of reconstruction. There is so much to do: walls and people to rebuild. Wounded to nurse, survivors to console, traumatized to analyze [...] Every morning, I put one foot in front of the other and I don't know if I am moving forward or backward. (ibid.: 47)[32]

Venant offers to take her to see a psychiatrist, but she refuses violently: 'So you think I've lost my marbles? You think that I am nuts? That I am crazy?' (ibid.). However, all the while she fears that he might be right: 'Have I escaped from it? I think about madness, so I cannot be mad. I hang on as much as I can to the little bit of reason that I still have' (ibid.: 47–8). Without Venant, she knows, she would have been either dead or 'in the asylum' (ibid.: 48).

The motif of the shadow, so strongly felt in Tadjo's text, is equally present here. It comes to symbolize loss and destruction and those survivors who have been reduced to 'carcasses' or walking corpses, having lost the capacity to embrace life fully: 'One day in June 1994, my life came to an end. [...] It was at the side of this path in the middle of nowhere that I should have died for good. Fate decided otherwise. Thanks to Venant, the carcass was brought back to life. But ever since, I wander about aimlessly, like a shadow, the shadow of my [former] self' (ibid.: 45, 47).[33]

She tries bravely to overcome this feeling of being only half-alive, but like many other survivors, guilt haunts her and she suffers from the inner conflict between feeling both fortunate and guilty for having survived (Gasengayire 2005: 149).[34] 'I am aware of my good fortune,' she says, a 'lucky chance of which I am almost ashamed' (Ilboudo 2000: 22). So she makes a tremendous effort to try and embrace this chance that she has received, while others died: 'Every evening, I make strong resolutions. I decide to snap out of it, to get back my energy' (ibid.: 47). However, for various reasons, she fails.

Murekatete seems powerless to restore the severed connection between herself and humanity, even to the point of being unable to give herself to her husband: 'I was ashamed. Ashamed of waking him up every night with this obscene laugh, ashamed of my incapacity to respond to his love. Without a word, Venant switched off the lamp and went back to bed. I sensed his arm encircling me in a vain gesture of protection' (ibid.: 10).[35]

Trauma, Rape, and Betrayal

The traces of trauma take on different forms in the lives of Murekatete and her husband. Murekatete is tormented by a recurring dream, a nightmarish flashback to the day she was attacked and left for dead. In her dream, her attackers are transformed into a pack of savage dogs and she sees how her head is torn from her body (Ilboudo 2000: 9–10). A chance meeting with an arrogant and impenitent perpetrator again triggers the nightmare. Her incapacity to integrate the trauma into her life story profoundly influences her present. She refuses to live in her old home, too afraid to face the ghosts that wait there for her (ibid.: 16).

Where Murekatete suffers from too many memories, Venant seems to have too few. Her 'guardian angel', the soldier who saved her, has his own painful story. He is described by Murekatete as gentle, patient, and indulgent (ibid.: 15, 48). Abandoned in an orphanage by his father after his mother's death, he tells his life story to Murekatete 'in one breath, as if afraid of not being able to come back to it' if he stops talking (ibid.: 20). Murekatete notes that death's shadow has also come to define his life: Venant is the 'opposite of life'. To tell his story demands much courage:

'Pain, hardship, solitude. Not a single moment of happiness, no joyful memory [...]' (ibid.).

Venant remains considerate to Murekatete, in spite of his own painful past. However, their pilgrimage to the genocide sites, which they undertake in order to mourn and to try and understand what happened, traumatizes him completely and destroys their marriage. The physical proof of the inhumanity of genocide reduces him to an individual who loses control:

> Since our visit to this accursed place, nothing is right anymore. In the beginning they were only slight agitations to which I did not pay enough attention. Then it became a tidal wave which crashed over us, submerged us, and drowned what he had tried to protect in this universe of chaos. Venant the sensible one, Venant the one beyond reproach started drinking. (ibid.: 61)[36]

Murekatete senses that Venant has lost his faith in humankind and that, even worse, he has somehow come to associate her with the monstrosities of genocide. The loss of his confidence in her becomes her most painful death experience:

> From the day that we visited Murambi, I never again saw the same trusting look in Venant's eyes. As if he had become wary of part of me, almost as if he assimilated me with the brutality of Murambi. He, the architect of my resurrection. I sorely felt this *final blow*. I will never recover from that specific *death*. (ibid.: 72; my emphasis)[37]

This is ironic, as Murekatete too had doubted herself when she saw Murambi, wondering whether she too possibly harbored such a 'vile beast' in herself (ibid.: 60).

Venant is transformed, from an attentive, loyal husband to a tormented man who uses drugs, starts drinking heavily and eventually rapes her: '"You can scream as much as you want, no-one will come. I am your husband for heaven's sake! And you know what a husband does with his wife?" While speaking he tore away my nightclothes, stripping me with his left hand, holding my wrists above my head with his right hand' (ibid.: 69).[38] During this trauma of being raped by her husband Murekatete disassociates herself completely from her body. She looks down from a distance, a passive spectator to a scene in which they are transformed into two characters on a stage. She no longer recognizes herself or her husband:

I was paralyzed. I didn't scream anymore, I no longer moved. I saw him going fiercely at my body with the sensation that it didn't belong to me. I did not recognize myself, neither did I recognize him. From above the two characters, I stared at the unusual scene. The roaring of a wild animal coming from the man above *the body that was not mine* brought me back for a moment to reality. I burst into the same spasmodic laugh that woke me up every night. (Ilboudo 2000: 69; my emphasis)[39]

Sadly, the same 'spasmodic' laugh that characterized her recurring nightmare which she associated with her haunting memories of the genocide will henceforth be associated with the brutal act of her husband. Here, Venant is transformed into the 'wild animal' that haunts her nightmares, and thus the author underlines the transformative effect of trauma on the victims, who in turn may become perpetrators.

Ilboudo's description is strangely reminiscent of the rape experience described by Tadjo and discussed earlier in this chapter. For both Anastasie and Murekatete, being raped serves as an act of profound alienation, the estrangement from their own bodies that results from the experience of being reduced to an object. Both descriptions illustrate the psychological fragmentation and multiplication of the traumatized self, described by Ursula Tidd, who compares it to a form of death (2005: 412).

In both these narratives, the rape victims are not necessarily Tutsi women, the perpetrators are not necessarily Hutu and the rape incidents do not necessarily take place during the genocide. Furthermore, they are raped by those who are closest to them and apparently love them; a brother and a husband. These choices, though surprising, seem to be deliberate choices made by the authors. Being raped by a band of marauding strangers is different from being raped by someone close, and yet both authors situate this event in the intimacy of the home. It would seem that the authors have placed their narrations of rape in contexts which endow them with additional metaphorical meaning. For example, Murekatete's rape after the genocide by her own husband is clearly a secondary effect of the genocide on their lives, underlining the prolonged effects of trauma, which are not confined to the period of the genocide. Furthermore, as Josias Semujanga suggests, in this narrative, rape comes to symbolize the evil that has beset the community to the degree that people harm those that are closest to them (2008: 217). The same can be said of Tadjo's narrative of Anastasie. A further important point is implied; neither suffering nor evil distinguishes between ethnicity, race, or gender. As Tadjo suggests in the final pages of her book, our whole humanity is in danger (2002: 118).

After raping her, Venant leaves Murekatete to go and work in a war zone, 'as if he wanted to punish himself for his vile behavior' (Ilboudo 2000: 71). This appears to be Venant's expression of a death wish, which echoes Murekatete's own desire to end it all: 'Venant has left, and the house, invaded by emptiness, is nothing but an echo of the nothingness of my life. Some days, I long to put an end to this nothingness. Only the fear of falling into the eternal void keeps me from doing so' (ibid.: 72).[40] After this, Murekatete will never again feel 'at ease' with life or experience the blessing that her father had intended for her. In any case, Venant's rape has left her with a 'final gift', which ensures that she will not have long to live anyway (ibid.).

The motif of the gaze, which is so powerful in Tadjo's text, is equally present in Ilboudo's novel and seems to embody the failed relationship that it narrates.[41] This motif is illustrated through Murekatete's remarks on how the couple avoids looking at each other in the eyes: 'I opened my eyes. Venant switched on the bedside lamp, and leaning on an elbow, smiled at me gently. I turned my back on him and covered my head with a part of the sheet, in order to escape from that look filled with love. I was ashamed' (2000: 10).[42] Because Murekatete remains imprisoned in the past, she cannot appreciate Venant's loving gaze until she has lost it: 'When he came back to the room from the bathroom, he avoided looking at me until he left [...] I try to meet his eyes, but it is impossible to attract his glazed drunkard's eyes' (ibid.: 62, 69).[43] Murekatete and Venant cannot even look in the same direction toward a shared future any more, ostensibly because of their shame and their inability to overcome the horror of genocide. By creating a couple who is incapable of integrating the genocide experience into their life story, Ilboudo transmits the failure of mimesis, as understood by Paul Ricœur (1983), and the subsequent impossibility of making sense of what happened to them. In Freudian terminology, the couple remains trapped at a place of 'acting out': Murekatete is tormented by her recurring nightmares and Venant develops an obsession with genocide sites and macabre stories. This leads to the logical conclusion of 'ruin and desolation' in their lives (Ilboudo 2000: 66). The sequence of healing prescribed by Ricœur, namely memory–forgetting–forgiving (1995), cannot even be contemplated by the survivors in Ilboudo's narrative: they have not been able to successfully remember, let alone forget or forgive.

The motif of the gaze however takes on a different form at the end of the narrative in the description of the couple, Aloys and Soline, whom Murekatete sees from her balcony and who provides a contrast to her and Venant's story. Aloys, a moderate Hutu who refused to participate in the killings, and Soline, a Tutsi who endured multiple rapes, are also marked by the genocide, both in 'body and soul' (ibid.: 73). Soline was raped by a neighbor under the pretext of 'protecting' her and, when she tried to flee, again by a group of drunk militia 'louts', high on drugs, who lined up to rape her one by one and ended up throwing a bottle of acid into her vagina (ibid.: 2000: 74). The text emphasizes the tension between appearances and the invisible but profound destruction she has endured. At first sight, Soline appears 'intact': Murekatete notes that she is beautiful, and unlike her partner, Aloys, has no missing body parts (ibid.: 73). However, it is her eyes that tell of her experience, which has in fact damaged her entire identity. 'I am no longer a woman', she says to Aloys when they meet after the genocide, 'Everything has been burnt, scraped away' (ibid.: 73, 74).

Soline's eyes may carry the traces of her suffering and, yet, the couple's combined gaze contains the only hope that this novel offers. Unlike Venant and Murekatete, they 'dare to dream' of a future together instead of dwelling on the ravages of the genocide: 'The time will come when they will have the courage to set sail, sure of being responsible for the ship. They can then turn their eyes away from this vision of horror, and gaze at the open sea, in order to see the future. For now, they were undecided travelers, searching the skies' (ibid.: 74).[44] Aloys and Soline are at least able to look in the same direction, with their questions, their love and their dreams (ibid.: 75). They are able to look away from the past toward the future, which offers possibilities, however uncertain.

In terms of resilience, Esther Mujawayo's literary testimony forms an interesting contrast to Ilboudo's novel. I do not provide an in-depth analysis of her co-authored text, as she does not form part of the project, but I do reference it because of the helpful comparisons it provides.[45] Mujawayo talks at length about the strategies she adopted in order to be 'fully alive', and the title of her text, *SurVivantes*, reflects this choice.[46]

Esther is a Tutsi who lived through the genocide and although she was not raped, she recounts the stories of others who were, and who shared their stories with the women from AVEGA (AVEGA is an acronym for Association des Veuves du Génocide which can be translated as Association of Widows of the 1994 Rwandan Genocide). She speaks from her experience as a social worker and, as Souâd Belhaddad reminds us, her focus is not her own story, but the 'despairing universality of genocide' (Mujawayo and Belhaddad 2004: 10). Esther identifies strongly with her namesake from the Bible, whose task was to save her people (ibid.: 18).

If we were to view both Esther and Murekatete's 'stories' as authentic versions of a typical genocide experience, although one is indeed a testimony and the other a fictional novel, there are some interesting parallels: although one is Hutu and the other Tutsi, both women are bereaved and have suffered. Both have physically survived the genocide. Both were given prophetic, life-giving names at birth by their fathers.

Both women experience their survival as a choice made for them, even imposed on them by fate, and feel that they have been 'condemned' to live (Mujawayo and Belhaddad 2004: 34). Although Esther seems to succeed better in doing so than Murekatete, both of them make a conscious effort to choose life. Murekatete says: 'Because I am not dead, I must live' (Ilboudo 2000: 47) and Esther pronounces her choice as follows: 'It so happens that I survived. Today, I live. They are not the ones, my killers, who left me alive; from now on it is I who choose to live' (Mujawayo and Belhaddad 2004: 29).

Only Esther, however, truly seems to succeed in embracing life after the genocide. It appears that the reasons are as follows: firstly, Murekatete is isolated in many ways and does not seem to have a strong social support structure. Esther, on the other hand, becomes part of an association of widows who work through and narrate their genocide experiences as a group, providing opportunities for active listening, where the group carries the individual who is telling her story through difficult moments. This sense of community is embedded in Esther's title, which is in the feminine plural form. It is clear that Esther has the social advantage of being what Brison calls 'reconnected with humanity' (Brison 1999: 45), which Murekatete does not.

Murekatete remains isolated. She does not reintegrate herself into a supportive community, 'reconnect with humanity' or reach out to help others (ibid.). Murekatete's world is reduced to her relationship with her husband (who eventually also deserts her) and one friend who supports her. Even her children, who might have provided her with a reason for living, are dead. Esther, on the other hand, displays a strong sense of agency toward the future, related to her daughters: 'I am hanging on, for my daughters. They are my life' (Mujawayo and Belhaddad 2004: 31). This role is extended beyond her immediate family through her strong sense of responsibility toward her community, a characteristic which is related to her surname, Mujawayo, which means 'servant of God' (ibid.: 24). Esther's focus is more collective than personal: she says that she doesn't feel a strong need to tell her story (ibid.: 17), but that she will fight to the end for the few remaining survivors, because it is 'not worth surviving in 1994 only to die stupidly afterwards, or to be completely weakened or run-down' (ibid.: 14, 17). Esther appears to have regained her 'voice' and her sense of agency: 'From now on it is I who choose to live' instead of feeling 'condemned' to live (ibid.: 29–30). When she speaks of survivors who go for therapy, she says: '[I]nitially condemned to live, today they have *chosen* to live' (ibid.: 30).[47]

This notion of overcoming by being reintegrated into a community and re-establishing a sense of agency contrasts sharply to Murekatete's despairing words, which prove her inability to overcome the destructive experience of the genocide: 'I love Venant. From the bottom of my wounded heart. With all the strength of my mutilated body. I know that he loves me. But I am dead. I have been for a long time' (Ilboudo 2000: 10).[48] Her poetic use of words and assonance emphasizes the sense of having already died: '*mon cœur meurtri*', '*mon corps mutilé*'. Her poignant affirmation 'I am dead. I have been for a long time' calls to mind Ernst van Alphen's observation that 'the basic feeling of being dead, or of continuing living as a dead person, is not narratable […] a figurative reading does not acknowledge the unrepresentability of the experience […]. On the contrary, it denies it […]. Something has really died, not in a figurative, but in a most literal way' (1999: 35). Murekatete does not have a community to turn to, for she has lost her parents, husband, children, and friends. Neither does she regain her voice or her subjectivity for telling her story, which is so essential in re-establishing the self after undergoing trauma.

Finally, when we consider these narratives, it is clear that Ilboudo refrains from introducing aspects which could empower her protagonist in the aftermath of genocide to overcome this experience, whereas Mujawayo's testimony displays many of the resilience processes identified by researchers as common to those who embrace life after the genocide experience. Examples exist in her testimony of processes such as meaning making, being a resource for others, caring, connecting, rejecting death, imparting advice, being emotionally present with others, cultivating inner peace, encouraging crying for emotional relief, and so forth. Mujawayo's text suggests that the ability to engage in resilience processes such as '*kwihangana* (withstanding)', '*kwongera kubaho* (living again)', and '*gukomeza ubuzima* (continuing life/health)' (Zraly and Nyirazinyoye 2010:

1656)—and to thereby move from a position of merely surviving to fully living—is influenced by factors such as the opportunity to verbalize the experience and being integrated in a social support structure. Perhaps the reason for the difference between Mujawayo's narrative and that of Murekatete lies in the fact that Mujawayo is herself a survivor. She is thus in a position to trace the journey toward redeeming the shattered life of the victim, whereas Ilboudo—as an intellectual witness only—demonstrates the consequences of trauma in the life of her protagonist but does not presume to suggest possible pathways to healing. It is also possible that Ilboudo, who is not Rwandan, was not familiar with the cultural notions of resilience as explained above, and therefore not able to incorporate them as naturally in her story as Mujawayo does.

Mujawayo suggests that the ability to move from a position of merely surviving to fully living is influenced by factors such as the opportunity to verbalize the experience and society's (in)capacity to listen in an appropriate way to these stories. It is significant that the fictional character Murekatete is portrayed as not having the opportunity of telling her story to others who could respond appropriately. This was indeed the case for many survivors. Brison states that society lives with the unbearable 'by pressuring those who have been traumatized to forget and by rejecting the testimonies of those who are forced by fate to remember' (1999: 49). Thus, the life-restoring experience of recovering and remaking the self that has been undone, destroyed, and shattered by trauma was not granted to many survivors of the genocide. And therefore many of them have, like Murekatete or the Zairean girl in Tadjo's novel, survived the experience, but only some are fully alive and not all will be able to choose life the way Esther Mujawayo has done.

Tierno Monénembo and the Children of the Genocide

Another voice that is rarely heard is that of the orphans who embody the uncertain future of the continent and carry within them the potential seeds of violence. Tierno Monénembo engages with their plight by narrating his novel, *L'aîné des orphelins (The Oldest Orphan)*, from the perspective of a Rwandan boy, Faustin Nsenghimana.[49] Many try to forget the genocide, but the orphans are there to remind us of it. They are a less obvious presence in the project, but they are nonetheless an integral part of the aftermath of genocide, and Monénembo and Tadjo are the two authors who focus explicitly on them.

Tadjo describes her visit to a youth center, where the children who roam the rubbish dumps of Kigali become the sad future of Africa; life holds little value for them and they are ready to be given weapons and enrolled in 'barefoot' armies (2002: 87–8). They are introduced to us as 'children of the genocide', 'the open wound of memory' that has the potential to 'kill the country all over again' (ibid.).

As with prisoners, who attempt to re-establish some sense of community after the genocide, the orphans organize themselves according to a strict hierarchy. This too is reminiscent of the tradition of submission to figures and structures of authority that existed both before and during the genocide, and which continues to exist after the event. On the 'lunar landscape' of the rubbish dump on which these children make their existence, Tadjo notes, there are 'well-established rules': 'There are leaders, deputies, a whole rigid hierarchy. The highest ranking gets first pick, choosing the best finds: nails, tin, tiles, empty bottles, boxes, jerry cans' (ibid.: 87). This aspect is also depicted in Monénembo's text, both in the way in which the genocide orphans interact with each other and in the prison cells; in both contexts, a role and position is assigned to each member and this dictates interaction.

In Tadjo's description of the children at the orphanage and in Monénembo's characterization of Faustin, the orphans are portrayed as unreliable narrators, too traumatized to provide coherent stories of what they have experienced:

> If you push them to talk, to speak of their former life, they retreat further into lies, lies that shield them against the cruelty of adults. They will tell you what you want to hear. It is only at night, when darkness has fallen, that occasionally you will hear a few snatches of the truth. The fragments of their stories overlap with each other, and finally a picture emerges. (Tadjo 2002: 86)

These two authors evoke the plight of these children, who are forced to find their own ways of surviving. Monénembo, who shies away from the term 'engaged writer', and does not aim to judge, moralize, or even analyze, sees his task as that of disturbing and profoundly troubling the reader: 'The novelist is not a conscience. He is a troubled soul [...] He does not analyze, he does not judge, he does not arbitrate. He is moved, and if he has a role to play, it is firstly that of moving others' (in Mongo-Mboussa 2004; my translation).[50]

His choice of title is highly significant. Faustin is not only an 'orphan', with all that that entails; he is also the 'oldest' in more ways than one. It is the polysemous character of the notion of being at once the oldest and an orphan that informs my reading of his novel. I explore this somewhat contradictory status, as depicted in the life of the protagonist. I also look at the child narrator and the theme of exile as a recurring figure and theme in Monénembo's work and the particular form they take on in this novel on the genocide.[51]

Recent medical and sociological research states that more than ten percent of Rwandan children were orphaned due to the genocide and rape-related AIDS. These are victims who carry an enormous burden of trauma; often they witnessed acts of extreme violence, including the death of their parents and possibly the rape of their mothers (Talbot et al. 2013). Most child survivors believed that they would die during the genocide. They experienced extreme humiliation and a large number of them survived by hiding under the corpses of other victims (Ng et al. 2015: 303). Often these child survivors set up households together, the oldest becoming the head of the household, watching over the younger siblings and caring for other child survivors (Schaal and Elbert 2006). Journals sometimes include examples of questions asked of child survivors in their studies. These provide us with a sense of the experiences the children were subjected to. Typically the following questions are included: have you been raped? Have you witnessed a massacre? Have you witnessed the murder of your mother or father? Did you believe that you yourself would die? Did you have to hide under dead bodies? (Schaal and Elbert 2006: 99).

If he had been handed such a questionnaire, Faustin, the protagonist in Monénembo's novel, would have answered yes to most of these questions. He is discovered in the church at Nyamata by an old woman, a few days after his parents' death, 'gripping his mother like a newborn' and 'nursing at her breasts': 'You're not a man like others. You were born twice in a way; the first time you were suckling her milk and the second time, her blood' (Monénembo 2004: 96). Like Murekatete, Faustin is an example of one of those who miraculously survived. Like Gérard Nayinzira, in Diop's text, he drank blood in order to survive.[52]

As for many survivors, escaping the death of genocide seems to be a second chance, but taking hold of this opportunity turns out to be more complicated than one can ever imagine. Faustin incarnates the disorientated generation of orphans and the degeneration and perversion of their sense of morality. When an RPF soldier mistakes Faustin for a *génocidaire*, refusing to believe in his innocence, he sketches a sad but rather accurate picture of the society in which these children find themselves:

'[…] You really think I'm a *génocidaire*?'
'Everyone is! Children have killed children, priests have killed priests, women have killed pregnant women, beggars have killed other beggars, and so on. There are no innocents left here.' (ibid.: 23)

The constant shift in the text between past and present, between Faustin the little boy and Faustin the hardened adolescent, underlines this loss of innocence. It is a violent and hardened society that Monénembo depicts, filled with bitterness and the incapacity to forgive or show remorse.

Michael Syrotinski describes this text as the most 'problematic' of all the texts produced for the project, largely due to the 'coarseness' of the novel and the use of 'a decidedly antipathetic child-narrator, whose grasp of events is often tenuous at best' (2009: 431). Initially, the callousness and disdain of the narrator is alienating, and his apparent bravado, cynicism, indifference, and vulgarity make it hard for the average reader to identify with or even have compassion for him. Faustin shows no appropriate remorse for his act of murder and, in spite of the efforts of the human rights activist, Claudine, this 15-year-old is condemned to death by the judge, who says: 'You're a monster Faustin! You don't deserve to be part of the human race' (Monénembo 2004: 84). To this judgment, Faustin replies: 'I never thought that being part of the human race was praiseworthy' (ibid.). The irony of the judge's declaration is that Faustin, who at ten years old was still a child playing with his kite, has become the 'monster' that he is through the lack of humanity of the society in which he lives. It is only at the end of the novel that the reader grasps the extent of the trauma Faustin has experienced and begins to comprehend its impact on his behavior. It is clear that Faustin's moral decline and emotional detachment is a direct consequence of the genocide. Yet society, and in particular its adults, judge him without admitting their role in his degeneration.

Critics have reacted in a variety of ways to the challenge of reading this novel, and my aim is to share my own point of entry into the text. An obvious first approach to the novel, and one which is rightfully proposed by various critics,[53] is to view this unsettling novel as a story narrated by a severely traumatized child who suffers from repressed memory.

This implies looking at narrative devices that alert us to the presence of trauma, memory loss, and the protagonist's inability to narrate his experience in a reliable manner. Furthermore, although the subject matter is clearly the genocide, the genocide is seldom mentioned—and is euphemistically referred to as the 'events' or, in the words of the child narrator, the 'advents' (*les avènements*) (ibid.: 6). This device further foregrounds the absence of memory that dominates Faustin's life and what Audrey Small calls his 'innocence (or ignorance)' (2006: 207). Faustin embodies the phenomenon of a repressed memory and, haunted by it, he bears the traces of his incapacity to integrate his traumatic memory with the rest of his life narrative. This argument is supported by the many references in the novel that remind us that Faustin is indeed still a child. He comically mispronounces words that he doesn't understand and, as Small points out, he obviously cannot 'have any sophisticated understanding of the long history of colonial and postcolonial identity-engineering and political events that led to the genocide' (ibid.: 208).

Like Ilboudo's text, the structure of the novel imitates the hesitant and non-linear, labyrinthine functioning of memory; snatches of memory suddenly and inexplicably appear, taking the protagonist by surprise: 'The rest, I was told later, or it resurfaced on its own in my tattered memory, in spurts, like muddy water pouring out of a clogged pump' (Monénembo 2004: 96). Certain incidents are repeatedly evoked, sometimes modified and fragmented, and the constant moving between past and present is at first confusing to the reader. There are, in fact, two cyclical, intertwined storylines: Faustin's life after the genocide (including his wanderings, the HQ—the headquarters or the abandoned building where the orphans live, the orphanage, the murder, hiding in the mine, prison life, and his trial), and his life before the genocide (childhood and village life), culminating in the Nyamata massacre narrated in the final pages of the text.

Faustin is characterized by the tendency to lie, exaggerate, and fabricate stories. As Rodney, the English cameraman, notes, to Faustin lying has become 'as easy as breathing' (ibid.: 65). What is even more tragic is that he lies to himself, telling himself that his parents are still alive, while in reality he has witnessed their death. Small rightly points out that 'Monénembo constantly indicates to the reader that they should be wary of Faustin's version of events, and read him as a traumatised survivor *throughout* his narrative' (2006: 209).

His testimony is presented to us as a 'grotesque' mockery of what really happened—that is to say, through the stories he fabricates in front of the camera, encouraged by Rodney. In these stories he is the protagonist, but they do not reflect the truth of his own story; this becomes a process of depersonalization in which his 'mute suffering' is exploited by the violence of the media (Germanotta 2016: 86). In this regard, Syrotinski notes that it is important to distinguish between 'self-serving, manipulative' lies and those unconscious untruths which can be attributed to denial and amnesia (2009: 435).

Researchers like Germanotta, Small, and Syrotinski emphasize the link between Faustin's behavior and his genocide experience. Syrotinski provides us with a list of symptoms that are associated with children suffering from attachment disorder, found among children whose early attachment to their primary caregiver has been severely disrupted. These symptoms correlate in an astonishing manner with Faustin's erratic behavior: his emotional detachment, tendency to lie, lack of remorse, 'poor speech development', 'inappropriate sexualised behaviour', 'fundamental lack of trust', underdeveloped conscience, 'inability to form close relationships', and so on (Syrotinski 2009: 434). This insight helps us to comprehend Faustin's reaction to the traumatic context in which he finds himself. In this regard Syrotinski evokes Faustin's 'regression to early childhood' by citing the closing paragraph, in which he again nurses at his mother's breasts (ibid.). Syrotinski's aim is to demonstrate how the author takes us to the 'realm of performative language' (ibid.: 434–5). He suggests that such a performative text, which does not 'stand in' for but rather 'stands alongside the event' and thus only gives us indirect or partial access to it, in turn solicits a response from the reader, reminding us that 'trauma testimony […] needs a listener or reader to work as testimony, and that sharing in the work of remembering and mourning is an ongoing collective responsibility, and not simply a civic duty we perform so as to then forget' (ibid.: 437–8).

Such a reading, though valid and extremely helpful, still does not put the reader at ease, because Faustin is not the innocent, vulnerable, and powerless character the reader might expect in a traumatized child (Small 2006: 208). This becomes particularly evident in his problematic relation with Claudine (as discussed further on). Faustin's innocence as a child victim is constantly undermined by the callousness of the adolescent murderer that he becomes.

Orphanhood and Exile

Faced with the paradoxical image of callousness and innocence combined in the protagonist, I propose a closer look at the central notions of 'orphan' and 'oldest', emphasized by the title. I take my cue from the title, which leads me to consider the meaning of what it is to be not only an *orphan*, but to carry the weight of being the *oldest* orphan in a context where child-headed households are the order of the day. I interpret the novel as a literary representation, grounded in the reality of post-genocide Rwanda, of how society has failed the children of Rwanda and the consequences of this abandonment. As will become clear, Faustin is failed by his parents, by the adults who surround him and by their value and judicial systems.

Furthermore, I read the novel as suggested by Sélom Komlan Gbanou (2003), by focusing on the ubiquitous theme of exile, and on the recurring and marginalized figure of the child as present in Monénembo's oeuvre in general. Gbanou notes that Monénembo inscribes in his child protagonists the profound unease linked to the distance and suffering associated with a life of exile (2003: 41). Exile, as presented in Monénembo's work, says Gbanou, is a space outside geographical borders, characterized by solitude, alienation, and distance with regard to society and loved ones (ibid.: 41, 59). The child protagonist is a recurring figure in his work: exiled and scorned by the society in which he or she drifts around (ibid.: 49). Their only refuge is drugs, alcohol, and sexual debauchery. They are left to fend for themselves, develop a taste for risk and adventure but also for violence and the transgression of social and moral norms (ibid.). Like Faustin, Monénembo's other protagonists are often tragic victims of their circumstances, condemned to flee from prison, death, and misery (ibid.). Gbanou's reading of Monénembo's oeuvre enables us to see the child protagonist, not as a choice made solely for the purpose of writing about the Rwandan genocide, but as recurring figure, marginalized by the African landscape which his characters inhabit.

The theme of exile is present in this text, not as literally as in Diop's or Lamko's text, but implicitly, for Faustin experiences a constant inner state of exile. This only really becomes obvious when considering this theme as a pervading element of both Monénembo's life and his oeuvre. Gbanou interprets the work of this author, who has lived in various African and Western countries, as a form of 'disguised autofiction', remarking that he often inscribes in his child protagonists the unease that is characteristic of a life lived in exile (2003, 49–50, 55; my translation). Even if the only moments of physical exile in this novel unfold when Faustin leaves his village after the death of his parents, and when he flees to the mine after killing Musinkôro, Faustin corresponds, in many ways, to this figure of exile described by Gbanou.

Gbanou suggests that exile is often linked to an identity quest and a search for points of reference in the face of the limbo and insecurity that characterize nomadic life (ibid.: 41, 43, 59). Exile is described as a 'rupture with an imaginary or real identity', a loss of self, aggravated by the loss of parents and family (ibid.: 43). When considering Faustin's character through this lens, it is clear that he is constantly in 'rupture' with his own identity: first he distances himself from his trusting and open childhood self by becoming an independent, hardened adolescent. Then, when he is confronted with the 'wild' children, whose 'inhuman cries' had been haunting him and who turn out to be his own siblings, he evolves into a caring maternal figure for them, nurturing them in the safety of the orphanage (Monénembo 2004: 39, 40). Unfortunately, his existential displacement does not end there, for, as Gbanou reminds us, for the exiled, 'every potential refuge represents a possibility of hope which, sadly, when they think it is within their grasp, seems to elude them' (2003: 43; my translation).[54] The need to flee, both physically and figuratively, follows him wherever he goes. Even in the orphanage, where 'the food [is] good' and they sleep well and laugh well (ibid.: 46), Faustin has the inexplicable desire to escape: 'If someone were to ask me today why I ran away from the City of Blue Angels, I wouldn't know what to reply. In reality there was no reason or, rather, yes, there was; there's always a good reason behind every stupid act' (ibid.: 46–7). It seems to be the strict discipline and his disagreement with the 'Hirish woman', the figure of authority at the orphanage, which prompt him to finally take the step of running away (ibid.: 47).[55]

Thus Faustin again takes on a different identity, becoming someone who lives from invented lies and who ends up committing a murder for which he shows no remorse. This hardened adolescent has no regret, no respect for society, or even fear of being judged by another human. One can establish a link here with the notion of 'parental transgression', a term used by the author when speaking of his own life and his choice to change his name (originally Tierno Saïdou Diallo) when his parents divorced. His new name means 'son of Néné Mbo' (referring to his grandmother), and it evokes the 'distance' in his relationship with his parents (Gbanou 2003: 44). This too is a form of exile, which entails turning to oneself when substituting a place in which one feels naturally at home with another one, which can at least guarantee one's survival and possibly offer some form of happiness (ibid.: 45).[56]

This is the type of substitution choice which Faustin makes when distancing himself from the wisdom of his father and falling back on other forms of support, such as the community of orphans, Claudine, or Rodney. Eventually, after murdering his 'old friend' Musinkôro, he even isolates himself from those support systems and turns to himself, hiding in an old tin mine (Monénembo 2004: 61). It is during this self-imposed exile that he expresses the paradoxical and heart-breaking condition of thus estranging oneself from others:

> The world of refined men and I were now an ocean apart. I was comfortable in my hole. I didn't need the outside world. My parents, my sisters, my brother? Their memory had deserted my head all on its own. I regretted nothing. I felt no blame. I didn't need any other place: neither Kigali, not Tanzania, not this green paradise in the Psalms that Father Manolo had so often promised. I had blotted out the world and believed that in return the world had done the same with me. (ibid.: 77)

The words 'I had blotted out the world' (*'j'avais annihilé le monde'*) (ibid.) evoke the 'revolutionary' spirit that characterizes the exile who develops the capacity to take sole responsibility for himself or herself, without needing or fearing others (Gbanou 2003: 49). When the lawyer scolds Faustin for 'acting like a child' and encourages him to 'keep his composure' like a real man, even 'at the brink of the grave', he answers flippantly: 'I've learnt enough in here that I can go before the judgment of God alone. A human eye will never scare me again' (Monénembo 2004: 70).

However, the need for some frame of reference and system of guidance continues to haunt him. Isolating himself from others makes him aware that he still needs them. In spite of his apparent indifference and independence, he constantly yearns to be recognized and to belong. When he finds himself in the RPF camp after losing his parents and wandering around, people draw him in. They put him in charge of the cattle and allow him to hunt for them, upon which he notes: 'I had found a new family. There's nothing I'd have liked better than to end my days there' (ibid.: 26). Unfortunately, this was not to be and Faustin ends up roaming the streets of a newly liberated Kigali and sleeping on a deserted veranda.

When he meets up with Musinkôro, his friend from the RPF camp, it is as if he has found family again: 'All I could say was that name. Incredible. It wasn't just the game of *igisoro*,[57] my slingshot and his harmonica that linked us, it was a whole bloodline [...] *itumba* [the rainy season] had purified my soul and Musinkôro's and reunited us in the heat of a new blood relationship' (ibid.: 28). At HQ, the abandoned house where Musinkôro lives with a gang of other children, stealing, using drugs, sharing spoils, Faustin regains a sense of family and belonging; they work in teams, are assigned 'territor[ies]' in which to work, and look out for each other (ibid.: 31). It is a time that he idealizes: 'Those were happy times, among the best of my life. In fact I rarely thought about my parents. It was an ordinary life, fulfilled and orderly, and it distracted us from thoughts of the past or the future' (ibid.: 32).

When someone calls out his name in prison, he remarks: 'It had been a long time since anyone had called me. There was still someone who remembered me; that filled me with joy [...] I had run mainly because of the sound of my name—a name is so important, at least no-one can take it away from you' (ibid.: 15). And when he realizes that Claudine might start losing faith in him, he fears losing her: 'Perhaps she had finally decided to see me as I really was: a real bastard and not the little martyr her complicated mind had invented for itself [...] I shivered [...] I was afraid of losing her. It's like that, even when you're irredeemable, even when you're in hell, you need someone as a link to the world' (ibid.: 52). Thus, in Faustin's world, the 'vicious cycle' of exile (Gbanou 2003: 43) comes in the form of being torn between looking out for himself and needing others, for, as Claudine reprimands him through an old proverb when he claims not to need anyone: 'He who thinks he can do without others will die!' (Monénembo 2004: 35).

Becoming an orphan automatically implies going through a process of loss. For Faustin, who describes the genocide as the 'season for losses' (Monénembo 2004: 24), this process represents much more than losing his parents. He loses his childhood innocence, his roots, all moral and religious landmarks, any sense of belonging to a community, and the financial and physical protection that having a family typically offers.

Faustin is more disillusioned, vulgar, and cynical than is fitting for his age; it is in this way that the text powerfully demonstrates the loss of innocence. This process is underlined when the mispronounced words[58] that characterize the child narrator are gradually replaced by the vulgar obscenities uttered by the foul-mouthed adolescent narrator that he becomes.

'Watch it, lady, I'm no longer what you think!' he warns Claudine, who treats him like a child, patting his hair and his forehead: 'Ask Gabrielle, Séverine, Alphonsine! I've had them all! Of all my pals, I'm the one with the longest thing. When I'm really hard, it's longer than a big soup spoon, and it fills my hand when I'm pleasuring myself in front of the women selling banana beer' (ibid.: 15).

The constant slippage of the narrative between Faustin the innocent child and the hardened adolescent foregrounds this loss of faith, of innocence and humaneness. When his invented stories of the genocide requires him to show emotion, Faustin manufactures tears in front of the cameras and interviewers, but in a moment of real sadness, he realizes that he has also lost his capacity to cry, along with all his other childhood capacities: 'To cry openly and sincerely this time. Only, not a single tear came to dampen my eyes. I had lost that habit as I had lost the habit of swimming, trapping tree squirrels, and ground squirrels, or washing my hands before meals. That's how it is' (ibid.: 71).

His childhood memories are filled with nostalgia, warmth, and caring; before the genocide life seemed good, 'worthwhile, and very often fantastic' (ibid.: 72). As he lies on his back, looking at a 'big crescent moon', the harmonious sounds of a flute and of calves lowing in the background, he thinks back to his boyhood: 'All that was missing was the husky voice of my father (soaked with alcohol as was often the case) grappling with the wizard kings and the valiant warriors of yesteryear and, of course, the tireless breathing of Mama struggling with her pots and pans between the hut and the well' (ibid.: 67).

Faustin seems to have inherited his childhood faith and naivety from his father, Théoneste. When Funga, the witch doctor, bursts into the house to talk about Habyarimana's plane that has been shot down, his father has no idea what is going on and Funga shouts: 'Théoneste, you'll always be more stupid than others. They shoot down the President's plane and you don't even know it!' (ibid.: 86). A 'shower of bad omens' accompanies this event (ibid.: 87), but Théoneste continues to believe that no harm will come to the peaceful village of Nyamata. Théoneste and the Mother Superior assure Faustin the *génocidaires* will not cross the Nyabarongo bridge. Faustin blindly trusts his father's judgment, and even when the first wounded survivors start arriving, he feels secure: 'I reacted with the same happiness I felt on dark nights when I'd imagined the miseries of a child abandoned in the forest, trembling with cold, threatened by wolves and hyenas, while I was warm and under the jovial protection of Théoneste, my father' (ibid.: 87). It only dawns on him at the last moment, when they are all gathered in the church, that his father and the nun's promises are worth nothing. Later, we will understand his disillusionment with these two figures, who represented security in his childhood.

Faustin's apparent naivety in the face of the impending horror of the genocide is so perturbing to those around him that they scorn him for it. Even after the *Interahamwe* militia have arrived, and houses have been marked with large crosses, he takes his kite and runs through the village, letting it fly 'as majestic as an eagle soaring over the trees' (ibid.: 92). It is in fact the recurring motif of Faustin's kite which most poignantly reminds us of his destroyed innocence and naivety: 'Oh that's Théoneste's son. Look at him playing with his kite! The killings are about to start and he's playing with his kite. There's no doubt about it, idiots are born to be happy!' (ibid.). In the church, as he watches his mother folding her hands above her head in the mourning posture, and his father's blood-covered jacket, he starts screaming when someone takes his kite from him: 'Shut-up! Said Nyumurowo grabbing the kite from my hands. "Look at this kid, he brought his kite! ... You think we're here to play?"' (ibid.: 95).

Faustin's growing disenchantment with society finds its most eloquent expression in his remarks about his own father. They represent a second type of loss, sorely felt by this boy, namely that of the comforting presence of his father. The image that we have of Théoneste is slightly contradictory: he is an honest, hardworking, and generous man who loves his alcohol a bit too much and is considered to be simple and naive—the village 'idiot', a title that he gladly accepts: 'There's a need for people like me. A village without an idiot is a village without a future' (ibid.: 73). The 'Italian woman', however, sees him as someone with more common sense than the other villagers (ibid.). He is also courageous and loyal: at the time of the massacre, he is invited to leave the church with the other Hutu inhabitants, but he chooses to be killed along with his Tutsi wife.

Before Théoneste's death, he taught his son about life through his constant use of local proverbs, fables, and the words of the elders. The content of these suggests that he is in fact not a fool, but rather 'lucid' (ibid.: 86). Théoneste's character is explicitly linked to these forms of ancient and local wisdom: in almost every instance in the novel that he is mentioned, his appearance is marked by a proverb or pearl of wisdom that others apply to him (often in mockery), or that he cites in order to teach his son some life lesson. Even when they are gathered in the church and Nyumurowo grabs Faustin's kite, he retorts: 'So you think that's the enemy you need to destroy? It's obvious you don't understand the words of the ancients. "If you hate a man let him live!" That's what the ancients used to say' (ibid.).

In many of the decisive moments in his life, Faustin evokes the presence of his father, thinking about what he would have said or thought if he had been there: 'Oh, if my father had seen me [...] "Don't let the sharp tongues tell you the milk of your mother is not as good as that of others! Understand?"' (ibid.: 21). However, as his disillusionment grows, he speaks in more disparaging ways of his father. His father had taught him through a fable that Lying, the 'gifted' younger brother, is the one who 'runs the world' and triumphs over Truth, even though he was the first-born of the two (ibid.: 63). He directly links his own loss of innocence, symbolized by the kite, with his loss of faith in his own father, the 'inno-cent', simple-minded idiot who had not foreseen the massacre, and had in this sense failed his family: 'From the day Corporal Nyumurowo snatched my kite from my hands, I learned that playing the innocent serves no pur-pose' (ibid.). Thus, in spite of his father's words of wisdom, we have the impression that Faustin blames his father for not having protected him against the world. The value system and attitudes proposed to him by his father were not enough to help him survive the ordeal of genocide and its aftermath.

Faustin's sense of loss regarding his father and the security he should have provided becomes synonymous for the way in which society and its value systems failed him. The motif associated with this loss is that of the slingshot that his father had made for him out of prickly pearwood and the rubber from the old inner tube of a bicycle tire. This too he loses, at a moment when he has already lost everything else and is looking for some-thing to wager in a game of *igisoro* at the RPF headquarters, where he is being held. He makes the decision easily, especially because he hopes that he might win something out of the game: 'I was very fond of it but since this was the season for losses, might as well lose that too' (ibid.: 24). It is significant that, while the kite of his innocence was taken away from him, he is the one who willingly gives up the slingshot symbolizing his father's protection and provision, hoping to win something more valuable in return. Faustin's losses progressively transform him into an estranged ado-lescent who isolates himself. Sometimes he rediscovers his faith in life and in God, but these instants become increasingly rare.

A further loss in Faustin's life is that of a dependable reference system in terms of values and beliefs. In this regard, Monénembo's choice of adult characters surrounding Faustin is significant. The author seems to make a deliberate choice to fill his protagonist's life with adults who fail him and whose presence simply aggravates his loss and derailment. His parents fail and abandon him by dying, his father by not preparing him for the harshness of the world. This is equally true for Funga and Father Manolo, the two spiritual figures that inhabit his childhood. These adults represent different spheres of influence in his life: Funga embodies traditional forms of wisdom and religion and Father Manolo represents the Catholic Church.

Here too, it is possible to draw certain parallels between Monénembo's life and that of his protagonist. Faustin experiences an identity conflict, similar to that of the author's,[59] and Faustin's experience is depicted by Monénembo through the tension between Catholic (Western) values, embraced by his parents, and those of the indigenous culture, represented by Funga, the local witch doctor. This is already made tangible in the first few pages of the text, when the author juxtaposes a Rwandan proverb with a citation by Edmond Rostand. The Rwandan proverb teaches that 'The pain of others is bearable', whereas Rostand's citation says: 'You kill a man, you're a murderer. You kill millions, you're a conqueror. You kill them all, you're god' (Monénembo 2004: 2). The irony is that both these epigraphs, one of African origin and the other from a Western source, cynically announce the breakdown in humanity and callousness that Faustin will first be subjected to and eventually perpetuate through his own actions.

Funga is another unreliable adult in Faustin's life. Faustin introduces him to the reader with the unflattering declaration that 'Funga the witch doctor is a liar' (ibid.: 6). Although some of the villagers respect him for having healed one or two of their ailments, Faustin admits to not liking him very much, because at church he has learned to 'adore Christ and to mistrust witch doctors' (ibid.).

The Catholic priest, Father Manolo, is equally unable to prevent the massacre of Faustin's parents. He is Funga's counterweight: 'Father Manolo had taught me to read the Holy scriptures and say some "Our Fathers" to protect myself from pagan devils like [Funga] who still haunted the village a hundred years after the white man arrived!' (Monénembo 2004: 6). Both Funga and Father Manolo offer threats and warnings rather than loving and supporting words of encouragement: Manolo makes his congregants 'tremble in the church pews' with his references to the last judgment, enjoys talking about the 'famous Flood' and warns them that God is 'as likely to call you to Him while you're brimming with happiness and health as He is to force you to live amid burning coals, it depends on His own pleasure!' (ibid.: 20, 72).

Faustin is exposed from a young age to both value systems. He is sent to Father Manolo, who teaches him to assist at Mass (ibid.: 6), but his mother also regularly sends him to Funga, with his 'turtle skulls and antelope horns', so that he can 'read her fortune' (ibid.: 7).

These two spiritual leaders delegitimize each other and Faustin is torn between them: 'But you never listen to me' says Funga, '[t]hat white Father corrupted your head. You don't believe in Funga's powers anymore, and that will be your ruin' (ibid.). Faustin's ambiguity toward these two figures remains throughout the text. He doesn't really trust either of them and suspects that they invent 'stories to amuse the white beards and scare the children' (ibid.: 85). He despises both of them for the threatening tones they take: 'I resented old Funga for interpreting any old lightning strike as a sign of threat from the heavens and I resented Father Manolo for so often invoking his Christian god, so quick to fry you for all eternity for a mere sin of gluttony' (ibid.: 84). When Faustin needs divine help, he calls on any possible divinity that he can think of: 'I stopped humming the lullaby and began to pray to all the powers I could think of: Imana and the Holy Spirit, the rock of Kagera and old Funga's charms. I hoped they'd all pool their miracles together [...]' (ibid.: 44). In spite of the fact that his parents encouraged him to adopt the Catholic faith—the white people's religion—he realizes that, in many aspects, their ways and culture are irreconcilable with the local ones. When the 'Hirish woman' tries to talk to him about his '*taumatrisms*', he says: 'It's hard to talk with whites; our worlds were made as if the feet of one were the head of the other' (ibid.: 55).

After the massacre at Nyamata, Funga invites Faustin to flee with him, but the boy prefers to stay and look for his parents. Funga's departure, however, seems to symbolize for Faustin a final break with his childhood world and the security it offered. He realizes that Funga was his 'only link with the world', but he stays behind in spite of the inner voice that urges him to follow Funga and at least not be alone (ibid.: 9). Years later, in prison, the rather cynical inner voice that encourages him or tells him how to react to life has somehow become 'Funga's voice':

'Hang on, son of Théoneste! Just another day or two and you'll have croaked for good! The dead don't suffer, it's their time to recover from

living.' It might have been Funga the witch doctor's voice. Now that nothing is left, neither the house where I was born, nor the church tower,
Funga's voice is all I have. I mustn't doubt him anymore; I'm protected by
his charms. (ibid.: 14)

It is clear that it is not only the physical presence of the house or the
church tower that Faustin misses, but rather the security and stability symbolized by these two buildings which represent his childhood nostalgia
and systems of faith. What is left for him then is Funga's voice—is this
perhaps Monénembo's way of pointing him back to traditional culture
and faith? If it is, it is a very tenuous attempt, for Faustin never had much
faith in Funga's powers.

If Faustin's parents and religious systems have failed him, the adult
characters that could provide guidance after the genocide are equally incapable of doing so in any adequate way. Claudine, an exiled returnee, is
kind but naive, and the relationship between them is troubling, and as far
as Faustin is concerned, highly ambiguous. She attempts to help him, but
he harbors a range of sexual thoughts and ambitions toward her.
Furthermore, as Small correctly points out, she fails to understand him
and her reaction to him is equally inappropriate (ibid.). When Faustin
insults the lawyer who is defending him, she treats him like a little child
who needs to be soothed: 'Listen young Faustin. This is not the place for
you. It's understandable that you're a little depressed' (Monénembo
2004: 71). Faustin, on the other hand, can only think of 'mounting'
Claudine 'in a real iron bed with a mosquito net and some flowered pil-
lows' (ibid.: 15). 'I'm a real man,' he says, 'but you think of me as a little
kid, as if I were still one!' (ibid.). She does nothing to encourage his sexual
fantasies; in fact, she constantly acts in a motherly manner toward him,
with her 'mother hen ways' and scolds him 'as if she were [his] mother'
(ibid.). However, he is more comfortable with fantasizing about her 'sexy
rump' than depending on her or seeing her as some sort of mother figure
(ibid.: 36). He questions her motives and doesn't trust her altruistic
kindness:

You almost hold it against her that she's so kind, so different from the others. You stuff yourself with her meatballs and her manioc roots, you fill your
pockets with her ballpoint pens and her coins, and as a result, you hold more
resentment toward her than gratitude. You get to the point where you wish
she'd croak too, once and for all. (ibid.: 14)

It seems then that Faustin is afraid (and justifiably so, given his previous experiences of the adults in his life) of depending on Claudine. In a twisted act that can be seen as an attempt at self-preservation—to avoid coming to rely too heavily on her—Faustin wishes her dead, almost as if he expects her to abandon him the way his real mother did. It would seem then that, in this case, it is not Claudine who necessarily fails Faustin, but he who has become too afraid to trust anyone.

Rodney, the unscrupulous English cameraman who represents in many ways the foreigners who arrive in the wake of the genocide, encourages Faustin not only to lie about his genocide experiences but also to 'get sloshed' and use drugs: 'Now that you're rich, go wherever you want to sniff glue or stick a needle in your arm. Do it to your heart's content, just don't do it where I can see you. It's not morality making me say this. It's so I won't have anything to reproach myself for in case you croak. I hope you don't sell your little behind?' (ibid.: 61). Instead of trying to help the boy to remember the true story of what happened to him, Rodney uses his fabricated testimonies to make 'sensational' films about the genocide. Ironically, not guessing—or maybe not caring—that Faustin has indeed seen indescribable things, Rodney presents him to the world as a 'kid who has lived through things and with the eyes of a child', and therefore as the one who will tell them the 'truth' about the genocide (ibid.: 65).

It seems then that Faustin's exile includes being abandoned and betrayed by all the figures of authority that could have helped him and all the value systems that are meant to guide him. He eventually rejects the value systems proposed by society, both the Catholic religion, taught to him by Father Manolo, and the traditional system, propagated by Funga and the Rwandan proverbs that permeated his childhood. Perhaps this is Monénembo's way of suggesting that none of these is able to solve the problems that survivors face in the aftermath of genocide and that these values cannot automatically be expected to continue to flourish in a post-genocide society.

On Being the Oldest

The existential exile experienced by Faustin seems to have been brought on by the ambiguous position which genocide has imposed on him and which is emphasized by Monénembo's title. This anti-hero is not only an orphan who has experienced a whole range of losses, but also the oldest, and this exacerbates his identity crisis. Under these circumstances, being the oldest is an almost unbearable responsibility. It implies becoming, all at once, mother and father of the Nsenghimana family (McNee 2004: 4–5). Faustin is the oldest remaining member of his family, and thus responsible for his three siblings. The moment which most poignantly underlines this responsibility is when he assumes the role of affectionate and protective mother: he tries to reach out to his traumatized siblings by imitating their mother and the way she used to sing them a lullaby. He embraces his little brother, who has rolled into a ball like a kitten: 'I threw my arms open wide as mother used to when she'd return from the fields with ripe avocados and delicious passionfruit juice. He curled up in a ball like a kitten and began to sob, but finally he let me kiss him. I walked around rocking him, trying my best to imitate Mother's voice and gestures' (Monénembo 2004: 43).

This glimpse into a private and touching moment of this hardened character's life invites the reader to not condemn him before getting to know his story. He is the one that coaxes his siblings back from the regressed state into which they have fallen. Henceforth, he will care for them, wash them, delouse them, and feed them. He will not only be their protective father, but also their mother who nourishes, watches over, educates, and consoles them. Syrotinski suggests that Faustin takes on the role of 'resilience tutor', someone who listens to them and lets them talk about their experiences, and yet, 'as the oldest orphan, there is no one to assume this role' for him (2009: 436). He also becomes a father figure for his siblings, dreaming that all is well again and he is back home with them:

> I'll watch them grow, and a day will come when Esther and Donatienne will marry. Then I'll kill two strong buffaloes, and I'll give them the horns to hang outside their huts. I'll drink like six warriors, I'll dance the dance of the *intore*, and I'll challenge with a spear the husbands of the twelve mistresses I'll have acquired in the meantime. (Monénembo 2004: 46)

Thus, in his role as oldest orphan, he forms a stark contrast to the cynical teenager that the reader has started to become accustomed to. When Rodney offers him a way of making money, his main reason for accepting is that he will then be able to take care of HQ for a few weeks, and he will 'finally be able to give Ambroise the ball he'd been wanting' (ibid.: 57).

His siblings are not the only ones he adopts this role for. He meets Sembé on the sidewalk, with his 'crooked legs', 'beady eyes', and 'slim bundle' (ibid.: 18). Sembé starts to follow him around everywhere and

Faustin soon finds a mattress and an old piece of tarpaulin for him. He is only about a year younger, but Faustin talks of him as of a younger child, with his 'little hands' that grip the gun during a robbery they perform together. Sembé clearly becomes a type of protégé and Faustin sends him off to 'Mukazano the Madwoman' when no woman will 'have him' because he is so ugly (ibid.). What is perhaps most telling is Faustin's rage when, years later, he learns that Sembé has died of AIDS at the age of 14: 'If she hadn't been there, I'd have hit someone. The warden, the guard, that giant jabiru we call Cerberus—I'd have hit someone! Sembe. I'll never forget his crooked legs [...]' (ibid.: 17). It is this violent reaction to the death of someone he felt responsible for, even though he was not even a family member, which gives us an inkling of the reaction Faustin will have when his sister, who is under his protection, is brought to harm.

It is then in this adopted role of one who is responsible for his siblings that he commits a murder, as contradictory as it may seem. He seems to realize the weight of the burden he has shouldered, and this is transmitted in an ironic, exaggerated remark that he makes when the orphanage management expects of him to solve the problem of his siblings' trauma. He somehow gets the impression that they blame him for it: '[T]hey were observing me as if I were a demon. It might as well be my fault! The famine, the cholera, the boiling lava flow in Karisimbi's crater,[60] they were all my fault!' (ibid.: 43).

Faustin's ambivalent behavior seems to stem from his paradoxical position of being, both an orphan who has lost just about everything, and a responsible oldest brother. The fact that he transferred his responsibility of watching over them to Musinkôro (ibid.: 61), who, instead of doing so, has sex with Faustin's little sister, only serves to reinforce the ambiguity of his crime. Musinkôro himself is a type of father figure; he introduces the gang of about 20 children living in HQ as his 'little family' and speaks of HQ as 'our home' (ibid.: 29). He is clearly considered by them as 'a schoolteacher or head of a family' and not a 'gangleader' (ibid.: 29). As we have seen, he is also Faustin's 'blood' brother (ibid.: 28). This is then what makes his abuse of trust even more severe.

Lisa McNee analyzes the notions of guilt and judgment, as presented in the person of Faustin, who is 'both victim and murderer, child and man, innocent and guilty' (2004: 2). It is the gray areas, the ambiguity, and paradoxes presented by this character that interest her, and the embodiment of that 'limbo' which is survivor's guilt by a character who survived by accident or by luck, because he was small and went unnoticed where he lay under the body of his mother (ibid.: 3). The story of Faustin and his other orphaned friends reminds us that survivor stories are often not pretty, and that they had to resort to desperate measures to survive during and after the genocide: stealing, lying, doing drugs, and selling themselves.

Having the double identity of being both orphan and the oldest implies being simultaneously a genocide victim and a perpetrator who commits a crime in order to fulfill his role as the protector: 'You, if I slept with your sister, you'd do what I did to this swine', he says to the judge, 'Family honor isn't debatable anywhere in the world, at least not with the Nsenghimanas' (Monénembo 2004: 82). McNee deduces that in certain value systems, Faustin's act of murdering Musinkôro would not be interpreted as a crime, but as an act of protecting the virtue of his little sister, for whom he is responsible as the oldest brother of the Nsenghimana family (ibid.: 4–5). His actual crime then would be the 'negligence' of having assumed that his sister was safe with his friend (ibid.: 4). Although this behavior does not follow the logic of colonial, Christian, or legal systems, it can still be interpreted as an 'honor code' which puts to shame the adults that inhabit Faustin's world, for 'an orphaned child has shown more respect for honor than the adults' (ibid.). Furthermore, the example that Faustin has been given by his own father to follow is that of 'the man who heroically died alongside his Tutsi wife rather than deserting her' (ibid.).

This perspective is confirmed by Old Bukuru, who defends Faustin by evoking the traditional moral value system and reminding the judges that this 'child is not a *génocidaire*, he simply avenged his sister. Crime of passion, family honour! […] Just because there's been a genocide, it doesn't mean Rwandans have lost all moral sense' (Monénembo 2004: 82). Of course, nothing is indeed black and white, because in many ways, Faustin does seem to have 'lost all moral sense'.

In conclusion, Faustin's story is inscribed not only into the narrative of the genocide orphans, but also in the recurring figure of the exiled child. Monénembo's own life and oeuvre unfolds over three modes or moments of exile: childhood exile, African exile, and European exile (Gbanou 2003: 48–9). Faustin's life seems to emulate these same three moments: at the age of ten, when he is forced to take responsibility for himself after his parents' death, and then again when he finds that he cannot count on either the traditional African value system or the adopted Western one.

Monénembo's representation of the genocide in this text offers no redemptive ending, and Faustin can attribute no positive meaning to his traumatic past. His future is in any case somber—he is condemned to death. The novel closes with the event that has disrupted his whole life and ultimately condemned him to orphanhood and all this entails. The old lady who saved Faustin's life seven days after the massacre exclaims (and this is the final sentence of the novel): 'Oh, God, three survivors, and seven days after the massacre! There's always some life left, even when the devil has passed through' (Monénembo 2004: 96). If his miraculous survival is something to celebrate, the question clearly remains: if there is indeed life after genocide, will it be worth living for Faustin and orphans like him, the ones we read about in the medical and psychological journals?

When we apply the model of the transformative journey to the two novels discussed in this chapter, we find that they trace a type of transformation that is the opposite to that depicted in, for example, Lamko's and Diop's texts in which protagonists arrive at new, life-affirming perspectives and develop the necessary capacity to narrate the stories they need to tell. This is perhaps an unfair comparison, for neither Pelouse (Lamko) nor Cornelius (Diop) are depicted as direct victims of the genocide, but rather exiles. Be that as it may, the contrast is clear: in both Ilboudo's and Monénembo's representations, the focus is on the loss of equilibrium and the characters' inability to understand, integrate, and work through what has befallen them. The journeys they undertake only serve to exacerbate the consequences of the genocide and augment their sense of failure and despair.

These texts leave the reader with no doubt about the consequences of the genocide, especially where orphans, widows, and victims of rape are concerned. Instead of focusing on possibilities of hope for the future, the authors choose not to write what LaCapra has called a 'redemptive narrative' (2001: 254). Rather, through their refusal to create a 'happy ending' or some form of closure for their protagonists and narratives, they focus on the complexity and pain of the aftermath of genocide.

NOTES

1. All English translations of Ilboudo's text, which was written in French, are mine. Where necessary, I supply the original citations in endnotes or brackets.
2. « Je n'ai pas encore compris pourquoi j'y avais échappé. Pourquoi moi ? Pourquoi pas les autres ? Pourquoi pas mes enfants, deux petits innocents si pleins de vie ? Pourquoi pas ma mère, mes sœurs, mon frère, tous les

autres ? Ils méritaient tous de vivre. Ils sont tous morts. Je suis vivante. Je méritais pourtant de mourir » (Ilboudo 2000: 22).

3. « Abrutie par des décennies de brimades, d'humiliations, et de terreur, l'ethnie tutsi, culpabilisée et complexée, était dans son ensemble résignée. Ses membres acceptaient leur condition de sous-hommes, de citoyens de seconde zone. C'est tout juste si la plupart d'entre nous ne s'estimaient pas heureux qu'on les laissât seulement vivre ! » (Kayimahe 2001: 44).

4. I use this term, not in reference to the notion of 'zombies', often depicted in horror films or literature, but rather to refer to those who have experienced such suffering that they feel it would have been better to die.

5. Whether intended or not, the image of ashes immediately evokes the ever-present theme of mourning.

6. Jennie Burnet speaks about the 'amplified silence' that is prevalent in post-genocide Rwanda, noting that silence is often a form of protection (2012: 114) or a 'culturally appropriate coping mechanism for their violent experiences' (ibid.: 115) or even a form of hegemonic power (ibid.: 117–8).

7. For further discussion of the representation of rape in narrative texts within the context of the Rwandan genocide, consult Eleni Coundouriotis's (2013) insightful article, which combines aspects of legal theory, testimonies, and visual theory on this issue.

8. 'Nous avons libéré les femmes Tutsi, nous avons libéré ces arrogantes …' (Mujawayo and Belhaddad 2004: 195, 196).

9. Citing a number of scholars, Maggie Zraly and Laetitia Nyirazinyoye have defined resilience as a characteristic which includes adapting well to adverse circumstances, coping with traumatic experiences, and maintaining emotional integrity in the face of human horror, and they add that social and community relationships and structures play an important role in promoting resilience (2010: 1657). They furthermore underline the importance of the culture and context relevant to the person who shows resilience (ibid.: 1658).

10. This is the girl who refuses to name herself, telling Jessica only that she wants to die, that she knows she is going to die but needs to shares her horrible secret of how the priest raped her because she cannot die alone with it.

11. « Là-bas, la séance de torture reprend, plus mécanique, plus méthodique. Pour commencer, tout le monde est prié de se mettre la tête en bas, les pieds en haut appuyés contre le mur, et de rester dans cette position pénible et incongrue jusqu'à ce qu'ils soient permis de se reposer. […] Tout le monde est en sang, plus personne ne crie et les tortionnaires eux-mêmes semblent se fatiguer. C'est alors que le plus terrible survient.

Avisant tout à coup l'une des deux jeunes filles, les bêtes immondes décident de la violer […] Mais elle continue à se débattre, à pleurer, à refuser et à repousser ces corps hideux qui se pressent contre elle. […] Le reste de la famille s'est tu. Face à l'horreur, à l'indicible, tout le monde a pudiquement détourné le regard » (Kayimahe 2001: 203–4).

12. At the time of the writing residency, her body was still displayed. In the meantime, the Nyamata site has been altered and Mukandori's remains are buried in a coffin inside the crypt.

13. ' Et quand on nous a dit qu'elle s'appelait Théreza Mukandori, j'ai vu tout le monde prendre note. Au fond, cela voulait dire, et l'on s'adressait un peu aux tueurs: « vous vouliez la tuer, mais nous, nous allons la faire revivre. » […]. Moi, j'ai changé beaucoup de noms, d'autres ont changé beaucoup de noms. Mais pour Théreza, personne n'a voulu changé. Personne. Parfois on met « Mukandoli » ou « Mukandori », mais n'oublions pas qu'en kinyarwanda, le « l » et le « r » sont équivalents. Je crois que cela a été quelque chose de très frappant. Elle revient dans la totalité des romans' (Diop, in Bénard 2001).

14. « Et en vérité, le cas de Théreza Mukandori revient dans tous les romans. Au fond, cela donne le sens profond de cette démarche. […] Je crois que cela a été quelque chose de très frappant. Elle revient dans la totalité des romans » (Bénard 2001).

15. « Furieux, il court traîner l'énorme croix en ébène massif, réservée aux grandes messes de Pâques […]. Il se précipite sur moi avec le crucifix, écarte violemment mes jambes flasques, l'enfonce d'un coup sec dans mon vagin, […] » (Lamko 2002: 46, 109).

16. Josias Semujanga (2008: 161) has commented on this reductive form, which makes no allowance for embellishment or poetic description, and Alexandre Dauge-Roth (2010: 134) has described it as a 'quasi-forensic mode' of writing which suggests that 'images and metaphors' would be 'inappropriate' to describe the violence of her death.

17. « J'ai rencontré Mukandori, ma sœur bien-aimée. Ligotée, violée, meurtrie. Mukandori, sortie de la fosse d'aisance, statufiée dans sa posture de prière, de vaine supplication. Quatre ans après sa mort, j'ai entendu ses cris de détresse, ses râles. 'Pitié !', implorait-elle. Comment ont-ils pu ? Ce pieu dans sa féminité endolorie, dans sa féminité bafouée ! Comment ont-ils osé ? Je l'ai vu exposée, sa pudeur violée » (Ilboudo 2000: 65).

18. Ilboudo's first novel, *Le mal de peau*, also addresses themes of mixed parentage, rape, and the condition of women.

19. Ilboudo is not the only author to give the main voice in her text to a protagonist from mixed parentage—Monénembo's Faustin and Diop's Cornelius are other key examples.

20. Rwandan children inherited their ethnic category from their father, irrespective of the mother's ethnicity.

21. Monique Gasengayire analyzes the discursive and narrative strategies used—such as dramatization, hyperbole, registers pertaining to that which is unheard of and impossible to believe, the unreal feeling created by the description of the dream, and the presence of the unsaid—all used in order to transmit the 'impossibility' of truly narrating the genocide (2005: 151–7).

22. This frequent slipping from the imperfect to the present tense is remarked on by journalist Souâd Belhaddad when discussing Esther Mujawayo's testimonial narrative. She suggests that the present tense represents the moment of trauma in which the victim remains suspended: « Tout au long de ce livre, le lecteur observera régulièrement un fréquent glissement du temps de l'imparfait à celui du présent, bousculant toute convention des concordances des temps. […] comme l'explique Marie-Odile Godard, […] le présent est le temps du traumatisme. […] Comme si cette période de l'horreur était, pour tout rescapé, un temps suspendu » (Mujawayo and Belhaddad 2004: 11–12).

23. « Prise de vertige, je perds tout contrôle. Une sensation d'étouffement. L'air me manque. Je me mets à haleter comme une noyée sauvée en extremis. […] j'étais tétanisée. Je ne criais plus, je ne bougeais plus » (Ilboudo 2000: 69).

24. Ilboudo notes that Murekatete means « laisse-la vivre ! laisse-la se sentir à l'aise ! » which I have translated with 'May she live! May she be happy!' (Ilboudo 2000: 12).

25. I have previously made a comparison between the work of three female authors on this theme, and some of the elements of that analysis have been incorporated into this section on Ilboudo's work. Consult De Beer and Snyman (2015).

26. « Je n'étais pas née pour vivre. Je suis morte à la naissance. La petite tombe était déjà creusée. Tout le monde était prêt pour mon enterrement. Seule ma mère se cramponnait à ce petit corps fripé, refusant de le laisser ensevelir » (Ilboudo 2000: 11).

27. When analyzing artistic representations of trauma, there are certain devices embedded in the texts that provide us with signs of the trauma. There are also different levels of witnessing (what is said, how it is said, and how it is received). Irene Kacandes claims that texts can be described as 'successful' or 'unsuccessful' portrayals of trauma because: 'we can think about narratives 'of' trauma, but also narratives 'as' trauma; that is to say, literary texts can be about trauma, in the sense that they can depict perpetrations of violence against characters who are traumatized by the violence and then successfully or unsuccessfully witness to their trauma. But texts can also 'perform' trauma, in the sense that they can 'fail' to tell the story, by eliding, repeating, and fragmenting components of the story' (Kacandes 1999: 55–6).

Certain elements in the text can be interpreted as signs of trauma, testifying to the victim's inability to verbalize the experience: interior monologues, fragmentation, repetition, euphemisms, and silences or gaps in the stories.

28. « La mort était partout. Une mort inhabituelle. Il n'y a rien de plus normal que la mort. Tout ce qui vit meurt un jour. Mourir est donc naturel, et nous l'acceptons en naissant. [...] La mort n'est pas normale lorsqu'elle frappe collectivement des êtres qui n'aspirent qu'à vivre » (Ilboudo 2000: 34).

29. Jorge Semprun evokes the enigmatic concept described by many Holocaust survivors of 'passing through death' (*avoir traversé la mort*) (1996: 26). For Semprun, those who have survived such a traumatic experience are often not survivors, but rather '*revenants*'—literally, those who have returned from the dead (1996: 121).

30. « Ce fut ma deuxième résurrection. Venant en est l'artisan. Comme autrefois ma mère, il a fait un miracle » (Ilboudo 2000: 16).

31. « Pourtant, ce qui devait être une seconde vie n'est jusque-là, qu'une pénible survie » (Ilboudo 2000: 22).

32. « Puisque je ne suis pas morte, je dois vivre. Au réveil, je me retrouve aussi désemparée que la veille. Je ne trouve pas l'énergie nécessaire pour me mettre dans le bain qui mousse autour de moi, le bain frénétique de la reconstruction. Il y a tant à faire: des murs et des hommes à reconstruire. Des blessées à soigner, des rescapés à consoler, des traumatisés à psychanalyser [...]. Chaque matin, je mets un pied devant l'autre, et je ne sais si j'avance ou si je recule » (Ilboudo 2000: 47).

33. « Ma vie s'est arrêtée un jour de juin 1994. [...] C'est au bord de ce sentier au milieu de nulle part que j'aurais dû mourir pour de bon. Le sort en a décidé autrement. Grâce à Venant, la carcasse a été ranimée. Mais depuis, je déambule, comme une ombre, l'ombre de moi-même » (Ilboudo 2000: 45, 47).

34. « [...] le combat entre la chance et la culpabilité de survivre [...] » (Gasengayire 2005: 149).

35. « J'avais honte. Honte de le réveiller chaque nuit avec ce rire indécent, honte de mon incapacité à répondre à son amour. Sans un mot, Venant éteignit la lampe et se recoucha. Je sentis son bras qui m'entourait, dans une vaine tentative de protection » (Ilboudo 2000: 10).

36. « Mais c'est Murambi qui a bouleversé notre existence à deux. [...] Depuis notre visite en ce lieu maudit, rien ne va plus. Au début ce furent de légères turbulences auxquelles je ne prêtai pas toute l'attention due. Puis ce fut une lame de fond qui déferla, nous submergea et noya ce que nous avions tenté de préserver dans cet univers de chaos. Venant le sage, Venant l'irréprochable s'était mis à boire » (Ilboudo 2000: 61).

37. « Depuis ce jour où nous avons visité Murambi, je n'ai plus rencontré le même regard confiant dans les yeux de Venant. Comme s'il se défiait d'une partie de moi, comme s'il m'assimilait à moitié à la barbarie de Murambi. Lui, l'artisan de ma résurrection. Je ressentis cruellement ce coup fatal. Je ne me remettrai jamais de cette mort-là » (Ilboudo 2000: 72).

38. « 'Tu peux crier autant qu'il te plaira, personne ne viendra. Je suis ton mari que diable ! Et tu sais ce qu'un mari fait à sa femme ?' Tout en parlant il m'arrachait mes vêtements de nuit, me dénudant de la main gauche, tenant mes poignets au-dessus de ma tête de la main droite » (Ilboudo 2000: 69).

39. « J'étais tétanisée. Je ne criais plus, je ne bougeais plus. Je le vis s'acharner sur mon corps avec la sensation que ce n'était pas le mien. Je ne le reconnaissais pas, lui non plus. Au-dessus des deux personnages, je scrutais cette scène insolite. Les rugissements de bête fauve de l'homme au-dessus du corps qui n'était pas le mien me ramenèrent un instant à la réalité. J'éclatai du même rire saccadé qui me réveillait chaque nuit » (Ilboudo 2000: 69).

40. « Venant est parti, et la maison, envahie par le vide, ne résonne plus que du néant de ma vie. Certains jours, me prend l'envie de mettre un terme à ce néant. Seule la crainte de tomber dans le néant éternel me retient » (Ilboudo 2000: 72).

41. Ilboudo's choice of cover image, entitled *Un corps étranger* (A foreign body) enhances the sensation of a breakdown in communication. This illustration by Bruce Clarke shows the profile of a man in the foreground, staring in one direction, and two seemingly feminine figures in the background, looking the opposite way. This creates the impression that they are looking toward each other without seeing each other, almost as if they were all looking at their past or their future without looking each other in the eye.

42. « J'ouvris les yeux. Venant alluma la lampe de chevet, et penché sur un coude, me sourit gentiment. Je lui tournai le dos et tirai un bout de drap pour me couvrir la tête, pour échapper à ce regard plein d'amour. J'avais honte » (Ilboudo 2000: 10).

43. « Quand il revenait dans la chambre après sa toilette, il évitait mon regard jusqu'au moment de son départ [....] J'essaye de rencontrer son regard, mais ses yeux vitreux d'ivrogne sont incapables d'accrocher un regard » (Ilboudo 2000: 62, 69).

44. « Le temps viendra où ils auront le courage d'appareiller, certains d'être responsables du navire. Ils pourront alors détourner les yeux de cette vision d'horreur, pour regarder le large, pour regarder l'avenir. Pour l'instant, voyageurs indécis, ils scrutaient le ciel » (Ilboudo 2000: 74).

45. For a more detailed discussion on Esther Mujawayo's literary testimony, consult De Beer and Snyman (2015).

46. She deliberately modifies the typography by using a capital letter in the middle of the word, thus highlighting the term '*vivant*', which means 'to be alive', and contrasting it to '*survivant*', which refers to surviving. This decision is confirmed in the preface, in which she describes being fully alive ('alive-alive') rather than mere survival as a form of revenge on those who wanted her dead (Mujawayo and Belhaddad 2004: 5).

47. « d'abord condamnés à vivre, aujourd'hui ils ont *décidé* de vivre » (Mujawayo and Belhaddad 2004: 30).

48. « J'aime Venant. Du plus profond de mon cœur meurtri. De toutes les forces de mon corps mutilé. Je sais qu'il m'aime. Mais je suis morte. Depuis bien longtemps » (Ilboudo 2000: 10).

49. The original French text was published in 2000. My quotations are from the 2004 English translation by Monique Fleury Nagem.

50. « Le romancier n'est pas une conscience. C'est une âme inquiète [...] Il n'analyse pas, il ne juge pas, il ne tranche pas. Il est ému, et s'il a un rôle, c'est celui d'abord d'émouvoir » (Monénembo, in Mongo-Mboussa 2004).

51. Parts of this analysis of Monénembo's novel are based on an article which I translated from French and edited for this chapter (De Beer 2016).

52. Both Faustin's and Gérard's stories have religious or mythical undertones: they miraculously survive or are 'rebirthed' by drinking blood.

53. Such as Audrey Small (2006), Lisa McNee (2004), Maria Angela Germanotta (2016), Paul Touré (2009), Josias Semujanga (2008), and Michael Syrotinski (2009).

54. « chaque asile rêvé est un espoir qui, une fois entrevu, malheureusement se dérobe » (Gbanou 2003: 43).

55. McNee interprets Faustin's flight from the orphanage as a subconscious refusal to recall the massacre: 'This flight from a comfortable home in the orphanage marks a flight from memory of all sorts' (2004: 7).

56. « [...] l'obligation de se tourner vers soi en substituant au contexte dont on est naturellement le plus proche un lieu qui a valeur d'ultime solution offrant des garanties minimales de survie, voire de bonheur » (Gbanou 2003: 45).

57. A traditional game played with stones or marbles on a wooden plank.

58. Such as *pernangamate, merchrocome, pellicinine, pédrophile, taumatrismes, Ouatican, Notions-Unies,* and *busenessman.*

59. Monénembo knew the vicissitudes of orphanhood: as a child he had to stay with his grandmother, due to his parents' divorce (Gbanou 2003: 44). He was exposed from a young age to the difficulties and unease that characterizes what Gbanou calls '*l'entre-deux cultures*' (being between two cultures): he first attended the Koranic school and then the colonial French school (ibid.: 46). At the colonial school, he was punished for not speaking French, but outside school, the Muslim community in which he lived

detested this language and he was reprimanded for using the 'language of the white man, the Christian, the colonizer' (Monénembo, cited in Gbanou 2003: 47; my translation). Monénembo acknowledges that language was one of the aspects that caused trauma in his youth, as he was torn between the two cultures that the different languages represented (ibid.); for him, language was thus already a form of trauma and alienation. In an attempt to complete his schooling, at a time when Guinea was experiencing great turmoil, he moved successively to Dakar and Abidjan, and finally lived in exile in Brussels and Lyon.

60. This is the volcano where the deceased allegedly spend the afterlife.

References

Bénard, Marie. 2001. Entretien avec Boubacar Boris Diop. Accessed July 18, 2018. http://aircrigeweb.free.fr/ressources/rwanda/RwandaDiop1.html.

Brison, Susan. 1999. Trauma Narratives and the Remaking of the Self. In *Acts of Memory: Cultural Recall in the Present*, ed. Mieke Bal, Jonathan V. Crewe, and Leo Spitzer, 38–54. Hanover: University Press of New England.

Brounéus, Karen. 2008. Truth-Telling as Talking Cure? Insecurity and Retraumatization in the Rwandan Gacaca Courts. *Security Dialogue* 39 (1): 55–76.

Burnet, Jennie E. 2012. *Genocide Lives in Us: Women, Memory, and Silence in Rwanda*. Madison: University of Wisconsin Press.

Coundouriotis, Eleni. 2013. "You only have your word": Rape and Testimony. *Human Rights Quarterly* 35 (2): 365–385.

Dauge-Roth, Alexandre. 2010. *Writing and Filming the Genocide of the Tutsis in Rwanda: Dismembering and Remembering Traumatic History*, After the Empire: The Francophone World and Postcolonial France. Lanham, MD: Lexington Books.

De Beer, Anna-Marie. 2016. « La saison des pertes » dans *L'aîné des orphelins* de Tierno Monénembo. *French Studies in Southern Africa* 46: 30–45.

De Beer, Anna-Marie, and Elisabeth Snyman. 2015. Shadows of Life, Death and Survival in the Aftermath of the Rwandan Genocide. *Tydskrif vir letterkunde* 52 (1): 113–130.

Diop, Boubacar Boris. 2006. *Murambi: The Book of Bones* (Kindle edition). Translated by Fiona McLaughlin. Bloomington: Indiana University Press.

Gasengayire, Monique. 2005. Murekatete, un témoignage (im)possible. In *Dix ans après: réflexions sur le génocide rwandais*, ed. Rangira Béatrice Gallimore and Chantal Kalisa, 143–160. Paris: Harmattan.

Gbanou, Sélom Komlan. 2003. Tierno Monénembo: la lettre et l'exil. *Tangence* 71: 41–61. https://doi.org/10.7202/008550ar.

Germanotta, Maria Angela. 2016. L'écriture de l'inaudible. Les narrations littérai-res du génocide au Rwanda, *Interfrancophonies*, Nouvelles formes de l'engagement dans les littératures francophones, ed. Alessandro Crostantini. 70: 73–100. https://doi.org/10.17457/IF7_2016/GER.

Gourevitch, Philip. 2000. *We Wish to Inform You that Tomorrow We Will Be Killed with Our Families: Stories from Rwanda*. London: Picador.

Ilboudo, Monique. 2000. *Murekatete: Roman*. Bamako and Lille: Le Figuier and Fest'Africa.

Kacandes, Irene. 1999. Narrative Witnessing as Memory Work: Reading Gertrud Kolmar's *A Jewish Mother*. In *Acts of Memory: Cultural Recall in the Present*, ed. Mieke Bal, Jonathan V. Crewe, and Leo Spitzer, 55–71. Hanover: University Press of New England.

Kalisa, Chantal. 2005. Le gos au Rwanda: entretien avec Koulsy Lamko. In *Dix ans après: réflexions sur le génocide rwandais*, ed. Rangira Béatrice Gallimore and Chantal Kalisa, 259–280. Paris: Harmattan.

Kayimahe, Vénuste. 2001. *France-Rwanda: les coulisses du génocide: témoignage d'un rescapé*. Paris: Dagorno.

LaCapra, Dominick. 2001. *Writing History, Writing Trauma*. Baltimore: Johns Hopkins University Press.

Lamko, Koulsy. 2002. *La phalène des collines*. Paris: Le Serpent à Plumes.

McNee, Lisa. 2004. Monénembo's *L'Aîné des orphelins* and the Rwandan Genocide. *CLCWeb: Comparative Literature and Culture* 6 (2). https://doi.org/10.7771/1481-4374.1228.

Monénembo, Tierno. 2000. *L'aîné des orphelins*. Paris: Éditions du Seuil.

———. 2004. *The Oldest Orphan*. Translated by Monique Fleury Nagem. Lincoln: University of Nebraska Press.

Mongo-Mboussa, Boniface. 2004. L'inutile utilité de la littérature. *Africultures* 59: 5–11.

Mujawayo, Esther, and Souâd Belhaddad. 2004. *SurVivantes: Rwanda, dix ans après le génocide*. La Tour d'Aigues: Éditions de l'Aube.

Ng, Lauren C., Naphtal Ahishakiye, Donald E. Miller, and Beth E. Meyerowitz. 2015. Narrative Characteristics of Genocide Testimonies Predict Posttraumatic Stress Disorder Symptoms Years Later. *Psychological Trauma: Theory, Research, Practice and Policy* 7 (3): 303–311.

Ricœur, Paul. 1983. *Temps et récit*. L'Ordre philosophique. Paris: Seuil.

———. 1995. Le pardon peut-il guérir? *Esprit (1940–)* 210 (3/4): 77–82.

Schaal, Susanne, and Thomas Elbert. 2006. Ten Years after the Genocide: Trauma Confrontation and Posttraumatic Stress in Rwandan Adolescents. *Journal of Traumatic Stress* 19 (1): 95–105.

Semprun, Jorge. 1996. *L'écriture ou la vie*. Collection Folio: 2870. Paris: Gallimard.

Semujanga, Josias. 2008. *Le génocide, sujet de fiction? : Analyse des récits du massacre des Tutsi dans la littérature africaine*. Quebec: Nota bene.

Small, Audrey. 2006. Tierno Monènembo: Morality, Mockery and the Rwandan Genocide. *Forum for Modern Language Studies* 42 (2): 200–211.

Syrotinski, Michael. 2009. Monstrous Fictions: Testifying to the Rwandan Genocide in Tierno Monénembo's *L'aîné des orphelins. Forum for Modern Language Studies* 45 (4): 427–440.

Tadjo, Véronique. 2002. *The Shadow of Imana: Travels in the Heart of Rwanda*. Translated by Véronique Wakerley. Oxford: Heinemann.

Talbot, Annie, Chaste Uwihoreye, Charles Kamen, Philip Grant, Lawrence McGlynn, Isaac Mugabe, Martin Nshimyumukiza, et al. 2013. Treating Psychological Trauma Among Rwandan Orphans Is Associated with a Reduction in HIV Risk-Taking Behaviors: A Pilot Study. *AIDS Education and Prevention: Official Publication of the International Society for AIDS Education* 25 (6): 468–479.

Temple-Raston, Dina. 2005. *Justice on the Grass: A Story of Genocide and Redemption*. New York: Free Press.

Tidd, Ursula. 2005. The Infinity of Testimony and Dying in Jorge Semprún's Holocaust Autothanatographies. *Forum for Modern Language Studies* 41 (4): 407–417.

Touré, Paul N. 2009. L'Aîné des orphelins de Tierno Monénembo et l'écriture de la mémoire traumatique. *Nouvelles Études Francophones* 24 (2): 171–186.

Van Alphen, Ernst. 1999. Symptoms of Discursivity: Experience, Memory, and Trauma. In *Acts of Memory: Cultural Recall in the Present*, ed. Mieke Bal, Jonathan V. Crewe, and Leo Spitzer, 24–38. Hanover: University Press of New England.

Waberi, Abdourahman A. 2016. *Harvest of Skulls* (Kindle edition). Translated by Dominic Thomas. Bloomington: Indiana University Press.

Zraly, Maggie, and Laetitia Nyirazinyoye. 2010. Don't Let the Suffering Make You Fade Away: An Ethnographic Study of Resilience Among Survivors of Genocide-Rape in Southern Rwanda. *Social Science & Medicine* 70 (10): 1656–1664.

CHAPTER 6

Poems, Testimonies, and Essays: Nocky Djedanoum, Jean-Marie Rurangwa, and Vénuste Kayimahe

This chapter deals with the work of Nocky Djedanoum, Jean-Marie Vianney Rurangwa, and Vénuste Kayimahe. We explore *Nyamirambo!*, Djedanoum's volume of poetry, Rurangwa's *Le génocide des Tutsi expliqué à un étranger: essai*, written in an argumentative tone, and Kayimahe's factual but personal eyewitness testimony, *France-Rwanda: les coulisses du génocide: témoignage d'un rescapé*. From a genre and stylistic perspective, these works are clearly very diverse and reading them together allows us to consider the different approaches and positionings they offer.

Djedanoum, although he has lived elsewhere, is originally from Chad and this volume of poetry was his first published text (Djedanoum, in Achariant 2002). The other two authors are the only Rwandans who participated in the project: Rurangwa as an exiled Tutsi and Kayimahe as a Tutsi survivor. Kayimahe tells his own story and although Rurangwa was not in the country during the genocide, he identifies strongly with the victims of this event. The mere fact of being Rwandan or non-Rwandan understandably influenced certain narrative elements and possibly even the intentions and aims of the authors in question. The two Rwandans had certain objectives in common with the other authors, but their unique contexts deserve to be taken into account.

Although the texts of the Rwandan authors are acknowledged as forming part of the project and are usually briefly summarized or mentioned, they are frequently excluded from in-depth analyses, often for practical reasons, such as the researcher's focus on fiction, novels, or specific themes.

© The Author(s) 2020   217
A.-M. de Beer, *Sharing the Burden of Stories from the Tutsi Genocide*, Palgrave Studies in Cultural Heritage and Conflict, https://doi.org/10.1007/978-3-030-42093-2_6

It may also be because the inclusion of these two voices complicates notions of intellectual witnessing and transnational solidarity as frameworks for analyzing the project. Indeed, many of the characteristics that I discuss in the first two chapters that pertain to such frameworks are not necessarily applicable to these two authors. In addition, the genres adopted by Rurangwa and Kayimahe lend themselves less to the use of literary devices and poetic language, which could influence the texts' capacity to compel the reader on an emotional level or attract the attention of literary critics. Indeed, judging by the amount of critical material dedicated to the project, it is clear that those works from the project which can be described as possessing a higher level of 'literariness'[1] (Miall and Kuiken 2009), such as the novels and travel accounts, have attracted more attention. These imaginative and largely fictional texts are also more often included in literary programs intended for students.

Djedanoum's poetry has strangely enough also received less attention than the other texts in terms of critical analysis and the reason for that is not clear. Perhaps this is due to the fact that it is the only work written in this form, which makes it both unique and difficult to include in a comparative study. Also, not one of the three texts discussed in this chapter have been translated into English, a fact which may have led to this paucity of critical attention.[2]

Djedanoum, a journalist by training, admits that he made the choice to express himself through poetry because he was convinced that the only way to attempt this endeavor was through the slow and constant process of self-interrogation that poetry requires. This is what he calls its '*lent travail*': the slow and meticulous searching for the right word in an attempt not to 'betray' the impact of the atrocities that took place (Achariant 2002).[3] Certainly, his choice of genre makes particular sense in the light of Rwandan oral tradition; poetry and songs have long been associated with storytelling and the transmission of history in this country.[4]

The anthology is divided into three parts; it is indeed its combination of prose and poetry—with its absence of rhyme and regular meter, and its abundance of rhythm, imagery, and repetition—that enables him to not 'betray' the violence of the subject he is writing about. The first and third parts are written in prose and serve as introduction and conclusion. Inserted between them is a collection of 16 poems, composed in free verse and in which typography plays an important role. Djedanoum is critical of the result he produced, admitting that his poetry leaves him dissatisfied, that it is 'limited' because of its 'introspective' nature and 'narcissism', and that it doesn't go beyond his own experience of visiting Rwanda (in Marcelli 2000).

The choice on the part of the two Rwandans to write an essay and a testimony is a logical one and speak to their positions: in the first place, they personally experienced the genocide, one as a survivor and the other as a displaced Tutsi. They are ideally positioned to write texts based on facts and personal experience. Furthermore, the project took place a mere four years after the genocide, giving them little time to obtain any type of distance from it—at least not the type of distance that would be required to write fictional and literary works.

Diop's intuition on this matter was clearly that the writers participating in the project were precursors (2006a). Theirs was a provisional attempt—by mostly non-Rwandans—to tell the genocide stories until such time as the Rwandans had found their own voices and the necessary distance to do so themselves. He emphasizes that the only two Rwandans in the group were also the only ones who did not write fictional works and that this is an issue of distance and time; more stories and more in-depth stories would be written in the future by those who had seen and experienced the atrocities (ibid.). 'I am convinced', says Diop, 'that the pain can only be expressed by being passed on over generations, thus gradually being sublimed/transferred and refined' (ibid.). He adds that, paradoxically, it seems easier for someone who did not experience the genocide, to write an account that gives the impression of what really happened than for those who were there, because the overwhelming desire of many eyewitnesses is to forget, rather than remember (ibid.).[5]

One can imagine that a survivor might not necessarily welcome having some or other poetic or literary format imposed on the telling of such a traumatic experience. Time has shown, however, that Diop's assessment was correct; an increasing number of survivors have by now written and continue to publish their own stories, some co-writing with experienced writers or artists, in French, English, and Kinyarwanda, and in a variety of forms. Esther Mujawayo's co-authored work, for example, offers an eye-witness testimony which is also written in a compelling and literary manner.[6]

In the case of the two Rwandan participants, Diop's assumption also proved to be accurate: after the project both of them went on to write subsequent texts on the genocide. Kayimahe co-directed a documentary series on a parliamentary mission investigating the role of France during the genocide and produced, 20 years after the genocide, what his publishers describe as a 'testimonial novel' (*roman témoignage*), entitled *La chanson de l'aube* (2014). Although it is fictional, this novel is infused with his own experience as a survivor. Catherine Mazauric notes that the publication of this fine novel, his second text on the genocide, indeed confirms the pact between the imaginary and the duty of memory (Mazauric 2015). Although he has returned to his native country, both of his books were written largely while in exile, the first in Germany and the second in Mexico (ibid.).

In 2005, Rurangwa published a book that he admitted was a text on his own life lived in exile: *Un Rwandais sur les routes de l'exil.* He also published *Au sortir de l'enfer* (2007), the story of a Tutsi journalist survivor, and in 2013 completed his thesis on the question of ethnicity in Rwanda, subsequently published in book form. In 2016, he published an essay on identity issues, entitled *Les identités lourdes à porter.* Before analyzing the three texts focused on in this chapter, I briefly look at the notion of exile which is a strong presence in all three texts as well as throughout the project.

TALES OF EXILE

As has become clear, the plight of the diaspora is very much a part of the Rwandan genocide story and to omit it in a narrative on the genocide would be unfortunate. Edward Said has stated that exile 'is strangely compelling to think about but terrible to experience. It is the unhealable rift forced between a human being and a native place, between the self and its true home: its essential sadness can never be surmounted' (Said 2000: 173). This 'essential sadness' and the thirst for being rooted somewhere is a burning issue among the Tutsi diaspora, which stretches over the African continent and beyond. The polyphonic narrative of the project extends the problem of otherness and exile beyond the borders of Rwanda, acknowledging it to be not only an African but a human problem that contemporary society faces. Exile and its 'unhealable rift' (ibid.: 173) is a central theme in Djedanoum's poetry and is also embodied in the protagonists of the other project texts: Lamko's wandering character, Fred R., and Pelouse, the script-girl who grew up in Paris; Cornelius, in Diop's novel, who returns to write a play on his country of birth, and his childhood friend Jessica; Seth and Valentine in Tadjo's travel account; and Faustin and his existential exile in Monénembo's novel.

Kayimahe tells of the Tutsis' dilemma of being torn between two impossible options: remaining in their country and facing persecution or going elsewhere where they were unwelcome:

> We were caught in a terrible impasse: flee and abandon everything, without the slightest guarantee of arriving anywhere, with a family of ten, hunted by the henchmen of the regime, or else stay there and wait for the next attack, and most likely torture and death. (2001: 31)[7]

Even in their country of exile, they become victims of xenophobia. We find an example of this in the story of Fred R., who is rejected by his class-mates in his parents' adopted country:

> 'Filthy little Rwandan!' Fred listened carefully. The nasty boy repeated loudly: 'Filthy little Rwandan, go away!'
> The class burst out laughing. Fred R. violently shot back:
> 'You're lying! I am neither filthy, nor Rwandan.'
> Another kid chimed in.
> 'He's right, it's true that you're a Rwandan. Look, you're not like us. You're a Rwandan; everybody says so.' (Lamko 2002: 51)[8]

This incident serves as a reminder that the problem of alterity and preju-dice was not just something the Tutsis experienced in their own country—they also faced it in exile in the form of xenophobia. In another incident, Fred R. loses his place in a shop queue because he picks up a newspaper. When he tries to reclaim his place, the woman behind him refuses to let him in, saying: 'Do you think that you have a place here? Just look at your-self! And tell me if you have a place!' (ibid.: 126). He reacts by talking to her in his own language, upon which she complains that she has been insulted by a 'foreigner' speaking in an 'uncivilized language' (ibid.). This encounter hardens his heart and he proclaims himself a 'son of the unlim-ited realm of the dream and the nightmare', thus evoking the painful life of a refugee (ibid.).

Jessica, who has lived in Burundi and elsewhere, metaphorically describes the existential crisis that refugees experience:

> Between our futures and ourselves, unknown people had planted a sort of giant machete. Try as you might, you couldn't ignore it. The tragedy would always end up catching you. Because people came to your house one night

and massacred all your family. Because in the country where you live in exile, you always end up feeling in the way. (Diop 2006b: 376–8)

Waberi touchingly describes the despairing existence of those living in exile, their lives characterized by the constant physical and emotional absence of their motherland, desperately hanging on to her language, her smell, and her culture: 'The exiled, vivaciously amassed on the perimeter of the motherland, breathing in her unique fragrance, live in subhuman conditions—hopeless young people enlist for distant campaigns, as far afield as Mozambique. They hold on to the grittiness of their mother tongue' (2016: 258–60).

Furthermore, the suffering of the diaspora does not necessarily end when the exiles return to their country after the genocide. They were not welcome there before the genocide and, as Philip Gourevitch (2000) notes, their return (understandably) causes tension between them and those who had stayed behind. A massive return of the diaspora from all the corners of the earth included many who had been in exile for years, even decades, and some of those who had remained behind ended up feeling less at home than those who came from elsewhere. These 'new arrivals', motivated by a desire to belong, but also eager to rebuild and reclaim a country that had been destroyed, demanded their share of the abandoned properties and goods, often leaving the survivors to feel misunderstood and judged:

> 'They come here, they see us, and they say: "How did you survive? Did you collaborate with the *interahamwe*?" They think we were fools to have stayed in the country—and maybe we were—so they disdain us. They don't want to be reminded. It shocks us to the bones.' […] '[…] we thought the survivors would be taken care of, that it would be the first task of the new government. But only those returning from outside are getting homes […].' (Gourevitch 2000: 232–3)

The plight of the returnee is addressed in Diop's text, in the character of Cornelius. Upon his return, he comes to realize that he will always feel like a stranger, an outsider, because he was not there during the genocide: '[H]e felt that he would never be able to understand the pain that had not been his. His return was almost becoming another exile' (2006b: 1435–6). After living in exile for years, Cornelius realizes that even his concept of his homeland is not necessarily realistic: 'After all, Rwanda is an imaginary country. If it's so difficult to talk about in a rational way, maybe it's because it doesn't really exist. Everyone has his own Rwanda in his head and it has nothing to do with the Rwanda of others' (ibid.: 724–5).

Esther Mujawayo testifies to the difficult cohabitation between survivors, perpetrators, and returnees:

> In Rwanda they tell us: 'We've talked about this enough.' We're stuck, us survivors, between the Hutu, our longtime neighbors who killed us, and the Tutsi, our brothers who returned from exile after more than 30 years [...] who always dreamed of coming back to Rwanda, but who didn't expect that they would return by walking on the corpses. (Mujawayo and Belhaddad 2004: 19; my translation)[9]

Monique Ilboudo evokes this tension caused by the return of the refugees and the naive expectation that their reintegration into the community would be easy: 'All I could think of saying was that Rwanda is a real mosaic, that every refugee had returned, with the habits and customs of his former country of refuge inside his hastily assembled bags, and that I wondered how we were going to deal with all of this' (2000: 63; my translation).[10]

Tadjo writes of her encounter with a refugee preparing to return, noting that although the desire to return is clearly overwhelming and irresistible, she worries about him. How will he adapt when his expectations turns out to be unrealistic?: 'Suddenly, I am concerned about him. Leave the United States for Rwanda with his whole family? The call of the country is indeed powerful. It is like the life-blood that pulses through the veins and arteries and makes the heart swell' (2002: 77). This ubiquitous theme is integrated in different ways in the work of Djedanoum, Rurangwa, and Kayimahe.

NOCKY DJEDANOUM AND THE TIGHTROPE OF SOLIDARITY

Djedanoum describes his initial reaction to the genocide as a knee-jerk reaction ('*reaction épidermique*') (Mongo-Mboussa 2000). The effect of his evocative, lyrical poetry is equally visceral, teeming with images and symbols, and possessing a rhythm that carries the reader along in its nostalgia, anger, and despair. The repetition of words and rhythmic units accentuate the many themes and emotions evoked by the poet: the pain of exile; the duty of remembering; the strong call of the land; the victory of life over death; and, above all, the dream of a continent 'turned towards the sun' (Djedanoum 2000: 34). For Djedanoum, going to Rwanda meant listening and sharing but also appreciating the beauty of the Rwandan culture, landscapes, and language, thus creating an atmosphere of dialogue and respect for those whose stories they were going to tell and moving toward a better understanding of the continent (Djedanoum 1999).[11]

Djedanoum's work displays the spirit of *ubuntu*, or communitarianism, not only in his role as an initiator of this collective project, but also in the poetry that he writes. This author was ostensibly driven by a desire to participate in creating a 'global vision' of the African continent and thus show solidarity with his Rwandan brothers and sisters in light of the isolation that this country experienced during the genocide. He is deeply convinced of their 'common destiny', in the first place as Africans, and in the second place as human beings (Djedanoum 1999).[12] He admits that the Rwandan youths they met appeared to have no sense that they all belonged to the same continent, and that when the authors showed them on a map that it was indeed so, the young people reproached them for not coming to Rwanda earlier, when genocide was being prepared and unfolding (ibid.).[13] It is this debt that Djedanoum seems to want to repay.

In the face of erasure and silencing, the project attempted to insert the genocide into the history of the continent and even of the world, thus signaling an act of irrevocable solidarity and connectedness:

> Djedanoum's solidarity is played out in the sense and in the hope of being more than a gesture but less than an invasive appropriation of the genocide as, for those who had not been involved, it would be impossible to identify with the experience of survivors in any way which could constitute a solidarity in that sense. But these texts, [...] may arguably create a space in which the perceived isolation of post-genocide Rwanda is broken. Through (the writing of) these texts, the genocide becomes part of Africa as a whole, part of the literature, history and actuality of African people, and inevitably not as a result or by extension, but simultaneously, part of humanity. (Small 2007: 88)[14]

The challenge then, as pointed out above, would be to do so without 'invasively' appropriating the Rwandans' story or over-identifying with survivors and victims: a trap that the writers who were not genocide survivors could easily fall into.[15] As we will see below, Djedanoum directly speaks in his poetry to his awareness of this potential danger. It seems that one possible solution, apart from assuming the role of appropriate listener and remaining sensitive to the Rwandan culture of mourning and remembering, was to write about experiences that they had in common with the Rwandans, both as Africans and as human beings. One of the most pertinent of such issues that Djedanoum raises is that of exile.

The task of these writers is a balancing act and in the first lines of his volume, Djedanoum introduces the powerful image of a tightrope walker, moving forward with her arms raised; the rope then is transformed into water in which she swims and finally dances toward a sort of 'utopia' (Djedanoum 2000: 9).[16] This dream of a better world is not, the poet states, an impossible dream, and not 'God's business' either, but ours—ours to remake our world (ibid.: 9). This possibility comes to us only at certain unique moments, and when they do come, we need to embrace them fully (ibid.: 9–10).

The creative 'dance' of remembering, sharing, and writing, which he embraces, leads him to wander over the Rwandan soil, like the refugee who finally finds his or her longed-for homeland (ibid.: 9). This journey takes him through Nyamirambo and to Nyanza, to the hills of Rwanda, to places of solitude and disillusionment, to his own memories of other emblematic places of suffering and beauty on the African continent. Finally, it leads him to a place where he reaffirms the duty of opening eyes and ears, of telling so that future generations will not forget.

In Djedanoum's poem entitled '*Mémoire*'[17] (Remembrance/Memory), he invokes the posture of respectful and active listening which transforms the poet-traveler. The theme of solidarity and shared responsibility is embodied; the poet lowers his eyes in shame, reaches out with a brotherly embrace, and musters the courage to walk through the hills and the tombs of Nyamata (ibid.: 23). It is the physical contact with the soil and sites, impregnated with memories, that unleashes a personal reaction in the writer—a reaction which is as much corporeal as it is mental and follows the contours of the country itself; he speaks of his thoughts 'meandering like rolling hills' beside Lake Kivu, of 'diving' into the 'swamps of collective madness' and of the odd sensation of the grains of sand beneath his feet (ibid.: 22). Rwanda becomes a 'soil of *pilgrimage* and *contemplation*' evoking a meditative stance which, in turn, speaks of the possibility of being transformed by what one hears (ibid.; my emphasis).[18]

The soil is not what it seems at a first glance; it contains corpses and hides their stories. Djedanoum personifies it as a storyteller which yields its whispered stories to his 'trembling feet', 'parched ears', and 'dazed, dry eyes' (Djedanoum 2000: 20). He offers himself to the soil in order to listen to the stories of 'millions of destroyed lives', to participate in mourning the millions of 'wandering souls', and to find the words to talk of and 'sing the void' left by the genocide (Djedanoum 2000: 21, 22). The poet metaphorically evokes the burial rites and the mass graves by comparing the soil to a vast 'shroud' covering unburied bodies and wandering souls (ibid.: 21). The relationship depicted between the poet and the soil is deeply evocative of interconnectedness, that invisible connection between man and nature, it is a mutual giving and taking, based on the presence and stories of the departed souls.[19]

The soil changes shape and function; in his poetry it is gradually transformed into an abstract space, that of remembrance. It invites the poet to 'bow down' and then opens up like a 'small window', lifts itself like a 'theatre curtain', revealing the scene of tragedy that took place (ibid.: 23, 24). The word *Mémoire* is repeated eight times in 11 lines, becoming the refrain of the poem, emulating the nature of traumatic memory and its 'repetitive haunting music' (ibid.: 24). In his position as fellow African, the poet is assaulted by the memory of this land; he does not have the luxury of turning a deaf ear and a blind eye to this tragedy:

> .....
> No. This is no place to close your eyes
> No. This is no place to block year ears
> No. No. No.
> (Djedanoum 2000: 24)[20]

Djedanoum evokes different ways of remembering and mourning. The work of the poet is not only to listen, he is also an accountant who must take accurate stock; will I have enough memory, he asks, 'to become a bookkeeper of my departed ones?' (ibid.: 23).[21] He acknowledges that a single approach will not suffice; the fate of the dead must be evoked in a poetic manner, but at the same time, numbers and statistics cannot be ignored because every number represents a human being.

Nyamirambo: Ode to Life

Despite its tragic subject matter, Djedanoum's slim collection of poems and poetic prose is a lyrical tribute to life and hope, an aspect that its title,

Nyamirambo!, highlights. He urges the 'sons and daughters of the continent' (ibid.: 39) to participate in the creation of a better future:

> .....
> Nowhere other than Nyamirambo
> Where I feel myself born again to the world
> Where at dawn, I see humankind smiling
> Where I still believe in mankind
> Where I again believe in life
> .....
>   (ibid.: 28)[22]

This eponymous title refers to a historic neighborhood in Kigali and holds possibilities of both symbolic and literal interpretations. Popular websites describe Nyamirambo as a lively multicultural neighborhood with a noisy, cosmopolitan vibe, known for its Muslim community (Guttman 2015). It is also the area where the authors participating in the project stayed during their writer's residency four years after the genocide. They evoke its lively streets, markets, cabarets, bars, and nightclubs, the cosmopolitan mix of Rwandan music and music from other countries and continents (Diop 2000: 67; Kayimahe 2001: 68–9).

At the same time, Nyamirambo is a symbolic place of remembrance, a site of pilgrimage (Mongo-Mboussa 2001: 1).[23] The name hints at the ostensibly clashing connotations that the neighborhood evokes, as it is a site of both life and death. The back cover of Djedanoum's text describes it as an 'immense cemetery' hosting mutilated bodies and souls, a place where human beings' most bestial instincts have been incarnated. Nyamirambo allegedly means 'a place of dead bodies', because in past battles with neighbors, bodies were deposited here (Tumwebaze 2009). Jean-Claude Awono (2004: 1) suggests that *Nyamirambo!* is not really a title but a 'pretext' for drawing our attention to a reality which is at the same time as esthetically pleasing as it is tragic.

Lamko compares Nyamirambo to a miniature Africa assembled around a mosque at sunset (2002: 148). Waberi calls it an 'oasis' in humanity's desert, reminding us that during the genocide, members of this neighborhood refused to divide themselves into Hutu and Tutsi, with Hutus protecting Tutsis and refusing to participate in the killings (2004: 84). As we will come to see, Djedanoum speaks of Rwanda not in isolation, but by constantly connecting it to the rest of the continent and its collective memory. It is therefore perhaps this cosmopolitan mix within a 'miniature' Africa, as well as the humanity of the Muslim inhabitants which motivated the author to use the name of the neighborhood as the title and theme of inspiration for his work. Djedanoum compares this modest little community—which is known as a place where various religions and cultures, locals and foreigners, live side by side—to a living, breathing lung (in Marcelli 2000).[24]

Djedanoum is constantly searching for signs of hope and life, and it is in Nyamirambo that he finds these: in its humaneness, its everyday scenes of life, the dried papaya tree branches on the roofs, the hens in the courtyards, the water that flows through the taps, the cleanly washed floors and children screaming happily, and the sound of cars and a hotel telephone (ibid.: 29, 30). After their visit to this neighborhood, Djedanoum would affirm that life, although fragile, indeed triumphs, and that we can best see that in the banana groves, the thunder, the rain, and the hills; he urges us to open our arms to life and embrace her, to look at her with new eyes for she needs our humanity as she silently breathes and bravely reconstructs herself (Djedanoum 1999).[25]

Djedanoum likens this neighborhood to his mother's comforting breasts, his childhood cradle, and the bliss of daybreak (2000: 28). It is a symbol of resistance, a war cry raising its fist to the world, a 'giant flame of hope', and the 'cradle' of all other neighborhoods. The author uses this physical site in Rwanda as a point of departure to comment on Africa and its place in the world. It could be a site of hope for the continent (Djedanoum 2000: 20). It is the 'most alive' neighborhood, the 'anti-genocide' (Djedanoum in Marcelli 2000)[26] and this is perhaps his most poignant way of providing a counter-narrative to the Afro-pessimism that plagues the continent and frames the way in which many interpret the genocide. In this neighborhood which opens its arms wide to all other continents, Nyamirambo buries the Africa where pessimism, despair, and fatality reigns (ibid.: 30).

Africa and Its Diaspora

The theme of exile is present throughout the anthology but in particular in '*Terre de tous les noms*' (Land of many names). The typographical layout creates the impression of a voice calling out, increasingly louder and louder. This 'voice' of the Rwandan soil, which has an ever-increasing hold on the diaspora, is at the same time 'single and polyphonic' (Djedanoum

2000: 13). The poet insists on the ambiguity of the call of the mother-land—its 'contradictory' nature—by positioning each adjective in its own line, contrasted to the others (ibid.). It is a poem which evokes the life of a refugee, filled with paradoxes and longing.

The poem pays homage to the beauty of this enigmatic country which is personified as being omnipresent, omniscient, a land of dreams, and the center of all desires, but also a country that has been sacrificed and set alight (ibid.: 14, 19). She calls her children to enroll for war and needs only to lift her finger or nod her head in order to rule them. Djedanoum equates the motherland, not to a mother, but to an unborn child, with whom the refugee has an ambiguous relationship characterized by close-ness and belonging on the one hand, but also distance:

> .....
> This land
> I have carried her in me forever
> This eternal pregnancy
> [...]
> Embrace other lands
> Go, go, she whispered in my ear
> Pushing me away with one hand
> Holding me back with the other
> Go and bear other children
> Go and give birth elsewhere
> Our planet is infinite
> .....
> (ibid.: 15–19)[27]

She holds back her inhabitants, while urging them to discover the joys of constantly wandering around and going 'elsewhere', of finding all the forests, deserts, oceans, rivers, lakes, colors, and diverse beauty that the planet has to offer (ibid.: 15–16). Like Lamko does with Fred R., Djedanoum paints a picture of those who wander on roads that lead to nowhere, in suspended time, having lost their direction and roots, and who dream of their native land; those who follow the wind, whether it goes up, down, or in circles; those who live lives filled with curious sights, joys, and disap-pointments (ibid.: 17).

The poem ends with the stark reminder that this land, which has been idealized and yearned for, is also the land where the 'sun was eclipsed behind the hills' in April 1994 (ibid.: 18). And still, this 'land of many names' remains 'my land' to its people (ibid.: 19).

The themes evoked in this poem are not unique to the Rwandan people. The pain of being far from one's native land is one that many Africans have in common, and Rwanda is depicted as a place of 'many names', creating the impression that the poem could just as well be describing the Congo, Burundi, Chad, Djibouti, Guinea, or many others (ibid.: 13). With its focus both on the country in which the genocide took place and on the painful experiences of people from other African countries, the poem sets the tone for the rest of the anthology, which constantly flows between Rwanda and the rest of the continent.

Awono notes that although there are many references to 'places of hope' in this text, they always lead us to Africa and its collective memory (2004: 1). Djedanoum himself explains that the goal of the project was to embrace Africa in its entirety and reflect on its shared history, a history which he defines as transversal/cutting across the continent, noting that both the liberation of black South Africans and the Rwandan genocide form part of its shared memory (Djedanoum 1999). He, perhaps more than the other participants, links their goal to his pan-African vision for the continent, his desire to create a 'global vision' of the continent (Djedanoum 1999).[28]

A theme therefore that preoccupies the poet is his position as a non-Rwandan writer who is at the same time African and thus has much in common with the Rwandan people. In his poem entitled 'I am from here and I have returned' (*Je suis d'ici et je suis de retour*) he admits that one could accuse him of making a fortune from the suffering of others; of 'trading' in words of gold, diamond, and emerald, fashioned from the 'congealed blood' and 'gaping wounds' of others (Djedanoum 2000: 31). He directly addresses the doubts of those who question the motives of writers coming from outside the borders of the country, on a mission which could be considered as a 'plundering' and the hypocritical abuse of the painful plight of others (ibid.: 31).

Djedanoum's defense is to frame the genocide within the context of African history, and thus part of his own history. As such, he goes as far as to speak of his 'regained memory' (*retrouvée*) which he wishes to work with and 'reproduce' (ibid.: 33), referring to the collective memory of the continent, available to the poet as an African and which he can in turn transmit to others (ibid.). In the face of possible accusations and questions, he simply responds that he is 'from here' and he has returned, begging them to allow him to 'transmit', 'export', 'be proud of', and 'appropriate' the memories (ibid.). In this poem, (*Je suis d'ici et je suis de retour*), the 'I' is simultaneously the Rwandan, the African, and the poet who fights against death by transmitting memories from 'hand to hand, mouth to ear and mind to mind' (ibid.: 10).

This collective identity is a growing motif in Djedanoum's anthology and he moves freely between the singular 'I' and the collective 'us', evoking places on the continent steeped in history and memory. In this sense, Djedanoum seems to embrace the traditional African worldview in which the community overshadows the individual. In many instances, he appears to appropriate the memory of the Rwandans, arguably more than any of the other non-Rwandan participants of the project.

In his optimistic poem, 'Dream of a perfect continent of love' (*Rêve d'un continent d'amour rêvé*), he intermingles references to culturally significant places in Rwanda (such as the royal city of Nyanza, 'the cradle of our traditions'), with the memory of emblematic places in the rest of the continent (ibid.: 34). Thus he creates cultural links between Rwanda and the native countries of the project participants, stating that they will 'bow down before the memories of our slave grand-parents' from Gorée island (Senegal), 'plant seeds of love' on the beaches of Mombasa (Kenia), 'kiss the blazing sun' in N'Djamena (Chad), 'drink sorghum beer' in Bobo-Dioulasso (Burkina Faso), 'follow the footsteps' of the Fulani (Guinea), and 'play at tightrope walking' in the horn of Africa (Djibouti) (ibid.: 35). All this is enveloped in a 'child's dream' of an Africa in which traditions are celebrated, an idyllic continent of love and words of love—'Babel-words' which will inhabit the continent (ibid.: 34, 35).

However, in the poems which follow this celebration of Africa, Djedanoum admits that this dream is fragile—in reality, his faith in humankind entails 'believing in man again and again, without really believing' (ibid.: 36). The tightrope walker, who bravely set off on her journey of remembrance toward 'utopia' (9) in the first lines of the anthology, now finds herself in a macabre circus, where tightrope walkers have 'lost their illusion of magic' and the 'naive public' has been 'caught in the trap of absurdity': the show is starting, but there are no nets for the artists (ibid.: 37). This is a circus of death in which the child's dream is shattered and innocence destroyed (ibid.: 38). Thus, the anthology vacillates between determined faith and despairing disillusionment.

Remaking the World Through the Word

A constant refrain in Djedanoum's work is the firm belief that Africa should take up its own destiny: 'They thought that we were eternally lost', he writes, but 'here we are again', 'the history book henceforth belongs to us' (ibid.: 41). He expresses his frustration with the way in which Africa is viewed and calls on his fellow Africans to declare war on this status. 'Enough of everything', he says: enough of being last in the row, of being the 'laughing stock'; enough of the orphans, widows, and street children, imported food, 'religious passivity', and powerlessness (ibid.: 39). Let us take up our pens, he exhorts, and 'sharpen our voices' (ibid.). Let us rewrite history, 'sons and daughters of the continent' (ibid.).

For Djedanoum, this process is a type of 'journey of emotion' that takes place through an exchange of 'reincarnated words' (ibid.: 43). They are 'syncretized' words; words which carry the force of emotions like 'stilts'; words like wading birds on long legs, rising 'above the sky'; words which are the 'reality of who we are, ourselves and no-one else' (ibid.: 42, 43). This is a shared process, an exchange, a joint enterprise: the words belong to both those who say them and those who listen to them, and their 'spirits dance shoulder to shoulder' (ibid.: 43).

Once again, however, this poem, in which solidarity and shared words and emotions triumph, is followed by three poems which undermine the tone of hope. This is perhaps the tightrope that Djedanoum evokes, constantly wavering between hope and despair, solidarity, and solitude. Two of these three poems deal with the overpowering and living presence of the emblematic hills of Rwanda, which symbolize community life, but which seem to have stopped breathing and the poet searches in vain for their 'pulse' (ibid.: 45). The hills accuse the arrogant and the powerful; they 'weigh on our conscience', 'watch us', and 'surround us' (ibid.: 44, 45). The third poem sets itself in opposition to the solidarity and humanity that Djedanoum has been pursuing. It is a 'Eulogy to solitude' in which he acknowledges man's loneliness; the poet states that his name is 'SOLITUDE', that he belongs heart and soul to this solitude, and that anything else is but a mask (ibid.: 46). 'How can we understand each other?' he asks, for peace is but an 'invention', a 'drop in this ocean of inhumanity which is the world' (ibid.: 47). In spite of this, his next poem is entitled '*Dire*' (To speak) for he cannot but continue this interminable journey of remembering, listening, seeing, and speaking out, which is the duty of memory to which he has committed himself (ibid.: 48–9).

Djedanoum seems to consider his participation in the project as a modest but creative way of contributing to the collective enterprise of 'remaking the world and that which surrounds us' and of 'turning the face of our destiny towards the sun', a task which he undertakes through the creation of words, images, song, and dance (ibid.: 9, 34). This is best understood when reading the first and last parts of the collection together. The anthology starts with a dreamlike description of the poet being drawn into a stream of lyrical memories, glimpsing a possible utopian world which he knows will only come about if we fashion it ourselves.

The notion that we have seen repeatedly in the work of the other writers, namely that death is an integral part of life, is also present here, from the start. Death is not something we can contain or reduce, writes Djedanoum; the best way to overcome death is to 'cast it into the mold of life' by telling the story and passing it on to others and through opening up to one another (ibid.: 10). This sets us on a voyage of discovery and our strength, according to Djedanoum, lies in our 'journey of emotion' (ibid.: 11, 43).

The poet, who, in this introductory part, is borne away and invaded by a stream of lyrical memories, submits to the memories and the ever-increasing musical process of the word, which in his closing lines he describes as the 'verb that creates' (ibid.: 51). He acknowledges, however, that there are limits to solidarity and listening: there is a place where another's trauma becomes impossible to conceive of, where one cannot be accompanied by another, it is a place of 'intense solitude' where soliloquies reign, where some images and experiences are beyond representation (ibid.: 12).[29]

The anthology ends with his 'Manifesto for life' (*Manifeste pour la vie*). This final poem in prose form, which is also Part III, takes on the form of a declaration, an exhortation. Djedanoum's 'Manifesto for life' stands in opposition to the renowned Bahutu Manifesto[30] which led to the death of thousands of Tutsis (ibid.: 50–1). Djedanoum's manifesto again reinforces the notion that he writes on behalf of and to the children of the African continent, not limiting himself to Rwanda: 'yes, we've had enough of dying in Rwanda, in Burundi, in South Africa, in Sierra Leone, in Algeria, in Chad, in the Congo, in the Democratic Republic of the Congo, in Angola, in Nigeria, in the Central African Republic, in South Africa ...' (ibid.: 50).[31]

Boniface Mongo-Mboussa interprets this declaration as an expression of the poet's desire to align himself with those writers who have participated in the struggle of commitment (*engagement*) and in particular with those associated with the *Négritude* movement. This critic sees in Djedanoum's work the faith in the 'miraculous weapons' that words can sometimes become, thus evoking Aimé Césaire's poetry of engagement (Mongo-Mboussa 2001: 1).[32]

Djedanoum ends the manifesto, and thus his anthology, by claiming the right to life, which is not exclusive but belongs to every human being. Furthermore, he reaffirms the commitment of the authors involved in the project to celebrate life through the creative impetus of writing, singing, painting, and any other activity that creates life in the face of death and destruction (Djedanoum 2000: 51).[33] If Djedanoum's text is not a redemptive one in the sense suggested by Dominick LaCapra (2001), it is, at the very least, in a way similar to Lamko's text, an invitation to go beyond the trauma, a declaration of faith in humankind and their ability to do so. What remains crucial, however, is that Djedanoum constantly situates this process within the context of solidarity and sharing. The work required by the duty of memory is best done, says Djedanoum, in the company of the other—we are to 'lean on another's shoulder' when we face the unimaginable and the inexpressible (ibid.: 11).[34]

JEAN-MARIE VIANNEY RURANGWA AND THE DISPLACED WITNESS

The playwright, poet, academic and author Jean-Marie Rurangwa, like many of his fellow Rwandans, became a child refugee at an early age; when he left Rwanda he was barely two. He would spend many years in exile, first in Burundi, where he grew up and, after completing his studies, taught French and wrote plays. In 1992, he moved to Italy and in 1999 to Belgium. In 2000, he returned to his country of birth, where he taught at the National University of Rwanda and directed a theater troupe, Izuba. He then moved to Canada. One of the main themes in his work is, understandably, the ordeal of exile.

The title and opening pages of his essay project provide us with important indications of this writer's position, as contrasted to a non-Rwandan participant like Djedanoum. The title, *Le génocide des Tutsi expliqué à un étranger* (The genocide of the Tutsis explained to a foreigner/stranger), suggests a clear pedagogical stance and implies that the envisaged readership is not Rwandans, but rather those from elsewhere, whom the author assumes are not well informed about the history of the genocide. In spite of being in exile at the time of the 1994 genocide, Rurangwa makes it clear from the beginning that he is not himself an outsider or a foreigner, like most of the other participants in the project, but rather someone who writes on behalf of '[his] people' (ibid.: 7).[35]

Apart from the intertextual reference to Tahar Ben Jelloun's text, *Le racisme expliqué à ma fille*, the (in many ways ironic) title does not immediately lend itself to imaginative interpretations. However, it is not to his own daughter (*fille*), or his people, that Rurangwa explains the genocide. We soon discover that the title refers to his chance encounter with a 'foreigner', a young Italian history student, Gianluca Perfetti, whom he, apparently, met during the writer's residency in Kigali in 1998 and who asked him some questions about the genocide in the course of a three-day interview (ibid.: 14). It is not made clear in the text itself whether this refers to an actual event or if it is a narrative invention by the author, employed in order to allow him to make use of an interview format for his text. The tone of the essay, then, is that of a political or scientific document, written in order to instruct, clarify, and correct misunderstandings about the genocide, and as with Kayimahe's text, the intention is not to write a fictional or even a literary text. The author's perspectives on the genocide are communicated in no uncertain terms and the idea is clearly not to include a host of other voices; he is speaking, as he claims in his dedication, on behalf of his own people and he expresses his frustration, often in an antagonistic tone, with strangers' ignorance regarding what happened in Rwanda.

Thus the essay, which is notably shorter than, for example, Kayimahe's testimony, takes the form of an interview in which the history of the genocide is explained to a stranger. The interview is reconstructed over time; the introduction is dated December 1998 and the interview June 1999, both indicating Rome as place of writing. This suggests that the author had the discussion (or multiple discussions) with the young Italian that he met in Rwanda and subsequently proceeded to reconstruct their discussion.

In contrast to the novels produced for the project, and even Kayimahe's testimony, this essay does not primarily tell a story. The guiding principle is not a storyline, but rather the questions and answers shared between the author and the student. The questions do not systematically follow on from each other in a specific order; the speakers move freely from one topic to another, as is often the case with an interview.

The questions that structure the text are largely issues that the other writers have also focused on: the duty of memory; the origins of the genocide and genocide ideology; the effects of colonialism and the Hamitic myth; the stereotypes and misconceptions around identity and the alleged Hutu, Twa, and Tutsi physiognomies; the role of the West and the Catholic Church. In addition, he writes about political abuses, the fate of refugees, the hope for unity and reconciliation in his country, the political situation in Burundi, and the difference between dying as a victim of genocide and dying due to a political crime.

This last one is an important theme because by engaging in this debate, the author indirectly addresses genocide denialism. This is also probably why in his introduction, Rurangwa takes great pains to make a list of the different categories of whom he considers to be perpetrators, victims, and survivors (ibid.: 9–12). He speaks at length about genocide denial and revisionism and the relationship between Hutus and Tutsis living in the West. Other points on which he debates adamantly is the varying reactions of Hutus and Tutsis living in Europe to genocide commemorations— because of the differing connotations and meanings these events hold for them—as well as the ignorance of Westerners on the genocide.

In response to some questions on his personal experiences, the author moves from the general to the personal, and this is where the text increasingly takes on a more autobiographical tone, discussing the humiliation and frustration associated with being a displaced Tutsi, and the 'shame' of being Rwandan (ibid.: 41). He also speaks passionately of the birth of the Rwandan Patriotic Front (RPF) and their use of cultural events and pamphlets in order to mobilize and create a sense of pride and love for the mother country and its language among exiles and to restore a sense of cultural identity.

Explaining the Genocide: Silence Kills

Through the title of the essay, Tahar Ben Jelloun's text, with his insistence on the evocative power of language in the fight against racism, is used as a frame which allows Rurangwa to introduce the paramount role that words play in the creation of genocide ideologies and societies (ibid.: 38). This title however has the unfortunate potential of alienating a non-Rwandan reader; in spite of the original intention of the author, who is merely seeking to explain and clarify, the label of 'foreigner who needs to be explained to' might have an (unintended?) negative effect. Instead of foregrounding the inclusive notion of solidarity, of sharing the story and journey of the victims, there is an implicit (probably justifiable) reference to the uninformed outsider who does not understand what happened.

In his text the embodiment of this ignorant foreigner becomes the old Italian woman whose comments display her Afro-pessimism and lack of understanding of the context: 'You Africans, I don't understand you at all. You are primitive barbarians, savages and racists. We educated and Christianized you' (ibid.: 58). She 'claims to be knowledgeable' about Africa and 'to love the Africans' (ibid.: 59), but Rurangwa labels her as a racist 'Tutsiphobe' whose knowledge is based on stereotypes, and who eventually becomes a genocide 'denialist' (ibid.: 58, 59). The ignorance and harassment of this woman and ignorant foreigners, in general, appears to be a significant part of his lived trauma as a refugee.

This choice of negative relationship with the implied reader can be contrasted to, for example, that of Tadjo, who describes the genocide as a universal event which involves and implicates all human beings, and her text which continuously invites the reader to participate in the journey of horror. This contrast is reinforced by the use of the word 'explained' (*expliqué*) in the title of Rurangwa's essay, which in a sense pre-empts and directs the reaction of the reader—one is to attempt to 'understand' the genocide.

Such an objective is, admittedly, completely in line with the typical expectations of an argumentative essay, and so the author remains true to the format that he has chosen. It is also true, however, that some readers might desire to move beyond comprehension, and that is something that literary works such as the novels and travel diaries can offer: initiating someone who was not there into the experience, relating to the reader on a deeper emotional level than mere comprehension would entail. Furthermore, if all is explained by another, how much encouragement is given to self-interrogation, to further thought on justice, evil, and one's own reactions to genocide ideology? I say this with great hesitation, because I am fully aware that the luxury of reflecting on the 'need' of the reader is probably one that is accessible only to what one can call a foreigner-writer—a listener who does not have to deal with the immediate brutal reality of genocide. This would not be the case for a survivor-author or other Rwandan people, whose main concern is that the facts of the genocide be known and for whom genocide denial is a real and overwhelming threat.

Rurangwa therefore defends his choice not to 'mince' his words (ibid.: 9) and not to transform reality into fiction, in the light of the danger of denialism. The use of lies, euphemisms, and word games in order to deny the truth of the genocide is precisely what he vehemently opposes (ibid.: 11).[36] It is clear that he prioritizes providing facts and figures—and rightly so. He engages the fight against those who would play with words: 'This is why, when we speak of "genocide of the Tutsis"—an indisputable reality—they speak of "mass anger", of "legitimate defense", "of interethnic war"' (ibid.: 10). Rurangwa grounds his discussions in examples from history and citations from other well-known scholars. He focuses on 'testimony', rather than story or fiction: 'To testify is to expose oneself to the wrath of all those who fear to tell things as they are. The genocide survivor embarrasses and annoys those who fear the truth. That is why they prefer him to be silent' (ibid.: 12–13). For Rurangwa, however, it is silence which 'kills' the survivor and, worse, which may lead to further genocides (ibid.: 13).

Therefore, while many of the other participants create a space for imagination and the fallibility of memory, Rurangwa sets out to provide precision. It becomes clear that his generic and stylistic choices are aligned to his objective of debunking the misconceptions propagated by Western media. Rurangwa writes: 'And it's the truth about the genocide of the Tutsis that I undertook to tell when I accepted to become part of this team of African artists' (ibid.: 13). Furthermore, as he notes, there are a thousand and one ways to write about the genocide, ranging from analysis to chronological accounts, to telling the story of one survivor and, finally, to works of art that are based on historical truth but that 'arouse emotion and invite reflection' (ibid.: 17). This is no competition, says Rurangwa, only an attempt to supplement and complement one another (ibid.: 16–17).

A further question begs to be asked with regard to Rurangwa's choice of title and his position as witness: how can he, as an exile who left the country at the age of two, 'explain' the genocide to foreigners? In a sense, he is himself a foreigner, defined by his perpetual situation of exile and absence from the mother country. In my opinion, this issue can, however, not be raised without remembering that the genocide and crimes against the Tutsis was not an isolated incident that happened in 1994, but that there had been a history of incidents which forced huge numbers of Tutsis into exile long before the 1994 genocide. This is why Rurangwa identifies himself as survivor of the 'first genocide' of the Tutsis, perpetrated in

1959, reminding the reader that it is a common misconception that the genocide of 1994 was the only massacre of the Tutsis that ever took place (2000: 38). The history of Rwanda and of the genocide cannot be told fully without considering the trauma of exile and this, for me, is Rurangwa's main contribution to the project: his insistence on telling the pain of being absent, exiled, displaced, and far from the motherland.

The underlying theme of Rurangwa's essay and of his subsequent works is indeed that of exile. He admits that his 2005 publication, *Un Rwandais sur les routes de l'exil*, is a text on his own life lived in exile. Of this work, he wrote: 'I will not write a novel on exile [...] but a book on my life in exile. And when people read it, they will think it is a novel' (2005: 10; my translation). In its prologue he confirms that the experience of exile has haunted and defined his life and drove him back to his motherland, the 'poor little country of Rwanda': 'Exile, it's a thorn driven into one's flesh and that you can never get rid of. Exile, it's the torture of Tantalus, the eagle of Prometheus, the rock of Sisyphus! Exile, to be honest, is a never-ending ordeal' (ibid.; my translation).[37]

It is in fact when Rurangwa starts talking about his own experience of exile that his project essay takes on a more poetic, imaginative, and even mythical tone: 'Listen, I am going to tell you a fable', he says to his young interviewer, who had asked him about Nyarunazi, the camp in Burundi to which his parents fled (Rurangwa 2000: 39). He clearly has the same idyllic and archaic image of the motherland (the land of milk and honey) as Lamko's protagonists, Fred R. and Pelouse, an image transmitted by parents in exile to their children. The cyclical repetition and the insistence on recurring images and memories which haunt the mind of the refugee reflect the trauma of those living in exile:

> We had a country that we loved dearly and that our fathers called Rwanda rugari rwa Gasabo (literally: vast Rwanda of Gasabo), a country of milk and honey. [...] And there we were sick at heart, on the road of exile [...] And there we were, right next to tigers, leopards and panthers [...] I remember that by day, our fathers were cutting trees [...] I remember that honey and those wild fruits [...] I also remember that older brothers and sisters learnt to read and write under the trees [...] I remember that they wrote on their legs and on their hands [...] I remember that the teachers were all Rwandan refugees [...]. (ibid.: 39–41)

Rurangwa describes the shame he felt at being Rwandan, because it implied being a refugee and this equaled misery, humiliation, frustration, death, and despair.[38] Being Rwandan meant being a young refugee girl who has to sell herself on the sidewalk or work as an unpaid housemaid, or a boy who has to steal and deceive in the cities of Burundi to have bread for tomorrow; it meant being unemployed in spite of having a qualification; it meant being driven to delinquency and alcohol; and, for Rurangwa and other artists, it meant having their plays and Rwandan cultural performances censored by the Burundian government (ibid.: 39–45).[39]

Drawing Borders, Blurring Boundaries

Rurangwa has been criticized for identifying wholly with the ideology and politics of the Tutsi diaspora and the RPF, thus 'allowing his writing to justify the view that the Tutsis are permanent victims even though a Tutsi-led government is occupying the seat of power' instead of presenting a more nuanced perspective (Diawara 2002). Those who criticize him suggest that this stance might be detrimental to the possibility of maintaining one's critical judgment (ibid.).[40] Furthermore, Rurangwa clearly is not politically neutral; his narrative suggests that he engaged in activities of awareness raising and mobilization of the exiled Tutsi diaspora through 'socio-political' plays that he wrote, denouncing the discrimination and dictatorship that was rampant in the homeland (Rurangwa 2000: 44).

Here again, Kayimahe's and Rurangwa's situations are different from that of the non-Rwandan writers: can one even expect them to act as 'intellectual witnesses' and keep the distance which Geoffrey Hartman (1998) and Manthia Diawara (2002) call for and the neutrality that a transnational project demands of its participants? Can they be expected to offer a global, nuanced perspective when they are describing their own experience and that of their people who suffered? Kayimahe is clearly an eyewitness, a genocide survivor, but Rurangwa's position is more complex. As a Rwandan Tutsi he appears to identify with the genocide survivors, but, like the foreign reader to whom he is explaining the genocide, he was not physically present in 1994; he spent the largest part of his life outside the borders of Rwanda.

However, when one looks closely at his categorization of perpetrators, victims, and survivors, two things become clear. Under the label 'victims' he includes not only Tutsis who were killed, but also moderate Hutus. Similarly, with the term 'survivors' he names not only Tutsis who were in

Rwanda and survived the genocide ('direct survivors'), but also Tutsi refugees, whom he calls 'indirect survivors' (Rurangwa 2000: 11–12). Rurangwa maintains that all Tutsis are genocide survivors, including the refugees who were elsewhere during the genocide, because if they had been in the country, they would have been targeted as well. Based then on his definition of genocide survivors, he is a survivor albeit 'indirect'.

With regard to Diawara's second claim, namely that Rurangwa supports the view that Tutsis are permanent victims and that he fails to question the RPF's ideology, it is helpful to take into account the comments of Mahmood Mamdani (2002), Kenneth Harrow (2005), and Ervin Staub (2006) on the real danger of victims becoming perpetrators under certain circumstances. Staub suggests that victimized people 'feel diminished and vulnerable, seeing the world, other people, and especially members of groups other than their own as dangerous' (2006: 871). Furthermore, if healing has not sufficiently taken place in a victimized community and a new conflict arises, 'it will be difficult for them to consider the needs of the other and to trust the other, and thereby to resolve conflict peacefully. In response to threat they may strike out, believing that they need to defend themselves, but actually becoming perpetrators' (ibid.).

The title of Mamdani's book, *When Victims Become Killers*, similarly suggests that with time and under certain circumstances, the victims of a certain period of history can in turn become perpetrators (2002: 270–3).[41] Mamdani posits that, instead of viewing oneself as a victim, or even conqueror after the genocide, and pursuing a type of 'victor's justice' (which could easily become a sort of vengeance), it would be more helpful to pursue a 'survivor's justice' in order to move beyond polarized notions of victim and perpetrator.[42]

It is interesting to note then how both the Rwandan writers take great pains to clarify who they consider to be genocide victims, survivors, and perpetrators, a contentious issue which has received much attention in post-genocide Rwanda. This is one of the ways in which their texts seem to contrast with the writing of the other participants, who tended to blur or at least question the boundaries between these distinct categories. This blurring of boundaries speaks to the awareness of the fluid and complex relation between being a victim and being a perpetrator, as described by both Staub (2006) and Mamdani (2002). The fictional texts project texts often introduce the disquieting possibility that a victim can eventually become a killer. Tierno Monénembo's (2004) Faustin Nsenghimana is a case in point: he is simultaneously a victim and a killer, a genocide survivor but also a murderer condemned to death. Similarly, in Ilboudo's (2000) text, Venant, Murekatete's husband, assumes the roles of victim, savior, and, finally, rape perpetrator at different times of the narrative.

Tadjo touches on this complex issue when she evokes Camp Kibeho, where Hutu refugees had fled after the genocide 'for fear of reprisals' (2002: 114). During a stampede caused by shots fired into the crowd, many people, 'mostly women and children', were 'trampled underfoot', and those who tried to flee were fired on by soldiers of the new government (ibid.: 114). The details of what exactly happened and who was to blame remain unclear, but immediately after evoking this 'carnage of Kibeho', Tadjo writes the following unsettling words: 'History was going in reverse. The executioners were becoming the victims, the victims the executioners. As if violence would never cease to engender violence' (ibid.: 115).

By conferring on their characters this multiple status of being at once a victim, savior, killer, or passive bystander, the authors remind us how complex the entanglement of justice, forgiveness, and reconciliation can become. In some cases, ordinary citizens become perpetrators, driven by fear. This is suggested through Tadjo's sensitive depiction of the inner world of the young farmer turned murderer. In her narratives, the victims are not always and only those for whom the genocide was intended but there are those who sometimes accidentally, voluntarily or arbitrarily get in the way and become victims too. Perhaps the most valuable contribution to reconciliation that these authors make is not in their insistence on forgiveness, or in identifying victim and perpetrator, but in their portrayal of the moral entanglement of genocide.

I do not presume to understand exactly why the 'outsider' writers portray this issue in this complex way, refusing to draw too many borders, whereas the two Rwandans are very specific in their description of categories. Nor do I think it fitting to judge which approach is more acceptable. Perhaps what I can do is, once again, emphasize that intellectual distance and imaginative, multivocal depiction might be a luxury that only those who did not personally experience the genocide can be expected to have obtained, at least so soon after the event.

In the face of these complexities, Harrow (2005) submits that the value of literary texts potentially resides in their ability to invite the reader to move beyond binary categories—them and us, victim and killer, enemy and friend—in order to be confronted with his or her own role and responsibility. He adds that in complex contexts like these, there is never only a single story to tell, neither only one right way of telling it (ibid.: 40).

Rurangwa then offers us a different type of voice. It might be less successful in creating an intellectual distance from the story, or drawing the reader in with an imaginative storyline, but it nevertheless sets out to clear up misconceptions, explain the origins and consequences of the genocide, and bring home to us the suffering of the diaspora, adding an important voice to the multivocal contribution of the project.

Vénuste Kayimahe or the Accusing Witness

Vénuste Kayimahe, whose contribution is entitled *France-Rwanda: les coulisses du génocide: témoignage d'un rescapé* (France-Rwanda: behind the scenes of the genocide: a survivor's testimony), claims that he was never a writer, but 'became one due to circumstances' (Guillamo 2011; my translation).[43] He worked for almost 20 years for the Franco-Rwandan cultural center (CECFR)[44] in Kigali, first as projectionist and later as audiovisual technician.

During the genocide he took refuge with his wife and two of his children in the offices of the CECFR, but they were left behind by French colleagues and soldiers sent to evacuate the European employees. A part of his family was subsequently evacuated with him to Nairobi by Belgian soldiers, where he was obliged to remain, ostensibly in an attempt to prevent him from giving his testimony in France. In Nairobi he learned of the death of his 13-year-old daughter Aimée, his mother, brothers, and sisters—all of whom he had been unable to bring with him to Nairobi.

From Nairobi Kayimahe wrote a letter to a former French colleague, telling him of his plight. This letter was later published in *Le Monde* of 15–16 May 1994 and created great sympathy among the French public, leading to financial support for his family. He subsequently sent an open letter to the French president to protest against Operation Turquoise.

After the genocide, he returned to his country of birth and wrote his testimony. It focuses on the genocide and, in particular, on the relationship between the Rwandan and French governments and the role of France in what he describes in his title as the 'behind the scenes' of the genocide. The title pre-empts this main leitmotiv—the underhanded role played by the French government. As Waberi points out, Kayimahe's text is a testimony to the involvement of the French authorities in Rwanda who 'turned a blind eye' and to the cowardice of those responsible for Franco-Rwandan affairs (Waberi 2002).[45]

Kayimahe dedicates his text to the dead and the living, both his loved ones and the Tutsi victims in general, declaring his intention to fight against forgetfulness and remember their humiliation and suffering. He also evokes the inhumane acts committed by Rwandan brothers and sisters against their fellow human beings, who were 'mowed down', humiliated, hated, and had their 'throats slit' (Kayimahe 2001: 5).

On Testimony and Tact

Kayimahe defines his text as an account of his personal experience as a survivor and a rendition of a period in history illustrated by a few 'anecdotes' (2001: 8). This objective of testifying, from a personal, subjective point of view, is confirmed by his subtitle, 'a survivor's testimony', and by the inclusion of a copy of the letter he wrote to the French embassy as well as copies of letters from French acquaintances who supported him. His direct, unambiguous approach is demonstrated by the choice of a factual title and the realistic cover of the text (a photo of the author holding a microphone).

The perspective that Kayimahe offers is, like Rurangwa's, not multiple, but fiercely personal and singular. However, like Rurangwa, he pays homage to moderate Hutus who were 'guilty of loving Tutsis' and thus considered 'enemies' by the perpetrators; to his mind, they were as much victims of the genocide against Tutsis as the Tutsi victims, because they sacrificed their lives in order to protect Tutsis or by refusing to kill Tutsis (ibid.: 7–8).[46] Those moderate Hutus who survived the genocide, he equally categorizes as genocide survivors.

His contribution lies in the details he provides on the context and circumstances of the genocide: the hypocrisy, the manipulation of the masses and the propaganda, the threats, and looting of Tutsi properties. He describes the corruption, nepotism, ethnic segregation and the quota system, details on Operation Turquoise, and the activities of the RPF. He speaks of the hope sparked among Tutsis by the clandestine papers circulated by the RPF and members of the diaspora, and the consequences of the RPF attack in 1990.

General references are interspersed with examples of personal experiences, combining the genre of scientific essay with autobiographical testimony. On a personal level, he narrates his struggles to be allowed an education and the experiences of his own family, whose house was raided more than once, as well as the reactions of their Hutu neighbors. He also tells of the reaction of his best friend, a Hutu, when he discovered that they were not of the same ethnic group, and the betrayal of former friends, neighbors, and colleagues. The text ends with a plea to the reader to become involved in the struggle against forgetfulness and indifference by supporting the creation of an institution where a body of knowledge on the genocide can be produced.

Kayimahe's approach is concrete and factual and his account is logically structured, with limited recourse to literary devices such as metaphorical language and creative manipulation of time or focalization. Daniel Delas (2002: 49) highlights the difference between Kayimahe's work and the other more artistic works produced for the project, noting that this survivor is above all a 'conscience' who writes in a beautiful but modest way about himself and his feelings and experiences. Delas suggests that he is not the type of writer who uses fiction as a tool to reveal and unmask people (ibid.).[47]

Like Rurangwa, Kayimahe is very aware of the difference between his approach and that of the other writers. He characterizes his own writing as being 'without tact', but driven by a desire to share the information truthfully, faithfully, and in context. This concern, he acknowledges, may have negatively affected the form of his narrative (ibid.: 8–9).[48] He therefore excuses himself in advance in case the reader feels dissatisfied after completing his text (ibid.: 9).

In this first attempt to write about the genocide, he prioritizes faithful reporting above any concern for skillful stirring of emotion and imagination: he was to write what he himself 'saw', 'heard', 'experienced', and 'understood' (ibid.). With time, he would indeed write a novel with imaginary characters inspired by history and people that he knew, but for now he was able only to undertake this 'modest' enterprise of recording memories in the hope that other survivors would have the courage to do the same (ibid.). The factual tone and style that Kayimahe adopts does become noticeably bitter and accusatory in instances where he relates painful personal anecdotes.

Recurring Exile, Recurring Betrayal

One of the interesting parallels between Rurangwa and Kayimahe's texts is the fact that the trauma they write about and which clearly haunts them are not the genocide itself, but situations related to it. We have seen that in Rurangwa's case the trauma is the unbearable weight of exile and being absent, whereas in Kayimahe's text, a further trauma is added to this, namely the pain of betrayal, both before and during the genocide.

Kayimahe leaves his country for the first time in 1973 to go to Burundi, together with many other Tutsis who had been chased from schools and refused the right to continue their education. His life story includes this first failed period of exile: '[T]his exile did not work for me', he writes, telling of his inability to adapt to the humidity and heat of Bujumbura, his anxiety over the health of his mother, and his nostalgia for the hills of Rwanda (ibid.: 36). All of this brought him back to Rwanda after four months, only to discover that once one is a refugee, one becomes an 'enemy of the State' (ibid.: 40) and that 'absent refugees don't have a right to anything' (ibid.: 39).

During the genocide, he flees a second time, this time with his wife and two of his children. As they leave Rwanda on an airplane to try and find a country that will receive them, he thinks: 'We became refugees in space, wanderers, cumbersome and unwanted' (ibid.: 229). He furthermore includes a description of the 'hell' of the Kakuma refugee transit camp, situated in the desert between Nairobi and Somalia, and the horror stories that he had heard about refugees who had been sent to this camp (ibid.: 295–6). He describes the difficult life in Nairobi, the crime, the misery, and the fight for survival. It is also while in exile in Nairobi that he learns of Aimée's death, a day that marks the rest of his life, and the spiritual and emotional trauma, which he shares with the reader.

Betrayal comes in many shapes in Kayimahe's story and this is a recurring element of the text which displays the author's almost obsessive insistence on this aspect of the genocide. Instances of betrayal are told and retold, each time implicating different individuals and detailing different circumstances under which betrayal took place. The director of the CECFR, Kayimahe's Hutu colleague, the head of the evacuation mission, the French soldiers, and the French government—all of whom might have been able to help during the genocide—are guilty of acts of betrayal.

On 8 April, when France, Belgium, and Italy send soldiers to evacuate foreigners, the director arrives at the CECFR with a group of soldiers. At first Kayimahe thinks they have come to save him and his family, but they have merely come to collect files and vehicles. The next day, a group of French soldiers again arrive at the center. Once again, he expects them to offer help, but it turns out they have come to set themselves up there until their mission is completed and they assure him that they are under no circumstances to evacuate any Rwandans. Kayimahe tells of his interaction with two of the soldiers, who show him kindness, in spite of explicit orders to have nothing to do with the genocide victims. When the French soldiers leave a few days later, they take with them the audiovisual equipment that they have looted from the CECFR. Later that day, Belgian soldiers evacuate Kayimahe and his family.

Upon their arrival in Nairobi, they are separated from the other refugees, who are leaving for other countries through the help of HCR, the High Commission for refugees. The family members are given the impression by French officials that they are leaving for France, but they are in fact driven away to the French embassy in Nairobi, where they are told that some formalities must be handled before they can leave. In the end, they are obliged to remain in Nairobi, under the pretext that there are too many of them and that they have no family to receive them in France. Kayimahe comes to understand that this is a way of preventing him from revealing to the Western world the way in which they were treated by his French colleagues in Rwanda and the behavior of the French soldiers who pillaged the center (ibid.: 249, 303).

The embassy arranges housing, a job at the French cultural center, and schooling for his children. Kayimahe reveals in detail the embassy's misrepresentations and manipulation, and his continuous conflict with them as they keep offering him positions in other African countries. This is followed by his resignation from the cultural center and a letter he writes to the senior advisor at the embassy, expressing his frustration at being thus betrayed by French authorities and forced to remain in Kenia. Kayimahe narrates this part of the story by framing it as a discussion with his friend and fellow survivor Saïdi, whom he meets up with after the genocide. Thus he highlights the importance of being able to give one's testimony and having an appropriate listener: 'I was happy', he writes, 'to be able to tell my stories to a friend who understood' (ibid.: 210).

After many vain attempts to be allowed to leave, either to France or to Canada through contact with the HCR, Kayimahe takes his family back to Rwanda. He tells of the terrible return to a country where the fertile hills have lost their splendor, and where an idyllic village becomes a place of extermination (ibid.: 330–1). After the genocide, his 'soul no longer felt Rwandan': 'I was no longer drawn by Rwanda, and I no longer wanted to be called a Rwandan. And above all, the idea of living in this country again, side by side with all these assassins and their accomplices, who were calmly returning, repulsed me' (ibid.: 309).[49] He shares bitter images of how his mother died and pays homage to her, recounting her humiliation during the genocide, an ordeal of which she had been forewarned many years before by a prophecy. Kayimahe was not there and tells the stories as told by others and as he imagines it. He is, however, able to find his mother's remains and bury her according to the customary rites and in the presence of his family.

Each example of betrayal brings the author to the same painful realization: that of the unexpected betrayal of the West, and in particular of France, both on an individual and collective level: France has not been 'tarnished' by others, he notes, she has 'tarnished herself' (*elle s'est salie ell-même*) (ibid.: 12) by participating in the 'masquerade' which turned into a genocide (ibid.: 83).[50] He frames his discussion of France's role in the genocide and their refusal to acknowledge it by evoking an official visit by a French commission to Murambi, a genocide site situated in the former 'Zone Turquoise'.[51] Kayimahe's conclusion is that the commission sent by the French government was not there to 'establish the truth' of what had happened, but rather to prove themselves innocent, in their 'shameless self-absolution', a choice that would gravely undermine any form of real future reconciliation between Rwandan and France (ibid.: 12). This visit, of which Kayimahe provides factual details, is ostensibly the one that inspired both Diop's and Lamko's fictional accounts and scathing comments on the French involvement.

A whole chapter is devoted to what Kayimahe refers to as France's fatal involvement in the genocide ('*le doigt dans l'engrenage mortel du génocide*'), the diplomatic and political errors committed, the questionable friendships and military and other agreements between the two countries' authorities and presidents (ibid.: 66). In his capacity as an audiovisual technician, he attended many private meetings between the French ambassador and the president of Rwanda while setting up film screenings in their homes, which allowed him to take note of the easy camaraderie and friendship between them (ibid.: 51). He tells of the intimidation of Tutsi girls who dated Westerners, of the French government's stand against the RPF and the exiles who wanted to return, and of France's intervention in the civil conflict in 1990 (ibid.: 70–3).

Kayimahe devotes further chapters to the CECFR, which was run by French authorities. He describes its stance toward the political situation and its Tutsi employees as well as the involvement of the director, Anne Cros, in the political landscape. He details his confrontations and deteriorating relationship with her due to their differences of opinion on the RPF and the role of the French in Rwanda. He identifies the CECFR as an important link between the French and Rwandan authorities, and cites various dinners and exchanges between staff of the French embassy and extremists who were planning the genocide. He also records the victimization of Tutsis employed by the CECFR, as well as other ambiguities, misrepresentations, and political and military interventions by the French authorities and soldiers present in the country, in spite of their status as so-called neutral observers. He notes how they closed their eyes and ears to the atrocities that were taking place in Bugesera and elsewhere (ibid.: 62, 81–133).

The author's narration of the events leading up to the genocide is thus constantly framed within his discussions with colleagues from the CECFR and with individuals, such as the French captain, whom he befriends. This captain assures Kayimahe that he (the captain) does not understand France's support of the Habyarimana regime; however, as a military man, his duty is to obey without asking questions (ibid.: 124). The author's tone is bitter and critical, and the many examples of his broken relationships with French colleagues come to embody France's betrayal of the genocide victims. The theme of betrayal becomes the main recurring thread of the testimony and, to my mind, a clear trace of traumatism in Kayimahe's own story.

In this way, the text is not only an account of the genocide and of the loss of the author's dear ones, but also a demonstration of the author's quarrel with the 'French machine' after the genocide. The text includes copies of documents and letters pertaining to this quarrel (ibid.: 319). He scathingly accuses the French government of being an 'accomplice to the genocide', of being its 'sponsor and co-pilot', of not preventing the genocide when they could have done so, and evokes all the unanswered questions surrounding France's role in the genocide (ibid.: 323–6). Reconciliation between the two countries will only be possible, says Kayimahe, when France humbly admits its complicity, with a profound and honest '*mea culpa*' (ibid.: 327).

At the same time, he insists on testifying to the moral and financial support he received from French friends, colleagues, and acquaintances. For him, these are the people who 'saved' the image of France (ibid.: 321). In fact, the chapter entitled 'The lady from Gordes' pays homage to the memory of their support and tells of the letter and money that the lady from Gordes sent Kayimahe in spite of her own difficult situation.

Betrayal did not only come from the French government and the West; he also reflects on the betrayal of people such as his childhood friend Aster and his Hutu co-worker Anastase. Like Ilboudo, Kayimahe compares the *génocidaires* to the biblical figure of Cain, who killed his own brother (ibid.: 15–20). It is indeed the figure of Cain that the author evokes in his opening chapter. Here he contrasts the lyrical myths and legends of his country, with their typical happy endings and themes of friendship and brotherhood, to the 'symphony' of hatred and extermination that the country became after 1959 (ibid.: 19–20).

Betrayal moves ever closer to home and we realize that perhaps Kayimahe's deepest issue with betrayal is that he accuses himself of this act. The very first event that he relates is the death of his daughter Aimée, who was among a large group of Tutsis taking refuge in the Iwacu Center. Kayimahe was not with her, and again has to resort to narrating her death as it was told to him by others and as he imagines it. The narration moves from the past tense, which is the main mode of narration, to the present tense in order to bring her suffering into focus: 'Now Aimée is completely alone. She knows it, she can feel it' (ibid.: 18). The person who does witness how she is shot down is her little brother, whom, Kayimahe tells us, would afterward refuse to speak and would move around on his tiptoes 'like a frightened animal' (ibid.: 17). Somehow, the silencing of the brother embodies Kayimahe's initial silence and voluntary amnesia, a silence which he attempts to break by writing this testimony. Aimée's body was thrown into a common mass grave, or perhaps the Nyabarongo River, says Kayimahe, evoking the pain of a father who could not bury his own daughter (ibid.: 19).

Thus, in the end, betrayal is not only something that others have done to him, but becomes the sin for which he condemns himself. His betrayal is neither that of not avenging their death nor of forgiving the perpetrators, but rather of waiting for justice and allowing himself to start forgetting: 'I have a sense of having betrayed everyone: my God, my faith, my daughter, my mother, my sisters, my brothers, my relatives, my friends, my country' (ibid.: 354–5).

These then become the central driving forces behind his text; the trauma of having been betrayed on so many levels, the obligation to remember and remind others of what happened, and a sense of remorse and guilt for having abandoned his loved ones. Kayimahe's text closes with an affirmation of the truth of its content and, once again, shares with the reader the 'impossibility', for someone in his position as genocide survivor, of writing fiction about the genocide. 'This is no legend', he says, 'it's not a story of fiction', but a true story, 'I am but a mere witness of History, one amongst two or three-hundred thousands of other witness-survivors' (ibid.: 354).[52] In the end he acknowledges that his only refuge and the only way of countering his own betrayal of forgetfulness is this: fulfilling the duty of memory (ibid.: 355).

The Sword of Memory

As we accompany Kayimahe through his narrative, it becomes clear that he has very specific and personal reasons for writing his story. He is driven by a sense of moral obligation, an attempt to address his own guilt for having left behind five of his children when fleeing Rwanda and his remorse for having 'abandoned' the memory of his Tutsi brothers and sisters through his 'unjustifiable silence', a form of deliberate amnesia (ibid.: 7).[53] The thought of fulfilling this task has been tormenting him for a long time.

The complex paradox surrounding remembering and forgetting is not unique to Kayimahe's text, but is a strong theme in the project, and the authors are confronted with it as they journey into the heart of Rwanda and its sites of memory. The duty to remember, which appears to be mainly a public and social concern, stands in opposition to the private, individual need of many victims to work through and forget the trauma (Semujanga 2008: 10). It is a conflict imposed both socially and within the conscience of the survivor: Kayimahe illustrates this by opposing his own 'voluntary amnesia' (which for him represents a form of comfort) to the imperative and pressing 'duty' of bearing witness that he knows he is honor-bound to do (2001: 7).[54]

This paradox also exists in the opposite form: in some cases the private needs of survivors are to keep commemorating and remembering, and this can be opposed to the 'political injunction "to turn the page", "to go on with one's life", and "to contribute positively to Rwanda's reconciliation and renewal"' (Dauge-Roth 2009: 171). In this sense, conflict exists between survivors burdened with memories who are an 'embarrassment' to the society they live in, and other members of this society for whom remembering appears to stand in the way of progress: 'No one wants to be weighed down by that unbearable memory. Those who survived are there to remind us of the past, and we would prefer them not to be in the fore-front any more so that the country can rebuild itself more quickly' (Tadjo 2002: 111).

This painful tension between remembering and forgetting characterizes the lives of those who have experienced the genocide, and many seem unable to work through the process effectively. Waberi describes how the Rwandans harden themselves against their memories and lose themselves in a frenzy of activity, his short, forceful phrases demonstrating their determination and will power:

> The city is buzzing with activity, and there just isn't enough room for all this energy and these fresh ideas. [...] One refrains from awakening the still waters of memory, sheathing wounded hearts in leather. [...] Unrestrained, we perform the task we've assigned ourselves. (2016: 501–5)

Diop notes that the duty of memory seems to be a contradictory undertaking, as the aim of remembering also eventually encompasses the aim to start forgetting (in Brezault 2002),[55] a paradox which Paul Ricœur has written on at length in his essay on memory, forgetting, mourning, and forgiveness (1995: 80–1). However, Ricœur's proposed sequence of memory–forgetting–forgiving[56] cannot always be attained, and Ilboudo's two protagonists, Murekatete and Venant, are a striking example of this. Their individual traumas prevent them from remembering effectively, let alone integrating their traumatic memories into their life stories. They are incapable of remembering and even more so of forgetting.

Regardless of the perspective one takes, memory and forgetting represent significant challenges in post-genocide Rwanda, and the genocide sites attest to this. Muyango-the-cracked-skull, the sage in Lamko's text, understands the destructive effect of the genocide on the memories and value systems of Rwandans. He describes a type of apocalyptic meltdown in which physical sites have become 'amnesic', landmarks have been 'erased', people have become like 'islands in empty spaces' and all of this is an 'enormous abyss' of forgetfulness which transforms people into 'monsters' existing on a 'planet' that has fallen apart (Lamko 2002: 77).[57]

Diop's sage, Siméon, describes memory as a guide that confirms our roots and shows us the way forward: '[I]t's good to remember certain things. Sometimes it helps you to find your path in life [...] That's how we know what trials we had to overcome to merit being alive. We know where we come from' (Diop 2006b: 1324–6). Tadjo's soothsayer evokes the value of memory for a society recovering from genocide; it is a powerful sword, rain in times of drought, a garment to cover and comfort those who are broken and bruised (Tadjo 2002: 45). Memory might indeed be a sword, but it is a double-edged sword and the multivocal narrative of the project does not try to solve or simplify the contradictions it brings. Instead, it makes us aware of its complexities.

An analysis of the three works chosen for this chapter foregrounds the various positionalities of the writers, particularly regarding their relationship with the notions of victimhood and witness, and their varied attempts to demonstrate solidarity with the victims of the genocide. Djedanoum's lyrical poetry allows for the expression of hope and a celebration of life, whereas the texts of the two Rwandans attempt to assure that the reader grasps the enormity of what the victims have experienced. The two Rwandan authors narrate their trauma by relying less on what Jorge Semprun has called creating 'an artistic object',[58] and more on detailing their lived experiences (1996: 167). They make us aware of the unresolved anger and pain of those betrayed by their fellow citizens and the international community, and those who lived as strangers elsewhere, frequently constantly exposed to the dangerous ignorance of the uninformed foreigners surrounding them.

It is also in reading these three texts together that we become most acutely aware of the importance of the theme of exile. Once again, their approach to this differs: the notion of exile provides Djedanoum with the opportunity to talk of the ambiguous pull of the motherland and the richness of the countries to which those in exile have traveled. This motif enables him to link Rwanda with the rest of the continent and the suffering of the African diaspora in general. The theme of exile is treated differently by the other two writers: both of them describe it as an intensely personal and humiliating experience.

This diverse range of positions and perspectives serves to enhance the heterogeneous and polyphonic nature of the project. The two Rwandan writers made a choice to write texts that are not fictionalized and that focus on transmitting truth rather than on arousing emotion, texts that provoke self-reflection by transmitting the lived horror of the genocide. One can wonder whether this is why their texts have received less attention from literary critics. Furthermore, their choice to refrain from providing a plurality of voices and perspectives constitutes the most telling sign of trauma in their work. Once again, achieving the necessary intellectual distance to write imaginatively and poetically about the genocide may be a luxury that only a foreign writer can have access to. I would suggest, however, that rather than considering the failure to achieve this distance as a shortcoming, or blaming the other writers for being able to do so, one can but celebrate the diversity of voices.

NOTES

1. This term is somewhat controversial, but I use it simply to refer to certain aspects of a literary text, such as stylistic and narrative elements, which lead to 'defamiliarization' and transformation of a conventional concept, as described by David Miall and Don Kuiken: 'Briefly, literariness is constituted when stylistic or narrative variations defamiliarize conventionally understood referents and prompt reinterpretive transformations of a conventional feeling or concept' (2009: 123).

2. I have provided English translations for these texts throughout. For longer quotations, the original is given in the endnotes.

3. « A mon sens, c'est seulement dans un recueil de poésie que l'on peut passer du temps à s'interroger sur la façon dont on va exprimer telle ou telle chose: ' j'ai dit cela, comment le dire de manière plus forte, comment faire que les mots ne trahissent pas la force des faits, comment coller à l'atrocité du fait ?' Parce qu'on ne peut pas ne pas dire, sous prétexte que le langage avilirait la réalité et que les mots seraient toujours trop faibles. Le silence est coupable. Le silence tue. Dans ce cadre, le journalisme est immédiat. Il est important pour l'actualité et pour l'histoire, que certains décrivent la réalité au jour le jour avec tous les risques de manipulation que cela implique. L'actualité journalistique a souvent constitué la base de notre travail. Mais à mon sens c'est ce lent travail qu'il nous fallait faire. Dans un demi-siècle, il y aura cependant des gens pour dire que nous-mêmes, nous avons écrit trop tôt ! » (Achariant 2002).

4. Based on the observations of the Rwandan philosopher, poet, and linguist, Alexis Kagame, Anthère Nzabatsinda notes that the majority of traditional Rwandan literature took on the form of poetry that could be divided into three categories: pastoral poetry, poetry of war, and dynastic poetry that recounted the history of Rwandan kings (Nzabatsinda 2007: 410).

5. My comments are based on the following quotation: « [D]ans notre groupe d'auteurs, les deux Rwandais Jean-Marie Vianney Rurangwa et Vénuste Kayimahe sont les seuls à n'avoir pas écrit de fiction. Ils ont fait des essais. Cela me semble avoir un sens: les Rwandais ont besoin de se tenir à distance de l'événement. Et nos romans, écrits dans l'urgence du témoignage, ne disent encore rien en profondeur sur le génocide. Cela viendra plus tard et ce sera l'œuvre des victimes elles-mêmes. Ceux qui, à l'âge de quatre ou dix ans, ont vu des inconnus violer leurs mères avant de les tuer à coups de machettes, ceux qui ont vu mourir des êtres chers en parleront demain, car un roman s'élabore plus avec des souvenirs anciens qu'avec de la réalité brute, immédiate. Je suis convaincu que pour pouvoir être dite, la douleur doit traverser des générations, se sublimant ainsi progressivement. Quant à moi, si j'ai pu donner cette impression de réalité,

c'est que paradoxalement, je n'ai pas vécu ces événements. Les témoins directs ne demandent qu'à oublier. Il leur est pratiquement impossible d'en parler et beaucoup d'entre eux, s'ils livraient le fond de leur pensée, diraient leur désir d'oublier ces heures sombres » (Diop 2006a).

6. One can argue, however, that her first text was co-written with a non-Rwandan journalist and that the interaction between these two women ostensibly contributed to and enriched the process of mimesis and provided a space of listening, which not all survivors could necessarily have access to.

7. « Nous nous retrouvions dans une terrible impasse: fuir en abandonnant tout, sans le moins du monde être sûrs d'arriver quelque part, avec sur les bras une famille de dix personnes pourchassée par les séides du régime, ou alors rester à attendre la prochaine attaque et sûrement la torture et la mort » (Kayimahe 2001: 31).

8. « 'Sale petit Rwandais !' Fred R. tendit l'oreille ! Le méchant garnement répéta à haute voix: 'Sale petit Rwandais, va !'

La classe éclata de rire. Fred R. lui rétorqua violemment:

'Tu mens ! Je ne suis ni sale, ni rwandais.'
Un autre bambin surenchérit.
'C'est juste, c'est vrai tu es un Rwandais. Regarde, t'es pas comme nous. T'es rwandais; tout le monde le dit.' ». (Lamko 2002: 51)

9. « Au Rwanda on nous dit: 'On en a assez parlé'. On est coincé, nous les rescapés, entre les Hutu, nos voisins de toujours qui nous ont tués, et les Tutsi, nos frères qui sont rentrés d'exil après plus de trente ans [...] qui ont toujours rêvé de rentrer au Rwanda mais qui ne s'attendaient pas à y revenir marchant sur les cadavres » (Mujawayo and Belhaddad 2004: 19).

10. « Tout ce que je trouvai à dire fut que le Rwanda est une véritable mosaïque, que chaque réfugié était revenu, avec dans ses bagages hâtivement rassemblés, des habitudes, des mœurs de l'ancien pays d'accueil, et que je me demandais comment nous allions gérer tout ça' » (Ilboudo 2000: 63).

11. « Cependant, le fait d'avoir simplement mis les pieds au Rwanda, d'avoir pris le temps de visiter les différents sites du génocide, d'avoir écouté les rescapés de tous âges et d'avoir discuté avec eux, d'avoir rencontré les différentes associations qui cultivent l'esprit critique cher à la société dite civile, mais aussi d'avoir été sensible à la beauté de ce pays (son extase verdure, sa langue si lyrique, ses danses traditionnelles à la fois guerrières et séductrices, sa science de l'érotisme tout en finesse, sa riche et complexe diaspora etc.) est déjà un grand pas pour nous dans notre volonté de mieux comprendre notre continent » (Djedanoum 1999).

12. « Tout ce que je sais, en mon fort intérieur, c'est que les Rwandais et moi, avons un destin commun, en tant qu'Africains d'abord, et ensuite en tant qu'humains » (Djedanoum 1999).

13. I base these comments on the following remarks: « L'un de nos devoirs est de faire comprendre aux Rwandais et au reste de l'Afrique que nous devons avoir une vision globale de ce continent. Nous savons que dans les esprits, il en est autrement. Nous avons fait l'expérience dans un collège de Byumba, au Nord du pays, en présence de deux cents élèves, par ailleurs bien informés sur la situation sociopolitique de leur pays. Mais il nous a été difficile de percevoir chez ces jeunes la notion d'appartenance au même continent. Il nous a fallu, pour les en persuader, dérouler la carte de l'Afrique et l'accrocher au tableau, et leur expliquer d'où nous venions, et surtout leur faire comprendre que notre seul rêve est d'enjamber toutes ces frontières. Notre satisfaction, à l'issue de cette rencontre, est que ces élèves, dubitatifs au début, nous ont reprochés notre silence coupable. 'Vous dites que nous sommes tous des Africains et vous venez nous voir seulement quatre ans après le génocide. Est-ce normal ? Et puis, vous pouvez pas nous dire que vous ne saviez pas que se préparait un génocide ici'. La vérité, comme toujours, sort de la bouche des enfants. Que leur répondre, sinon que nous sommes là, devant eux. Enfin, nous sommes venus nous recueillir, écouter, observer, essayer de comprendre et réfléchir ensemble sur ce qui faut appeler la tragédie culminante de l'Afrique » (Djedanoum 1999).

14. Audrey Small's (2007) article provides an insightful discussion of the project as an attempt to demonstrate solidarity and the strategies used by the authors to do this, as well as the limits of this kind of endeavor.

15. Identifying too closely with the victim, says Geoffrey Hartman, hampers the possibility of remaining an 'intellectual witness', a task which requires a certain intellectual distance and is always a challenging place to be in: 'Artists like these reveal that the intellectual part of consciousness always keeps us in the position of spectator or bystander. It is a deeply uncomfortable place to be in, because we are exposed, at one and the same time, to trauma and the anxiety of not empathizing enough. In this crucial area little can guide us' (Hartman 1998: 42).

16. « Je march sur une corde raide, les bras levés et les mains ouvertes. Je ferme les yeux et je suis envahie par un flot de souvenirs lyriques » (Djedanoum 2000: 9).

17. Where deemed necessary, I have kept the typography of the extracts from the poems because in many instances, it enhances or emphasizes the content.

18. « […] terre de pélerinage et de recueillement » (Djedanoum 2000: 50–1).

19. Another poem that speaks vividly of the interconnectedness between the physical and invisible world is 'The castle of tombs' (*Le château des cata-*

combs). Here Djedanoum gives a glimpse into the life of one of the victims of the genocide that has become emblematic of the consequences of genocide, namely the child survivor. Petit-Jean, an eleven-year-old watches over the dead in silence; no living being can teach him anything for he has inherited the wisdom and the secrets of the dead. He lives amongst the dead, carrying their weight, and the knowledge of their names, communing with them, hears them breathing, their lives are reflected in his glance (ibid.: 25–27). This poem powerfully evokes the invisible world and the porous boundaries that exist between it and the physical world in post-genocide Rwanda.

20. « Non. Il n'y a pas lieu de fermer les yeux. / Non. Il n'y a pas lieu de boucher les oreilles. / Non. Non. Non. » (Djedanoum 2000: 24).

21. This metaphor is reminiscent of Lamko's comments who distinguishes between the role of the mathematician, guardian of statistics, and the poet, who brings those statistics to life (Lamko 2002: 12).

22. « Nul lieu autre que Nyamirambo / Où je me sens renaitre au monde / Où je croise à l'aube le sourire de l'humanité / Où je crois encore à l'homme / Où je crois de nouveau à la vie » (Djedanoum 2000: 28).

23. « *Nyamirambo*, nom d'un quartier populaire de Kigali, fut un haut-lieu du génocide, une façon pour Nocky Djedanoum d'immortaliser ce drame africain. Une façon de nous rappeler que le génocide a bel et bien eu lieu, et qu'on ne devrait jamais l'oublier. D'ailleurs, Nocky nous invite dans l'un de ses poèmes (p. 20) à faire de *Nyamirambo* une terre de pèlerinage » (Mongo-Mboussa 2001: 1).

24. « Comme un poumon qui respire… Il y a de la vie. C'est le seul quartier où on trouve des étrangers de condition modeste, qui tiennent des petits commerces. C'est aussi dans ce quartier qu'il y a une mosquée alors que le pays est très catholique » (in Marcelli 2000).

25. My comments are based on the following remarks: « Après les deux mois passés au Rwanda et les autres séjours qui ont suivi, nous avons envie de dire au voyageur aveugle qui passe, la tête lourde de préjugés: 'Regarde dans la rue. Regarde les champs de patates douces et de pommes de terre. Ouvre les yeux et lis les mystères de la nature. La vie rôde dans les bananeraies. Elle rase les murs […] Elle voyage à travers les collines, sans répit. Elle recherche le soleil qui n'appartient à personne. Regarde comme elle est fragile […] Colle ton oreille à la vie et écoute-la respirer'. Regardons se construire ce pays qui vient de loin, qui se bat seul avec ses larmes enfouies, qui n'en finit pas d'enterrer ses morts, mais qui en même temps est si vivante sous nos yeux » (Djedanoum 1999).

26. « Nyamirambo est l'anti-génocide, de par sa composition même. C'est un lieu de cohabitation.

La vie y reprend le dessus alors qu'il y a eu là beaucoup de morts. Après la résidence j'ai su que Nyamirambo signifie cimetière. C'était le quartier où il y avait le cimetière, pourtant c'est le quartier le plus vivant. C'est là qu'il y a de l'espoir ! » (in Marcelli 2000).

27. The typography of the poem certainly evokes the form of a human being, perhaps a pregnant woman:

> .....
> Cette terre
> Je l'ai portée depuis toujours en moi
> Cette grossesse éternelle
> [...]
> Embrasser les autres terres
> Va, va, me soufflait-elle à l'oreille
> Me poussant dehors d'une main
> Elle me retenait de l'autre
> Va, porter d'autres grossesses
> Va, pour d'autres enfantements
> Notre planète est infinie
> .....
>
> (Djedanoum 2000: 15–19)

28. « L'un de nos devoirs est de faire comprendre aux Rwandais et au reste de l'Afrique que nous devons avoir une vision globale de ce continent » (Djedanoum 1999).

29. « Il y a des images qui se situent au dessus de notre ridicule entendement, des images tellement inimaginables et impensables qu'il semble que seuls les yeux peuvent les représenter pour eux-mêmes et seulement pour eux-mêmes. [...] C'est une situation de solitude exacerbée que rien alentour ne peut ni distraire ni dissoudre » (Djedanoum 2000: 12).

30. The Bahutu Manifesto, drawn up by a group of Hutu intellectuals in 1957, was a political document that promoted Hutu ethnic and political solidarity and called for the liberation of the Hutu people, both from colonialism and from the Tutsi who are described as oppressors in this document.

31. « [O]ui nous en avons assez de mourir au Rwanda, au Burundi, en Afrique du sud, en Sierra Leone, en Algérie, au Tchad, au Congo, en République Démocratique du Congo, en Angola, au Nigéria, en Centrafrique, en Afrique du sud... » (Djedanoum 2000: 50).

32. « Le dernier poème de son recueil, une sorte de manifeste, répond bien à cette esthétique de l'engagement. Sans confondre le discours poétique et politique, il pense que les mots peuvent parfois être des « armes miraculeuses », pour reprendre la célèbre expression de Césaire, tout en s'interrogeant sur le silence des mots face à l'indicible (p. 27). Il se situe

ainsi dans la lignée des poètes de la Négritude qui refusèrent de dissocier l'éthique de l'esthétique » (Mongo-Mboussa 2001: 1).

33. « […] nous revendiquons cette vie à cor et à cri par notre verbe créateur, cette vie, si elle est à créer de nouveau, nous la re-créerons, au commencement le verbe créateur, la vie existe quand elle est dite, chantée, peinte, rendue en images, cette vie que nous voulons en mouvement, une vie sans cesse rêvée et renouvelée, cette vie qui bat dans la poitrine et le pouls, elle est à tous cette vie, unique et indivisible, si cette vie est à créer, nous voulons la créer ici et maintenant » (Djedanoum 2000: 51).

34. « Peut-être que c'est dans le naturel de l'homme, cette pudeur qui veut que l'on s'appuie sur les épaules de l'autre, que l'autre nous donne la main et nous essuie les larmes pour nous soulager de notre blessure ? » (Djedanoum 2000: 11).

35. « Pour m'avoir encouragé
Quand nous étions encore en exil
A écrire pour mon peuple. » (Rurangwa 2000: 7)

36. « Mais ils changent de langage, de nom et de lieu. Voilà pourquoi, quand on parle de 'génocide des Tutsi'—réalité pourtant incontestable—eux parlent de 'colère populaire', de 'légitime défense', de 'guerre interethnique'. Voilà pourquoi, quand on leur demande leur nom, ils se font passer pour des Congolais ou des Camerounais […] Fuir devant la vérité, mentir pour survivre et se cacher pour ne plus voir ceux qu'ils avaient voulu anéantir, voilà à quoi sont actuellement réduit ces bourreaux hutu » (Rurangwa 2000: 11).

37. « L'exil, c'est une épine plantée dans sa chair et dont on ne peut jamais se débarrasser. L'exil, c'est le supplice de Tantale, l'aigle de Prométhée, le rocher de Sisyphe ! L'exil, pour tout dire, c'est un calvaire qui n'a pas de trêve. Mes amis n'ont jamais compris qu'après trente-cinq ans d'exil, j'avais urgemment besoin d'aller vivre dans un pays qui allait enfin m'accepter comme citoyen à part entière. Je ne sais même pas s'ils le comprendront un jour. Seul quelqu'un qui a passé autant d'années en exil, pourrait comprendre pourquoi on peut quitter l'Amérique ou l'Europe pour un pauvre petit pays comme le Rwanda » (Rurangwa 2005: 10).

38. « Je me souviens qu'à un moment donné au Burundi, pour parler d'un pays que je connais le mieux, on avait honte d'être rwandais » (Rurangwa 2000: 41).

39. « Nous avions un pays que nous aimions beaucoup et que nos pères appelait Rwanda *rugari rwa Gasaboi* (littéralement: Vaste Rwanda de Gasabo), un pays où coulaient le lait et le miel. […] Et nous voilà la mort dans l'âme, sur le chemin de l'exil […] Et nous voilà voisin directs des tigres, des léopards des panthères […] Je me rappelle que nos pères, le jour, abattaient des arbres […] Je me rappelle ce miel et ces fruits sauvages […] Je me rap-

pelle aussi que mes aînés apprenaient à lire et à écrire sous les arbres [...] Je me rappelle qu'ils écrivaient sur leurs jambes et sur leurs bras [...] Je me rappelle que les enseignants étaient tous des réfugiés rwandais [...] Qui disait 'Rwandais' entendait ces jeunes filles réfugiées tutsi debout sur les trottoirs [...] Qui disait 'Rwandais' entendait tous ces jeunes réfugiés tutsi qui [...] Qui disait 'Rwandais' entendait tous ces diplômés réfugiés tutsi [...] » (Rurangwa 2000: 39–45).

40. « Finalement, ils ont permis que leurs écrits justifient le point de vue que les Tutsis sont les victimes permanentes, même si un gouvernement dirigé par des Tutsis occupe le pouvoir. Cette logique de victime permanente tutsi mobilise tout le pays contre un seul ennemi—les extrémistes Hutus au Rwanda et en RDC—au détriment de la reconstruction de la nation, de la paix et de la réconciliation. Le texte qui succombe à cette identification totale à l'idéologie du parti dominant au Rwanda est *Le génocide expliqué [à] un étranger*, par Jean-Marie Rurangwa » (Diawara 2002).

41. This notion has, in turn, been criticized by scholars such as Lisa McNee, who interprets it as a form of hypocrisy: 'Least of all do the onlookers who refused to make a move to prevent genocide wish to think about the lost opportunities and the hypocrisy of supposedly humanitarian pretensions that have led some to equate victim with killer' (2004: 2).

42. Instead of what Mahmood Mamdani calls 'victor's justice'—which implies that the only peace possible is armed peace, which believes that Tutsi power is the condition for Tutsi survival, which sees victory in civil war as a pre-condition for justice—Mamdani advocates 'survivor's justice'. This type of justice seeks to transcend bipolar notions of victim and perpetrator, blames the system instead of the agent, and thus puts emphasis on institutions of rule instead of individuals and reforms institutions of rule (Mamdani 2002: 270–3).

43. « Je me suis engagé en 1999 dans le projet *'Rwanda, [É]crire par devoir de mémoire'*. À l'origine, ce programme n'était tourné que vers des écrivains africains non rwandais, mais pour finir, il a encouragé aussi les Rwandais à y participer. Moi je n'étais pas écrivain, je le suis devenu par la force des choses » (Guillamo 2011).

44. Centre d'échanges culturels franco-rwandais.

45. « Si la compromission des autorités françaises au Rwanda ne fait plus de doute, au-delà de ce qu'on a appelé pudiquement 'la cécité au plus haut niveau', le témoignage de Vénuste Kayimahe nous plonge dans l'horreur et nous apprend beaucoup sur la veulerie, la lâcheté, la muflerie de ceux qui avaient en charge les affaires franco-rwandaises. Un seul exemple, les séances de cinéma dans la villa du président Habyarimana auxquelles l'ambassadeur de France de l'époque était toujours convié, ne sont en définitive que de longs apartés politiques. Le seul témoin muet de ces discrets tête-à-tête n'est autre que le petit projectionniste du CECFR, Vénuste Kayimahe » (Waberi 2002).

46. « S'ils devaient être distingués, des autres victimes, ce serait par un plus et non par un moins: ils constituaient parmi les Hutu, parmi cette immensité de sauvageries déchaînées, un groupe à part, celui des gens d'honneur, des hommes de cœur, respectueux de la vie au point de sacrifier la leur pour protéger, sauver ou refuser d'ôter celle des autres » (Kayimahe 2001: 7–8).

47. « Vénuste est avant tout une conscience, une très belle conscience d'ailleurs, et reste très pudique à l'égard de tout ce qui le concerne personnellement, ses sentiments comme son corps. Ce qui est tout à son honneur mais ne fait pas de lui un écrivain au sens étroit du terme, celui qui s'institue le sujet de son écriture et use de la fiction pour être impudique et dévoiler les hommes » (Delas 2002: 49).

48. « […] racontée sans tact peut-être, mais aussi influencée par le désir strict de rapporter l'information dans son contexte et sa vérité. Il se pourrait que ce désir de restituer de la manière la plus fidèle possible les événements ait nui à la forme du récit […] Seul le souci de mémoire a prévalu » (Kayimahe 2001: 8–9).

49. « Je n'avais plus aucune attirance pour le Rwanda, je n'avais plus envie d'être appelé rwandais. Et surtout, l'idée de revivre dans ce pays, côte à côte avec tous ces assassins et complices d'assassins qui revenaient tranquillement, me révulsait » (Kayimahe 2001: 309).

50. My observations are based on the following extracts:

   « Car la France n'est pas salie, elle s'est salie elle-même […] ». (Kayimahe 2001: 12)

   « Tandis que la Belgique et le Zaïre se désengageaient dès les premières semaines après avoir sauvé provisoirement le pouvoir de Kigali, la France, elle, s'engageait à corps perdu auprès du régime chancelant, gangréné par la corruption, le racisme et l'injustice, ce qui devait l'amener à jouer toutes les partitions de ce dernier, y compris celle du génocide ». (ibid.: 49)

   « Malheureusement la France avait pris part à cette mascarade dont les conséquences avaient été très lourdes pour plus de dix mille Tutsi et quelques Hutu réputés opposés au régime […] ». (ibid.: 83)

51. This visit seems to be the same commission of enquiry that inspired Lamko to frame Pelouse's journey to Rwanda as being part of an official French delegation.

52. « Tout ceci n'est pas une légende. Il ne s'agit pas d'un récit fictif. Ceci est une histoire. Une vraie histoire. Mon histoire. […] Je ne suis qu'un simple témoin de l'Histoire, témoin-survivant parmi deux ou trois centaines de milliers d'autres » (Kayimahe 2001: 354).

53. « Voici des années que, suite à mon injustifiable silence, mon esprit est sans cesse tourmenté par un remords profond et tenace: celui d'avoir le sentiment d'abandonner à l'anonymat et à l'oubli mes frères et sœurs victimes de la

haine de leurs semblables et de m'y complaire; celui de me réfugier, au détriment du souvenir et de la mémoire dans l'irréel confort de la lâcheté et de l'amnésie volontaire [...], j'ai finalement ressenti comme un impérieux devoir la mise au grand jour de ce témoignage » (Kayimahe 2001: 7).

54. I have provided English translations of Vénuste Kayimahe's text, as no English translation has been published. For longer quotations, the original text is given in the endnotes.

55. « Je crois, en l'occurrence, que notre démarche est paradoxale: à la fois le devoir de mémoire mais aussi l'oubli » (Diop in Brezault 2002).

56. Paul Ricœur suggests that remembering and forgetting are two necessary stages for coming to a point of healing; the work of memory must be followed by a work of forgetting and of mourning, which could potentially lead to forgiveness and healing (1995: 80–1).

57. « Ici, chaque homme, chaque femme est une île au milieu du vide. Les lieux physiques sont amnésiques, les repères gommés, l'histoire de chaque enfance, de chaque vie, lobotomisée. [...] Un océan de vide, un énorme gouffre dans la mémoire. Ici, l'on est dans l'anorme, tous plus ou moins monstres sur une planète effondrée » (Lamko 2002: 77).

58. Semprun (1996: 167) writes about the 'density' and substance of a traumatic experience which can be partially transmitted by creatively transforming a testimony into an 'objet artistique'.

References

Achariant, Céline. 2002. Entretien de Céline Achariant avec Nocky Djedanoum: Entretien réalisé pour le théâtre international de langue française. Accessed July 22, 2018. http://africultures.com/entretien-de-celine-achariant-avec-nocky-djedanoum-2588/.

Awono, Jean-Claude. 2004. Tchad: Nyamirambo de Nocky Djedanoum, une poésie du génocide et du manifeste pour la vie. *Africultures.* Accessed July 22, 2018. http://www.africultures.com/php/?nav=article&no=4006.

Brezault, Éloïse. 2002. A l'occasion de la sortie du dernier livre de B. B. Diop : Murambi, le livre des ossements. Entretien d'Eloise Brezault avec Boubacar Boris Diop. *Africultures.* http://www.africultures.com/php/index.php?nav=article&no=2577. Accessed 6 July 2018.

Dauge-Roth, Alexandre. (2009) Testimonial Encounter. *French Cultural Studies* 20 (2): 165–180.

Delas, Daniel. 2002. Entre fiction et témoignage: les chiens du génocide rwandais. *Notre librairie: revue des littératures du Sud* 148: 44–50.

Diawara, Manthia. 2002. African Literature and the Rwandan Expedition. Accessed July 22, 2018. http://africultures.com/african-literature-and-the-rwandan-expedition-5584/.

Diop, Boubacar Boris. 2000. *Murambi: le livre des ossements*. Paris: Stock.

———. 2006a. Entretien avec Boubacar Boris Diop par Lanfranco Di Genio. Accessed January 26, 2012. http://www.fieralingue.it/modules.php?name=News&file=article&sid=303 (site discontinued).

———. 2006b. *Murambi: The Book of Bones* (Kindle edition). Bloomington: Indiana University Press.

Djedanoum, Nocky. 1999. Le Rwanda, terre de recueillement de mémoire. Accessed November 1, 2011. http://nocky.fr/ecrits-inedits/ (site discontinued).

———. 2000. *Nyamirambo!: recueil de poésies*. Bamako and Lille: Le Figuier and Fest'Africa.

Gourevitch, Philip. 2000. *We Wish to Inform You that Tomorrow We Will be Killed with Our Families: Stories from Rwanda*. London: Picador.

Guillamo, Valérie. 2011. Vénuste Kayimahe, rescapé rwandais et écrivain. Accessed June 6, 2013. http://www.legrandjournal.com.mx/actu-mexique/venuste-kayimahe-rescape-rwandais-et-ecrivain (site discontinued).

Guttman, Amy. 2015. Nyamirambo: Kigali's Coolest Neighbourhood. The Rough Guides Limited. Accessed July 22, 2018. https://www.roughguides.com/article/nyamirambo-kigalis-coolest-neighbourhood/.

Harrow, Kenneth W. 2005. "Ancient tribal warfare": Foundational Fantasies of Ethnicity and History. *Research in African Literatures* 36 (2): 34–45. https://doi.org/10.2979/RAL.2005.36.2.34.

Hartman, Geoffrey. 1998. Shoah and Intellectual Witness. *Partisan Review—New York* 65 (1): 37–48.

Ilboudo, Monique. 2000. *Murekatete: Roman*. Bamako and Lille: Le Figuier and Fest'Africa.

Kayimahe, Vénuste. 2001. *France-Rwanda: les coulisses du génocide: témoignage d'un rescapé*. Paris: Dagorno.

———. 2014. *La chanson de l'aube*. Toulouse: Izuba.

LaCapra, Dominick. 2001. *Writing History, Writing Trauma*. Baltimore: Johns Hopkins University Press.

Lamko, Koulsy. 2002. *La phalène des collines*. Paris: Le Serpent à Plumes.

Mamdani, Mahmood. 2002. *When Victims Become Killers: Colonialism, Nativism and the Genocide in Rwanda*. Princeton: Princeton University Press.

Marcelli, Sylvain. 2000. Rwanda, mémoire d'un génocide—Le partage du deuil. Accessed July 22, 2018. http://interdits.net/interdits/index.php/Rwanda-memoire-d-un-genocide-Le-partage-du-deuil.html.

Mazauric, Catherine. 2015. Vénuste Kayimahe, La chanson de l'aube. Carnets de littératures africaines. Accessed July 22, 2018. https://apela.hypotheses.org/687.

McNee, Lisa. 2004. Monénembo's *L'Aîné des orphelins* and the Rwandan Genocide. *CLCWeb: Comparative Literature and Culture* 6 (2). https://doi.org/10.7771/1481-4374.1228.

Miall, David S., and Don Kuiken. 2009. What Is Literariness? Three Components of Literary Reading. *Discourse Processes* 28 (2): 121–138. https://doi. org/10.1080/01638539909545076.

Monénembo, Tierno. 2004. *The Oldest Orphan*. Translated by Monique Fleury Nagem. Lincoln: University of Nebraska Press.

Mongo-Mboussa, Boniface. 2000. « Nous avions l'obligation morale d'aller jusqu'au bout » : Entretien de Boniface Mongo-Mboussa avec Nocky Djedanoum et Maïmouna Coulibaly. *Africultures*. Accessed July 22, 2018. http://africultures. com/nous-avions-lobligation-morale-daller-jusquau-bout-1463/.

———. 2001. Rwanda 2000: Djedanoum et Ilboudo. *Africultures*. Accessed July 22, 2018. http://www.africultures.com/php/index.php?nav=article&no=1832.

Mujawayo, Esther, and Souâd Belhaddad. 2004. *SurVivantes: Rwanda, dix ans après le génocide*. La Tour d'Aigues: Éditions de l'Aube.

Nzabatsinda, Anthère. 2007. Passeur des langues: Alexis Kagame, poète du Rwanda et écrivain francophone. *Contemporary French & Francophone Studies* 11 (3): 409–416.

Ricœur, Paul. 1995. 'Le pardon peut-il guérir?' *Esprit* (1940–) 210 (3/4): 77–82.

Rurangwa, Jean-Marie Vianney. 2000. *Le génocide des Tutsi expliqué à un étranger: essai*. Bamako and Lille: Le Figuier and Fest'Africa.

———. 2005. *Un Rwandais sur les routes de l'Exil*. Paris: L'Harmattan.

Said, Edward W. 2000. *Reflections on Exile and Other Essays*. Cambridge, MA: Harvard University Press.

Semprun, Jorge. 1996. *L'écriture ou la vie. Collection Folio; 2870*. Paris: Gallimard.

Semujanga, Josias. 2008. *Le génocide, sujet de fiction? : Analyse des récits du massacre des Tutsi dans la littérature africaine*. Quebec: Nota bene.

Small, Audrey. 2007. The Duty of Memory: A Solidarity of Voices after the Rwandan Genocide. *Paragraph* 30 (1): 85–100. https://doi.org/10.3366/prg.2007.0016.

Staub, Ervin. 2006. Reconciliation after Genocide, Mass Killing, or Intractable Conflict: Understanding the Roots of Violence, Psychological Recovery, and Steps Toward a General Theory. *Political Psychology* 27 (6): 867–894. https://doi.org/10.1111/j.1467-9221.2006.00541.x.

Tadjo, Véronique. 2002. *The Shadow of Imana: Travels in the Heart of Rwanda*. Translated by Véronique Wakerley. Oxford: Heinemann.

Tumwebaze, Peterson. 2009. Nyamirambo: A Unique Suburb with More than One Face. *The New Times*. Accessed May 3, 2017. http://www.newtimes.co. rw/section/article/2009-10-23/80067/.

Waberi, Abdourahman A. 2002. *France-Rwanda: les coulisses du génocide, témoignage d'un rescapé* de Vénuste Kayimahe. Accessed July 22, 2018. http:// www.africultures.com/php/?nav=article&no=2559.

———. 2004. *Moisson de crânes: textes pour le Rwanda*. Paris: Serpent à plumes.

———. 2016. *Harvest of Skulls* (Kindle edition). Bloomington: Indiana University Press.

CHAPTER 7

Conclusion: The Mythical Universe of Storytelling

This project, like Siméon Habineza from Diop's text, is not prescriptive as to who reads it and how it is to be read: one is of course free to travel through each text on its own, or to select only certain authors. However, when reading the project as a collective text, as I have done here, it becomes a multilayered narrative which is connected through recurring elements and which provides a more comprehensive image of the genocide, leading us to a deeper understanding of this event.

When reading them together, we see more clearly how the authors portray in different ways the dehumanization and loss of personhood, the pain of exile, the unsettling journey to the heart of the sites, the destruction of traditional and cultural points of reference, and the conflict between remembering and forgetting and burying and displaying. Through their imaginative and varying insertions of supernatural signs, myths, proverbs, and sages, the project authors not only evoke and rehabilitate Rwanda's cultural and communal heritage but also demonstrate the different experiences of and reactions to the genocide.

In this final chapter, I emphasize the power of such a shared narrative by looking at a few key recurring themes as they appear throughout the project. I frame them on the one hand within the theme of the erosion of Rwandan traditional belief systems, and on the other hand, the authors' creative and even subversive endeavor to reinsert and dialogue with traditional frames of reference and storytelling devices.

© The Author(s) 2020   265
A.-M. de Beer, *Sharing the Burden of Stories from the Tutsi
Genocide*, Palgrave Studies in Cultural Heritage and Conflict,
https://doi.org/10.1007/978-3-030-42093-2_7

EROSION OF A MYTHICAL UNIVERSE

As we have already seen, the colonial project of discrediting traditional beliefs and rites and gradually replacing them with Western symbols and practices led to the dispossession of Rwandan cultural memory. Diop describes how the missionaries ordered them to change Imana's name and challenged the rituals and sacred elements such as the drum of Kalinga and the cowrie shells (2006: 1625–8).

Ceding the power to name one's god to another is highly significant, and the Mwami (king) warns his people that a terrible tragedy will befall them; they will lose power over their own lives because 'the world belongs to those who give a name to God' (ibid.: 1630). Those who control the religion of a people have much power and the 'foreigners' soon replaced the Mwami with a less 'recalcitrant' king (ibid.: 1361). An old man in Diop's novel questions this newly adopted religion, which is propagated through violence and coercion: 'What a bad god is yours, white man, that you can make me worship him only by force and not by persuasion!' (ibid.: 1629). Diop relates how the newly appointed Mwami's conversion to Catholicism confused the community and literally turned their world upside down, undermining their points of reference:

> When the padres gave him a car, he almost went crazy. For everyone, the Mwami was the very presence of God on earth. To see their god going to mass on Sunday was a terrible shock for those who did not want to change Imana's name under any circumstances. The world was no longer recogniz-able. Every day that passed was different from the others. The padres had won. (ibid.: 1634–6)

The Catholic Church, which is perceived to have perverted Rwandan society, has become one of the most contentious examples of the cultural dispossession that Rwanda underwent. Lamko portrays the change in their belief system as a tension between 'Black' Imana and 'White' Imana (2002: 40) and Semujanga interprets this juxtapositioning of Imana *Lenoir* and Imana *Leblanc* as an 'opposition of two moments in Rwandan culture' (Semujanga 2009: 46; my translation).

Lamko frames this conflict within an argument between Muyango, a survivor, and a black, foreign Catholic priest. Muyango is clearly critical of the Church's role in manipulating the people of Rwanda, but also of the rest of the continent. He scathingly accuses Rwanda of becoming a 'true colony' of the Catholic Church (Lamko 2002: 105). He blames the priest for having chosen to give up his own cultural identity and become a 'white priest', claiming that such an alignment leads to a loss of 'freedom of conscience' (ibid.: 106).

When Muyango affirms his own belief in Imana and emphasizes the value of knowing the 'true myths', the priest expresses his frustration with the people's tendency to confuse Imana, the traditional deity, with the Christ (ibid.: 109). 'Alas!' he retorts, 'there is Imana and Imana. You used to say Imana to indicate who you worshiped before Christianity. And now you still say that Imana is part of the Church. The Christian god is not necessarily Imana' (ibid.: 107).[1] Muyango, however, is disillusioned with the Catholic Church and claims that their hypocritical behavior has 'killed' the Christ they are representing and that their religion was neither socially relevant nor helpful in this context:

I want to speak about Christ.

Leave him out of it! With everything you've made of him in this country! You've killed Christ a million times. Besides, why do you keep yourself busy with those who are not here? Christ is among the absent here. Misery, that is present … the widows … the orphans … the crippled, the unemployed. (ibid.: 107–8)[2]

In his testimony, Kayimahe sheds more light on the conflict between 'White' and 'Black' Imana. He explains that, although Rwandans continued to serve both gods with equal devotion, they did not do so equally visibly and they served them for different purposes. The god of the whites was deemed to be more evolved and symbolic, whereas the god of their ancestors was believed to be more efficient (Kayimahe 2001: 19–20).

Religion, however, remains a controversial matter, both due to the combined veneration of deities from two different belief systems and due to the tendency to justify acts of genocide through religion. Kayimahe tells, for example, how perpetrators would wield the Bible in one hand and a machete or a club in the other, declaring to the tortured victims that they were in fact being killed by the divine hand of God, who was delivering them (ibid.: 20).

It is common knowledge that historically Rwandans have had 'the same language, the same God, Imana, the same beliefs' (Diop 2006: 710). This belief in Imana, which had traditionally been a unifying factor, had been undermined by the arrival of the missionaries, and one could see how the logical next step during the genocide was to deny this unifying belief, an assumption confirmed by the following anecdote from Diop's text: 'Our commander answered the old woman with an air of false astonishment, "Ah! Mama, didn't you know? We spent the night in heaven and we fought the God of the Tutsis there until dawn! We killed him and now it's your turn." With a single stroke of his machete he sent her head to the devil' (ibid.: 855–7). Thus the idea is introduced that the Tutsis and Hutus never served the same god.

One could draw the origin of this argument straight back to colonial times when the Catholic Church favored Tutsis in terms of education and positions in the Church, suggesting that the god of the white man did not see Hutus and Tutsis as equals. Now this favoritism was being turned against them. Waberi indeed suggests that the Catholic Church had a direct impact on the genesis of the genocide. He attributes the 'deeply entrenched hatred' between the Tutsis and Hutus to the arrival of the missionaries, who, with their 'pernicious teachings', had 'succeeded [...] in irrevocably damaging ancestral religious beliefs and in altering both the temporal and the eternal balance of power' (2016: 546).

Lamko represents the erosion of traditional beliefs as a type of symbolic rape. By ascribing the Tutsi Queen's rape to 'Father Théoneste', he metaphorically attributes the 'rape' of Rwanda to the Catholic Church, or at least to the 'hypocrite[s]' within that institution (Lamko 2002: 46, 109). Through this metaphor, the author emphasizes the people's estrangement from their indigenous 'mythical universe' and its religious values, which had previously fostered unity among them:

> For me, the rape of the Queen [Mukandoli] was in the first place committed by a member of the clergy. What does it mean to tear away a whole people from its mythical universe, from everything on which its religious values are based, that's to say its unifying values? They did this all over Africa. Rwanda opened itself up wholly and completely to this. (Lamko, in Kalisa 2005: 275)[3]

The rape then speaks of a violation of culture, values, and moral and religious frameworks.

The church buildings which were turned into sites of massacre are highly symbolic of this process of cultural dispossession taken to the extreme, and Lamko labels them 'church-museum-site[s]' (2002: 13). They symbolize the tension between conflicting belief systems and the authors use them as a space to reflect on this tension. Nyamata, Ntarama,

Nyarubuye, and Musha—these were ambiguous places which were supposed to protect their people, but instead became sites of betrayal and destruction. In times of crisis, the people had for many decades fled to these places of worship, which were experienced as havens. During the genocide, they became traps in which large numbers of Tutsis could be assembled and where they were easy targets. Like the hills, these buildings have become symbolic points of reference in the Rwandan landscape: sites of mourning, of remembrance, but also of controversy.

It is then no small wonder that the rape in Lamko's text takes place in the setting of a church. Given the history of dehumanization, it also seems fitting that the rapist, Father Théoneste, is progressively transformed into an animal during the narration of this event; a donkey, a pig, a perverse 'devil incarnate' (ibid.: 38). This is significant, as, from the queen's perspective, it is not just the priest who is raping her; she claims that it is God himself who is committing this act (ibid.). Thus follow her bewilderment and anger when faced with the contrast between the wise, bountiful Imana that she used to believe in and the perverted image of him proposed by the white man's religion and represented by the priest:

> God, Imana or whatever name pleases you! Just understand that I am troubled because I don't know who you are anymore. Imana, the one from the olden days, Black Imana was wise and generous, demanded neither cathedral nor incense nor devout woman rapist in a large cream robe. You, today's Imana, White Imana that they snatched from who knows which hurricane, and who rips me apart in black, listen to my very last prayer. (ibid.: 40–1)[4]

Her sense of betrayal and disorientation echoes the bewilderment experienced by the genocide victims.

Kayimahe demonstrates the tension between the two belief systems by comparing the narratives which characterize each of them. He first evokes the lyrical Rwandan myths and legends, which typically have happy endings and encourage hope. In contrast to this are the biblical stories introduced by the foreigners, of which he cites the case of Cain who murders his own brother (ibid.: 19, 20). A parallel is thus established between Cain, from the Christian faith, and the perpetrators senselessly killing family members and close neighbors.[5]

Ilboudo too cites Cain and Abel's story. However, she transposes it to and mixes it with what sounds like a traditional myth on the history of Hutu and Tutsi. Ilboudo's transformation of the biblical story into a type of traditional tale with a moral lesson which has parallels with the Rwandan story is noteworthy. It speaks to the confusion and intermingling of Western and indigenous belief systems but also introduces the element of invasion by the 'cattle owner':

> The first crime of mankind was a fratricide. Cain and Abel were brothers. […] Adam's son killed his brother. A crime that remained unpunished. 'If anyone kills Cain, vengeance shall be taken on him sevenfold' warned the Creator. The ways of the Lord are mysterious. Amen. So it's the story of two brothers. Born from the same father. Born from the same mother. The oldest cultivated the soil, the youngest let his cows graze. They lived happily without problems until the day that the cows invaded the fields of the older brother. (Ilboudo 2000: 27)[6]

The parallels between this story and the genocide are clear and yet it is narrative clothed in the shape of a myth, inviting the readers to make their own deductions. Is the implication here perhaps too that killing their brothers is something the Rwandan people did because of their contact with the 'white people's religion' and its primal example of fratricide? The teller of the tale evokes 'the motifs of crop farmer and cattle owner to speak of the rivalry in Rwandan mythology between *Gihanga*'s children', Gahutu becoming Cain and Gatutsi reminding us of Abel (Semujanga 2008: 187).[7] In her tale, the oldest sibling takes revenge on his brother, who has humiliated him in front of his guests, and the tale ends with a moral lesson: 'Woe to those who stir up trouble between brothers' (Ilboudo 2000: 28).

Semujanga suggests that these intertextual references, which evoke both the biblical story and the foundation myths of Rwanda, constitute an attempt at providing a 'mythological explanation for a cosmic human evil' and for how this evil, characterized by hatred and revenge, progressively becomes historical and collective (2008: 187; my translation).

An interesting feature of this part of Ilboudo's narrative is that it speaks to the contrast between an analytical, rational mode of explaining the world and a more traditional, mythological mode. This is the only chapter in Ilboudo's novel that is not told from the point of view of the protagonist. Rather, it seems to feature the omniscient voice of the author, who is reflecting on the origins of the genocide. It reminds one of Tadjo's chapter on the wrath of the dead, with its sudden change in tone and genre. In both cases, the authors allow oral, mythical tales to intrude into the more analytical, rational narratives within which they appear. These are the textual signs of the African context from which they write and the fact that they move so effortlessly from one narrative world to the next demonstrates the link between the rational, physical world and the invisible, mythological world.

Ilboudo makes another link between the Bible and the Rwandan context which illustrates the conflict between White Imana and Black Imana. She compares the Nile to the emblematic Nyabarongo River. This conjures up a different type of myth: the notorious colonial Hamitic myth which prompted genocide propagandists to send the Tutsi 'foreigners' back to Ethiopia, where they allegedly had come from. Here, Ilboudo uses the same seamless transition from one context to another:

> 'He raised his staff and struck the water in the River in front of Pharaoh and his officials. All the water in the river turned to blood'. Miracle or magical spell? On the road to Nyamata, we crossed a bridge which straddles the Nyabarongo River. Its waters, which are grey today, became scarlet during the months of terror. (Ilboudo 2000: 64)[8]

For God's chosen people, the turning of a river into blood was a miracle, but during the genocide it spoke only of death and destruction. Even the opposition between 'miracle' and 'magical spell' emphasizes the uneasy co-existence between indigenous beliefs and those to which people were exposed by the Western missionaries.

Lamko metaphorically depicts the rejection of these imposed worldviews. The Butterfly, who represents tradition, reacts with nausea when she witnesses a religious ceremony taking place in a church (formerly a genocide site), during which a *musungu* (white) church official exorcizes a possessed woman. This is a clear symbolic expression of her rejection of the practices introduced by the white man's religion, whose place it seems is to 'exorcize' that which does not fit within their religious framework (Lamko 2002: 18). Lamko's character rejects not only the Catholic Church, but any religious institution which may have eroded the traditional way of thinking. She has equal disdain for the 'hallelujahs in the churches', the 'requiem's and eternal burials in which 'lecherous bishops', pastors, and 'hysterical imams' rub shoulders.

As we have already seen, Monénembo's text, through the fate of his youthful protagonist, suggests that neither belief system is able to resolve the dilemma in which the country finds itself and that the genocide has undermined people's ability to have faith in any of them.

Restoring Through Storytelling

Chantal Kalisa suggests that the Rwandan people's sense of loss is much deeper than God's perceived absence during the genocide. As we have seen above, it also includes the 'death' of large parts of Rwandan culture, including its myths, symbols, rituals, and even language:

> In the light of the annihilating force of genocide, this question is rather about a society's shocking discovery of the death of meaning in normal language, which goes hand in hand with the death of myths, rituals, and symbols that were part of Rwandan culture. Language that defines a people loses its meaning in the act of genocide. (Kalisa 2013: 164)

She posits that writing in ways that 'revive' these cultural elements—through, for example, dances and popular songs—can be seen as a creative way for authors to respond to a part of this void left by the genocide (ibid.). One can argue that a possible response to the overwhelming 'annihilating force' of both colonialism and genocide is to textually reinvest the genocide narrative with traditional cultural elements.

This endeavor is indeed attempted by the project authors. In many instances, they do not merely integrate these elements into their narratives, but engage with them in unconventional and unexpected ways in order to explore the complexity of the genocide.

The most obvious textual motifs and oral devices which draw on traditional African culture and which the writers weave into their storytelling are the acknowledgment of the link between nature and the immaterial world, the incorporation of proverbs, myths, and oral legends, and the inclusion of the traditional voice of wisdom, represented through elders and sages.

As in many other rural and traditional societies, natural phenomena such as the wind, storms, rain, and drought are imbued with great significance and read as bearers of divine messages. Signs in nature dictate everyday life: 'We're just waiting for the rain to come, for a sign from heaven to start the seeding' (Waberi 2016: 286–7). They also reflect the state in which society finds itself. Tadjo's soothsayer, who is closely attuned to signs, both in nature and in the behavior of the community, says: 'The signs are telling us: the nation is in mourning' (2002: 48).

References are made to warnings in nature and local prophecies that foretold the genocide. In Monénembo's novel, Faustin relates how the falling of the president's plane is accompanied by 'a shower of bad omens': 'We saw a herd of topis running through the village, asps and chameleons coming out of everywhere, and, in broad daylight, a flight of owls perched on the church roof. Flasks of palm wine filled up with blood and rows of ants invaded homes and wells' (2004: 87).

Funga the witch doctor fears the supernatural consequences of abandoning the traditional god(s) and allowing foreigners to interfere with their beliefs and traditions:

> If you outlive me, Théoneste, remember to put this rock of Kagera back in its right place. Otherwise there's much to fear and not just for the village, but for the whole world. Strange things are parading behind my eyes; hybrid beings, mountains of eyeless heads being carried along rivers of blood. Oh, it's the fault of the older generation like us. We've been neglecting the gods lately. We've served the god of others. We shall pay! (Monénembo 2004: 90)

Tadjo expresses the unease which haunts the country through the motif of the shadow.[9] The troubling question that her ambiguous title evokes is this: does the shadow signify Imana's comforting presence or his profound absence? Is this country blessed or is it cursed? On the one hand it is abundant, lush, and green, and the myths, proverbs, and historiography of the country portray it as being favored by Imana. Rurangwa cites a fable in which the ancestors spoke of a land in which milk and honey flowed (2000: 39).

Yet it is also a land in which signs of being cursed and abandoned abound. Funga highlights this ambivalence: 'The devil is all around here! […] His fire is in our mountains; his cruelty in our hearts […] Poor Rwanda! They call it a paradise! But it's more like hell!' (Monénembo 2004: 6).

Kayimahe describes nostalgically how the physical landscape has been transformed by the genocide(s). He evokes the 'pretty little' hill of Butare from his childhood, with its fertile ground, its belt of eucalyptus trees, and the clear water of the Agatobwe River (2001: 331). The valley that he sketches is green, populated with peaceful herds of cattle and cheerful herdsmen, a place in which one good season followed another and the arrival of the children were 'punctuated' by the births of calves—in short, a type of paradise on earth (ibid.). However, after the violence of 1959 and subsequent years, and the exile of many Tutsis, the landscape tells a different story. Herds were destroyed and the Agatobwe River became troubled, filled with mud, sand, and red earth before partly drying up—a phenomenon which Kayimahe describes as 'one of those inexplicable revolts of nature' followed by barrenness and poverty (ibid.).

Waberi expresses the bewildering transformation of a green, idyllic country into a 'land of sorrow and ossuaries' (2016: 294). Its status as the paradise is undermined by the irreversible 'damaging' of the ancestral beliefs (ibid.: 551). The country has undergone some sort of 'eclipse', both through the sense of Imana's perceived absence, and due to the disempowerment of myths, legends, symbols, taboos, and rites (ibid.: 277). Throughout the texts, this unsettling motif symbolizes the darkness that has overtaken the country: 'We allow people to say, lead them to believe, that it was only a partial eclipse' (ibid.). Djedanoum states that the sun 'eclipsed behind the hills without warning' (Djedanoum 2000b: 18).[10] In Ilboudo's text, the eclipse is a direct metaphor for the genocide:

> That day, the sun did not rise. How could it have? A whole country had just sunk into darkness [...] There was no more place for the light. We were in the impenetrable kingdom of hatred and violence. The eclipse would last three long months. (Ilboudo: 34)[11]

Like the shadow, the eclipse speaks of the absence of light and life and is a sign that God (whichever form of god the people rely on) has abandoned them or that they have lost their own way in the darkness. Tadjo merges these two motifs; her shadow metaphor becomes a destructive eclipse that swallows the earth: 'Darkness has hidden the sunlight and shadow has engulfed the earth. "We shall emerge from this long and terrifying eclipse"' (2002: 117).

Not being able to bury the dead according to the traditional customs is another transgressed rite and the societal unease caused by this uncompleted process is also reflected in nature. Tadjo links the anger of the unburied to disturbances in the weather patterns—a shrieking rain, and a 'torrential downpour' partner with the dead to haunt the living (ibid.: 42). Waberi prefaces his discussion of Rwanda's unpredictable weather by citing Césaire's work on the anger of the dead:

... of the dead circulating in the veins of the earth
who at times come and break their heads against the walls [of our ears]
and the screams of revolt never heard [...]
(Césaire, in Waberi 2016: 327–28)

He evokes the impersonal and anonymous state of the piles of unearthed
bodies, the 'open holes' in the ground (ibid.: 331, 449). He associates this
unnatural state of affairs with the unexpected changes in nature: The 'skies
are inclement', and the country wavers between drought and destructive
downpours (ibid.: 331–6). This makes the Rwandans wonder whether the
'God of the Christians' is perhaps angry because of what happened in the
country (ibid.: 463–8).

Another traditional motif with which the authors reinvest the genocide
narrative is that of the sage. This useful figure of authority in the traditional African community tells us much about a community itself. As with
proverbs, the sages that populate the texts not only incarnate and confirm
the indigenous worldview, but equally serve to subvert and problematize
it. Sages come in different forms and fulfill a variety of roles, ranging from
the conciliatory elder to the prophetic soothsayer, and even the slightly
ridiculous sorcerer or healer.

Tadjo's sage is a soothsayer, initiated into the 'secrets of time', who
represents traditional customs and beliefs (2002: 43). He is respected in
the community, his advice is not questioned, his words do not aim to subvert, and his tone is sincere. He is wise and fulfills a well-defined role: that
of mediating between the physical and spiritual world. He is simultaneously a negotiator, advisor, interpreter of the supernatural, and guardian
of morals. Furthermore, he seems at times to assume the voice of the
author, who takes note of certain realities in this unsettled society.

He is endowed with the ability to speak frankly and from a position of
authority. The author acknowledges that this figure exists in traditional
Rwandan culture, but that she 'added the function of truth-teller to his
role because his particular status allows him to be directly in contact with
the gods' (2000; my translation). He is a type of intermediary, for both
the dead and the living listen to him: 'He connects them to each other'
(ibid.).[12]

His role as 'truth-teller' places him in a position to speak on forgiveness
and reconciliation. He gives advice on issues of guilt, hatred, and violence.
He urges the men and women of Rwanda to remain 'master' of their emotions (Tadjo 2002: 48). He promotes peace, hope, respect for the dead,

and memory. He is also the one to accompany them in their work of mourning, the one who intervenes between the dead and the living and performs the traditional rites (Tadjo 2002: 43–4). Tadjo's sage seems to live isolated from everyday life and keeps his distance; he comes when summoned by his people, gives advice, and then '[turns] on his heel' and disappears into the hills once his mission is fulfilled, retreating, it seems, from daily life to a more spiritual world (ibid.: 48).

The character who incarnates wisdom in Diop's novel is Siméon Habineza. He is Cornelius's 'symbolic' father' (Arnould-Bloomfield 2010: 508). In contrast with Tadjo's sage, Siméon is integrated into everyday life. He personally lived through the genocide, the rape of his wife, and his brother's betrayal. He lives in Murambi, among those who know his story and his connection with the 'famous Butcher of Murambi' (Diop 2006: 1123). The members of his community can identify with him and listen to his advice. He is not endowed with supernatural powers, but is rather a figure of wisdom, a respected elder who plays a significant role in the community. Cornelius describes him as one filled with a 'great spiritual force', 'a sober and reserved being, with a great inner strength', a 'free man' who reminds him of the proverb 'The man who has no fence around his house is a man who has no enemies', as 'Simeon has no fence around his mind' (ibid.: 464, 1306–7, 1580–1).

Whereas Tadjo's sage is all-knowing, Siméon seems disillusioned and baffled by the world he lives in. He has lost faith not only in Imana, but in the traditional wisdom of the elders: '"[T]hese days Simeon detests proverbs and everything else that they call ancient wisdom," remarked Gerard. "He's changed a lot." [...] "Even with regard to religion, he is more or less indifferent now, the old man. He thinks that our people were betrayed by Imana"' (ibid.: 1581–3).

Siméon does not ascribe the onset of the genocide to the supernatural world, as do some of the other sage figures, who evoke signs, omens, and portents in nature. This might lead to events being interpreted in a symbolic, less literal manner, or to blame somehow being shifted to fate and Siméon resists this possibility:

> 'Monsters drinking the blood of Rwanda. I understand the symbol, Siméon Habineza.' 'It's not a symbol,' said Siméon softly. 'Our eyes saw it.' [...]
>
> 'No, there was no sign, Cornelius. Don't listen to those who claim to have seen spots of blood on the moon before the massacres. Nothing of the sort happened. The wind didn't howl with sorrow during the night, nor did

the trees start to talk to each other about the folly of men. It was all very simple. Here in our region one of the prefects had said: "No, none of these barbarous crimes here." They immediately killed him. We knew that our turn would come.' (ibid.: 1458–64)

He represents a new type of wisdom, which is possibly less naive than that of the traditional sage, and offered by one who is profoundly disturbed by the reality and complexities of post-genocide Rwanda. When the inhabitants of Murambi want to destroy the house of an infamous local genocide leader (Siméon's brother), Siméon prevents them from perpetuating the circle of violence and shows them a new way, one which is not based on rejecting and othering (ibid.: 1578–9).

In Lamko's text, traditional wisdom is personified by the character of Muyango-the-cracked-skull, who can read not only a person's exterior, but knows everyone 'from inside as well as from outside' (2002: 76). He has lost his whole family but has become the storyteller, poet, and truth-teller in his society. There is no distance between him and the society he operates in, and if he leads, it is by example, through his own difficult path of mourning.

Es'kia Mphahlele has described poetry as a way of 'seeking to touch the Highest Reality beneath the surface of things' (2002: 139). Seen in this light, it is meaningful that Lamko endows Muyango with the role of poet. It is Muyango who urges Pelouse to open her eyes to the hidden world and enhance her writing and her photos with new 'rhythms' and 'emotions' which 'celebrate' what she sees and appreciates in nature (Lamko 2002: 113). This advice brings to mind Mphahlele's evocation of the 'harmony between humans and nature' brought about in a 'triumphant, inviolable, pantheistic union that negates death' (2002: 135).

When compared to the sages depicted by Tadjo and Diop, Muyango seems young and inexperienced, but he fulfills the same role—that of demonstrating the path of mourning to others and of resuming and even embracing life after suffering: 'Here, we have learnt to laugh at our misfortunes', he says (Lamko 2002: 111). In this sense, he is a true sage who leads others in his society.

In Ilboudo's text, Murekatete's father is the voice of reason and figure of wisdom. However, being a sage does not offer him impunity or supernatural protection—he will suffer for it. His wisdom and strong principles make of him a loving father and husband who makes his own choices in spite of what politics dictates. As a moderate Hutu, he chooses to marry a

Tutsi woman in spite of the possible consequences. When his daughter is born, he knows that he needs to give her a strong name to protect her against the world. His wisdom goes against the prescriptive rules of the Bahutu Ten Commandments, and it will eventually cost him his life.

Like many of the other sages found in the texts produced for the project, he is associated with the proverbs that he uses. When his daughter warns him to be careful, he answers: 'The lie has caused too much harm to our nation. [...] Remember my daughter: "Aho kuryamira ukuri wari-yamira ubugi bw'intorezo" ("It is better to lie down on the edge of an axe than to lie down on the truth")' (Ilboudo 2000: 25).[13] This cynical remark is ambiguous and therefore difficult for the uninitiated to interpret, but seems to speak of his awareness that untruthfulness and deceit has long reigned in their society and caused much harm; conversely, it might suggest that telling the truth can be very dangerous. Through her treatment of Murekatete's father, Ilboudo implies that it is naive to think that in a world where genocide is possible, the wise will be safe, listened to, and respected.

In Monénembo's novel, the figure of the sage plays an even more unsettling role.[14] His role and character are subverted and do not meet traditional expectations. He is not a typical sage who is wise and venerated. In fact, he often ends up in grotesque situations and usually does not have the necessary answers or appropriate responses to difficult situations.

Funga's behavior does not comply with what one expects of a sage who serves his community. When Faustin wants to stay behind to find his parents while the others are fleeing the country, Funga encourages him to think about 'saving his own skin' (ibid.: 7).

Funga, who often speaks through proverbs and prophecies, is filled with superstition and warns Faustin not to fly his kite, as he might 'dislodge a star'; it wouldn't serve to try and be 'cleverer than the gods' (ibid.: 72). He is a prophet of doom, characterized by the use of negative proverbs and utterances, such as 'Life marches on, but often in the wrong direction' (ibid.: 28). He is constantly predicting Rwanda's demise by interpreting signs and omens: 'here, the gods have become heartless [...] this country is going to its ruin [...] I told them that soon there'll be signs from heaven' (ibid.: 7–8). He warns that the sacrilegious acts of the white people, who have ignored the old customs, have brought bad luck to the country:

'[…] The really bad stuff hasn't started yet. By the way, did I tell you the legend?'

'A thousand times, Funga: no one must move the sacred rock of the Kagera! The whites knew that when they deliberately moved it. That's why they conquered us, and that's why there are catastrophes.' (ibid.: 9)

Ironically, in spite of his premonitions, Funga does not manage to save those around him from disaster. In fact, it is the representative of the 'White people's faith', the Mother Superior, who also has had a premonition, who saves Faustin's siblings from being slaughtered (ibid.: 91).

Another less obvious, but still important, figure of wisdom in Monénembo's text is Faustin's father, who is strongly associated with proverbs and the words of the elders, and who likes to 'compose songs for his cows and recreate scenes' from the ancient epics (Monénembo 2004: 62). He embodies the awareness of the connection between humans, nature, and the cosmos: 'My father, Théoneste, used to say: "Eat grasshoppers, eat lizards, eat frogs, just eat! It's in the taste of food that God's spirit can be found"' (ibid.: 21). This harmony with the world around him is something that he shares with the Italian nun who lives in their village and who is as much at home in Théoneste's family home as they are in hers: 'Like us, she believed that there is dignity in working the soil and living is not shameful' (ibid.: 74).

Although the others in the village scorn Théoneste as being unintelligent, he has a type of wisdom, courage, and 'common sense' that sets him apart. Faustin describes him as one whose 'soul knew neither anger nor resentment' (ibid.: 73). Like Murekatete's father, he stands up against the dictates of his time and marries a Tutsi woman.

Another addition to this gallery of sages which is especially interesting is that of Kayimahe's friend Saïdi, particularly because Kayimahe is not presenting a fictional depiction of the genocide, but his own testimony. Kayimahe describes Saïdi as someone with 'immense courage' and faith in the future, in spite of being crippled by the moral and physical suffering that he has gone through (2001: 309). Kayimahe relates how, when he has lost all faith in Rwanda, Saïdi encourages him. He reminds Kayimahe of the universal wisdom that 'There is no place like home', and that the elders of their country always said: '*Amazi arashyuha ntigibagirwa*: water boils but never forgets to cool down again' (ibid.: 308). Saïdi also concludes that their lives lie in the hands of '*Imana, Allah Akbar*. God is great' (ibid.: 310). Like Diop's Siméon and Tadjo's sage, Saïdi addresses the issue of how to cope with post-genocide life in Rwanda. He reminds Kayimahe of all that he still has to live for and that, in Rwanda, there are orphans to look after and a country to reconstruct (ibid.). Kayimahe closes this part of his narrative with an interesting observation. At the end of the conversation, Saïdi remains optimistic, while Kayimahe cannot shake his pessimism. However, he concludes that these two interlinked visions of the world are probably what makes the world and post-genocide Rwanda the heaven and the hell that it is (ibid.: 310).

Michael Syrotinski has suggested that Funga's character represents, in an allegorical way, how the Rwanda that used to be organized and comprehensible through the traditional myths and symbols seems to have lost this coherence (2009: 436). To my mind, this comment is applicable in general to the figure of the sage as discussed above. The sages represent a range of problems faced by a post-genocide society: disillusionment, the erosion of culture and tradition, and the fear that the beacons that served to guide society in the past may no longer be relevant. At the same time, they provide new and alternate forms of wisdom and coping mechanisms, situated as they are at the crossroads of tradition and modernity.

Transitional Spaces and 'Memory Traces'

In the context of the growing call for trauma theory to be less Euro-American centered and more inclusive of 'minority traumas' (Craps 2014: 46), and of 'collective' experiences of colonial and postcolonial trauma (Craps and Buelens 2008: 4), it is my view that this project offers us useful references to local forms of 'coping mechanisms' (Craps 2014: 54). Written by authors from the African continent about an important African-based historical trauma, the polyphonic nature of the project is on its own already one such reference, purely because it proposes both collective and individualistic approaches to this trauma.

Certainly, the authors participating in the project do not restrict themselves to creating narratives that can be contained within the 'enclosure[s]' of African—and in particular Rwandan—traditions of mourning and storytelling (Waberi 2011: 105). Neither, however, do they ignore those cultural aspects; rather, they enter into dialogue with them, looking at them from different angles, questioning or affirming their relevance in contemporary post-genocide Rwanda, and constantly pointing the reader to the fact that there are multiple stories to be told and multiple ways of telling them. The authors' engagement with collective memory, burial traditions, the invisible world, different forms of orality, porous boundaries, and voyages of initiation and transformation all contribute to the Afropolitan lens they provide. Thus, local and indigenous coping strategies and social realities are woven into the very fabric of the narratives: mourning customs; views of the afterlife; deference to traditional healers and healing practices; proverbs, tales, fables, and other forms of oral and societal wisdom. And yet, in spite of the texts' collective contribution, they still remain what Bernard de Meyer would call 'individual and authentic voices', each one offering a unique reading of the genocide (2015: 191; my translation).

The project certainly contains examples of 'failed' narratives (fragmented, elliptical, and non-linear), a phenomenon which has become closely associated with the typical esthetics of trauma writing. Some of them suggest that verbalizing the experience can be useful in the process of working through, whereas others convey the overpowering sense that silence may be more helpful. Most of them emphasize the 'social and historical context' in which this trauma unfolds, together with the structural violence, systematic oppression, and ongoing problematic social aftermath that it entails (Craps 2014: 51). In some instances, trauma has taken the protagonists beyond Western strategies of coping. The sense remains, however, that even local coping mechanisms are not always enough. The heterogeneous nature of the project proposes, through its stories and counter-narratives, a variety of spaces in which diverging and contesting voices can be safely explored. The project becomes then what Éloïse Brezault has called a form of 'memory traces' (as opposed to monuments), which offer 'alternative' forms of sites of memory, and which create a space for reflection, for 'discordant' voices and memories (Brezault 2016: 235, 237). The texts from the project serve as a type of alternative memory to the official history simply because they can express criticism and are less 'institutionalised' than certain other forms of memory (ibid.: 234).

What becomes clear as we as readers journey through the project is that there are not only different stories and different types of storytellers, but also different types of listeners. The texts act as mediators, creating transitional spaces in which we can begin to listen. These are spaces in which facile judgment is suspended and in which parallel stories or silences are allowed, in which authority is fluid and in which stories can be open-ended. Such a project demands a price from its readers; we are urged to reflect on our own experiences, our own fear of the Other, our own cultural taboos and coping mechanisms, but also on how to read atrocity ethically. When we look at or listen to the genocide experiences of others, do we gaze in a way that again dehumanizes? Many of the images—such as that of Mukandori, or the dogs feasting on blood, or the piles of bones—are, as we have seen, recursive, and the texts provide us with multiple ways of looking at them. Staring at them can be dehumanizing. Telling the stories over and over again can be dehumanizing. Ignoring them or silencing them can be dehumanizing too.

The writer-listeners may have been the ones to pave the way for us, but we as listener-readers also have a responsibility. Who will we be when we come face to face with Nyamata, Ntarama, and Murambi? How will we look at and how will we read genocide? Will we 'avert' our gaze, 'be shocked', 'weep', 'remain silent', or ask questions and try to understand or rationalize? (Tadjo 2002: 14).

These authors achieve an extraordinary thing—the 'encounter' that Djedanoum evokes between the writer and the survivor also becomes our encounter through imagination, and this is how we as readers come to feel that the possibility of showing solidarity has somehow been extended to us, as we share the burden by listening and reacting (Djedanoum 2000a).

The texts never take the responsibility away from us, but rather encourage us to grapple with the story. They do not try to contain our reading and seldom presume to teach us a lesson. Rather, the stories that prompt our imagination are riddled with spaces, silences, and contradictions through which we have to make our own way, like the 'solitary traveler' that Diop (2006: 1604) speaks of.

NOTES

1. « Hélas ! il y a Imana et Imana. Vous disiez Imana pour désigner ce que vous adoriez avant le christianisme. Et maintenant vous dites encore Imana au sein de l'Église. Le dieu chrétien n'est pas nécessairement Imana » (Lamko 2002: 107).
2. «—Je veux parler de Christ.
   ———Laissez-le tranquille ! Avec tout ce que vous lui avez fait dans ce pays ! Vous avez tué Christ un million de fois. Et puis, pourquoi vous occupez-vous des gens qui ne sont pas présents ? Christ est aux abonnés absents ici. La misère, elle est présente…les veuves…les orphelins…les infirmes, les sans-emploi » (Lamko 2002: 107–8).
3. « Pour moi, le viol de la Reine [Mukandoli], s'est fait d'abord par un religieux. Que veut dire arracher à tout un peuple son univers mythique, tout ce qui fonde ses valeurs religieuses, c'est-à-dire ses valeurs de rassemblement ? Ils l'ont fait un peu partout en Afrique. Le Rwanda s'est prêté à cela mais à fond » (Lamko, in Kalisa 2005: 275).

4. « Dieu, Imana ou n'importe quel nom qui vous réjouisse ! Comprenez bien que je sois troublée puisque je ne sais plus qui vous êtes. Imana, celui d'autrefois, Imana Lenoir était sagesse et générosité, ne réclamait ni cathédrale, ni encens, ni dévot en grand robe crème violeur de femme. Vous, Imana d'aujourd'hui, Imana Leblanc que l'on a saisi à je ne sais quel cyclone et qui me déchirez en noir, écoutez ma prière, la dernière » (Lamko 2002: 40–1).

5. « À la ressemblance de Caïn, ils tuèrent leurs frères de façon gratuite, inutile » (Kayimahe 2001: 19).

6. « Le premier crime de l'humanité fut un fratricide. Caïn et Abel étaient des frères. […] Le fils d'Adam a tué son frère. Un crime resté impuni. 'Si l'on tue Caïn, il sera vengé sept fois' prévint le Créateur. Les voies du Seigneur sont insondables. Amen. C'est donc l'histoire de deux frères. Nés du même père. Nés de la même mère. L'aîné cultivait le sol, le cadet faisait paître ses vaches. Ils vivaient heureux et sans histoire, jusqu'au jour où les vaches envahirent les champs de l'aîné. […] » (Ilboudo 2000: 27).

7. One can think here of the origin myths, according to which different parts of Rwandan society were alleged to have been the descendants of Gihanga, Kazi, or Imana. Gatwa, Gahutu, and Gatutsi, the ancestors of the Twa, Hutus, and Tutsis respectively, were put through a variety of tests which would determine their vocation and position in society.

8. « 'Il leva le bâton et frappa les eaux du Fleuve sous les yeux de Pharaon et de ses serviteurs. Toutes les eaux du fleuve se changèrent en sang.' Prodige ou sortilège ? Sur la route de Nyamata, nous traversons un pont qui enjambe la rivière Nyabarongo. Ses eaux, grises aujourd'hui, étaient vermillon durant les mois de terreur. Elles ont charrié des milliers de corps confiés à leurs soins par l'hystérie collective » (Ilboudo 2000: 64).

9. For more on the ambiguous motif of the shadow, present both in her title and in her portrayal of selected persons in her text, such as Consolate and Annonciata, read De Beer (2016a: 57–9).

10. « le soleil a éclipsé derrière les collines sans crier gare » (Djedanoum 2000b: 18).

11. « Ce jour-là, le soleil ne se leva pas. Comment aurait-il pu ? Tout un pays venait de sombrer dans les ténèbres. Les dernières lueurs d'espoir venaient de s'éteindre. […] Il n'y avait plus place pour la lumière. Nous étions dans le royaume opaque de la haine et de la violence. L'éclipse allait durer trois longs mois » (Ilboudo 2000: 34).

12. « Le personnage du devin existe dans la culture rwandaise traditionnelle. Mais je lui ai ajouté la fonction de diseur de vérités puisque son statut particulier lui permet d'être directement en rapport avec les dieux. Il a la force de dénoncer les tares du passé mais aussi celles du présent, puisque les morts et les vivants l'écoutent. Il fait la jonction entre les deux » (Tadjo 2000).

13. « Le mensonge à trop nuit à notre nation. […] Souviens-toi ma fille: '*Aho kuryamira ukuri wariyamira ubugi bw'intorezo*' ('Au lieu de se coucher sur la vérité, il vaut mieux se coucher sur le tranchant d'une hache') » (Ilboudo 2000: 25).

14. I have previously analyzed the conflict between the two systems and some of the points I make here are taken from that article, which was written in French and reworked in this chapter. Consult De Beer (2016b).

REFERENCES

Arnould-Bloomfield, Elisabeth. 2010. Commitment and Genocide Literature: Boubacar Diop's *Murambi: The Book of Bones*. *Contemporary French and Francophone Studies* 14 (5): 505–513.

Brezault, Éloïse. 2016. Les Œuvres du Fest'Africa: Les enjeux de la trace dans un « lieu de mémoire » déterritorialisé. *Contemporary French and Francophone Studies* 20 (2): 233–242. https://doi.org/10.1080/17409292.2016.1143740.

Craps, Stef. 2014. Beyond Eurocentrism: Trauma Theory in the Global Age. In *The Future of Trauma Theory: Contemporary Literary and Cultural Criticism*, ed. Gert Buelens, Sam Durrant, and Robert Eaglestone, 45–61. London: Routledge.

Craps, Stef, and Gert Buelens. 2008. Introduction: Postcolonial Trauma Novels. *Studies in the Novel* 40 (1, 2 [Spring, Summer]): 1–12.

De Beer, Anna-Marie. 2016a. « La saison des pertes » dans *L'aîné des orphelins* de Tierno Monénembo. *French Studies in Southern Africa* 46: 30–45.

———. 2016b. VÉronique Tadjo and the Masks and Shadows of Rwanda. In *Écrire, traduire, peindre—Véronique Tadjo—Writing, Translating, Painting*, ed. Sarah Davies Cordova and Désiré Wa Kabwe-Segatti, 43–63. vol. Les cahiers. Paris: Présence africaine.

De Meyer, Bernard. 2015. Posture et écriture. Le Mabanckou post-Renaudot. *Tydskrif vir letterkunde* 52 (1): 189–200. https://doi.org/10.4314/tvl.v52i1.14.

Diop, Boubacar Boris. 2006. *Murambi: The Book of Bones* (Kindle Edition). Bloomington: Indiana University Press.

Djedanoum, Nocky. 2000a. Discours d'ouverture de Nocky Djedanoum à l'ouverture du colloque international—Fest'Africa sur le génocide des Tutsi et le massacre des Hutu modérés. Accessed November 2011. http://nocky.fr/ecrits-inedits/ (site discontinued).

———. 2000b. *Nyamirambo! : recueil de poésies*. Bamako and Lille: Le Figuier and Fest'Africa.

Ilboudo, Monique. 2000. *Murekatete: roman*. Bamako and Lille: Le Figuier and Fest'Africa.

Kalisa, Chantal. 2005. Le gos au Rwanda: entretien avec Koulsy Lamko. In *Dix ans après: réflexions sur le génocide rwandais,* ed. Rangira Béatrice Gallimore and Chantal Kalisa, 259–280. Paris: Harmattan.

———. 2013. Theatre and the Rwandan Genocide. *Journal of Dramatic Theory and Criticism* 27 (2): 159–166.

Kayimahe, Vénuste. 2001. *France-Rwanda: les coulisses du génocide: témoignage d'un rescapé.* Paris: Dagorno.

Lamko, Koulsy. 2002. *La phalène des collines.* Paris: Le Serpent à Plumes.

Monénembo, Tierno. 2004. *The Oldest Orphan.* Translated by Monique Fleury Nagem. Lincoln: University of Nebraska Press.

Mphahlele, Es'kia. 2002. *Es'kia: Education, African Humanism and Culture, Social Consciousness, Literary Appreciation.* Cape Town: Kwela.

Rurangwa, Jean-Marie Vianney. 2000. *Le génocide des Tutsi expliqué à un étranger: essai.* Bamako and Lille: Le figuier and Fest'Africa.

Semujanga, Josias. 2008. *Le gÉnocide, sujet de fiction? : Analyse des rÉcits du massacre des Tutsi dans la littÉrature africaine.* Quebec: Nota bene.

———. 2009. Par-delà l'innommable, la littérature. *La phalène des collines* de Koulsy Lamko. In *Le génocide des Tutsi: Rwanda, 1994: Lectures et écritures,* ed. Catalina Sagarra Martin, 35–69. Quebec: Presses de l'Université Laval.

Syrotinski, Michael. 2009. Monstrous Fictions: Testifying to the Rwandan Genocide in Tierno Monénembo's *L'aîné des orphelins. Forum for Modern Language Studies* 45 (4): 427–440.

Tadjo, Véronique. 2000. Le pardon ne veut pas dire l'oubli: entretien de Boniface Mongo-Mboussa avec Véronique Tadjo. Accessed July 30, 2018. http://www.africultures.com/php/index.php?nav=article&no=1611.

———. 2002. *The Shadow of Imana: Travels in the Heart of Rwanda.* Translated by Véronique Wakerley. Oxford: Heinemann.

Waberi, Abdourahman. A. 2011. 'Fragments of an African discourse: Elements for a new literary ecosystem.' *Yale French Studies* 120:100–10.

Waberi, Abdourahman A. 2016. *Harvest of Skulls* (Kindle Edition). Bloomington: Indiana University Press.

Afterword: Safe Spaces of Reconstruction

The representation of the genocide has taken on and is still taking on a multiplicity of guises, ranging from literary texts by intellectual witnesses, to testimonies, works of art, co-authored texts and collaborations between Rwandan and non-Rwandans, interactions between written text and photographic images, and even fictional reconfigurations by survivors themselves. These stories are told in formal and informal ways—personally, collectively, publicly, and privately.

As I write this, I think of the recent encounters I have had in Rwanda, 25 years after the genocide. I think of the people I met who had never before told their stories to anyone and those who had told and retold them countless times. I think of the young people who worry about the unrecorded stories living in the hearts of their elders. These stories may forever be lost to our collective memory and imaginary.

The project authors knew that they were precursors. Time has proved that Rwandans are telling their stories. Not all of them can read and write, and many can only tell them in their mother tongue and yet there are initiatives that bring much hope.

There are those who have started to tell their stories in communal and informal ways, and I would like to conclude by paying homage to them. They seem to draw from traditional modes of storytelling and are reminiscent of Alfred Ndahiro's (2016) 'home-grown solutions', a notion that lies at the heart of this afterword.

© The Author(s) 2020   287
A.-M. de Beer, *Sharing the Burden of Stories from the Tutsi Genocide*, Palgrave Studies in Cultural Heritage and Conflict, https://doi.org/10.1007/978-3-030-42093-2

I think in particular of the *Cahiers de mémoire* writing project at *La Maison de quartier*, the community center at Kimironko, where a group of survivors from the neighborhood gathered regularly over a period of time to encourage each other and listen to each other's stories, many of which had never been verbalized before.

The center was created because so many of these survivors had lost the places they called home—not just the physical buildings, but everything and everybody with whom they had shared that home and their childhood memories. Florence Prudhomme, who helped them build their community center, envisaged it as a safe place where they could again belong, feel part of an 'us' (Prudhomme 2015: 29, 49).[1] She notes that in this safe environment, memory transformed into words takes on the function of the 'reconstruction' of the self and compares their writing project to an archive for future generations (ibid.: 81, 82). It is not only the individual work of each participant that is created here; instead, through the 'reciprocal listening' of the whole group, it becomes a shared work of memory (ibid.).

The writing project (*Atelier de mémoire*) was initiated in 2014 and when I visited them in 2017, they were still continuing with new groups. Those who cannot write were helped by those who can. A local lecturer and author encouraged and gave them advice. Here the responsibility to build that communal public story is inclusive and collectively owned. The survivors confirmed that the stories they had written in the year that I met with them had been collected and compiled in Kinyarwanda in one manuscript, so that each of them could read it. In the meantime, most of these works have been translated to French and two collective works have been published.[2]

A communal center such as this one also serves to preserve the memory of those cultural elements that the Rwandans were in danger of losing after the genocide: if whole families were wiped out, who would share the prayers, the legends, the rhymes, the dances, and the lullabies with the next generations? Prudhomme describes how the group of women built the center together and how they sing together and record their childhood lullabies. She speaks of how they revisit and learn the old tradition of *imigongo* painting: an abstract, geometrical decorative art traditionally transmitted from mother to daughter; a 'shared wealth' and heritage which is rooted in their culture and speaks to them all (ibid.: 44–7). These mural patterns too tell stories; like legends and epics, they speak of origins and ancestors (ibid.: 61).

Such initiatives embody the informal and participatory type of storytelling that is one of the necessary pathways to healing in a traditional community such as Rwanda. It is such communal efforts, together with the more formal ways of remembering, that contribute to the creation of the many-voiced narrative that I believe is necessary to build our collective African memory, not as individuals, but as a community in dire need of our own stories.

NOTES

1. All translations from Prudhomme's text are mine.
2. *Cahiers de mémoire*, Kigali (2019) and *Cahiers de mémoire*, Kigali (2014).

REFERENCES

Ndahiro, Alfred. 2016. Homegrown Solutions, Healing and Reconciliation. Paper presented at the International Conference on Healing and Social Cohesion: Healing and Social Cohesion: Understanding Reconciliation Experiences in Post-genocide and Extreme Violent Societies, Kigali, 9–11 November.

Prudhomme, Florence (dir.). 2014. *Cahiers de mémoire, Kigali, 2014.* Translated by Louis Munyaburanga Basengo, Charles Kalinda, and Leiny Munyakazi. Paris: Classiques Garnier.

———. 2015. *Rwanda, l'art de se reconstruire.* Paris: Atelier Henry Dougier.

——— (dir.). 2019. *Cahiers de mémoire, Kigali, 2019.* Translated by Bernard Kanyana Kabale, and Odette Mukantagara. Paris: Classiques Garnier.

Index[1]

[1] Note: Page numbers followed by 'n' refer to notes.

© The Author(s) 2020
A.-M. de Beer, *Sharing the Burden of Stories from the Tutsi
Genocide*, Palgrave Studies in Cultural Heritage and Conflict,
https://doi.org/10.1007/978-3-030-42093-2

Printed by Printforce, the Netherlands